DE 08 '18

DICKINSON AREA PUBLIC LIBRARY

3 3121 00190 0815

001.9092 J17
Jacobson, Mark.
Pale horse rider

WITHDRAWN

D1165572

Pale Horse Rider

blue
rider
press

Pale Horse Rider

WILLIAM COOPER,
THE RISE OF CONSPIRACY,
AND THE FALL OF TRUST IN AMERICA

Mark Jacobson

WITHDRAWN

Dickinson Area Public Library
139 3rd Street West
Dickinson, ND 58601

BLUE RIDER PRESS
New York

blue
rider
press

An imprint of Penguin Random House LLC
375 Hudson Street
New York, New York 10014

Copyright © 2018 by Mark Jacobson
Penguin supports copyright. Copyright fuels creativity, encourages diverse voices, promotes free speech, and creates a vibrant culture. Thank you for buying an authorized edition of this book and for complying with copyright laws by not reproducing, scanning, or distributing any part of it in any form without permission. You are supporting writers and allowing Penguin to continue to publish books for every reader.

Photo credits: p. 1: photo by James Hamilton; pp. 2, 63: *The Hour of the Time* photo collection; pp. 7, 17, 205: © Getty Images; p. 35: © Library of Congress; p. 101: © iStock by Getty Images; p. 140: courtesy of The Everett Collection; pp. 165, 189, 346: courtesy of the author; p. 173: Licensed from Regan Carmona, manager of permissions, Andrews McMeel Syndication; p. 281: photo by William Jacobson.

Blue Rider Press is a registered trademark and its colophon is a trademark of Penguin Random House LLC.

LIBRARY OF CONGRESS CATALOGING-IN-PUBLICATION DATA
has been applied for.

ISBN 9780399169953

Printed in the United States of America

1   3   5   7   9   10   8   6   4   2

While the author has made every effort to provide accurate telephone numbers, Internet addresses, and other contact information at the time of publication, neither the publisher nor the author assumes any responsibility for errors or for changes that occur after publication. Further, publisher does not have any control over and does not assume any responsibility for author or third-party Web sites or their content.

To the seekers of truth everywhere

Contents

PART ONE

A Minute to Midnight

Milton William Cooper, circa early 1990s

1

Even a broken clock is right twice a day; that's what they say about people who are supposed to be crackpots. It's the idea that there is a moment in time when even the most outlandish contention, the most eccentric point of view, the most unlikely person, somehow lines up with shifting reality to produce, however fleetingly, what many perceive to be the truth.

But to accept the notion of the "broken clock" is to embrace the established, rationalist parameters of time, twenty-four hours a day, day after day, years arranged in ascending numerical order, decade after decade, eon upon eon, a forever forward march to an undetermined future, world without end, amen.

For some people, people like the late Milton William (Bill) Cooper, collector of clocks, time did not work that way. American shortwave talk-show host, author, and lecturer during the millennial period of the late 1980s onward to the advent of the current century, Bill Cooper chose not to adhere to the mandated linear passage of existence.

This wasn't because Cooper, a voracious reader and self-schooled savant, was anti-science or anti-intellectual. He believed in evolution and, like his philosophical hero Aristotle, Cooper treasured the supremacy of knowledge and its acquisition. For Cooper, the entire span of time—the beginning, the middle, and the end—was all equally important, but there could be no doubt where the clock had stopped. A minute to midnight, that was Bill Cooper's time.

Cooper sought to dramatize the compounding urgency of the moment on *The Hour of the Time*, the radio program he broadcast from 1992 until November of 2001, his resonant, sometimes folksy, sometimes fulminating voice filling the airwaves via satellite hookups and shortwave frequencies. Nearly every episode of *The Hour of the Time* began the same way, with the show's singular opening, one of the most arresting sign-ons in radio history.

It starts with a blaring air-raid siren, a blast in the night. This is followed by a loud, distorted electronic voice: "*Lights out!*" comes the command, as if issued from a penitentiary guard tower. "Lights out for *The Hour of the Time*! . . . Lights out for the curfew of your body, soul, and mind."

Dogs bark, people shriek, the bleat of the still half-sleeping multitudes. There is the sound of tramping jackbooted feet, growing louder, closing in.

Now is the time, a minute to midnight, sixty seconds before total enslavement, one last chance. Some citizens will rise, if only from not-quite-yet-atrophied muscle memory. They will shake themselves awake as their forebears once did at Lexington and Concord, heeding Paul Revere's immortal call. They will defend their homes, families, and the last shreds of the tattered Constitution, the most close-to-perfect political document ever produced.

The vast majority, however, won't even get out of bed. Some will cower under the covers, but most will simply roll over and go back to sleep. They slept through life, so why not sleep through death?

This is how it will be at a minute to midnight, according to Bill Cooper. At the End of Time, a broken clock is always right.

Reputed instances of Cooper's prescience are legion. An early roundup of these forecasts can be found in the August 15, 1990, edition of the newsletter of the Citizens Agency for Joint Intelligence (CAJI), an organization Cooper created, billing it as "the largest private intelligence-gathering agency in the world." Published on a dot matrix printer, carrying the tagline "Information, not money, will be the power of the nineties," Cooper ran an article entitled "Every Prediction Has Come True." He listed sixteen of his most recent prognostications that had come to pass "or will soon be fulfilled."

These included the disclosure that "the CIA and the military are bringing drugs into the United States to finance their black projects."

Cooper also predicted that "the rape of the Savings and Loans by the CIA is only the tip of the iceberg. At least 600 banks will go under in the next two years." The current monetary structure, Cooper said, "will be replaced by a cashless system that will allow the government to monitor our every action by computer. If you attempt to stay out of the system you will not be allowed to buy, sell, work, get medical care, or anything else we all take for granted."

Cooper continued to make predictions in his watershed book, *Behold a Pale Horse*. Published in 1991 by Light Technology, a small New Age–oriented house then located in Sedona, Arizona, *Behold a Pale Horse* is something of a publishing miracle. With an initial press run of 3,500 (500 hardcover, 3,000 paperback), by the end of 2017, the book was closing in on 300,000 copies sold.

"*Behold a Pale Horse* is the biggest-selling underground book of all time," Cooper often told his audience. Yet sales figures represent only a fraction of the book's true reach. For one thing, as its author often bragged, *Behold a Pale Horse* routinely topped lists of the most-shoplifted books in the country. To this day, Barnes & Noble stores keep *BAPH*, as it is sometimes called, behind the cashier's counter to reduce pilferage. This was because, as one clerk at the Barnes & Noble near my house in Brooklyn told me, "that book has a habit of walking out all by itself."

There is also the captive audience. Since its release, *Behold a Pale Horse* has been among the most popular "prison books" (in that prisoners read them), a distinction it shares with Robert Greene's *The 48 Laws of Power*. During the crack epidemic of the 1990s, it was not unusual for a single copy of *Behold a Pale Horse* to go through enough hands in the cellblocks of places such as Attica to break the book's spine.

Some of Cooper's best-known predictions appear in *Behold a Pale Horse*, which runs a densely typed five hundred pages. Eight years before the Trench Coat Mafia murders at Columbine High School, Cooper wrote: "The sharp increase of prescriptions of psychoactive drugs like Prozac and Ritalin to younger and younger children will inevitably lead to a rash of horrific school shootings." These incidents, he said, "will be used by elements of the federal government as an excuse to infringe upon the citizenry's Second Amendment rights."

For many, including those who would later claim that the seemingly endless series of school shootings were part of a plot by gun-control advocates to take away America's weapons, Cooper's words took on the air of prophesy.

But Bill Cooper never claimed to be a prophet. He never imagined himself in the line of Ezekiel, Jeremiah, and Daniel, the ancient Hebrew seers carried off by King Nebuchadnezzar II to a seventy-year captivity in Babylon. Neither did Cooper compare himself to John, an exile on the island of Patmos, author of the Book of Revelation, which is where the title *Behold a Pale Horse* comes from. The phrase appears in chapter 6, verse 8, in which John is witness to the opening of the Seven Seals, the preview of God's secret plan to once again destroy the world prior to its rebirth as the Kingdom of Jesus Christ.

When the Fourth Seal was revealed, John wrote, "And I looked, and behold a pale horse: and his name that sat on him was Death, and Hell followed with him."

"I am no Prophet, I am no Nostradamus, I have no crystal ball," Cooper proclaimed. He was "just an ordinary guy." There was nothing supernatural about his predictions. Anyone could do it. It was all in the methodology, summed up in what he called his "standard admonition," the one rule every prospective *Hour of the Time* listener had to obey, "no matter what."

"You must not believe anything you hear on this show," Cooper declared. Nor was the listener to believe anything they heard from any other shortwave host, "or Larry King Live, Dan Rather, George Bush, Bill Clinton, or anyone else in this entire world, whether you hear it on radio, on television, or from the lips of someone standing right in front of you.

"Listen to everyone, read everything, believe *nothing* until you, yourself, can prove it with your own research," Cooper told the audience. "Only free-thinking, intelligent people who are prepared to root through all the crap and get at the truth should be listening to this show. Everyone else should just turn off their radio. We don't even want you to listen.

"*Listen to everyone. Read everything, believe nothing* . . . until you can prove to yourself whether it is true or false or lies between the many shades of gray. If you don't do this, if you cannot do this, or are just plain too lazy to do this, then I can assure you that you will march into the New World Order as a docile slave."

Then Cooper made the sound of a sheep. "*Baaa! Baaa! Baaaing* all the way."

September 11, 2001

Cooper's most famous prediction was made during the June 28, 2001, broadcast of *The Hour of the Time*. A little past his fifty-eighth birthday and drinking heavily, Cooper was doing his program from a studio he'd built in the den of his house at 96 North Clearview Circle, atop a hill in the small White Mountains town of Eagar, Arizona, fifteen miles from the New Mexico line.

"Can you believe what you have been seeing on CNN today, ladies and gentlemen?" Cooper asked the *Hour of the Time* audience that evening.

"Supposedly, a CNN reporter found Osama bin Laden, took a television camera crew with him, and interviewed him and his top leadership, lieutenants, and his colonels, and generals . . . *in their hideout!*

"Now don't you think that's kind of strange, folks?" Cooper asked with his signature chuckle. "Because the largest intelligence apparatus in the world, with the biggest budget in the history of world, has been looking for Osama bin Laden for years, and years, and years, *and can't find him!*

"But some doofus jerk-off reporter with his little camera crew waltzes right into his secret hideout and interviews him!"

This meant one of two things, Cooper told the audience. Either "everyone in the intelligence community and all the intelligence agencies of the United States government are blithering idiots and incompetent fools, or they're lying to us."

The fact was, Cooper told the audience, no one in the US intelligence services was really looking for Osama bin Laden. They knew where he was. They had since the beginning of the Soviet invasion of Afghanistan. Bin Laden, along with his entire family, was a wholly owned subsidiary of the Central Intelligence Agency.

"They created him. They're the ones funding him. They supported him to make their new utopian worlds . . . and he has served them well."

There were rumors floating around the mass media that bin Laden was planning attacks on the United States and Israel, but this was just subterfuge, Cooper said. "If Osama bin Laden is an enemy of Israel, don't you think the Mossad would have taken care of that a long time ago?" Cooper asked.

Something else was in the wind. There was no other reason for the government to allow the CNN report but to further stamp bin Laden's bearded, pointy face upon the collective American mind-set. Bogeyman of the moment, the Saudi prince was being readied for his close-up.

"I'm telling you to be prepared for a major attack!" Cooper declared. The target would be a large American city.

"Something terrible is going to happen in this country. And whatever is going to happen they're going to blame on Osama bin Laden. *Don't you even believe it.*"

Two and a half months later, on September 11, 2001, after two commercial airliners flew into the Twin Towers of the World Trade Center in a cataclysm that killed 2,996 people, including 343 New York City Fire Department personnel, Cooper's prediction came to pass.

By the time Cooper got on the air that morning, the towers had already fallen. Several hours passed before the name Osama bin Laden surfaced on the BBC feed Cooper was monitoring. The British station, which Cooper regarded as marginally more reliable than the American networks, was doing an interview with the former Israeli prime minister

General Ehud Barak and Richard Perle, chairman of George W. Bush's Defense Policy Board Advisory Committee.

Widely known as the Prince of Darkness, in part for his Reagan-era support of Edward Teller's $100 billion Strategic Defense Initiative, known as Star Wars, Perle said the attacks on New York and Washington were "clearly an act of war."

"All our Western civilization is under attack," Barak put in. The interviewer asked Perle if he thought the United States would be justified in firing cruise missiles at Kabul, the capital of Afghanistan. Perle, who along with fellow neocons Dick Cheney, Paul Wolfowitz, and Donald Rumsfeld would soon push hard for the reinvasion of Iraq, answered in the affirmative.

The Afghani authorities had "allowed Osama bin Laden to operate in their territory," Perle said. That alone was reason enough for a military strike. Bin Laden was involved, no doubt about it. Yes, Barak agreed, there was "every reason to believe" bin Laden was behind the attack.

It was then Cooper interrupted the transmission, shouting, *"How do they know who did it?*

"If the United States government had no warning like they say, if they didn't know who was going to mount these attacks, and there are no survivors from the people in these planes, *how do they know Osama bin Laden is behind it?"*

So, yet again, Cooper was right. Events were transpiring exactly as his research had indicated. Osama bin Laden, the Saudi mama's-boy prince, was about to be officially blamed for the most spectacular foreign attack on America since Pearl Harbor.

Not that Cooper was gloating about his latest successful prediction. What had happened in New York City—thousands dead, their bodies crushed beneath tons of twisted rubble, a toxic cloud rising over the metropolis—was just the beginning of a new torrent of death. On the radio feed, Perle and Barak were discussing logistics; Afghanistan would be a target, possibly, Iraq as well.

"How can they determine that they should bomb Afghanistan?" Cooper shouted with alarm. "Who are we going to be bombing? The terrorists, or the innocent people of Kabul?"

Cooper made another prediction. "Folks, I can assure you that seventy-two hours from now we will be at war. We will be bombing two or maybe three countries. . . . Because that's how it works. When governments are attacked, they lash out. Thousands of people who had nothing whatsoever to do with what is happening at the World Trade Center and the Pentagon are going to die.

"Nothing will be the same after today," Cooper said grimly.

"Get ready for it, folks, because that's what you're going to be hearing in the next weeks and months on radio and television: *Nothing will be the same after today.* . . . Because I'll tell you, ladies and gentlemen, that's what the people who *really* did this want you to think, that nothing, *nothing,* will be the same after today.

"And you know what? They're right. They're telling the truth about that. Within weeks the Congress will pass draconian legislation aimed at restricting the rights of American citizens. You're going to have surveillance cameras on every street corner. You think your phones are being tapped now, just wait.

"No one is going to gain from this except a very small group of people. Everyone else will lose. No one will lose more than the American people." This would be the most grievous casualty of the 9/11 attacks, Cooper told the audience, the nation itself, the America that could have been.

Freedom, the most elusive of qualities, best distilled in the inspired documents of the Constitution and the Bill of Rights, had been dealt a fatal blow. "From now on, freedom will be whatever the law allows you to do."

That wasn't going to stop him, Cooper told listeners. He'd stay behind his microphone up in his hilltop studio. He'd keep sending out *The Hour of the Time*, speaking truth to the ultimate power, if it was the last thing he did.

It was soon after that Cooper's final prediction came true.

"They're going to kill me, ladies and gentlemen," he told the audience. "They're going to come up here in the middle of the night, and shoot me dead, right on my doorstep."

And, around midnight on November 5, 2001, less than two months after the 9/11 attacks, that's exactly what happened.

2

Bill Cooper had been in the back of my mind for the better part of a quarter century, not that I noticed it much. His name, his book *Behold a Pale Horse,* and his radio show *The Hour of the Time,* had popped up here and there, in seemingly random bits of information and conversations, but no pattern emerged. Then, one late-fall morning in 2013, I woke up convinced that Cooper, a semi-obscure conspiracy theorist with a Cassandra-like knack for connecting the distressing dots of modern life, might hold a key to the ambient unease descending upon this great nation, land that I love. The sensation made little sense on the surface but established a haunting obligation that was difficult to shake.

Cooper's visions of things to come was much in the air as I turned off Arizona Highway 260 and drove up Udall Street toward North Clearview Circle on the evening of November 5, 2016, exactly fifteen years to the minute that Bill Cooper's final prognostication had come to pass. If an inquiring reporter was interested in communing with the man and his surprisingly persistent ghost, this seemed as good a time as any.

Much had changed on what Cooper used to call "my mountain." In 2001, the year of his death, Cooper's ranch-style residence was the only home up here. Now there were several dwellings. Pickups and minivans lined the narrow roadways. The town of Eagar, where Cooper lived the last nine years of his life, was growing. Down below, streetlamps spread vaporous orange light over once pitch-black roadways. The Circle K sign cast its LED glow. But up above, the night sky was intact, full of stars, primeval in spots.

The house where Cooper, by his own account, had experienced the happiest times of his life has been upgraded. The two-car garage has been added, animal skulls set out on posts, Georgia O'Keeffe–style, marking the edge of the gravel yard make for a nice touch. You would never guess the nature of the passion play that once unfolded up here.

Fifteen years after his death, it wasn't as if Cooper had been forgotten. On the contrary, he was probably bigger than ever. *Behold a Pale Horse* continues to sell at a brisk clip. It was still number one in Amazon's "Ancient and Controversial Knowledge" category. A whole new audience, many barely into their subteens at the time of Cooper's death, sprang up during the broadband era. With most of *The Hour of the Time* episodes available for download, a large number have been reposted to YouTube by a new generation of Cooperites operating under cyber handles like Behold a Messenger, Esoteric Riddler, FreedomVidz, TheyDwellBeneath-TheTemples, ThirdWorldAssassin, Gloomylunatic, A Graceful Watchman, and Cosmic089, to name but a few.

Cooper's digital-age lionization is epitomized by NoMad News's 2016 YouTube tribute. It begins with a Star Wars–type crawl reading, "In Loving Memory of a true American patriot; killed for Telling the Truth and LIVING IT! . . . He was murdered on his doorstep by the Federal Government!!!" If there is anyone who deserved to be called "the Truth movement Founding FATHER!!!" it was Cooper, NoMad News wrote.

Still, it was no surprise to arrive at the top of Cooper Hill shortly before midnight on November 5, 2016, Guy Fawkes Day, to find ourselves alone in paying homage to the martyred Father of the Truth Movement. Eagar is kind of out of the way for most net-based pilgrims. The town and the adjacent community of Springerville, where Cooper is buried in the town cemetery, is a four-hour drive from both Phoenix and Albuquerque.

My wife and I almost didn't make it ourselves. We were staying on a ranch east of Springerville with only one road out to the highway and that was blocked. A horse had gotten its leg stuck between the thick iron slats of a cattle guard.

The ranch hands, a bunch of sun-blasted Arizona cowpokes, were saying they hardly ever saw anything like it. Cows and horses are supposed to know better than to try to walk on cattle guards. You can barely get them to walk over a series of yellow lines painted on asphalt. It was a gruesome sight by truck headlight, watching the trapped horse trying to free his leg, only to fall back down in flailing spasms, blood seeping from its trapped fetlock. There was no way the leg wasn't broken, the hands agreed. Someone had already gone back to his cabin to get a .45.

As we waited uneasily, one of the ranch hands, a grizzled type with a ZZ Top beard, snapback cap, and vaguely subversive look in his watery blue eyes, asked me what I did "back in that New York City." Hearing I was a writer, he asked, "What kind?"

"A journalist," I said, "you know, a member of the lying mainstream media."

"The devil himself," said the cowboy, slyly, eliciting a balm of nervous laughter.

The man with the gun was back. The horse, perhaps recalling other such scenes, looked up in terror. But just then, in what seemed a magical reprieve, one of the younger ranch hands managed to free the horse's leg. A veterinarian arrived. To most everyone's surprise, the vet said the horse's leg was not broken. After shots of painkiller and antibiotics, the animal was on its feet. In a few days, it would be fine. Sometimes, the ranchers said, you get a little bit of luck.

It was a seemingly portentous event, an uncanny visitation of the animal spirits that still supposedly linger out here, on what used to be Apache and Navajo land. On the way to commemorate the death of the author of *Behold a Pale Horse,* it fit.

This was how it was with Bill Cooper, I thought to myself, not for the first time. In the opening paragraph of *Behold a Pale Horse,* Cooper writes, "There have been many related sequential coincidences all throughout my life, incidents that by themselves would have led nowhere. Statistically, the odds against the same or a related sequence of events happening to one individual are astronomically high. It is this series of incidents that have convinced me that God has had a hand in my life. I do not believe in fate. I do not believe in accidents."

I thought back to the first time I'd ever heard of Bill Cooper. It was in 1991, the year *Behold a Pale Horse* was published. On this particular day, I was at Mount Sinai Hospital in New York to say a last goodbye to a treasured friend and mentor, Harold Conrad.

Like Bill Cooper, Harold Conrad was one of those essential, if largely unrecognized twentieth-century American characters, in this case a prime specimen of the Ellis Island *boulevardier* variety. Keen to the nuances of post–World War Two popular culture, Harold's great talent was in being in the right place at the right time, once and maybe forever the hippest guy in the room.

The résumé was impressive. He'd been a gossip columnist for the *Brooklyn Eagle*, did "public relations" for Meyer Lansky's Colonial Inn in Miami, was a close friend of *Guys and Dolls* author Damon Runyon, had promoted Evel Knievel's failed jump over the Snake River Canyon. He was also the only person I ever met who had Humphrey Bogart play him in a movie (*The Harder They Fall*, 1956). But now he was dying. Barely able to speak above a whisper, he motioned for me to put my ear near his mouth.

"Did you bring a joint?" he asked. It was the last thing I ever heard him say.

I met Harold's son, Casey, a drummer, at the hospital. We went over to his apartment, talked about his dad. A man's life, especially to a son and a friend, inevitably boiled down to fathomless mystery, we agreed, as Casey suddenly changed the subject and put a tape into the VCR. He said he had something very important to show me. I assumed it had to do with Harold, but after a few moments of visual static, the images settled into a familiar, chilling tableau. There was President Kennedy's motorcade making its way through Dealey Plaza in Dallas.

We were watching the Zapruder film, the famous home movie shot by children's clothing manufacturer Abraham Zapruder with his Bell and Howell 8mm Zoomatic on November 22, 1963.

It was a terrible, washed-out copy, probably a fifth- or sixth-generation dupe. You could barely make out the young and handsome president, first lady Jackie beside him in her pillbox hat, the hopeful promise for the future they represented. But it was better than nothing. At the time, it was almost impossible to get a copy of the Zapruder film.

The original had been purchased for $150,000 by Henry Luce's head man at Time Life, C. D. Jackson, the former deputy director of the Allied forces' Psychological Warfare Division and member of Wild Bill Donovan's Office of Strategic Services, forerunner of the CIA. I'd heard rumors about various Zapruder copies circulating in the underground. Casey's copy appeared to be one of those.

By 1991, the gnawing conundrum of Kennedy's death had dragged into its twenty-eighth year. Every day of the week, murder cases were being cracked by municipal police departments. On TV they did it inside of an hour, with time out for commercials. However, here was the crime of the century, the assassination of a president in broad daylight, witnessed by hundreds of people. Yet in the minds of many, it remained a debilitating societal enigma, a national humiliation.

It was the sheer resistance to transparency that was so maddening. The Warren Commission, composed of the alleged best and brightest, offered nothing but the galling implausibility of Lee Harvey Oswald at the sixth-floor window of the Texas School Book Depository with his Italian mail-order rifle.

Over the years, there had been many proposed scenarios of what happened on November 22, 1963. The docket of usual suspects included the CIA, the Mafia, Cubans, gay southern businessman Clay Shaw, Lyndon Johnson, and a trio of bums, two of whom looked a lot like the Watergate burglars Frank Sturgis and E. Howard Hunt. There was the man with the black umbrella, shooters from the Grassy Knoll, and many others. It was the deepest of rabbit holes, one many felt a solemn, patriotic responsibility to jump into, often never to be seen again.

Still, I must say, in the byzantine annals of what came to be called assassinationology, I had never heard a theory so outside the accepted realm of possibility as the one I expressed that evening in the apartment of Harold Conrad's son.

The driver did it. That was the story. The limo driver, William Greer, a fifty-two-year-old Secret Service agent born in the village of Stewartstown, County Tyrone, Northern Ireland, killed the president. As the motorcade turned, Greer stopped the limo, turned from the steering wheel, and shot the president square in the forehead. He did this at the closest of ranges in full view of all those eyewitnesses, including those sitting right there in the car. Yet somehow no one noticed this. Or perhaps the shock of the moment made them forget.

Like David Hemmings continually enlarging his photograph in Michelangelo Antonioni's *Blow-Up*, a big campus date film in 1966, we sat there for a good while running the tape backward and forward, pushing the PAUSE button at what seemed the critical moment.

There could be no doubt that Greer slowed down the vehicle prior to the shooting. The brake lights come on. Sunlight glints off what appears to be a gun in Greer's hand.

In the sober light of day, killjoys suggested that "the gun" was actually the sun's reflection off the Brylcreemed hair of Roy Kellerman, the Secret Service man riding in the passenger seat. But a Brylcreem reflection was not what a nation starved for the Truth needed to see. After twenty-eight years, the country was desperate for an answer, something to hang your hat on. William Greer's alleged act provided that, if only for a fleeting instance.

Where did he get this? I asked Harold's son. He said it came from a man named Milton William Cooper. Cooper was touring around the country, selling his indistinct copies of the Zapruder tape at thirty-five dollars a pop.

"Don't watch the president, watch the driver," Cooper would instruct the audience as he played the film in the basements of VFW halls and hotel conference rooms. When asked how Greer had managed to escape detection on the scene, Cooper said that the driver had been abetted by the use of "an electrically operated, gas-powered assassin's weapon built especially for the Central Intelligence Agency which fired pellets of shellfish toxin."

The recoilless weapon was used, Cooper said, because "if the impact of the pellet did not kill the president, the toxin would." This was the reason Kennedy's brain was switched for another brain in transit between Parkland Hospital and the Bethesda Naval Facility in Washington.

This was, of course, crazy talk. Yet you had to appreciate the audacity of the scenario. Cooper, whom I had never heard of, was saying that the ever-more rococo theories of Kennedy's death were flights of fancy at best and deliberate dispatches of disinformation at worst. What hundreds of eyewitnesses had missed had been caught by the lens of Zapruder's Bell and Howell Zoomatic. Perhaps not everyone would be able to make out Greer's history-changing act. It took a certain gift, a specific frame of mind. But for those capable of accepting the hitherto hidden truth of the matter, the great mystery had been solved.

Ol' Dirty Bastard, Wu-Tang Clan, mid-1990s

My second interface with Bill Cooper and his work dates back to late 1992 or early '93, as I walked along Seventh Avenue in my as-yet not fully gentrified neighborhood, Park Slope, Brooklyn. There were many great hip-hop practitioners in the early 1990s; it was the Golden Age, the time of N.W.A., Tupac, Biggie Smalls, and the rest. But few consortiums engendered the love afforded the Wu-Tang Clan, at least among many New York fans. It was no stretch to imagine oneself watching the same kung-fu film in the same sticky-floored Forty-Second Street movie house with members of the Clan. This would be followed by a wide-ranging discussion about whether the ancient masters used the lethal "reverberating palm" to murder Bruce Lee for revealing too many martial arts secrets to the *lo fan* in films like *Fist of Fury* and *Enter the Dragon*.

Back then, most of the Wu-Tang, RZA, GZA, Raekwon, Method Man, Ghostface Killah, et al., were still living on Staten Island, which they called Shaolin after the order of warrior monks dating to the Sui and Tang dynasties. But Russell T. Jones, better known as Ol' Dirty Bastard or simply ODB, still hung around his mother's home near Methodist Hospital only a few blocks from my house in Brooklyn. Around the time of the release of the group's monumental *Enter the Wu-Tang (36 Chambers)*, I saw ODB sitting on a stoop on Sixth Street. He was reading *Behold a Pale Horse*. I said hello, but engrossed, he did not look up.

Over the following years, I began to notice that the Wu-Tang were far from the only rappers interested in Bill Cooper. The writer and his book have been name-checked thousands of times by any number of artists, big-time and not. Such luminaries as Tupac, LL Cool J, Busta Rhymes, CeeLo Green, Eminem, Jay-Z, Immortal Technique, and dozens of others have either invoked Cooper and his work in their music or talked about him in interviews.

Typical was the Wu-Tang's own "Gravel Pit," in which Method Man raps about a holocaust stemming from "the land of the lost, behold a pale horse, of course (of course)." (Leave it to the Wu-Tang to throw in the *Mr. Ed* reference.) As late as 2008, rapper Nas, the Queensbridge Houses project-raised lyrical nonpareil, paid tribute in "Testify." He was exposing shit, Nas rapped, likening himself to Cooper, "who told you *Pale Horse* is the future."

The fact that Cooper was a fat white guy living on top of a hill in Arizona, and was being described by liberal organizations like the Anti-Defamation League of B'nai B'rith and the Southern Poverty Law Center as a right-wing militia leader, mattered not at all. If anything, it was a plus. Cooper was a former Navy military intelligence man; if he was saying that George Bush and Bill Clinton were behind the CIA plot to move crack cocaine into the ghetto, and claiming that AIDS was a man-made virus cooked up to wipe out the African people, this was worth listening to. Why would someone from military intelligence say stuff like that if it wasn't true?

That was when the word on the street was don't buy a copy of *Behold a Pale Horse* with a credit card, if you happened to have such a thing. That put you on The List. Just to have the book in your possession was a risk.

But it would take ODB to truly explain the reason why Bill Cooper mattered. This didn't occur until early 2003, a decade after I'd seen him reading *Behold a Pale Horse* in Brooklyn. Cooper had been dead two years by then and Dirty wasn't looking so good himself when I went to interview him for a magazine piece. The composer and singer of "Brooklyn Zoo" and "Shimmy Shimmy Ya," was only thirty-six at the time, but that was like 3,600 in ODB years.

The stories were folkloric. One time, while on the lam, ODB showed up for a Wu-Tang gig at the Hammerstein Ballroom in Manhattan. He did a couple numbers to tumultuous response, then gave the waiting cops the slip, only to be picked up a few days later signing autographs for his fans in the parking lot of a McDonald's on Grays Ferry Avenue in Philadelphia.

Now, however, Dirty had thirteen children and almost as many stints in jail, including a just-completed two-year dope bid in Clinton-Dannemora, a notorious prison hellhole built in 1844. When I asked him how he was doing, ODB said only, "Haldol," the name of the powerful antipsychotic drug he was taking. Some record guys had the rapper under close watch in a condo apartment in Nanuet, New York, over the Tappan Zee Bridge. They were trying to keep him alive long enough to finish a record begun years before.

We'd been sitting there a while, ODB and me, watching the Robin Williams movie *Mrs. Doubtfire* on television, when I brought up seeing him those many years before, reading Bill Cooper's *Behold a Pale Horse*.

It took a moment, but ODB turned to me, his face swollen, eyelids leaden. "William Cooper . . . *Behold a Pale Horse* . . . *yeah*." A spasm of lucidity took hold. For an instant, he was as clear as a bell.

"Everybody gets fucked. William Cooper tells you who's fucking you." When you were someone like him, ODB said, "that's valuable information."

Now, a dozen years after Dirty's death, we were on Bill Cooper's mountain, looking at the stars. Betelgeuse and Rigel were up there in the southeast sky, gleaming jewels on Orion's Belt. So were the Pleiades, the cluster known as the Seven Sisters. During his flying saucer period, Cooper had said that's where the aliens came from, the evil long-nosed Grays who had met with Dwight D. Eisenhower at Edwards Air Force Base in 1954.

A bit of wine spilled for memory's sake, we drove back down Cooper Hill. The cowboys back at the ranch had told us we might not want to hang around too long. The gun laws in Arizona weren't like they were in Brooklyn. In Arizona, they've got open carry, concealed carry, every kind of carry. You go into Bashas' Supermarket on North Main Street in Eagar and middle-aged ladies pick through the broccoli with raspberry-pink-handled .380s strapped to their hips. The Castle Doctrine was in effect, which meant one step across the property line and the homeowner might be well within his rights to put one between your eyes, especially after midnight.

Besides, the icy wind was picking up, slicing hard through the Carhartt. The Navajos call November the time of the *nil-chi-tsosie*, or "small wind." This precedes *nil-chi-tso*, the "big wind" of December, when it can blow a steady sixty or seventy miles per hour for hours at a time. On bad days, when Cooper lived up here, trying to get by without proper insulation, he had to drape his windows with Pendleton blankets bought at the trading posts along old Route 66 in Gallup, New Mexico.

There was another kind of wind, too, whipping in from the north near Canyon de Chelly, former home to the vanished Anasazi people. This was the *hochxoo*, or the "dark wind."

3

If Bill Cooper's ghost was elusive on the night of November 5, it proved palpable only three nights later. It was November 8, 2016, when the results of the presidential election blindsided the mind.

Throughout the campaign, fans pointed out that Cooper had been the first to alert the country to the possible election of someone like Donald J. Trump. This dated back to an interview Cooper did with CNN in 1992.

Looking hale and hearty in his customary button-bursting plaid flannel shirt, a genial Cooper sat on a couch and said that in the current climate, with the vast majority of politicians in the pocket of Illuminati overlords, it was now "impossible for another Abraham Lincoln to be elected president of the United States." The only way to get rid of the corrupt cast of characters in office was "to stop voting for them."

"Kick all the members of the secret societies out of the bureaucracy. Try them for treason, because that's what they are, traitors," Cooper told the interviewer.

The only way to restore the Constitution to its place as the supreme law of the land was to elect a president "who had never served in government before." It would have to be done quickly, "in the space of a single election," Cooper said in 1992. Twenty-four years later, the campaign of Donald J. Trump seemed to fit that description.

It is hard to imagine Cooper supporting Donald Trump with his cheesy gold-plate George the Third patina. On the other hand, he'd rather have been beaten with a truncheon than to see Hillary Clinton assume the highest office in the land.

Cooper made his feelings known about the Clintons early on, in the run-up to the 1992 election, when he correctly predicted that Bill

Clinton, who was trailing in the polls at the time, would become the forty-second president of the United States.

The description of the Clinton skullduggery was classic Cooper, the product of a man who bragged that while others might be content to open "cans of worms, I open barrels of worms."

The scenario was a snap for those who did their own research. With the end of the Cold War in the early 1990s, the elites required a new man to preside over the American sector of the New World Order (NWO). George H. W. Bush, onetime CIA head, had been a faithful anti-Soviet servant. His presidency amounted to a gold watch for services rendered. But new times required new men, and Poppy didn't even know what a supermarket scanner was. A more down-home, hot-sauce-drenched figure was needed, someone like Bill Clinton.

The fixers had been grooming Bubba since his saxophone-tooting days in the piney-woods home of his single mom. They snatched him out of the Arkansas muck and made him a Rhodes Scholar—a power apprentice course founded by the ultimate globalist Cecil J. Rhodes, builder of the Cape to Cairo Road, master of the De Beers diamond mines, the only man to have three countries (Rhodesia, Northern Rhodesia, Rhodesia and Nyasaland) and a dog (the Ridgeback) bear his name.

Handicapping the election, Cooper said the third-party candidate, H. Ross Perot, was in the race "to make sure Bush lost." Once, Perot was a nobody, a Texarkana Community College student. But now, according to Cooper, Perot's longtime patron, David Rockefeller, was offering the deal of a lifetime. Perot's company, Electronic Data Systems, Cooper told a cable TV audience, had been secretly chosen to be the exclusive manufacturer of "the implant," the tracking device that would soon be inserted under the skin of every American.

The deal was worth billions. All Perot had to do, Cooper said, was run for president. His homey pie charts and psuedo-Libertarian tone would be a death knell for the hopelessly plutocratic Bush. As it turned out, Perot's 19 percent was more than enough to swing the election to Clinton.

"Bill Clinton!" Cooper raged to the *Hour of the Time* audience. "*Rhodes Scholar!* Member of the Council on Foreign Relations and the Trilateral Commission! *Draft dodger!* Spent time in the Soviet Union when no other American citizen was allowed to travel there! Socialist, par excellence!" The same went for Hillary Clinton, Bubba's First Lady *Macbeth* partner-in-crime.

This particular view of history was very much in play on November 8, 2016, as we settled in to watch the election returns at the Sugar Shack, a fun little joint in the unincorporated town of Concho, Arizona, about an hour's drive from Eagar.

The political leanings of the crowd at the Sugar Shack had been made apparent when we'd visited the place a few nights earlier to sample the excellent Surf n' Turf special, which proprietors Ray and Marie cook on a gas grill out on the porch. There was some drunkenness, and a soused lady took a header down the stairs. It looked bad, but after a quick check revealed no blood, people walked away.

"She's a Democrat, let her lie," someone said, to much laughter.

We were in Trump country. If anyone in the room had, however reluctantly, voted for Hillary Clinton, they weren't talking about it.

The reason we'd come to the Sugar Shack was to cheer on candidate Doyel Shamley. Like Trump, Clinton, and the immigrant-hunting Sheriff Joe Arpaio down in Maricopa County, Doyel, known to *Hour of the Time* fans as Bill Cooper's research partner and all-around right-hand man, was on the ballot this election day. He was running for supervisor in District 3 of Apache County.

This was no small thing. Apache County, a vast strip of land running along the New Mexico border from the Four Corners region down past the White Mountains town of Alpine, measures 11,218 square miles. That makes it the sixth-largest county in the country. With barely 70,000 people (Eagar, pop. 4,800, is the largest community), it is also one of our nation's least-densely populated. Few places in the USA have more wide-open spaces.

When I started researching Cooper, everyone told me if I wanted to get the real story, Doyel was the guy to talk to.

As representatives of successive generations of American fighting men—Cooper in Vietnam and Doyel in the first Gulf War—they had a lot in common. The wars may have been twenty-five years apart, half a world away from each other, but as far as Cooper and Doyel were concerned, the conflicts were part of the same, corrosive, never-ending process. That made them brothers-in-arms, natural allies. Both ardent patriots and prodigious readers, they shared research on many matters, from the extent of federal jurisdiction to the ancient secret society the Brotherhood of the Snake to the symbolism of the Phrygian cap worn by fighters during the French Revolution. When their libraries were combined, there were more than fifteen thousand titles.

Doyel also worked on the *Hour of the Time* broadcasts, often appearing on the air, sometimes hosting shows with Cooper's young daughter, Dorothy, whom everyone called Pooh.

After Cooper's death, Doyel kept *The Hour of the Time* on the air. Along with webmaster Rob Houghton, Doyel helped put together *The Complete Cooper*, a digital archive of all 1,926 *HOTT* broadcasts (including repeats). If anyone could be called the keeper of the Bill Cooper flame, it was Doyel Shamley.

At the outset of my research into Cooper, I googled Doyel's name. The first thing that came up was a six-minute YouTube video *The End According to Doyel Shamley*.

Accompanied by ominous strains of electronic music, the 2009 video begins with images of a cloud-crowned primeval forest, an untouched Eden. There is a stark image of the Java man, among the earliest of the *Homo erectus* species, followed by a home movie of a man berating his son. This morphed into a mass rally with swarms of faceless people holding up giant placards of Mao Tse-tung and Chou En-lai.

"Ever since the first slimeball came out of the ocean and developed into a stronger man than his neighbor, someone had the inclination to control someone else," Doyel's Okie-inflected narration begins. The life of the common man had been reduced to the constant hand-to-hand combat of Hobbesian natural selection. You could fight it, and if push came to shove, he would, Doyel said, in the front lines "alongside good friends." But then again, he mused, perhaps it would be better to let the whole thing implode. That way, the survivors, "those who want to prosper and be free again," could set about rebuilding a world worth living in.

A busy man, Doyel was abrupt when I first contacted him. After all, I was far from the first person to come around asking about Bill Cooper. Following the shoot-out on the hill, it seemed important to tell Cooper's story and Doyel did, spreading details on the radio and in a 2003 documentary, *The Hour of Our Time*. But after a while, there were simply too many Internet posts saying things like "Bill Cooper Told the Truth about 9/11. Two Months Later They Killed Him for It." Cooper had become a god to an increasingly eccentric flock.

You never knew who might turn up. One day a man appeared uninvited inside Doyel's house. Reacting as any homeowner with Special Forces training might, Doyel pounced on the guy and jammed a large-caliber firearm into his midsection. The man explained that he found Doyel's home via an arcane triangulation of coordinates based on images of Cooper's home available online.

The stars had been rearranging themselves since the beginning of time, the intruder told Doyel. Soon humanity would look up and see the name JESUS spelled out across the firmament. The man thought anyone who had been Bill Cooper's right hand needed to know that information. His message delivered, the man left.

After a period of text tag, Doyel drove up to my motel in a mud-splashed Toyota pickup with a battering-ram-type shield attached to the front bumper. Sporting an early sixties George Jones–style flattop, attired in camo pants and a sheepskin vest against the morning frost, Doyel leveled the gaze of his blue-steel eyes and said he wanted to get one thing straight from the get-go.

"I swore I would never spend another minute of my time talking about this, so let's go," Doyel said. I was to be the last reporter to hear what he knew about the Bill Cooper story.

As we drove around the cinder cones of the Miocene-vintage Springerville volcanic field, Doyel filled me in a little about his background. His people were Okies; they'd come to California during the Dust Bowl days. That was the old joke, about how there were supposed to be more Okies in Bakersfield and Stockton than in Oklahoma, Doyel said as we drove along US 191, which used to be called US 666 before the Mormons complained and the DOT got sick of people stealing the signs.

Several of his relatives were pickers, on the migrant circuit through the 1950s, Doyel said. "They went to Montana for the cherries, then to Washington for apples, back home for navels and Valencias. That was when the central valley of California was," Doyel said with a dismissive laugh, "the breadbasket of the world, not the breadbasket of bankruptcy that it is now."

Even if he was the sort of demographic that traditionally fill the ranks of the US Armed Forces, this did not appear to be Doyel's destiny.

"I'm not saying anything, but I always stood out from others my age. I was an Eagle Scout, won every badge you could win. Did really well in school, college-level science and math, economics and political theory. I've got a kind of photographic memory. I can really take in a large amount of information in a short amount of time and retain it.

"I was on the high school debate team. All the rich kids, these pricks from San Diego prep schools, they said we were a bunch of Okies, and we cleaned their fucking clocks. We went to the National Finals in Washington and got a tour of the House and Senate. For years I thought I would go into low-temperature physics, superconductors, magic sort of stuff. Then there was the symphony, playing cello.

"They said I was a prodigy. I was the youngest person in the local symphony. We played the greats. Beethoven's Fifth, *The Rite of Spring*, Mahler."

Mahler was "a real sick son of a bitch," Doyel said. "He was always writing in all these different time signatures just to torture the orchestra. Our poor conductor almost had a heart attack. We played *Carmina Burana* . . . I really liked that except when I was playing, I had images in my mind of all these monks running wild and raping nuns before they locked them up in the monastery. One time we went to the Azores to play for the king, that was cool.

"We already had these letters from Stanford. Probably could have gotten a free ride, on account of the cello," Doyel said. "I would have had it made.

"*But no.* No college, no first seat in the philharmonic for Doyel. I decided what I really wanted to do was *fight for my country.*"

His father, John Shamley, a surveyor by trade, was military, but a "special kind of military," Doyel said. He was attached to the Civilian Affairs Division as a photographer. He took pictures at events like Douglas MacArthur's funeral. "Dad got right in there, open coffin, better stuff than anything that came out in *Life* magazine," said Doyel.

"They sent him to New York and he'd walk around, taking pictures. As for what he was taking pictures of, who and why, he never said. There was one shot, a plane that crashed in the snow. I guess the idea was that he was supposed to be on the scene, but there were these other shots, too, where you'd see the plane was really a prop sitting on a soundstage.

"It was kind of humorous," he continued, describing the day he enlisted in the service. "It happened to be my sister's eighth birthday. They were having this little party. The recruiter brought me home. He went into the house and walks right over to my father, shakes his hand, and says, 'Mr. Shamley, I'd like to congratulate you. Your son just enlisted in *the United States Army.*'

"My father jumped right out of his chair. He was screaming at the recruiter. 'Get out of here! Whatever you told him is a lie! I know it and you know it.'"

Doyel went anyway, quickly sent off to Iraq to fight in Desert Storm. As an infantryman with top marksman scores, he sometimes carried the M60 machine gun, the one Sylvester Stallone rocks in *Rambo.* Capable of firing 500–600 rounds of large-caliber .308 bullets per minute, the M60 is a highly efficient killing machine. The main drawback was the weight. The fully outfitted M60 can weigh at least twenty-five pounds, not including the 100-round bandolier the operator straps across his chest like a modern-day Pancho Villa.

"The life expectancy carrying that kind of weapon is about eight minutes, so they like to give it to the short guys because you were a smaller target," said the five-foot-nine Doyel, who despite his relatively modest stature retains many of the deadly skills learned in combat training. Once asked the size of the mountain lions who roam the White Mountains, he said, "Oh, I don't know. Just imagine me on all fours."

Things between Doyel and me took a turn for the better when we drove over to the 26 Bar Hereford Ranch, west of Springerville. The handsome spread had once been owned by the Duke himself, John Wayne. Back in the 1960s and early 1970s, Wayne used to come in for the cattle sales, often stopping in for the first-class breakfast at the Safire Restaurant on Springerville's Main Street. The star's presence was a source of pride to the local community, which still holds an annual John Wayne Days festival. After Wayne's death in 1979, however, the

26 Bar was put up for sale. The buyer turned out to be the Hopi Indian Tribe.

"I love that," Doyel snickered as we sat in the truck, overlooking Wayne's old ponderosa. "He kills a million Indians, now they got his ranch. HAHAHA."

But what really broke the ice between us was the mention of the notorious punk rocker GG Allin. Reputedly born Jesus Christ Allin in New Hampshire in 1956, GG was legend for his transgressive, i.e., gross, live shows. He was known to defecate on the stage while playing songs like "Shoot, Knife, Strangle, Beat, and Crucify," "Darkness and a Bottle to Hold," and "Bite It You Scum."

Allin's name came up while we were barreling down old 666, listening to Cannibal Corpse, Deicide, and for old time's sake, Slayer, on Liquid Metal, Doyel's favorite Sirius XM channel. I mentioned that I'd once seen Allin and his band, the Murder Junkies, play in Tompkins Square Park in New York's East Village, and Doyel got a delightedly goony smile on his face.

"Oh, man, I love him. I got everything he ever did," Doyel said, breaking into a couple of lines of "Die When You Die."

After that, Doyel and I became friendly, at least friendly enough. My wife and I traveled to Eagar a number of times, attending the 2014 and 2015 Skills and Research Conference, a continuation of the meetings Cooper organized during the middle 1990s. While Cooper's conferences generally involved much sitting in classrooms listening to lectures on Freemasonry and tax protesting, Doyel's version tended to be a lot more hands-on, heavy on preparation for WROL (without rule of law) situations, and plenty of target practice. He would set up some targets supposed to be a guy hiding behind a bathroom stall door and yell to "shoot right through it."

As part of an ad hoc cultural exchange program, Doyel and his significant other came to visit us in Brooklyn. It was a kick, showing them around the Big Town, eating at Peter Luger's, taking them up to Arthur Avenue in the Bronx to have a real slice of pizza. We did the tourist things, riding on the Staten Island Ferry and going to the top of the Empire State Building. It was a different place, Doyel had to admit, riding the subway on the uptown Lexington Avenue line, reading a copy of

Battlefield Ballistic Wounds he bought at the Strand bookstore, wondering if his interpretation of the Second Amendment would hold up during rush hour.

Our guests loved the cheesecake at Junior's on Flatbush Avenue, so we sent them one for Christmas. When his brother-in-law, a cop, started to open the package by mistake, Doyel intervened, saying, "Keep your government dick-beaters off my cheesecake."

In 2016, however, there was no Skills and Research Conference. Doyel was campaigning full-time to win election as the Apache County supervisor in District 3. It was a job that would offer Doyel a larger opportunity to influence local policy, especially in the all-important issue of land rights. Surrounded by huge stretches of federal property, it was Doyel's position that the land should be under local control, with county jurisdiction playing a leading role.

When we first met, he was leading the fight against the US Fish and Wildlife Service's introduction of the Mexican gray wolf into the Apache-Sitgreaves National Forests. The feds claimed the forest was the animal's natural habitat. Doyel said this was crap. The Mexican wolf wasn't even a real species; it was a hybrid that had never been native to the area, he said. The animal was preying on ranchers' cows, destroying whatever mom-and-pop commerce remained in the area. The feds, making their environmental policies in Washington, DC, didn't care about that, Doyel said.

Asked what progress he was making, Doyel flashed his best Dennis the Menace smile and said he was kicking the butts of "the douche spout greenies. The lady from Sierra Club in Phoenix, she hates my guts."

Doyel had run for office before and lost. But his knowledge of local issues was impressive enough that his victorious opponent brought him in as the county natural resource coordinator, where he helped develop environmental policies for the county. For the current election, Doyel was putting in the maximum effort. By the beginning of November he'd put several thousand miles on his truck, driving great distances to drum up the vote. His black-and-white posters were slapped on fences from the ski resorts of Alpine to Window Rock, the capital of the Navajo Nation three hundred miles north.

The Navajo reservation, which makes up most of the county north of Interstate 40, was Doyel's chance. The vast majority of the tribe, solidly

Democratic, were for Hillary. But after years of battling the Bureau of Indian Affairs, the Diné, as the Navajo call themselves, liked what Doyel had to say about the overbearing tactics of the federal agencies. As one local leader said, the US government "stole our land once and they're not going to do it again."

Still, Doyel remained the underdog. His opponent, Gary Davis, held formidable advantages. He was a well-liked boss at the local Salt River Power Plant, where many in the southern part of the county worked. Far more imposing, however, was Davis's status as a bishop in the Church of the Latter-day Saints. The Mormons, everyone said, had controlled Apache County politics back to before Arizona even became a state. If he won the supervisor job, Doyel said, he'd be the first non-Mormon to hold the office since 1879. "That's one hundred and thirty-seven years," Doyel said, "which is a long time."

On election night at the Sugar Shack, the Trump victory was taking people by surprise. Even if they'd voted for him, few in town thought he was going to win. People favored Trump's position on Obamacare, which they hated, along with everything about else about Obama. Trump had his flaws, to be sure, but at least he was a human being.

"Hillary is Satan," said one of Trump's voters. Better known as "Killary" or "Hitlery," Clinton was the personification of the Evil One. Relatively speaking, that made Trump, as one supporter at the Sugar Shack said, "God's man in the race."

A woman wearing a MAKE AMERICA GREAT AGAIN cap said she was offended that corporate media outlets kept preaching it was her duty as a female to vote for Hillary. "I'm supposed to vote for her because we're the same sex? How insulting is that?" the woman said. Trump's lewd talk didn't bother her. It was disgusting, but that was how men were, disgusting. But how could Hillary put up with her husband's philandering? "She stood by and let him humiliate her because she couldn't bear to give up power."

The Clintons had to be stopped, another woman said, bringing up Pizzagate, the ambient conspiracy charge that the Democratic Party candidate was involved in a global pedophile ring run out of the basement of Comet Ping Pong pizzeria in northwest Washington, DC. The sexual trafficking of underage children—John Podesta, Clinton campaign manager, was said to be spending time in hot tubs with six-year-olds—was exactly the sort of satanic ritual that always went on in Washington, people said.

"Pizzagate is real," the woman in the Trump hat said. Asked how she knew that, she said she'd "done her research. . . . I try to read everything I can, I talk to as many people as possible. But I don't believe anything I read until I do my own research."

The phraseology rang a bell. I asked the woman if she was an *Hour of the Time* fan. She had never heard of it. I provided a short Cooper bio, including details of the fifteen-year-old shoot-out that occurred only forty or so miles away from where we sat. Again, there was no recognition.

The woman and her husband weren't native to the area. "We're snowbirds," the couple said in unison. But they agreed that Cooper's dictum to find your own Truth made sense. Who else could you trust?

It was about then that the TV networks declared Florida for Trump. The real estate developer was sweeping the battleground states. Ohio fell, then Pennsylvania. Jubilant shouts filled the Sugar Shack.

My cell phone was ringing. People from back east, friends from California, were calling, saying they couldn't believe it. Donald Trump? President? This couldn't really be happening, could it?

"Where are you?" one caller asked. "What's that cheering?"

I told him I was in Arizona, at the Sugar Shack, where everyone voted for Trump. That was why they were cheering.

"Well, everyone here is crying," the caller said, bitterly, before hanging up.

The lady in the MAKE AMERICA GREAT AGAIN hat was exultant. "Well, if this doesn't wake up the sheeple, I don't know what will."

"Wake up, sheeple," I replied. It was another famous Bill Cooper phrase, I explained.

"Really?" she said. "Well, everyone will be shouting it from the rooftops from now on."

We left the Sugar Shack before Trump hit 270. All things considered, it was better to be here, among the revelers, than in front of the TV in Park Slope, where everyone was slitting their wrists. It wasn't going to change the result.

Besides, we liked these people, in spots at least. We hoped they felt similarly. That was part of the mission: détente—an attempt to restore the supposedly washed-out transit between "our America" and "their America." To see if there was any "America" left between us and them.

These were worthwhile goals, but there was a limit. There was no way we were hanging around the Sugar Shack to watch the country go completely down the tubes. It felt a moment of real change, a point of no return. It made you think how you got to this precarious place.

Driving back to Eagar, the only car on US Highway 60, surrounded by the immense blackness of the Arizona night, my thoughts turned back to Bill Cooper holed up in his house on the hill, a lone and lonely soldier behind his microphone, hurling insults at his New World Order tormenters.

Within weeks of the shoot-out on Cooper Hill, the New York–based pulp house Global Communications released *William Cooper: Death of a Conspiracy Salesman*, edited by the mysterious "Commander X," whose other titles include *Mind Stalkers: UFOs, Implants, & the Pyschotronic Agenda of the New World Order* and *Invisibility and Levitation: How-To Keys to Personal Performance*.

Likely the least successful "quickie" book put out to capitalize on "celebrity" demise, *William Cooper: Death of a Conspiracy Salesman*, not unlike *Behold a Pale Horse* itself, has the aspect of a hastily thrown together collage of newspaper clippings, murkily reproduced photos, reprints, and memorabilia.

That said, Commander X's title cannot be beat. Bill Cooper was a conspiracy salesman as sure as Willy Loman carried a battered suitcase. Perpetually hard-up for money, in many ways he recalls the mythic figure in the green visor who sits in an office at the end of a long, narrow corridor, feverishly typing out every dirty joke you ever heard, ten dollars a punch line. A P. T. Barnum of dread, Cooper lived by the darkening edge of his conspiracy stories and his capacity to find an audience willing to hear and believe them. It was an ethic he practiced until the night of his death.

In one of the obits that appears in *William Cooper: Death of a Conspiracy Salesman*, Kenn Thomas, esteemed writer and a close observer of what he called "parapolitics," said that despite Cooper's often outlandish pronouncements, "he was right in his broad strokes. He certainly was not alone in looking into the political and cultural environment and see-ing an evil monster, but he was more articulate than most in getting across what that feels like."

By now I'd been listening to *Hour of the Time* programs for the better part of three years, reading Cooper's overheated works, tracing his incon-gruous, almost Zelig-like spread through the cultural landscape. Once you got through bluster, the hucksterism, and the name-calling, there was mostly anguish. The nation was in decline, sinking lower every day. If there was one thing every Fox News and MSNBC viewer could agree on, it was that America's assumed status as the land of the free and home of the brave was under assault. Cooper's prescience, and his curse, was to understand this quicker and more deeply than most. He went around the country asking his audience, "What is America, what's it all about?"

People raised their hands, and Cooper, the stern professor, called on them, one by one. "Recognition of God-given rights," "individual lib-erty," "no King but King Jesus," "sound money," came the responses. But the real answer was never in doubt.

"Freedom," Cooper said, that was what America was all about. The freedom of the individual human being as guaranteed by the Constitu-tion was what separated the US from every other country ever invented.

Cooper spent his whole life fighting the enemies of freedom. He fought them in Vietnam, or so he thought at the time. He fought them when he imagined they were coming from outer space. He fought them when he believed they were evil plutocrats, followers of secret reli-gions dating back to the beginning of recorded history.

Cooper found the enemy in the people around him, in those he tried to love, within himself. These realizations only made him more deter-mined to resist. And where had the fight got him? To the hilltop, with the blaring sirens, the barking dogs, the tramping feet.

Sometimes, he'd talk to his *Hour of the Time* audience with an air of quiet despair. "I'll tell you right now, folks, whether you're religious or not, it doesn't make a difference. Whether you believe in God or not, it doesn't make a difference. It is all a big battle between Good and Evil and most of it, I got to tell you, exists in the minds of men. Some of it is real, some of it isn't. The question is what's real? What's deception, what should we be paying attention to . . . what is it that is driving us *insane?*"

PART TWO

The New World Order

4

Milton William Cooper was born during the time of war, on May 6, 1943. On that same day, Allied troops under Dwight D. Eisenhower moved into Tunis, near Carthage, city of Hannibal Barca, the African general who defeated Rome at Cannae in 216 BC, killing fifty thousand legionnaires. Eisenhower's advance, coming on the heels of the defeat of the German army by the Soviets at Stalingrad, where over a million died, further diminished Nazi prospects to win the war.

By April of 1945, the New World Order as envisioned by Adolf Hitler, a dominion in which the free will of the vast majority of humanity would be subject to the mercy of a self-designated race of "supermen," had come to an end.

The cost of the Allied victory was enormous. No war had ever been so destructive. More than fifty million people perished. Much of Europe was in ruins. The atomic bomb, a new and inconceivably powerful weapon, had devastated the Japanese cities of Hiroshima and Nagasaki, killing over two hundred thousand inhabitants. No longer would it take forty days and forty nights to destroy a world; it could happen in an instant.

This was where the vaunted civilization of the Enlightenment had led. Humanity's self-regard, the belief that the species was created in the image of the ultimate Good, had not brought about the return to the utopian garden. Instead, it came to the dead end of Hugo Boss–clad executioners flipping switches in gas chambers and the blinding flash that President Harry S. Truman, a 33rd-degree Freemason of the Scottish Rite, declared to be "the greatest achievement of organized science."

Instead of a return to Paradise, humanity had turned the planet into a vast haunted house. Only a fool could believe all those ghosts were friendly.

For those who subscribe to the conspiratorial theory of history, it comes as no surprise that the building blocks of what would become the next New World Order were already being set in place well before Hitler bit down on the cyanide capsule. On July 1, 1944, even as the fresh-faced GIs who had stormed the Normandy beaches only three weeks before continued to advance to the Black Forest of northern Europe, an army of a different sort gathered at the venerable Mount Washington Hotel in the bucolic central New Hampshire town of Bretton Woods.

Led by such luminaries as British economist John Maynard Keynes and US Treasury secretary Henry Morgenthau Jr., the Bretton Woods talks established such institutions as the International Monetary Fund and the World Bank, key structures of the coming global financial system. No longer would the fate of civilization be left to the unchecked egos of larger-than-life politicians. There were to be no more Roosevelts, Churchills, Stalins, or Hitlers.

The romance of the nation-state and its ability to let loose the animal nature of the species would have to be blunted. From this point on, so-called national leaders were to be little more than front men, actors, buffoons.

The seat of real power would be more elusive, incomprehensibly complex, a centerless labyrinth of bureaucrats speaking the murky Esperanto of their respective domains—high finance, theoretical science, econometrics, academia. The immense suggestive power of the entertainment industry and media would be more precisely calibrated to manufacture the desired reality.

At meetings like the Yalta Conference, the new paradigm came into focus. Rather than a scrum of competing local interests, the planet would be divided into two spheres of interest, the United States of America and the Union of Soviet Socialist Republics.

The result was a highly addictive competition between basic elements of human nature. The romance of the individual spirit symbolized by the American cowboy was pitted against the hardwired need for the collective security of the group best depicted by the red hordes of

Communism. The goal was to play these two wholly normal behaviors off against each other.

Stasis was policed by the Bomb, eschaton of the previous New World Order and the fail-safe guarantor of the next. The fingertip slicing slo-mo toward the Button, the billowing mushroom cloud, flesh slipping from the bone, the empty *Twilight Zone* streets, all these indelible images fell under the rubric of "mutually assured destruction," the rollout of which commenced in the Baby Boom year of 1947.

The timeline began with the Soviet invasion of Poland on January 31, 1947, and the subsequent installation of the Communist regime in Warsaw. Six weeks later, on March 12, the American president responded with the introduction of his Truman Doctrine. It was endorsed by Congress as a counter to the advance of godless Communist rebels in Greece, the heralded cradle of western democracy. The elastically worded doctrine issued a virtual blank check that allowed the US government "to provide political, military and economic assistance to nations threatened by internal or external authoritarian forces."

On April 16, 1947, Bernard Baruch, aging lion king of Wall Street, point man for Wilson's League of Nations, was given the honor of presiding over the formal branding ceremony of the new model of control. "Let us not be deceived," Baruch said in what was supposed to be a simple speech on the occasion of the unveiling of a portrait before the legislature of South Carolina, the state where the Jewish financier owned the 16,000-acre former plantation he called the Hobcaw Barony.

"We are today in the midst of *a cold war*," Baruch said. "Our enemies are to be found abroad and at home. Let us never forget this: Our unrest is the heart of their success. The peace of the world is the hope and the goal of our political system; it is the despair and defeat of those who stand against us. We can depend only on ourselves."

The parameters of what came to be called the Cold War were further articulated by the Princetonian George Kennan in an essay, "The Sources of Soviet Conduct," published in the July 1947 issue of *Foreign Affairs,* the magazine of the Council on Foreign Relations (CFR). Author of the talismanic "Long Telegram," Kennan codified mutually assured destruction in his doctrine of "patient but firm and vigilant containment of Russian expansive tendencies."

Writing of these tendencies in his famous telegram, Kennan wrote about the occult nature of the enemy: "In atmosphere of oriental secretiveness and conspiracy which pervades this Government, possibilities for distorting or poisoning sources and currents of information are infinite. The very disrespect of Russians for objective truth—indeed, their disbelief in its existence—leads them to view all stated facts as instruments for furtherance of one ulterior purpose or another. There is good reason to suspect that this Government is actually a conspiracy within a conspiracy; and I for one am reluctant to believe that Stalin himself receives anything like an objective picture of outside world."

If the Bolshevik chess masters traded in black magic and deceit, then it was imperative that salt-of-the-earth Americans learn to fight fire with fire. If they spied, we must spy. If they used the tricks of psychology to propagandize the gray matter of men, we must do the same. It wasn't the aw-shucks, plainspoken American Way, but with the fate of the universe in the balance, the stakes were too high to do anything else.

Meanwhile, the agenda moved ahead. With the land (a former slaughterhouse) donated by John D. Rockefeller in 1947, the sleekly designed United Nations, the next incarnation of the New World Order, rose on the banks of the East River in New York City.

Many might have considered the UN Charter with its declared goals of maintaining "international peace and security," "to develop friendly relations among nations," and "strengthen universal peace" to be one large step forward for mankind. Lofty precepts, no doubt. Yet to a once small but still growing number of Americans that would come to include Bill Cooper, these fine phrases were nothing more than code for the ultimate formation of a One World Totalitarian Socialist Government aimed at undermining the sovereignty of the nation and curtailing the liberty of the individual.

The systematic plan to eliminate individual freedoms granted under the Constitution was launched in earnest on July 26, 1947. Aboard the presidential plane, the *Sacred Cow*, Harry Truman signed the National Security Act authorizing the creation of the Central Intelligence Agency, the Joint Chiefs of Staff, and the National Security Council. Deemed necessary to combat the Communist threat in the nuclear era, it was the official beginning of the American security state.

Meanwhile, the new social structure was being snapped into place. The year 1947 saw the birth of the American suburb. The model was Long Island's Levittown, open for business on October 1, 1947. In Levittown, the so-called nuclear family fleeing the raw tumble of New York City could settle into a segregated community of identical homes splayed out on gently curving lanes with succoring names such as Harvest Avenue, Shelter Road, and Homestead Street.

Inside each of these homes, behind sliding wooden cabinet doors disguised to look like any other piece of furniture, lurked a six-inch screen. This was the television, the black-and-white prototype of the single most powerful weapon in the battle for men's minds yet invented. Regular programming, as it would unashamedly come to be called, began in 1947 with the debuts of such habit-forming cornerstones as *The Howdy Doody Show* and *Meet the Press.*

According to students of the conspiratorial theory of history, another essential of the post–World War Two New World Order was set in place on November 29, 1947, when the fledgling UN General Assembly passed Resolution 181, paving the way for the establishment of the State of Israel.

Biblical references to what came to be known as the "in-gathering" of the Jews in the Promised Land dated to Deuteronomy. Ezekiel, prophet of the Hebrew Exile in Babylon, made clear that it was only when the Chosen People had returned to the Promised Land "from all places where they have been scattered on a day of clouds and thick darkness" that the Messiah would appear. Picking up the theme, many twentieth-century evangelicals believed that the return of Jews to Israel was a precursor to the Second Coming.

For a new era founded on the brinksmanship of instant annihilation, the architects found a powerful ally in the Book of Revelation, John of Patmos's graphic vision of ultimate destruction and rebirth.

The last book of the Christian Bible, Revelation had long been the subject of canonical dispute. Martin Luther dismissed John's cataclysm as "neither apostolic nor prophetic." John Calvin ignored it in his biblical treatises. However, as Americans began digging up their backyards to build fallout shelters, phrases like "there was a sea of glass like unto crystal" (Rev. 4:6), "the sun became black as sackcloth of hair, and the moon became as blood" (Rev. 6:12), and "heaven departed as a scroll when it is rolled together, and every mountain and island were moved out of their places" (Rev. 6:14) took on totemic power.

This was how the NWO architects of mass public opinion worked, Cooper explained in an interview in 1992. "Either these men are following the Book of Revelation like a plan, and bringing the prophesies in there to pass to manipulate and control those who believe in those prophesies, or there really is a God," Cooper said.

As Cooper tells it in *Behold a Pale Horse*, his autobiography is definitively American. His ancestors came from England, Scotland, and Ireland. They fought on both sides of the Civil War and moved west in covered wagons. His great-grandfather "was a real cowboy," Cooper wrote, describing seeing pictures of him "standing in front of a saloon with a six-gun stuck in his belt." Another ancestor was a horse thief. "I don't know for sure, but I think he got hung for it."

When he was growing up, Cooper sometimes heard "whispers" that there was some Cherokee blood in the family, but every time he asked about it, he was told to shut up. He couldn't understand it; he liked the idea of having Indian blood. It was only later he came to realize that hiding differences, especially in matters of blood, was a matter of survival. "In the old days on the American frontier, people lived by hard rules. If you weren't accepted by your neighbors you were more than likely to end up dead."

Born in Long Beach, California, Cooper grew up in a military family. His father, Milton Vance Cooper, whom everyone called Jack (Bill was "little Jackie"), was a pilot who had started his career flying open-cockpit biplanes in the Army Air Corps. Cooper loved to look at pictures of his dad in his flight jacket and leather helmet. In *Behold a Pale Horse*, he wrote that the gear made his dad look like Snoopy in the *Peanuts* cartoon.

Cooper recalled treasured moments, when things felt like home. Best of all was when he, along with younger brother and sister, the twins Connie and Ronnie, visited their grandparents in Garber, Oklahoma. The family had been "Sooners," part of the Oklahoma Land Rush of 1889, and had staked out a 320-acre spread not far from present-day Enid. His grandma made "the biggest breakfast I'd ever seen. We slept in real feather beds that swallowed us up," Cooper wrote, recalling with some distaste the chamber pots his grandmother kept under every bed. For the most part, the Cooper family moved from one military base to another, depending on where Jack Cooper was stationed. During the Cold War, with the Soviets thought to be ready to strike at a moment's notice, these moves tended to be frequent. Doom could be right around the corner. Once, while his father was assigned to Lajes Field on Terceira Island in the Azores, the young Cooper was sitting in the base rec room, watching a movie, when "the projector ground to a halt . . . the lights came on and a plea was made for blood donors. . . . I knew immediately something terrible happened." Running outside, Cooper saw that a B-29 Superfortress had crashed.

"I saw men on fire running through the night," Cooper wrote in *Behold a Pale Horse.* "I was only nine years old but felt much older." A year later his father was reassigned again. As the family prepared to leave Lajes, Cooper looked out the plane window. The wreckage of the B-29 was still there, piled up alongside a runway. No one had bothered to haul it away.

"I didn't always love my father," Cooper wrote in *Behold a Pale Horse.* "He was a strict disciplinarian. My dad did not believe in 'spare the rod' and his belt was put to use frequently in our family." Describing himself as "a very sensitive but willful child" to whom "rules didn't mean much until I got caught breaking them," Cooper says that he was often "the focus" of his father's anger. "I thought he was a tyrant."

Things were much easier with his mother, "a real Southern lady, the kind that used to be called 'a Southern belle,'" Cooper wrote, "the type of woman that men like to dream about when they're lonely. She is the kindest, gentlest woman that I have ever known. . . . Once she likes you, she cannot be driven away. She is loyal to a fault."

Never staying in one place long enough to make many friends, Cooper took refuge in the radio, listening to stateside dramas on the American Forces Radio and Television Service, or AFRTS, which, of course, everyone called A-FARTS.

"You could hear all the music you wanted on the Armed Forces radio," Cooper told the *Hour of the Time* audience one night in 1999. It was all there: Elvis, jump blues, the big bands of Ellington and Basie, urban street-corner doo-wop, the Platters, Nat King Cole, and Sam Cooke. No one ever sang better than Sam Cooke, Cooper always said.

While attending Yamato High School on the Tachikawa Air Base near Tokyo, where his father was stationed in the late 1950s and early 1960s, sixteen-year-old Cooper got his own AFRTS show, *Radio Teen*. It was the first time he felt the power of the radio.

"I was called the Mad Lad and my theme song was 'Quiet Village' by Martin Denny. Hundreds of teenagers all over Japan were dancing to the music I spun on my little machines," Cooper said. He was sure "millions" of Chinese listened in, too, at least until the Communists jammed the signal. That was really too bad, Cooper said, because what he was playing was called "rhythm and blues—rhythm and blues, and rock and roll."

That was the best America had to offer, the most convincing advertisement for the nation ever devised, Cooper later said, mournfully remembering how, instead of making Chuck Berry secretary of state "like he should have been," they put him in jail.

In 1962, at age nineteen, Cooper joined the Air Force. He would rather have gone into the Navy, he said, but he had "a tendency toward car and seasickness." The assumption had been that Cooper would become an officer like his father and uncles. But he chose to enlist instead. Instead of four years of walking around in dress blues at the Air Force Academy, he found himself at the Technical School for Aircraft and Missile Pneudraulics in Amarillo, Texas. He was then assigned to the 494th Bomb Wing of the Strategic Air Command (SAC) complex at Sheppard Air Force Base near Wichita Falls, Texas.

On October 14, 1962, a few days after Cooper's arrival at SAC, the Cuban Missile Crisis broke out. An American U-2 spy plane recorded pictures of Soviet surface-to-surface missiles with thermonuclear warheads at launching pads around Cuba, barely ninety miles from US shores. On television, President Kennedy said, "It shall be the policy of this nation to regard any nuclear missile launched from Cuba against any nation in the Western Hemisphere as an attack by the Soviet Union on the United States, requiring a full retaliatory response upon the Soviet Union."

Attached to a maintenance unit, Cooper was assigned to the care of the B-52s. It was an essential task. If the Russians were to launch their missiles, the B-52s, mainstay of the US airborne nuclear deterrence, would carry the response.

"I saw REAL atomic bombs," Cooper writes in *Behold a Pale Horse*. "I worked around them on a daily basis. Because of that I had to wear a dosimeter just in case I was exposed to radiation."

Nonetheless, Cooper says he was never really afraid until thirteen months later, on November 22, 1963. He was on duty as the CQ (Charge of Quarters) of the Field Maintenance Squadron at the time. "Most of the men were out on the flight line, the barracks orderlies had been assigned their tasks, the first sergeant was gone somewhere, and I was alone." It was then, Cooper claimed in *Behold a Pale Horse*, that he turned on the TV to watch the broadcast of the president's motorcade in Dallas.

"I stared in disbelief as the events unfurled in front of my eyes. I knew that something had happened, but what? I had seen and heard the assassination, but my mind was not accepting it. . . . I kept staring at the set to discover what it was that had happened when slowly the realization crept over me. . . . *I saw what had happened!* . . . President Kennedy had been shot right in front of my eyes!"

Within moments "a red alert at DEFCON TWO" was declared. That meant, Cooper wrote, that war was imminent. "I was scared shitless. . . .

"We had been told that we had about fifteen minutes to launch all of our planes before the first atomic bomb would hit us. . . . I just jumped in the first car I saw, rode to the SAC compound. . . . For the next three days I slept under the belly of a B-52 bomber, staring at the Armageddon that hid just inside the closed bomb-bay doors. . . . It was a great relief when the alert was ended."

In 1966, Cooper got his honorable discharge from the Air Force and, his seasickness a thing of the past, immediately enlisted in the Navy. At the time his plan was to serve in the Army, the Navy, the Air Force, and then the Marines. No member of the Cooper family, his father included, had ever done that.

After serving on a number of vessels, Cooper put in a request to be sent to a combat zone. He got his wish when he was assigned to the Naval Support Unit operating out of Dong Ha, Cua Viet River, Quang Tri Province. Barely a dozen klicks from the Demilitarized Zone that marked the border between North and South Vietnam, the Cua Viet, with its outlet to the Gulf of Tonkin, was a hairy place to be. The Tet Offensive, the all-out assault by North Vietnamese and Vietcong against American and South Vietnamese positions, was in its final stages when Cooper arrived. Not far from Khe Sanh, scene of the seventy-seven-day siege that was the longest battle of the war, rarely did an hour pass on the river without the sound of rocket fire. When one of the shells hit the US Dong Ha ammo dump by the river's mouth, all hell seemed to break loose.

A quartermaster second class, Cooper served as the commander of a Patrol Boat, River (PBR). As the "brown water" sailors said, the hulls of PBRs might be made of fiberglass, but if you planned to stay alive on the river, you better have balls of brass.

In training, Cooper made a good friend, Bob Barron. The two men had a pact. "We promised each other that if one of us bought the farm the other would drink a bottle of scotch in memory, then break the bottle on the rocks," Cooper wrote. Barron was shipped out to Cua Viet three weeks earlier than Cooper. On one of his first missions, Barron's boat was hit by the North Vietnamese. The PBR was later found with its hull shot full of holes, "twisted up like a pretzel," Cooper wrote.

Now it was "a personal war. They had killed a part of me." He felt responsible for Barron's death; they were brothers; it was no different than if Barron had been part of Cooper's crew. After he got his own boat command, Cooper wrote, "my boat engaged the enemy more times than any other boat that ever patrolled that river. We kept the enemy off the river, and I never lost another man."

In 1971, after nine months on the river and a year more of sea time, Cooper was reassigned to the Office of Naval Intelligence in Hawaii, where he worked on the briefing team of Admiral Bernard A. Clarey, Commander in Chief of the US Pacific Fleet (CINCPACFLT). His security clearance was upgraded to "Top Secret, Q, Sensitive Compartmentalized Information," which entitled him to view a wide range of classified material.

"It was a wonderful job, fat cat, *gedunk* duty," Cooper later told an interviewer about working in Naval Intelligence. He described how he would arrive at four in the morning, go through the message traffic that had come over the wires during the night, editing and preparing them for the general staff. "By nine or ten A.M. we were done, free for the rest of the day."

Now, instead of the leech-ridden river muck, Cooper worked in air-conditioned offices. He liked and admired Admiral Clarey, winner of the Silver Star for bravery at Guadalcanal in World War Two and a Bronze Star in Korea. Certified to operate the decoding KL-47 cryptography machine, Cooper was a valuable member of the team. The position came with a fair amount of setting up slide shows for often disinterested members of the upper command and occasional ashtray cleaning, but that was to be expected.

If Cooper had been destined to become a regular career armed forces guy, the Office of Naval Intelligence, the oldest and traditionally most advanced of the US military classified sections, would have been a sweet spot to land. At the rate he was going, it wouldn't take all that long to make MCPON (master chief petty officer of the Navy), the highest naval rank an enlisted man can attain. A ton of respect came with those three stripes. Even the snottiest officer would have to think twice before fucking with an MCPON, especially one with a combat V for valor Armed Forces Achievement Medal. There were worse things than being career military, maxing out the pay scale, padding the pension.

But soon, Cooper wrote, "I began to see things that at first made no sense to me. President Nixon was on television giving a speech, an incredible speech, saying that we were conducting no bombing raids in North Vietnam, Cambodia, and Laos. Five minutes later intelligence came into the office with KIA figures from sorties over exactly the targets Nixon said the Americans weren't bombing.

"I would shake my head and wonder what in the world was going on here. This wasn't right. I never said anything at the time. Most of us never did. I never imagined that the people in charge of the country would lie to the people like that. I was raised to think this was impossible."

Cooper issued a forehead-slapping chuckle. "Let me tell you, ladies and gentlemen, I was extremely stupid. Naive. Ignorant beyond belief. A sheeple. That was me."

He did, however, know enough to keep on looking, to dig deeper into the files. It was there, peeking behind the first of what would be many veils, that Cooper says he began to wake up from his lifelong slumber.

"Right away I knew I was seeing what I was not supposed to see, material never intended for my eyes," Cooper told an audience that assembled to see him at Hollywood High School in 1989. "The secrets were there, what had been covered up, the treasonous betrayal. *I looked right into the heart of it.*"

Everything about the war was in there. The story behind the alleged attack by the Vietnamese Navy in the Gulf of Tonkin, the death counts, the American dealings with the corrupt South Vietnamese government. One by one the scales dropped from Cooper's eyes. He was not the defender of freedom he had so longed to be but, rather, cannon fodder in a huge game of Risk played by powerful puppeteers.

"That's what I learned in Vietnam. I thought I was fighting for my country and I found out that I was really fighting for big business, the coming one-world government," Cooper told the audience. It was a devastating realization.

The worst of it was reading the files concerning the US government's involvement with the Kennedy assassination. It was in Admiral Cleary's cabinet, Cooper often told his audience, that he first learned of the treachery of Secret Service agent William Greer, the limo driver who had killed the president with the shellfish-toxin pellet gun. "Mortally shocked" and uncertain what to do with the truths he'd uncovered, Cooper decided to go AWOL with no intention of ever returning.

As he writes in *Behold a Pale Horse,* it was only talking with his great friend Bob Swan that convinced Cooper to stay. Swan was running a commercial dive shop on Oahu at the time. Cooper worked with him and they became buddies. The two had pulled each other out of the soup more than once.

And so, on June 1, 1972, the night before one in what would prove to be a long series of weddings, the oft-married Cooper opened a bottle of Chivas Regal and told Swan everything he'd found in the admiral's cabinet: the lies, the black ops, the cover-ups, the murders. Years later, introduced by the Beach Boys' "Still Cruisin'," Swan appeared as a guest on *The Hour of the Time.*

"What Bill told me that night blew my mind. I didn't want to believe it. I couldn't think about it for years."

Swan managed to talk Cooper into staying in the Navy. It was the only choice at the time, Cooper said. Where was there to run to? They'd find him, try him for treason, put him in the brig for the rest of his life, or simply throw him overboard. It was better to stay in, do his job. Keep his eyes and ears open, his mouth closed.

5

S oon after, Cooper left Naval Intelligence and spent his year in the service as quartermaster on the aging aircraft carrier USS *Oriskany*. Named for a critical, bloody skirmish during the Revolutionary War, the Mighty O, as it was called, earned two battle stars in Korea, five more in Vietnam. But by April of 1975, after twenty-five years of service and a catastrophic onboard fire that resulted in forty-four deaths, the *Oriskany* was a tired, outmoded Essex-class hulk, ready to be decommissioned, which it was the very next year.

The parallel between the used-up *Oriskany* and the hasty evacuation scene on the Saigon rooftops at the end of the war was impossible to miss. Once a bright and shining thing in the eyes of many, the Vietnam War had devolved to a corrupt burden upon the heart and mind. Protests had torn the country apart. In the last years of the conflict, as many as 15 percent of US soldiers returned home addicted to heroin.

As sickening as it was to watch Americans turn tail, what was happening to the South Vietnamese was worse. We were supposed to be there to save them. That's what Cooper told the children in the villages along the Cua Viet. Don't worry, kids, he'd said, the cavalry has come, everything is going to be all right, here's a piece of chewing gum.

Now US bureaucrats clutching briefcases were on the embassy roof. When the Vietnamese allies strained to reach for the landing gear of the departing helicopters, US personnel kicked at their hands, leaving those they'd sworn to protect to be murdered by the Communists.

A few months later, Cooper put in his retirement papers. He took his honorable discharge, his government insurance, his medals and said goodbye. At thirty-two, he was on his own for the first time. The eleven years of active duty was the least of it. As his father's son, he'd grown up in a world ruled by codes of conduct. The military was all he knew. It was a life in which he rarely had to go to a normal supermarket filled with screaming kids, cook his own meals, shop for clothes, or decide what to wear.

Originally, the plan was to go into the dive business in Hawaii with Bob Swan. It sounded good on paper. With his sea time, Cooper had every certificate any commercial diving operator needed. He was an ace underwater welder. Swan had a head for business and plenty of connections. When Swan was in the construction business, one of his clients was Clare Boothe Luce, wife of Henry, author of *The Women*, the best-known female anti-Communist of her day. It was a name that opened doors. Plus, Cooper and Swan figured they could set up a little dive-boat service for the tourists, play *McHale's Navy* with the bikini-clad coeds.

But Hawaii wasn't America, not really, not the one Cooper wanted. Until then, much of what Cooper knew of day-to-day life in the US had been gleaned from television shows he had watched in base rec halls. It was the America of *The Andy Griffith Show*, *The Donna Reed Show*, *The Life of Riley*, and *Leave It to Beaver*, a mostly untroubled idyll surrounded by loving family members and a wonderful, if a little cockeyed, set of neighbors. As for the 1960s, Haight-Ashbury, LSD, long hair, the Manson murders, and Woodstock, Cooper had missed all of that.

Settling in Oakland, California, home of the Black Panthers, Cooper was confronted with a vision of America in decline. Mired in the self-inflicted Watergate scandal, Nixon had resigned in disgrace. San Francisco's Tenderloin was filled with homeless people; a simple stroll in the park was to take your life in your hands. In the bars, they were playing disco music as if regular R&B was not enough to get oddly sexed young people up and dancing. It was a sign of the times, but to Bill Cooper, the times were fucked.

When Cooper's father, Jack, came home, he had been greeted with a ticker-tape parade. He traveled around in a big Caddy with an Airstream trailer hooked up behind. There wasn't a place where people didn't recognize and respect what he'd done, the risks he'd taken for his country.

When Bill Cooper came home, it was as a member of the first American fighting force to lose a war. Haunted by nightmares, perpetually in need of cash, he was a failure, a walking stigma, better off forgotten.

Yet, he hadn't arrived home empty-handed. He knew things, terrible, dangerous secrets, hidden information that could change everything, even save the world from itself.

Shortly after Cooper returned to the mainland, he attempted to leak what he'd found in Admiral Cleary's cabinet to a reporter. It seemed the way to go. Woodward and Bernstein had just broken the Watergate story, bringing down the Nixon government. A movie about the case had been released, starring Robert Redford and Dustin Hoffman. The newspaperman was a hero of the day, the defender of the Republic, a warrior of the First Amendment. Except this reporter was no Woodward or Bernstein.

Cooper was living in the Bay Area at the time, teaching mixed-gas saturation deep-diving. On his days off he liked to ride his motorcycle on Skyline Boulevard, the road that skirts the Berkeley Hills. There was no better view of the Frisco Bay than from up there. One afternoon he was putting the bike through its paces when a black Cadillac began following a bit too close. The Caddy moved as if to pass but instead veered sharply to the right, knocking Cooper's bike toward the guard rail. Cycle hurtling end over end, Cooper flew into the air, ending up at the bottom of the incline.

"Two men got out and climbed down to where I lay covered in blood," Cooper wrote in *Behold a Pale Horse*. "One bent down and felt for my carotid pulse. The other asked if I was dead. The nearest man said, 'No, but he will be.'"

Cooper managed to survive that time, only to be "forced into an another accident" a month later by the same limo. This time it was more serious. Cooper's right leg was severely mangled.

In *Behold a Pale Horse* Cooper describes lying in his bed one evening only to wake to find the two men standing over his bedside. "They only wanted to know if I would shut up or if the next time should be final," Cooper reported. "I told them that I would be a very good little boy and that they needn't worry about me anymore." Yet even as the two men were leaving the room, Cooper swore to himself he'd "spill the beans," tell everything he knew, sooner or later.

Cooper went through several painful, costly operations to save his leg, but it was no use. His leg was amputated above the knee. He'd walk with a prosthetic after that.

While he was convalescing at Stanford Medical Center in Palo Alto, one of Cooper's attendants was a twentyish nurse's aide, Janice Pell. Reached at her northern California home forty years later, Ms. Pell recalled the moment she first laid eyes on the young Bill Cooper lying in his hospital bed.

"I thought he was the most handsome man I'd ever seen in my life," Ms. Pell recalled. "I was just a kid, really innocent to say the least, but I remember saying to myself, 'I want to be with that man.'"

Cooper told Janice about the crashes on the road. "He said the government was after him. The FBI? The CIA? I don't remember which. I believed him. I would have believed anything he said back then.

"I'd never met anyone like him before. He was older but it was more than that. Intellectually, he was so far from the level I was at the time. He seemed to know everything. He was a great reader. He also had this incredible masculine aura about him, with these green eyes and the scars on his face. He just knocked me off my feet. The other nurses told me to stay away from him, that he was trouble. My parents warned me, too. But I wouldn't listen.

"It was so romantic. I was crazy about him and he knew it. When he got out of the hospital I took him back to my apartment to recover and he just stayed. We started living together."

In late 1976, Janice and Cooper were married. Janice knew that Cooper had been married before, but not how many times. "I was number four, I think," Ms. Pell said when we talked. "But I didn't know that at the time, of course."

Even now, the number of Bill Cooper's marriages remains unclear. In his voluminous FBI file, Cooper's father, Jack, is quoted as saying that his son had been married or engaged at least nine times. According to Jack, Bill was still in high school when he got engaged to a seventeen-year-old Japanese girl. The elder Cooper had to break it up. A year later, living on Tinker Air Force Base near Oklahoma City, Cooper again got engaged, to another young Asian woman.

"I had no idea what I was getting into," said Janice Pell. "One minute he'd be the sweetest, warmest guy. Then he'd change, start yelling at me for no reason. It was like living with Dr. Jekyll and Mr. Hyde."

Janice says she tried to make a go of the marriage, especially after she became pregnant with a son, Tony, who was born in 1978.

"We were living in Union City, near Hayward. Bill was working in Oakland at the diving school. He'd get up at six to drive to work. I tried so hard to be a good wife. Every day I'd clean, make dinner for him. I set a nice table, waiting for him to come home. In the beginning he'd rush home, give me a kiss, bring flowers. It was great. Then he got home later and later. It could be after ten, or midnight. Sometimes he didn't come home at all. I'd be beside myself, trying to find out if he was all right.

"It was really awful. I'd sit there at the dinner table, looking at the cold food, and cry my eyes out. When he did come back, he'd say he was tired and go straight to bed. I didn't understand what was happening. I thought it was all my fault."

Worse was the drinking. When Cooper was drunk he could be "a monster," Janice said. "He'd get abusive, mentally and, after a while, physically. I tried to make excuses for him. The war, his leg. He always told me the men in the car would come back and finish the job. That was what kept him on edge, he said.

"I was afraid of him. He was this huge man, really strong. Like a giant bear. If something happened, he always came back and apologized. He'd cry and say he didn't know what got into him. He didn't even remember what happened.

"One day he hit me, gave me a bloody nose, knocked me out. I called the hotline. They told me to get out of there. Tony was just a little baby then. The next day we drove Bill to work and just kept going. We moved in with my parents in Los Altos. I only saw him one more time after that, when he drove up to get his stuff. I thought he might stay a moment, talk to his son, but he just got the things and left. For years I thought about filing alimony papers, but I never did it. I just didn't want to be involved. My life improved, I married a very good man, but I still had feelings for Bill. I cried when I heard he was dead."

A few months following his breakup with Janice Pell, Cooper was back in Long Beach. Once the bustling Coney Island of the west, the town had fallen on hard times, its art deco housing in disrepair, the famous Pike amusement park an increasingly seedy ghost of itself. Cooper was working in the Naval Shipyard on Terminal Island when he ran into thirty-year-old Sally Elizabeth Jordan at Panama Joe's.

"She was the most the beautiful woman I'd ever seen in my life," Cooper later told the *Hour of the Time* audience. A self-identified California girl, Sally worked as a hostess and bartender at private parties, but she wasn't working that night.

"I was waiting for a friend," remembered Sally, speaking on the phone from her current residence near Eugene, Oregon. "I grew up in Long Beach. My brother was born in the same hospital Bill was. The town was changing, getting rougher. But Panama Joe's was still nice. A lot of sailors were there because of the port, but it felt a little special, a place to go."

From across the room on that particular night, Sally recalled, she could see this big guy looking at her. "I thought he was someone else, this policeman I knew. When I told Bill that later, he wasn't happy, he always hated cops. Anyway, he flashed a really big smile."

"Bill and I started talking," Sally said. "I liked him, but he was smoking. I told him smoke really bothered me. I'm allergic. He looked me right in the eye, said 'all right,' and crushed his cigarette into the ashtray. He said he'd been smoking since he was fourteen, a couple packs a day, but for me he was going to quit. I asked him when. He pointed to the cigarette in the tray and said, 'I already did.' He never smoked another cigarette as long as I knew him.

"We started dancing. He had this kind of old-world formality about him. That military thing, I suppose. He was a very graceful dancer. Very light on his feet for a big guy. It wasn't until later I realized that he had an artificial leg. You would have never guessed it.

"Plus, he made me laugh. He was zany, always acting out these incredible stories. He did these funny impressions. I loved to hear him talk; it didn't make a difference what the topic was, he knew everything about it. He had this tone in his voice, it just draws you in. You can hear it on the radio. He was perfect for that."

Soon enough, Sally and Cooper were living together. "He had this little apartment in downtown Long Beach with a Murphy bed in it," Sally recalled. For a while they lived on a thirty-four-foot cabin cruiser Cooper had bought cheap and fixed up.

"Bill could be a very personable guy when he wasn't being a complete asshole. We'd go on these little trips out into the harbor, just drop anchor.

"We got married on Catalina, on the steps of the Wrigley mansion. The party was at the El Galleon. Bill planned the whole thing, told the band what to play. It was great. But then he started drinking, and picking fights. I guess that should have been a sign. My girlfriends said I was crazy to marry him, but I really loved him."

After the marriage, Cooper and Sally opened the Absolute Image Photo Gallery near the corner of Seventh Street and Redondo Avenue in Long Beach. "Bill said he always wanted to have a photo gallery. He was a very talented photographer and loved looking at pictures.

"We turned the carport of the building we were living in into a business space. Bill was completely positive the place was going to be a fantastic success. He printed up thousands of sheets of stationery, all these business cards. I still have some of it in storage somewhere," Sally said, recalling that Cooper invited Ansel Adams, his favorite photographer, to the gallery opening. Adams didn't come but sent Cooper a signed postcard. "Bill was thrilled by that," Sally remembered.

Marrying multiple times herself, Sally was not aware that she was Cooper's fourth or fifth wife. "What I wanted was to settle down, have a family. I'd just gotten out of a long-term relationship with an older man. He was a wonderful person, but he already had four children from a previous marriage. He didn't want to have any more. That's why I left him. I really wanted to be a mother."

To Sally, Cooper seemed like someone who might be a great father. "He was never happier than when he was around kids. We'd go over to my sister's house and he'd read her kids hundreds of stories, doing these different voices. One time, it came up about his missing leg. He told the kids it had been bitten off by a shark. They loved that."

Sally remembered how happy she was when she found out she was pregnant. "It was the greatest day of my life. I ran home to tell Bill." But Cooper didn't say anything, just told Sally to get in the car. There was something he wanted her to see.

"We drove over to a movie theater where *Apocalypse Now,* the Vietnam War movie, was playing," Sally remembered. "'This is me, this is what I did,' Bill told me. It was unbelievable. I was happy about the baby and he takes me to watch these atrocities."

Things began to go downhill from there. At one of his dive jobs, Cooper got into a dispute with his boss. "Bill saw the guy inside the workroom and punched his hand through the plate-glass window to get at him. He got fired for that." Cooper soon fell behind in the rent at the Absolute Image gallery. Larry Wiese, a photographer who had one of the first shows at the place, remembered Cooper as "a friendly guy who talked about his hardhat diving experiences. Then one day I drove by and the place was cleaned out, like they left in the middle of the night."

After the birth of the baby, whom Cooper named Jessica Dovie after his mother, "Bill couldn't have been nicer," Sally said. "He was the most loving, attentive dad. He'd play with Jessica for hours. He seemed so happy. But then, just like that, he'd go off, start yelling. I blamed it on the drinking, but it was more than that. It was like he became possessed, not in control of himself. I'd tense up every time he came in the room.

"One night, when Jessica was little, we went to Chuck E. Cheese's. Bill was drinking. He got really abusive, calling me names. When that happened, you could feel it, like the temperature in the room dropped.

"I told him I'd had enough, to stop the car, let us out. I was holding Jess on my lap. We didn't deal with seat belts like today. I opened the door to go, when Bill turned and pushed me and Jess out of the car with his artificial leg. It was like getting hit by a four-by-four. We went flying. I was okay, but then I looked and Jess's tiny face was all cut up.

"That was it. If it was just me, I might have been able to take it. But when Jess was involved, I couldn't stand for that."

Soon after, Cooper had a breakdown in the office of Sally's pastor, David Reed, at the First Congregational Church on Cedar Avenue. "Bill had a job taking pictures of the church's stained-glass windows. The windows are really beautiful and Bill was doing a terrific job. We were in talking about the windows, and Bill, he started getting upset. Yelling about his experiences in Vietnam. All these atrocities. Pastor Reed called the VA. They came over and got him."

A glimpse into Cooper's state of mind at the time can be found in a composition he wrote while he attended Long Beach City College in 1982, when he was pursuing an associate's degree in photography. In a neatly printed essay, "Vietnam: Are We Still Suffering Casualties 10 Years Later?," Cooper took issue with former president Gerald Ford, who said it would be best if the country "put Vietnam behind us" and moved on. For Cooper and so many others, there was no moving on.

"On the campus of Long Beach City College a specter reaps its harvest," Cooper's essay begins. "Ghastly, it stalks the future of those who know its past; any of us who have stood against it and survived. The demon strikes down dreams, educations, and even minds. It is insidious in nature and rides upon an undercurrent of memories, ignorance and fear. It is not dead as many believe. Nor is it a figment of the imagination. It is real, as real as the earth we walk upon."

Writing that "in the years 1973 to 1978 more US Vietnam combat vets have died by their own hand than were actually killed in Vietnam," Cooper thought Long Beach City College was a perfect container to observe the war's ongoing effects. Much of the student body was made up of American war vets and immigrants from Southeast Asia. How individuals would react when "surrounded by people they fought against" was a "valid question," Cooper said.

He interviewed Kim Brigstocke, "a small, pretty Vietnamese counselor at the Indo-China Refugee Assistance Program." As Kim spoke about her difficulties sleeping and her bad dreams, Cooper found his heart going out to her. She seemed so nice; yet only a few years before, in different circumstances, he could have shot her dead. Just thinking of it, Cooper writes in his essay, made him so upset he had to pull his car off the road.

Seeking a rationale for his despair, Cooper engages in a seemingly unrelated historical reverie, invoking a French nobleman and professional soldier, Jean de Bueil, count of Sancerre, who in 1428 fought alongside Joan of Arc. "'A joyous thing is war,'" Cooper quotes de Bueil as writing in his memoir, *Le Jouvencel.* "'You love your comrade so in war. When he sees your quarrel is just and your blood is fighting well, tears rise to your eye. A great feeling of loyalty and pity fills your heart seeing your friend so valiantly exposing his body to execute and accomplish the command of the Creator.

"'Do you think that a man who does that fears Death? Not at all, for he feels so strengthened, he is so elated that he does not know where he is. Truly he is afraid of nothing.'"

This was one of the lasting sins of the Vietnam War, Cooper felt. The young Americans like himself who went to Vietnam possessed valor "no less intense than those who fought at Lexington and Concord." They suffered "pain no less severe than those at Normandy." But instead of Jean de Bueil's "delectation" of living or dying alongside his compatriots, those who served in Vietnam were assigned a DEROS, a loathed bureaucratic acronym that stood for "Date Eligible for Return from Overseas."

Like an IBM punch card, each soldier had their own personal DEROS, the exact moment when they could get their behinds out of "the shit" and reenter "the world." Even within a specific unit, everyone's DEROS was different. That meant, Cooper wrote, that the continuity "of those who preceded you and those who followed" was totally disrupted. Each soldier was now engaged in "a private war of survival." To be rotated out, to abandon one's buddies, created in the soldier's mind "a guilt that can never be overcome," Cooper wrote. Rather than Jean de Bueil's "delight," the American soldier in Vietnam received nothing but "a solitary plane ride home with a head full of grief, conflict and confusion."

Cooper's composition (he got an A) then turns more personal. "I was married and had a daughter," he writes, using no names. "My daughter became my life and for the first time since Vietnam I allowed myself to feel."

This unguarded moment proved disastrous. "I had opened the door and the demon took over completely," Cooper writes. "I was upset and irritated most of the time. . . . My photo gallery, The Absolute Image, had just started to pay off when my world crumbled to dust. My wife was fed up. She took our daughter and left. Just prior to the Fourth of July 1981, I walked across campus with my camera bag over my shoulder. As I walked through a crowd of Asian students everything changed. I saw the River, the jungle. I was wearing greens and my camera bag was an M-16.

"On the Fourth of July, as thousands of people watched and enjoyed the fireworks bursting in the sky, I returned to Vietnam. I relived all the terror and death over and over again." He considered killing himself right then, but luckily ran into a neighbor, "a Korean War veteran who knew what was happening," who took him in for a couple of days.

Diagnosed with what was then called Post-Traumatic Delayed Stress Syndrome (Vietnam), Cooper was an inpatient at the Long Beach Veterans Administration Medical Center on two separate occasions, first from July 7 until September 25, 1981, and then again from March 8 until April 28, 1982.

When Cooper was released from the VA, he pronounced himself "a new man altogether." After "being depressed for thirteen years," Cooper said that even if he still had nightmares, he could deal with them now. "I still have occasional flashbacks but I know they're not real and I can handle them, too. I just put my rifle on my shoulder and keep on walking."

After the collapse of his marriage to Sally, he moved in with a woman only a few blocks away. The relationship was short-lived, ending shortly after Cooper reportedly kicked the woman's toy poodle across the room. In 1986 he married again, this time to Roxanne Whiteside, in an impromptu ceremony in Las Vegas. That one didn't take, either.

By the middle 1980s, after an extended period of outpatient treatment at the VA, Cooper was hired by United Education and Software (UES). A pioneer in the corporatization of vocational, for-profit colleges, UES had a number of facilities in the LA area. Working at several of these schools, Cooper moved up from an associate admissions representative at Airco Technical Institute, to assistant director at the Adelphi Business College, and then executive director at the National Technical College.

Cooper claimed to be making $75,000 a year, but his for-profit education career came to an end when the California Attorney General's Office filed a $24 million suit against UES, saying the company had defrauded hundreds of students, often collecting tuition for nonexistent classes. As one student who had attended the Pacific Coast Technical Institute (where Cooper was the executive director for a time) said, the college "promised me a job in computer repair. All I got was telephone calls from creditors. But I'm better off. I started my own carpet-cleaning business."

In the 1980s, when Cooper did the bulk of the research that eventually became *Behold a Pale Horse,* high-performance computing power was still the property of the government and big university libraries. An independent researcher, someone like Bill Cooper, often found themselves in the back shelves of musty bookshops where the books on the so-called occult were kept. As always, the truth was in the hidden.

His family gone and feeling he had nothing to lose, Cooper decided that was the time to expose everything he'd seen while in Naval Intelligence no matter what the consequences. To do that, Cooper knew he would have to go back to the beginning of the New World Order in 1947, more specifically to the evening of July 7, 1947. It was on that night, the story goes, in the midst of a raging thunderstorm, a spaceship from another planet crashed on a ranch near Roswell, New Mexico.

PART THREE

Put the Aliens in the Middle and You've Got All the Answers

6

The Roswell Crash/Retrieval, as it is semiofficially described, is without doubt the best-known case in ufology, i.e., the study of unidentified flying objects. The story of what may or may not have happened on that dark and stormy July night in southeastern New Mexico has long been a staple of the paranormal, the basis of dozens of books, movies, and TV shows. Like "Hollywood," "Wall Street," or "Watergate," "Roswell" is a cultural shorthand; its mere mention sets off a galaxy of associations.

In the context of the New World Order that emerged in 1947, if a spaceship from another planet were to come to Earth, Roswell, a high plains drift of a town west of the Pecos River, would be a culturally resonant place to land. At the time, the Roswell Army Airfield was home to the 509th Bomb Wing, the same unit that wheeled out the *Enola Gay*, the B-29 Superfortress that its pilot, Colonel Paul W. Tibetts, named for his mother, to drop the atomic bomb on Hiroshima. Now, less than two years later, the local paper was reporting that the 509th had taken possession of a flying saucer.

According to the July 8, 1947, edition of the *Roswell Daily Record*, a disk-shaped machine crashed into a sheep pasture tended by W. W. "Mac" Brazel. Brazel was the nephew of Jesse Wayne Brazel, who in 1908 shot dead lawman Pat Garrett, the famous tracker and killer of the outlaw Henry McCarty aka William Bonney, Billy the Kid. Brazel contacted Major Jesse A. Marcel, an intelligence officer with the 509th, about the falling debris he said had spooked his livestock. Major Marcel came by, inspected the remains, which were, the *Record* reported, "flown to higher headquarters."

The very next day, however, the *Record* ran a follow-up article that repudiated the previous day's report. Now, rather than a "flying saucer," the object that crashed in Brazel's pasture was a high-altitude weather balloon. The paper quoted an Army spokesman as saying that the so-called wreckage contained nothing more unusual than "tinfoil, paper, tape, and sticks. . . . There was no sign of any metal in the area which might have been used for an engine, and no sign of any propellers of any kind. . . . Considerable Scotch tape and some tape with flowers printed upon it had been used in the construction."

This being a time when Americans tended to believe what the authorities, especially the military, told them, the tale of the Roswell crash soon dropped from the headlines. It would rarely be mentioned for more than three decades.

No matter, there were plenty of other saucer stories around. Only two weeks before Roswell, on June 24, 1947, Kenneth Arnold, thirty-two, a fire safety equipment salesman from Boise, Idaho, who piloted his own small plane, made what is generally regarded as the first modern UFO sighting. A C-46 transport plane with thirty-two US Marines aboard had gone down in a remote section of the Cascade Mountains in Washington State. A $5,000 reward was offered for anyone who could locate the wreck. Arnold flew over the area in his CallAir Model A-2. He looked for several hours but, seeing nothing, headed to Yakima for the evening.

Near Mount Rainier, Arnold later told authorities, he was startled when he noticed "a terrific blue flash pass the nose of my plane." His first thought was that "some wildman lieutenant in a P-51 had given me a buzz job across my nose and it was the sun reflecting off his wings that had caused the flash."

A moment later, however, Arnold saw "to my left and to the north, a line of peculiar-looking aircraft, nine in number, flying north to south at approximately 9,500 feet elevation, going in a definitive direction of 170 degrees." The objects were arrayed in a diagonal "echelon formation," Arnold said, likening them to "snow geese, flying in a diagonal chain-like line, as if linked together but traveling at tremendous speed."

Believing he was looking at "a new type of jet," Arnold was baffled "because if they were jets they didn't appear to have any tails.

"Everyone is going to think I'm nuts," Arnold told Bill Bequette, a reporter for the *East Oregonian* the next day. "If someone else reported seeing those things I might feel the same. But I saw them. It seems impossible—but there it is."

Arnold's "sighting" was the first of many that even the most casual UFO fans can tick off at will. Among the classics is the story of Captain Thomas F. Mantell, a war hero and fighter pilot with more than two thousand hours of flight time, who in 1948 chased what he believed to be a craft of unknown origin until he blacked out at twenty-five thousand feet and crashed. In 1952, a forebodingly slow-moving flotilla of circular craft was seen above the Capitol dome in Washington, DC. In 1957, numerous Levelland, Texas, motorists reported their engines stalling out after a giant egg-shaped machine passed by, low in the sky.

There was the curious case of Betty and Barney Hill in 1961. An interracial couple, active in both the Unitarian Church and the NAACP, the Hills were driving through the White Mountains wilderness in New Hampshire when they found themselves confronted by a large, snaredrum-shaped object. The Hills lost consciousness only to wake up still driving, thirty-five miles closer to their home. After undergoing extensive hypnosis, the Hills came to conclude that they had been taken into the spaceship, where they were given invasive physical tests by aliens from another star system. It was one of the very first of the so-called abductee cases.

"The phenomena," as it came to be called in UFO circles, caught the attention of psychologist Carl Gustav Jung. Surveyor of what he called "the collective unconscious," Jung spent many of his final, atom-bombhaunted years at his desk in Zurich, thumbing through news clippings about strange aerial displays.

In his late-career book *Flying Saucers: A Modern Myth of Things Seen in the Skies*, Jung, whose concept of "synchronicity" or "meaningful coincidence" is at the core of all modern conspiracy theory, admitted to being "unable to make out whether the whole thing is a rumor with concomitant singular and mass hallucination, or a downright fact."

Such confusion was not unexpected, Jung said. "At a time when the world is divided by an Iron Curtain . . . we might expect all sorts of funny things." Still, the psychologist concluded that "when people are beginning to see that everything is at stake, the projection-creating fantasy soars beyond the realm of earthly organizations and powers into the heavens, into interstellar space, where the rulers of human fate, the gods, once had their abode in the planets." In such a case, Jung concluded, "it might be better to accept the possible reality of flying saucers than not."

The United States government did not accept Jung's analysis. Reports of UFOs were invariably met with indifference or outright ridicule from government officials and other bastions of supposed rationalism. People were seeing things, to be sure, but they were not ships from outer space. They were balloons, glare from airplanes, clouds, the planet Venus, swamp gas. People whose lives had been turned upside down by what they believed to be an encounter with an extraterrestrial presence were sent to psychiatrists. Some accepted these official explanations, but many did not. Indeed, flying saucers were the first populist Truther issue, the first time the authorities denied something that a large percentage of the population believed to be real.

Bill Cooper came of age along with the saucers. As a kid growing up on air bases during the 1940s and 1950s, he often had overheard his father and the other fliers going on about odd objects in the skies. "I can remember the pilots gathered around the kitchen table talking about the planes and telling stories. Sometimes they discussed strange things called foo fighters, UFOs."

The pilots were able to get pictures of the strange craft. When his dad "got out the projector and showed Kodachrome slides" of the phenomena, "that was a special treat," Cooper wrote.

As a boy, Cooper grew up reading UFO magazines. Among his favorites were back issues of *Fate*, edited by Raymond Palmer. A hunchback, barely four feet tall as the result of an injury sustained when he was run over by a milk truck at age seven in his native Milwaukee, Palmer is without doubt one of the great unsung architects of the American pulp mentality that came to dominate the overheated thought processes of people like Bill Cooper.

Perhaps the original sci-fi fanboy, Palmer, who often presented himself in a waistcoat and bow tie, took over the editorship of *Amazing Stories* magazine in 1938 from Hugo Gernsback (for whom the annual Hugo Awards are named). Palmer published eighteen-year-old Isaac

Asimov's first piece, along with the early writings of Ursula K. Le Guin, Theodore Sturgeon, and Scientology founder L. Ron Hubbard. But in modern conspiracy circles, he is best known as the impresario of the spectacular Shaver Mystery, the odd and deeply troubling ravings of Richard Sharpe Shaver.

It was Shaver's contention that through "some freak of the coil's field attunements" of the welding machines at the shop where he worked he had acquired knowledge of Mantong, the root tongue of all languages. This enabled Shaver to understand the true story of life on Earth. Key to Shaver's conception was the idea that the planet was split between two groups, the surface-dwelling humans and a race of vengeful underground-dwelling creatures. The subterranean beings created a breed of Deros, or "detrimental robots," which they programmed to torment the hated surface people. Foremost of the Deros was "The Ray," a malevolent beam that coursed through the everyday household appliances used by the sun dwellers, making them fear the machines supposedly created to make their lives more convenient. Eschewing boundaries of the real and made-up, Palmer, after some heavily punched-up editing, published Shaver's stories as nonfiction, i.e., the truth.

It was also Palmer who brought the flying saucer to the fore as a pop obsession. He published Kenneth Arnold's story in the first issue of *Fate* in June of 1948 and later expanded it into a full-length book, *The Coming of the Saucers*. Cooper, always a collector, had a first edition.

"I had noticed that there was a lot of UFO activity in Vietnam," especially over the DMZ, Cooper writes in *Behold a Pale Horse*, telling how he heard of an incident in which "an entire village disappeared after UFOs were seen hovering above their huts. I learned that both sides had fired upon the UFOs, and they had blasted back with a mysterious blue light. Rumors floated around that UFOs had kidnapped and mutilated two Army soldiers, then dropped them in the bush." No one knew what to make of the story, Cooper said, adding that later he "found out that most of these rumors were true."

For more than three decades Roswell slept, one more roadside attraction that didn't pan out. As the classic early sightings of the late forties and fifties passed into folklore, subsequent decades proved a slack period for

UFOs. The Cold War "space race" had reduced the wonders of the heavens to one more politicized sphere of contention between the US and the USSR. Rocket launches became jingoistic exercises that wound up on the cover of *My Weekly Reader* sounding like so much more school. Even the epochal 1969 landing on the moon—the corporate/techno boot heel imprinting on the enchanted preserve of poets—had an oddly demystifying, deflating effect. By the 1990s, the moon landing, hailed as one of the greatest feats in human history, was widely suspected to have been faked in a Hollywood studio.

Between Roswell and "Roswell," much had happened, most of it guaranteed to undercut post–World War Two American unanimity. Among these documents was the 1975 report of the United States Senate Select Committee to Study Governmental Operations with Respect to Intelligence Activities. Chaired by Senator Frank Church, the committee exposed what had been whispered about for years. So it was true, the CIA *was* assassinating leaders of other countries, everyone from Mohammad Mossadegh in Iran (1953), Patrice Lumumba in the Congo (1960), to the Diem brothers in Vietnam. Eisenhower *did* approve hiring the Mob to rub out Castro. Military intelligence *had* worked with the CIA's MKUltra program during which soldiers were given large doses of LSD without their knowledge to see exactly how much stress the human mind could take before snapping completely.

For those in the ufology field, the issue had never been whether flying saucers existed. Of course they did. Too many people had seen them. For many, it became the central moral issue of the time. If beings from another world and/or dimension were not only in our midst but also communicating with humans, wasn't that the biggest piece of news short of the coming of the Messiah? What right did the United States government have to keep such monumental information to itself?

Then, in 1977, the UFO narrative was changed in one fell swoop with the release of Steven Spielberg's *Close Encounters of the Third Kind*. Soon to become the official delineator of the renewed American optimism embodied by the sunny-faced Reagan administration, Spielberg had dreamed of making a flying saucer movie since he was a kid watching a meteor shower with his dad outside their suburban New Jersey home. Now *Close Encounters*, with its everyday people, mashed potato

mountains, and color-coded intergalactic tone communication channeled through Buddhist monks, had revived the saucer genre. It was in
the formidable slipstream of Spielberg's commercial success that Roswell
shrugged itself awake.

The story's resurrection began in 1980 with the publication of *The
Roswell Incident* by Charles Berlitz, grandson of the language school
founder and author of the paranormal bestseller *The Bermuda Triangle*. Berlitz's coauthor was the thirty-seven-year-old William Moore, a
former English teacher from Minnesota. The two had previously
worked together on *The Philadelphia Experiment*, the story of the
destroyer USS *Eldridge* that had supposedly dematerialized while
docked at the Philadelphia Naval Shipyard. The book did well, getting
picked up for a B movie starring eighties demi-icons Michael Paré and
Nancy Allen.

Hopes were even higher for *The Roswell Incident*, which was based in
large part on Moore's interviews with several of the original participants.
Here we get the basic elements of what would become the dominant Roswell
story: the crash, the phony weather balloon explanation, the confiscation of
the craft wreckage, along with the chilling money quote from Jesse Marcel,
who originally handled the case for the Army Air Corps in 1947. Apparently now willing to come clean, Marcel told Moore that whatever came
down that night, it was "nothing made on this earth."

Now the weaknesses of the Roswell narrative—the insufficient eye-
witness testimony, the lack of compelling physical evidence—became
the case's greatest selling point. If Roswell was relegated to obscurity,
someone at the top must have wanted it that way. It was an axiom of
modern life: The extent of the obfuscation is in direct proportion to what
the authorities felt they needed to hide. The bigger the secret, the bigger
the cover-up.

Still, *The Roswell Incident* did not make the commercial impact its
authors hoped for. It did okay, but nothing like *The Bermuda Triangle*,
leading Berlitz to sever his relationship with Moore. "Roswell" could
have once again slipped toward obscurity, but things changed when on
December 11, 1984, a parcel postmarked Albuquerque, New Mexico,
with no return address, arrived in the North Hollywood mailbox of TV
documentary maker Jaime Shandera. A friend of William Moore,

Shandera claimed to be surprised when he opened the package to find an unprocessed roll of Kodak Tri-X black-and-white 35mm film.

The film was blank save eight frames, each displaying a page of alleged highly classified information pertaining to the Roswell incident. Accompanied by a letter signed by President Truman indicating that from "hereafter this matter shall be referred to only as Operation Majestic Twelve," the pages consisted of a "TOP SECRET/EYES ONLY" memo informing President-elect Dwight D. Eisenhower of the existence of a governmental program dealing with UFOs.

The "Eisenhower Briefing," as it was called, was part of the orderly transfer of secrets from one leader to the next. Fact #1 was that those wacky stories about flying saucers were true, much, much more true than the new president or anyone else knew. Aliens had visited Earth, perhaps often. The United States government had known about it all along. The Majesty-12 papers were the proof.

On the first page was a listing of the members of MJ-12. It was a formidable group, exactly the type the government would be expected to trust with control of an ultimately explosive issue like extraterrestrial life. They included three former, present, or future directors of the CIA (Vice Admiral Roscoe H. Hillenkoetter, General Hoyt S. Vandenberg, and Sidney William Souers), head of the Joint Chiefs of Staff General Nathan Farragut Twining, national security advisor Gordon Gray, aeronautics executive Jerome Hunsaker, astrophysicists Donald Menzel and Lloyd Berkner, and Dr. Detlev Bronk, president of Rockefeller University.

The MJ-12 committee head was Vannevar Bush (1890–1974, no relation to presidential bloodline), who at fifty-seven represented the very ideal of the successful mid-twentieth-century American male, a consummate figure of the late Enlightenment. Once a fourteen-dollars-a-week equipment tester for General Electric, by age thirty-two, Bush, son of a Universalist minister, founded the Raytheon Company, which would become one the world's most successful military contractors. By 1939, Bush was FDR's top science adviser, on the scene right beside J. Robert Oppenheimer on July 16, 1945, for the testing of the first atomic bomb in the New Mexico desert. Bush also developed the memex machine, an essential forerunner of the personal computer. If anyone should represent the United States in dealings with beings from other planets, Bush was the man.

"On 07 July, 1947," the Eisenhower Briefing document read, "a secret operation was begun to assure recovery of the wreckage of this object for scientific study. During the course of this operation, aerial reconnaissance discovered that four small human-like beings had apparently ejected from the craft at some point before it exploded.

"These had fallen to earth about two miles east of the wreckage site," the briefing memo continued. "All four were dead and badly decomposed due to action by predators and exposure to the elements during the approximately one week time period which had elapsed before their discovery."

Operating under "an effective cover story that the object had been a misguided weather research balloon," the memo revealed, after conducting autopsies on "the four dead occupants," Dr. Bronk had come to the "tentative conclusion" that although the creatures were "human-like in appearance," their "biological and evolutionary processes" were quite different. Dr. Bronk suggested that the creatures be called "Extra-terrestrial Biological Entities," or EBEs, "until such time as a more definitive designation can be agreed upon."

The briefing document ended on a disturbing note. Being as "the motives and ultimate intentions of these visitors remain completely unknown," it was the unanimous opinion of the MJ-12 members that in interests of "the strictest security precautions," the committee work "should continue without interruption into the new administration."

If the documents were legitimate, it would expose the biggest cover-up in history, said Jaime Shandera, who was now working with William Moore and nuclear physicist turned ufologist Stanton Friedman.

When the story of the MJ-12 papers appeared in the Los Angeles publication *UFO* magazine, Cooper later told his audience, "I could barely believe my eyes."

This was, Cooper explained, because he already knew all about MJ-12. He knew about the EBEs, how the National Security Agency had been formed on November 4, 1952, primarily, he said, "to decipher the alien communication and language, and to establish a dialogue with the extraterrestrials." Cooper said he knew all this because he'd already read these documents and many, many more while in Naval Intelligence.

For sixteen years, Cooper had not revealed what he'd seen while poking through Admiral Clarey's cabinet. It hadn't been easy. Knowing what he wasn't supposed to know had turned his life into a living hell, made him drink, sent him into rages. Attempting to unburden himself of the secrets had taken his leg, almost gotten him killed. It was the reason his marriages failed. For so long he'd kept quiet. But now, armed with what he knew, Cooper "decided to enter the arena."

7

It was the summer of 1988 when Bill Cooper first went public. He did it via the new alchemy of the 8088 microprocessor chip and the 14.4 kbps dial-up modem. In those pre-broadband days, the big news was the "computer bulletin board," or "BBS," endless screens of quivering green letters where, for the first time in the history of the planet, thousands of like-minded but geographically dispersed individuals could converse in something close to real time.

Cooper's first post appeared on ParaNet, a BBS that had been founded by a twenty-four-year-old ufologist and systems operator (SYSOP) named Jim Speiser in his Fountain Hills, Arizona, home. Up only a few months, ParaNet had already become the place to discuss UFO phenomena.

Speiser introduced Cooper's post by writing, "The question is often asked, why don't more military UFO witnesses come forward publicly and provide names, dates and places? . . . ParaNet is deeply indebted to, and a little honored by, user Bill Cooper of Fullerton, California, for this, the first known report of a multiple-military-witness sighting that occurred onboard the submarine USS *Tiru* in 1966."

Cooper's post told of the journey the *Tiru* made from Hawaii to Seattle "during the month of the Rose Festival in the Pacific Northwest United States." Serving as the port lookout, Cooper noticed "a strange contact at a range of 2 miles bearing 315 degrees relative." Unsure whether he was dreaming, Cooper alerted the officer on deck (OOD) and the starboard lookout to the area.

"The three men looked through their binoculars . . . and were astounded to see a metal craft larger than a football field tumble from the clouds into the ocean," Cooper wrote.

"Then the object dove into the ocean, sending huge geysers of water into the air." A moment later the giant ship "rose from the water" and shot back into the clouds once again. By now a number of other crew members, including the captain and the chief quartermaster, were on deck. Together the crew watched as the object flew from the clouds and back into the water before it shot off beyond the horizon.

"There was no doubt as to what we had seen," Cooper continued. "It was a metal craft, with machinery on and around the outside of it. It appeared to have windows or lenses placed around its perimeter. It made no noise that we could hear. It did not disturb the sub's electrical systems nor did it affect the gyro compass. . . . It had the shape and form of a saucer with a bowl inverted in the saucer and it was huge. I will never forget it as long as I live. . . . This is the first time I have ever mentioned it since the moment that the captain told me that it was classified."

What happened next is described in *Behold a Pale Horse,* in which Cooper writes how he was summoned before a commander from Naval Intelligence.

"When I entered the stateroom the commander was holding my service record in his hands," Cooper writes.

"What did you see out there, Mr. Cooper?" the commander asks.

"I believe it was a flying saucer, sir," Cooper replies, after which the commander begins to "visibly shake and he screamed obscenities," threatening to put Cooper in the brig for the rest of his life. It is at this point Cooper remembers what his father told him about getting along in the military, namely that if something you say makes a ranking officer blow his top, "the next thing out of [your] mouth had better be something completely different."

"Let's start all over again," the commander says. "What did you see out there?"

"Nothing, sir," Cooper answers. "I didn't see a damn thing."

"Are you sure, Cooper?"

"Yes, sir. I'm sure."

"You're a good sailor, Cooper," the commander says in conclusion. "The Navy needs men like you."

The ParaNet post was Cooper's introduction to the ufology field. He'd done it the right way. It was a protocol established in a thousand

AA-sanctioned group therapy rooms. Announce yourself. Be open, tell your story before you ask anyone about theirs. There was every reason to be careful. Even forty years after Kenneth Arnold's sighting, there was a stigma attached to seeing a UFO. It pegged you as a certain kind of person.

Still, as fantastic as it was, the *Tiru* incident itself would not have done much to make Cooper's name in ufology. That opportunity came only a few days later in the form of another ParaNet BBS entry, this one from John Lear, who on August 25, 1988, posted "The John Lear Hypothesis."

The Lear Hypothesis began with "two truths." The first, Lear wrote, was that "the sun does not revolve around the earth." The second was that "the United States Government has been in business with little gray extraterrestrials for about 20 years." The first truth, the Hypothesis said, "got Giordano Bruno burned at the stake in 1600. . . . The second truth has gotten far more people killed . . . than will ever be known."

This was the "horrible truth" at the core of his Hypothesis, Lear wrote, that the leaders of the country, "those we trust with our lives have sold us out to aliens from another world."

These were astounding claims, but Lear was not exactly a nobody. He was the son of William Lear (1902–1978), a classic self-made American who used his Tom Swift ingenuity to invent the first car radio for a company he called Motorola. The elder Lear soon sold his Motorola shares, using the money to follow his dream by creating the Learjet.

John Lear was another kind of American hero, albeit in a rambunctious first-generation son-of-wealth kind of way. Born in 1942 (his middle initial, *O*, commemorates the father of Bill Lear's fourth wife, Moya Olsen, daughter of Ole Olsen, half of the Olsen and Johnson vaudeville team), Lear was always interested in getting "off sea level." Sent to boarding school in Switzerland, he became the then-youngest American to climb the Matterhorn. But flying was his thing. First learning to handle a plane at age fourteen from his father's buddies at Clover Field in Santa Monica, by the time he was twenty-five, Lear held seventeen separate air-speed records, including flying solo around the world in sixty-five hours and thirty-eight minutes.

It was a soldier-of-fortune career possible only in the 1950s–1970s, when the tech was available and the clandestine services were still willing to hire semi–loose cannons like John Lear, whose swashbuckling résumé includes a 1966–1973 stint flying for the CIA fleets Air America and Continental Air Services, skimming jungle treetops in Convair 440s and Twin Otters, and delivering small arms to people like Laotian general Vang Pao, an agency client. Later on, Lear was widely rumored to have been the pilot who flew Reagan campaign figures to Paris to make the "October Surprise" deal with the Iranians. He was also spotted in Afghanistan, Beirut, and other skullduggerous locales. By the 1980s, he was largely flying freelance commercial airline flights, racking up record mileage in his preferred Lockheed 1011.

This history, along with personal friendships with legendary aviation figures like General Jimmy Doolittle, and a fun-loving, approachable manner (his phone number, unchanged for decades, is in the book) made Lear a go-to guy among ufologists looking for someone to bankroll their research. Most assumed that Lear was rich, heir to the fabulous Learjet fortune, but this wasn't so. After many arguments with his mercurial father, Lear had been disinherited. Most of the time he was dead broke.

"When the Hypothesis came out, everyone said I was crazy," Lear told me when we spoke at his Las Vegas home on a mind-numbingly hot day in the summer of 2014. "They said I'd become addicted to LSD. That was one of the main drawbacks of the UFO field and kind of why I've withdrawn from it over the years. Too many literalists. I told everyone: 'I never said it was true. I said it was a hypothesis. A hypothesis is something that *might* be true.'"

Freed from the stilted interoffice prose of the Eisenhower Briefing document, Lear's version of the ongoing Roswell story, now part of a greater scheme he called "The Grand Deception," took on a *Creature Features* aspect. Describing the MJ-12 members' first contact with The Other, Lear wrote, "imagine their horror as they actually viewed the dead bodies of those frightening-looking little creatures with enormous eyes, reptilian skin and claw-like fingers."

The tech was no less exotic. Lear wrote of the mystification of even the most brilliant scientists as they attempted to determine how these strange "saucers" were powered, only to find no part even remotely like components they were familiar with: "No cylinders or pistons, no vacuum tubes or turbines or hydraulic actuators."

The US government's obsessive need to possess such fearsome, magical technology became the cornerstone of John Lear's Roswell narrative. Forty years after the original incident, the *real* story of the nation's most famous UFO incident came down to a deal, a negotiation between species.

The Cold War was a major driver of the arrangement. Atomic power was no longer the sole property of the United States. The Soviets had bigger bombs and, the propaganda said, far less compunction about using them. If there was one sure way to guarantee US military hegemony over the Communists, and not coincidentally make fabulous amounts of money, it would be by patenting and controlling this otherworldly engineering.

This phantasmagorical scenario required several amendments to the original Shandera/Moore/Friedman MJ-12 narrative. Dr. Bronk pronouncing the EBE to be dead was now dismissed as disinformation. In reality, the EBE was alive and in government hands. There were other EBEs too, kept in secret locations. This was the human race leverage used to bring the aliens to the table to meet with MJ-12 at Holloman Air Force Base in New Mexico. It was essentially a hostage negotiation.

According to Lear's Hypothesis, the terms of the deal were as follows: In exchange for the return of an undisclosed number of aliens and know-how to manufacture the sort of "black tech" that would become stealth weaponry like the B-2 bomber, MJ-12 agreed to a number of concessions.

The first was to keep the existence of the alien presence a secret. The second, and more troubling, was MJ-12's pledge "to ignore" alien abduction of US citizens. As Lear wrote, "The EBEs assured MJ-12 that the abductions (usually lasting about two hours) were merely the ongoing monitoring of developing civilizations."

But the aliens lied. The abductions may have lasted only two hours, but their consequences would stain the human helixes for all time. Lear listed six invasive events likely to happen during the alien abduction process, including "the insertion of a 3mm spherical device through the nasal cavity" for the "biological monitoring, tracking, and control of the abductee" as well as "impregnation of human females and early termination of pregnancies to secure the crossbreed infant." By the 1960s, more than twenty thousand children a year were being abducted, Lear wrote.

In the end this was MJ-12's unforgivable sin. In their lust for wealth and control, a cabal of blue-blood hierarchs had bartered away the purity of God's masterpiece in exchange for a pile of shiny trinkets. The aliens had set up vast underground medical facilities. One such site was located near the small northern New Mexico town of Dulce.

"This jointly occupied (CIA-alien) facility has been described as enormous with huge tiled walls that go on forever," Lear wrote. "Witnesses have reported huge vats filled with an amber liquid with parts of human bodies being stirred inside." The working relationship was tense. At one point the aliens took a number of human hostages. An attack on the aliens by US forces resulted in the deaths of sixty-six soldiers "and our people were not freed," Lear's Hypothesis reported.

No longer able to delude themselves about their great mistake, MJ-12 was torn by dissension. One faction believed the public should be told about the alien presence. But they were overruled by other members who argued that full disclosure would deal a fatal blow to citizen confidence in government. It was their hope that Earth scientists could develop a special weapon to destroy the aliens before the secret came to light.

Even "as these words are being written," Lear noted, "Dr. Edward Teller, 'father' of the H-Bomb, is personally in the nuclear test tunnels of the Nevada Test Site, driving his workers and associates, in the words of one, 'like a man possessed.'"

Now in his seventies and often unable to move without great pain due to injuries suffered in various crashes, Lear was seated amid the chiaroscuro of his home office, which he calls Lear's Lair. He was surrounded by the blinking lights of outmoded computer monitors and mementos of his matchless career as a flyboy for hire: Lear in Africa, Lear in Vientiane, Lear flying a Douglas A-26 Invader at the Reno Air Races in 1968.

It is part of the great charm of talking to John Lear that he can be in the middle of a perfectly reasonable discussion of Middle Eastern politics or the kick-ass capabilities of the Fairchild A-10 Warthog fighter plane, and then he'll be saying there are half a billion inhabitants on the moon and will bring out official NASA photographs of the dark side to prove it. "Most of the individuals there are slaves, working in mining colonies," Lear told me.

You never quite know if Lear is kidding, not that it seems to matter. "Everything I think is just so much bullshit," he says genially. "But it is bullshit I happen to believe in, at least today." If you persist in churlish skepticism, questioning Lear's contention that the planes that hit the World Trade Center were not real 767s but rather holograms, he will smile and reach up to a shelf and pull down a shiny derby hat.

"This is the official John Lear Tinfoil Hat," he says. Every main player in the conspiracy field, from current heavyweight champ Alex Jones, on to David Icke, Jim Marrs, Texe Marrs, and dozens more, relentlessly hawk their books, DVDs, MP3s. But the John Lear Tinfoil Hat "remains my only product," Lear remarks.

Chances are his Hypothesis would have followed the path of many of the pilot's more flamboyant notions, "into the crapper," Lear said.

"Except then I heard there was this guy on ParaNet who was supporting what I said. Bill Cooper. He was writing into the bulletin board saying he'd worked in the Office of Naval Intelligence and seen this incredible amount of top secret material and could vouch for—word for word—50 percent of what I said.

"'Fifty percent,' I thought to myself. 'Well, that's not bad.'"

Lear contacted Cooper through ParaNet. "I gave him my phone number, told him to call, which he did, pretty much right away. A few days later he was at my house, ringing the doorbell."

Lear and Cooper spent a lot of time together from 1988 through 1990. "I liked him from the beginning," Lear recalled. "He was smart, had a good sense of humor, an amazing memory. He also could drink me under the table, which wasn't so easy to do back then. When I saw him put away a fifth of scotch before lunchtime, I knew he was my kind of guy.

"We'd stay up nights, talking, get into these deep conversations. We were pretty much the same age, but he treated me like I was a guru. A father figure of some type. He wanted to make his peace with his dad, but I told him he was talking to the wrong person if that's what he wanted.

"Then he'd be off on something else. That was Bill. One minute he'd be wrapping himself in the flag, standing up and reciting parts of the Constitution verbatim. Then he'd be like a beatnik in a jazz club. *Hey daddy-o this, hey daddy-o that.* He must have pulled a gun on me three or four times. Then again, I pulled a gun on him, too."

When he first came to see Lear, Cooper was deep into what would become his first major self-published work, "The Secret Government: The Origin, Identity and Purpose of MJ-12." A revised version of the essay later appeared in *Behold a Pale Horse.* As Lear used the original Shandera/Moore/Friedman MJ-12 papers to build his Hypothesis, Cooper took Lear's "human souls for alien tech" narrative as the linchpin of his own reworking of the story.

The Cooper version was full of new, bristling details, ostensibly gleaned from the top secret papers in Admiral Cleary's files. Cooper claimed to have top secret information revealing that "at least 16 crashed or downed craft, 65 alien bodies, and 1 live alien" were recovered from 1947 to 1952. This collection included a massive disk, 100 feet in diameter, discovered near Aztec, New Mexico. The number of incidents spiked in 1953, Eisenhower's first year in office, during which there were "at least ten crashes" that yielded "26 dead and 4 live aliens."

Still, it was only when a large number of human body parts were found on two of the crashed spaceships that "a demon had reared its ugly head and paranoia quickly took hold of everyone then in the know," Cooper said.

Unsure of how to deal with a potential enemy from outer space, Eisenhower turned to his prime benefactor, Nelson Rockefeller. It was Rockefeller and his Who's Who Council of Foreign Relations cronies, people like the Dulles boys, Allen and John Foster, John McCloy, Zbigniew Brzezinski, Dr. Henry Kissinger, and Cold War policy virtuoso Paul H. Nitze, who really controlled MJ-12, Cooper said. This was not the relatively ecumenical public servant list presented by Shandera, Moore, and Friedman. As far as Bill Cooper was concerned, the alien cover-up was a straight New World Order operation.

An additional perpetrator of Cooper's "Secret Government" was the Jason Society, aka Jason Scholars. Founded in 1960 by the most elite scientific minds in the nation, and funded in large part by the Defense

Advanced Research Projects Agency (DARPA), Jasons were perhaps the most-low-profile group of the coming New World Order.

But Bill Cooper knew them from his time in Vietnam. The Jasons were the ones who created the McNamara Line, a so-called electronic infiltration anti-personnel barrier that was built in Quang Tri province not far from the Cua Viet River. Costing millions, with several lives lost during construction, the barrier proved ineffective.

Cooper's rewrite of Lear's Hypothesis added new items like a "particle beam weapon" and "machinery for cloning and synthetic genetic duplication of humans" to the shopping list of Lear's unholy "tech-for-flesh" deal. He also tweaked the timeline of government-alien interaction. Now there were three separate meetings, the most significant being the signing of the formal agreement, which took place on February 20, 1954, at Muroc (now Edwards) Air Force Base near Lancaster, California.

"The historic event had been planned in advance and the details of the treaty had been agreed upon," Cooper writes in "The Secret Government." President Eisenhower had been vacationing in nearby Palm Springs when he was "spirited away to the base" on the pretext that he had an appointment with his dentist, who happened to be Dr. Tim "Tote" Leary, father of LSD guru Timothy Leary.

"President Eisenhower met with the aliens and a formal treaty between the Alien Nation and the United States of America was signed," Cooper's "Secret Government" continues, noting that the aliens displayed the triangular logo of the supersecret Trilateral Commission "on both their craft and their uniforms." The meeting was filmed, Cooper said, and unseen by all but those with the highest clearance.

The essay went on from there, detailing how MJ-12 deceived a docile Eisenhower into signing a treaty that has led to alien control of "an army of human implants, which can be activated and turned upon us at will."

In 1989, not content to limit his "Secret Government" information to the narrow confines of ufology, Cooper made 535 copies of everything he knew about the aliens and sent it to every member of the US House and Senate; the mailing cost $27,000, Cooper said.

Cooper provided, among other things, an item called "The Species Classified," detailing the taxonomic traits of the nine alien races in contact with Earth governments. These included the Roswell insect-like "Zeta Reticuli Greys—Small," the "Orion Greys—Tall" (currently based in the Aleutian Islands), the "Pleiadians" ("the forefather race of the genetic creation of humankind"), the eight-foot-tall nocturnal "Draco Mothmen," and the "Deros/Teros." In an apparent shout-out to Shaver Mysteries, Cooper described the Teros as "friendly" surface beings and the Deros as "demented" creatures who lived in underground tunnels. Maintaining that he saw this information while in Naval Intelligence, Cooper's letter to Congress included an offer to "undergo hypnotic regression" therapy to prove the veracity of his claims.

Cooper received only two replies, from Senators Richard Lugar of Indiana and Daniel Patrick Moynihan of New York; both were glorified form letters.

At least one good thing had come out of his mailing campaign, however, Cooper said in *Behold a Pale Horse*; just having the information out there "prevented the government from arresting me or harming me. Any move by them would be interpreted as total confirmation of everything that I had revealed." Few issues split "the field" like MJ-12. If John Lear's Hypothesis had proved divisive, Cooper's even more outlandish claims and far less congenial personality created outright dissension in the already touchy UFO community.

Things came to a head at the 1989 symposium of the Mutual UFO Network (MUFON), the best known of the ET-centered groups. Then, as now, it was MUFON practice to hold its national convention in a different location every year, with the organization's "state director" serving as host. As it would happen, the 1989 conference, entitled "The UFO Cover-Up: A Government Conspiracy?," was scheduled for the Aladdin Hotel in Las Vegas, where the state director was John Lear.

The symposium was contentious from the start. Seeing the schedule was dominated by mainstream ufologists like Stanton Friedman and French UFO researcher Jacques Vallée, with programs entitled "UFO Car Pursuits: Some New Patterns in Old Data," "a cluster analysis" of "two-hundred UFO reports involving witnesses traveling in automobiles," Lear demanded that he be allowed to submit a list of presenters. These included himself, Don Ecker, then the research director of *UFO* magazine, ufologist Bill English, and Bill Cooper, who would read his "Secret Government" paper.

That idea was vetoed by the crusty sixty-nine-year-old founder and head of MUFON, Walt Andrus. A driving force behind MUFON's attempt to legitimize ufology through an intricate system of field research, Andrus had no use for wild speculation that he regarded as "unscientific" and "unpatriotic." He refused to allow Lear's speakers to present their papers.

"I blew up," Lear told me when I visited him. "Andrus was taking my own conference away from me. I told him if he wasn't going to let us talk, I'd hire another hall down the Strip. The people would follow us there and our speakers would outdraw his. He must have known I was right because we wound up speaking at the Aladdin after all."

Lear and Cooper were given speaking slots on Sunday, July 2. Before this, however, the symposium was thrown into further uproar during a Saturday evening appearance by MJ-12 originalist William Moore. Moore stunned the packed house at the Aladdin by tearfully confessing he'd colluded with Richard C. Doty, a shadowy figure reputedly working for the Air Force Office of Special Investigations (AFOSI), to spread false information to UFO researchers. Most glaringly, Moore admitted to "disinforming" one Paul Bennewitz, owner of a small electronics firm and NASA contractor who lived on the outskirts of Albuquerque not far from the high-security Kirtland Air Force Base.

Bennewitz, an avid ufologist, built a high-powered antenna on the roof of his house in an attempt to pick up alien transmissions. Apparently nervous that he might stumble on information about classified projects, the AFOSI supposedly decided to encourage Bennewitz's increasingly delusional UFO theories, thereby neutralizing anything he might say.

This job fell to Moore, who fed the credulous Bennewitz forged documents and told him grisly stories about the mendacity of Grey aliens. Bennewitz came to think aliens were stalking him, passing through walls in his house and attempting to inject him with genetically altered DNA vaccines. He suffered a mental breakdown and was hospitalized.

Now, guilty over his part in the plot, a remorseful Moore told a hall of angry, booing ufologists, "What we are hearing about malevolent aliens, underground bases, and secret treaties between the aliens and the US government has its roots in the Bennewitz Affair."

This was particularly troubling for the Lear/Cooper contingent since Lear had included a fair amount of Bennewitz's material in his Hypothesis. It brought the galling possibility that much of the MJ-12 story that revealed Washington malfeasance was itself part of a government-directed disinformation program. Following Moore's speech, Cooper turned up at Lear's home in a rage. "He was roaring drunk, screaming that he'd been set up and demanding to know who I was *really* working for," Lear recalled. "That was one of those times I thought he might kill me."

By the next day, Cooper had calmed down. Who cared what William Moore said anyway? The man was a liar, a fake, less than a pawn in the larger game. The original MJ-12 papers were bogus, Cooper said, a pile of crap designed "to lead you right through the rose garden." The truth, the real truth, the one he'd learned while looking through Admiral Clarey's cabinet, was still out there, ready to be told.

Such was Cooper's stance as he stood dressed in a white poplin suit and striped tie to present the first public reading of "The Secret Government" in the Aladdin ballroom right down the hall from where Elvis married Priscilla in May of 1967.

At forty-six, Cooper had never spoken to a large audience before. Yet as he scanned the room, he appeared confident, in charge. He'd been waiting for this moment for a very long time.

Even now, watching a nearly thirty-year-old, heavily scan-lined YouTube video of Cooper's MUFON speech, the urgency in his voice is palpable as he begins with a quote from Winston Churchill. Humanity had now entered a period when, the internationalist Churchill said, "we are drifting, steadily, against the will of every person, every race, and every class, toward some hideous catastrophe. Everyone wants to stop it, but they do not know how."

From there, Cooper engaged in a massive info dump, citing a blizzard of classified documents that he'd seen in Naval Intelligence. He mentioned numerous National Security Council Acts and several operations, with names like Project Pluto, Project Plato, Project Pounce, and Project

Sigma that were designed to establish "a common binary computer language" to communicate with various alien races.

Everything that happened in the country since the end of World War Two had been colored by the alien presence, Cooper told the Aladdin audience. When an "idealistic and religious man" like Defense Secretary James Forrestal objected to dealing with the duplicitous alien creatures, Cooper said, "agents of the CIA came to his hospital room, tied a sheet around his neck, and threw him out the sixteenth-story window, to make it look like he'd hung himself. When Secret Service agent William Greer shot John F. Kennedy in the head in Dallas, it was because the president was about to blow the whistle on the alien cover-up.

"Without the aliens, you can't make sense of anything that has happened in this country for the past forty-four years," Cooper told his MUFON audience. "Put the aliens in the middle and you've got all the answers."

It was somewhere near the end of Cooper's speech, as he spoke of how the US colonized the moon, and Mars, too, working out of "a joint US/USSR/alien base," that a woman's voice in the back of the Aladdin ballroom rang out.

"Oh, stop it. Just stop it already," the woman shouted. "This is outrageous."

Cooper looked up at this unwanted noise that had broken his flow. He narrowed his eyes and said, "If you think it is outrageous, just wait a few years and you'll see how outrageous it is."

He stared out at the audience. He said he knew when he came to the conference that there was every chance he wouldn't be believed, but that didn't matter because "I am not one of you, I am not a ufologist."

He had no other agenda beyond his belief in the sanctity of the Constitution of the United States, which had been sorely subverted by the actions of the secret government. What truly mattered was that Americans had lost their freedom. The sacred gift of the Founding Fathers had been bartered away to an alien race. This was evil and had to be stopped.

"I don't care what you think of me," Cooper declared with a leveled gaze. "I don't care what you call me. I do care what you do with this information because it is important to our survival as a species. It is important to our planet. . . . What happens to me is of no consequence and I knew that when I started this. Over the last seventeen years I knew that someday I was going to have to get up and say this whether I wanted to or not. Whether I was afraid or not.

"Now I am here and now it is done and I feel an overwhelming relief. You have the information. You can laugh at it, you can throw it in the trash can. You can burn down my house if you want to. But I'm telling you that your future, your children's future, your grandchildren's future depends on what you do with this.

"Your own government is selling your children drugs and you don't seem to care. Your own government has given away the power of the people and you don't seem to care. There is an apathy that is running rampant in this country that is deadly. Whether or not there are aliens, we are truly now a nation of sheep. And ladies and gentlemen, I assure you sheep are always led to the slaughter.

"But it does not have to be that way. There is tremendous power in knowledge, there is also tremendous power in secrecy. Take away that secrecy, you make sure you're informed, and you can change things," Cooper said to great applause.

8

ooper described his MUFON speech as "a moment of relief and re-
demption," but his weekend was far from over. Two days later, on
July 4, 1989, the 213th anniversary of the signing of the Declaration of
Independence, Cooper got married again, at a wedding chapel on South
Las Vegas Boulevard. This time his wife was a twenty-eight-year-old Tai-
wanese woman, Annie Mordhorst.

It didn't take him long to realize that Annie was the right woman for
him, Cooper later told the *Hour of the Time* audience. They'd been married only a short time when Cooper gave a lecture at the Vegas Showboat
Hotel and Casino. After Cooper finished his presentation, a scuffle broke
out in the lobby. Annie stepped in front of Cooper with her hand shoved
into her purse.

"She was clutching the handle of a twelve-inch kitchen knife," Cooper proudly told listeners. "She was going to protect me!"

Annie came by her nature honestly, Cooper said. She was the daughter of a Nationalist Chinese official who had fought the Communists
before being forced to leave his homeland for Taiwan along with the
remnants of Generalissimo Chiang Kai-shek's Kuomintang army. There
were thousands of so-called patriots out there screaming about the government, Cooper told the audience. But Annie was someone who really
understood the horrors of totalitarian socialism, the yoke of Maoist slavery. She'd stared it in the eye. Annie was his "soul mate," Cooper said.
He planned on spending the rest of his life with her.

It was a heady, hot-button time for ufology. The MJ-12 controversy
had disinterred Roswell. Now there was the disclosure of activities at Area
51, a vast, off-limits Air Force facility in the Nevada desert northwest of

Las Vegas. Something funny was going on at Area 51, which was soon to become the most famous top secret base in the world. A new, more foreboding energy had been pumped into the flying saucer narrative and, overnight, Bill Cooper had become its most sensational voice.

One of Cooper's best-known early appearances was a November 5, 1989, lecture at Hollywood High School in Los Angeles. Announced as "An Evening with Bill Cooper, Former Naval Intelligence Briefing Team Member," the speech was arranged by Norio Hayakawa, who remains a well-known figure in ufology.

"Bill Cooper had a big effect on me. You could say I was one of his first followers," said the now seventy-year-old Hayakawa, who was nattily attired in a gold sweater and matching Kangol cap when we met at a Weck's coffee shop in Rio Rancho, New Mexico, north of Albuquerque.

Born in Yokohama, Japan, in 1944, a year before the bomb blast at Hiroshima four hundred miles south, Hayakawa first learned of UFOs from his father. "After the war ended he went night fishing in Yokohama Bay. One time he saw a UFO. He ruined his health with that night fishing. But he kept going out there hoping to see another UFO. You could say it stuck with me."

Moving to Los Angeles in 1980, Hayakawa took a job at the Fukui Mortuary in Little Toyko. "They said all I had to do was answer the phone at night. Also, they said I could live there, in a little room. I wound up staying twenty-eight years. I became a licensed funeral parlor director.

"The funeral parlor is an interesting place because it is where the living are forced to face issues they might rather ignore, the transition from life to death. To me a lot of the UFO experience is about that."

In the late eighties, Hayakawa, who moonlighted from his funeral job by playing country and western music with Native American bands, was attending a monthly meeting called UFORUM in West Hollywood. "A lot of UFO meetings can be dull," Hayakawa commented. "But on this night they had Bill Cooper. I hadn't heard of him. He looked like a normal, middle-aged guy, huge but paunchy with receding hair. He could have been anybody. He made a couple of remarks and then read his 'Secret Government' paper. He didn't look up, just read, for an hour and a half. But what he was saying—the authority with which he said it—was very interesting.

"Most of ufology avoids politics. But with Bill Cooper *everything* was political. He was the first person to really take the UFO phenomena and extend it out as a way to talk about global politics, history, religion, and society. It sounded so fresh to me, so intriguing." Hayakawa became a Bill Cooper fan. "The most important thing, I thought, was to get Bill bigger and better venues so more people could hear what he had to say.

"For the Hollywood High lecture, we printed up handbills and put them up on telephone poles all over town. There were ads in the underground newspapers. The show was a big success. That lecture really put Bill Cooper on the map outside of just ufology circles."

On a roll, Cooper expanded upon a concept from Lear's Hypothesis in which a high-ranking official at Edwards Air Force Base is quoted as saying "the EBEs have a device that has recorded all of Earth's history and can display it in the form of a hologram." This meant, Cooper posited, that the celebrated 1917 sighting of the Blessed Virgin Mary by three shepherd children in Fátima, Portugal, was in fact "an alien manipulation" to test "the extent to which religiosity remained in the human psyche" after the horrific carnage of World War One. As if to top this, Cooper further claimed that aliens had shown MJ-12 members a hologram of "the actual crucifixion of Christ," which they had filmed with a time-traveling camera called a Chronovisor.

The purpose for these exercises, Cooper said, was to perfect various tools to better control humanity "through religion, Satanism, witchcraft, magic, and the occult."

As Norio Hayakawa said, "There are basic questions in ufology, things you need to know. You need to know who they are. You need to know where they come from. But mostly you need to know *why* are they here? What do they *want*? Are they friend or foe? Good guys or bad guys?"

Inside the realm of early ufology, it usually boiled down to a binary, a neo-Zoroastrian dualism between the "light" and the "dark." For every *Angry Red Planet* and *Earth vs. The Flying Saucers*, there were people like George Van Tassel.

Born in 1910, the airplane-obsessed Van Tassel left his Ohio home at the start of the Great Depression to seek employment in the rising aeronautics industry of Southern California. He got jobs at Douglas (later McDonnell Douglas), Lockheed, and Hughes. By 1947, Van Tassel, now a licensed pilot, was living and working inside a four-hundred-square-foot burrow dug into the base of Giant Rock, a seven-stories-high piece of granite near the Mojave Desert town of Landers, California.

It was here that Van Tassel said he first began receiving telepathic communications. At first, he believed himself to be in touch with local Native American deities, but soon the voice he heard was revealed to him as that of Ashtar, a space-dwelling "Ascended Master" and time-traveling manifestation of Lord Sananda. Ashtar said he had chosen Van Tassel to "channel" a message of "spiritual evolution" to humanity.

Word spread and people began to show up at Giant Rock to hear Van Tassel "channel" Ashtar's commentary on the human condition. After the 1953 H-bomb tests, the size of the crowds increased. Throngs traveling in buses marked FLYING SAUCERS ARE REAL came to sit on folding chairs beside Joshua trees in shiny smocks and "space glasses," hoping that Ashtar and his cohort of Ascended Masters might lay upon them a portion of the cosmic good. The assemblage, word had it, included Van Tassel's old boss, Howard Hughes.

"Channeling was supposed to be the light," Norio Hayakawa said. "Then, on the dark side, were people like Bill Cooper and John Lear."

It wasn't anything Lear denied when I talked to him at his Las Vegas home. He'd been talking about "false light" as far back as his Hypothesis. Supposedly uplifting films like *Close Encounters of the Third Kind* and *E.T.* were a clear "deception," Lear wrote in 1987, an attempt on the part of MJ-12 "to get the public used to 'odd-looking' aliens that were compassionate, benevolent, very much our 'space brothers.'" But MJ-12 had outsmarted themselves. They "sold" friendly EBEs to the public and now realized "that quite the opposite was true."

Lear's resolutely dark-side view was summed up in the final lines of his Hypothesis: "The best advice I can give you is this: Next time you see a flying saucer and are awed by its obvious display of technology and gorgeous lights of pure color—RUN LIKE HELL!"

"That was the way I used to think. I guess you could say I was paranoid," said Lear. "I used to think people were looking around corners at me. Spying on me." Part of him had always been that way, Lear supposed. Asked to describe his first-ever memory, Lear thought a moment and said, "I was lying in my crib, I don't remember where, but there were sirens out the window. Like the world was on fire."

Yet as bleakly as he regarded the world to be in the late 1980s, Lear said, "Bill Cooper was in a much darker place. I couldn't hold a candle to his darkness."

Cooper's ascent to the heights of ufology did not prove sustainable. An early sign of slippage occurred when he agreed to sit for an interview with Jacques Vallée, the single-most-respected investigator in the history of the field. Educated at the Sorbonne, an astrophysicist and futurist, model for the part played by François Truffaut in *Close Encounters of the Third Kind,* Vallée brought a rare touch of continental class to the US military/nerd-dominated ufology subculture.

Flattered when the esteemed author of *Passport to Magonia: From Folklore to Flying Saucers* asked to meet him, Cooper suggested getting together at the Chelsea, a seafood restaurant on HMS *Queen Mary.* Once the crown jewel of the Cunard transatlantic fleet, from the 1970s on, the ocean liner had been transformed into an allegedly haunted hotel moored in the scruffy Long Beach harbor only blocks from where Cooper once ran his Absolute Image Photo Gallery.

Vallée wrote about the meeting under the title "The Cooper Briefing" in his 1991 book, *Revelations.* Arriving with Annie, Cooper was "a big fellow with a fleshy face marked by a scar on the right side of his forehead and another scar down the length of his nose, suggesting a life of action and real danger," Vallée wrote.

As Cooper downed shots of Chivas Regal, the two men got into a discussion of alien biology. Vallée quoted Cooper as saying, "They are air-breathing creatures like us, although the heart is connected to their lungs as a single organ. Their digestive system is atrophied. They are chlorophyll-based—plantlike, if you will. They absorb nourishment through the skin, and they excrete through the skin, too."

"What about their brains?" Vallée asks.

"They have two brains, separated by a bone partition, but going into the same spinal cord," Cooper replied. Vallée managed to keep a straight face through this, but soon Cooper took what the Frenchman called "a more confidential tone."

"You know, I'm not a religious man," Vallée quotes Cooper as saying. "But if you look at the Bible . . . the Angels could be the Nordic types and the Grays could well be the demonic ones. After all, the Bible talks about a pact with the Devil in the last days, after Israel is reinstated. Leading to Armageddon."

"What did the aliens have to say about that?" the now openly dismissive Vallée asks.

By the time they leave the boat, Vallée writes, Cooper had turned "suspicious." The astrophysicist attributes this attitude on Cooper's part to the fact "that I hadn't shown the absolute, unconditional enthusiasm he was obviously seeking.

"Is that how the whole machine of myth and fantasy works?" Vallée concludes the chapter. "Have the legends of MJ-12 and Area 51 been created out of whole cloth by a few people like Cooper, taking every word they heard, every shade of meaning, out of context? Or were they driven to such desperation by real events in their lives?" Either way, Vallée resolved never to speak to Bill Cooper again.

There were other naysayers. ParaNet had put Cooper on the map, but now SYSOP Jim Speiser feared his site "was becoming a home for unwed paranoids."

Speiser said he couldn't tell whether Cooper "was engaging in fantasy role-playing, or something more sinister." Lear was no better. "Lear is known to have been a CIA operative," Speiser wrote, pointing out that the pilot had "an autographed picture of G. Gordon Liddy on his wall."

Few ufologists detested Cooper more than Don Ecker. A fellow Vietnam veteran and former law enforcement official from Idaho, Ecker was the "research director" of *UFO* magazine, which was owned and edited by his wife, Vicki Cooper, no relation to Bill.

An original member of the "dark side" contingent that John Lear brought to the 1989 MUFON convention, Ecker soon came to regard Cooper as "one of the most repellent human beings I had ever had the misfortune to meet during my entire life." Angered by "the disgusting lies" that undercut "the mission to find the truth" about the ET problem, Ecker wrote a two-part series in *UFO* magazine aimed at exposing Cooper's methods.

"Who are the UFO whistle-blowers?" Ecker's 1990 article began.

"They come out of relative obscurity and burst into the center of ufological attention, making incredible claims of alien activity on Earth and the government's deep but covert involvement. . . . But is it legitimate? Who are the ruthless Pied Pipers forging a trail of lies and deception?"

A full dossier of Cooper's outrageous claims and bullying behavior followed. Ecker even investigated Cooper's bizarre assertion that "real aliens" had auditioned for and received roles in the TV show *Alien Nation*. "That's not true," Irene Kagan, casting director of the program, told Ecker. "All the *Alien Nation* actors on the show are human. I hired them myself."

Cooper's response to this criticism was typically over-the-top. He claimed that Ecker's wife, Vicki, had been arrested while serving as the chief bookkeeper for Sydney Biddle Barrows, the infamous "Mayflower Madam." To avoid jail, Vicki agreed to turn *UFO* magazine into "a CIA front organization," disseminating misleading information regarding the alien cover-up.

Cooper said his source for this information was Ecker himself, claiming the ufologist was "spending every night drunk, raving about his intelligence connections and proclaiming the Russians have already crossed the arctic and are lined up at the Canadian border ready to invade the United States."

Twenty-five years later, when I called him up at his San Fernando Valley home, Ecker was still mad. Hearing that I wanted to talk about Cooper, Ecker said, "What's your e-mail address? I'll send you something."

It was an MP3 of a 2011 episode of Ecker's satellite-radio show, *Dark Matters*. As Ecker explained, he'd seen a YouTube post in which Cooper was described as "a father of the patriot movement," someone who "told it like it was." This ticked Ecker off. He felt it was important to "tell people what a despicable, truly vile man Bill Cooper was."

The climax of Ecker's show is a series of messages Cooper left on the answering machine of actor Michael Callan. As a prospective Fabian-style heartthrob Callan played Riff, the leader of the Jets, in the original Broadway production of *West Side Story*. He also played Jane Fonda's would-be love interest in the Oscar-winning *Cat Ballou*. Moving into the management business, Callan and his partner, Douglas Deane, heard Cooper talking about MJ-12 on *The Billy Goodman Happening*, a Las Vegas radio show dealing with the paranormal.

Callan and Deane believed Cooper had qualities that could make him into a major star on the lecture circuit, but things quickly went south. A dispute arose about the ownership of the masters of the Cooper shows promoted by Callan and Deane's Need To Know Productions, Ecker narrated.

At that point, Ecker's commentary is interrupted by an earsplitting bellow. It is Cooper, totally drunk, yelling into Michael Callan's answering machine. "*Get down on your knees!*" Cooper screams. "I've come to get them, those *knees!*" There is a momentary pause, after which Cooper's voice returns, now affecting a heavy Southern accent.

"Michael," a wholly composed Cooper says. "This is Bill, your old pard-ner." He was just calling to put Callan's mind at ease. He'd been supplied some bodyguards, Cooper said, "so nothing is going to happen to me . . . because I know you were really concerned about that, so don't worry." Callan should give him a call, Cooper says, "in case you've got a hankering to talk about old times."

Until then, Cooper went on, "I'd suggest you be real careful . . . don't ride no bucking broncos, don't do nothing you haven't done before . . . because I guarantee you, no one is going to hurt me and get away with it. Take care, Mike. Love you . . . and we're going to make sure you amount to something, even if it's a pile of horseshit. . . . We miss you. We really do. And next time we see you, we're going to get you a real good present."

The next morning, Doug Deane, who lived not far from Cooper at the time, came out to find the tires of his car slashed. Cooper denied any part in this, charging Deane had slashed his own tires and then filed "a report to the sheriff that I had done it." This had been Callan and Deane's "goal from the very beginning," Cooper wrote in *Behold a Pale Horse*, "to try and destroy my efforts at educating the American people."

John Lear recalled the moment he realized Bill Cooper had contracted UFO Disease. "We were in Salt Lake City, on a show, 1991 maybe, I think it was called *PM Magazine*," Lear said, chowing down on a bowl of homemade chili in his office. "The show hadn't begun yet. I was standing offstage a bit when I heard Bill talking to the host about the Krill Papers."

The name referred to the papers' alleged author, O. H. Krill, the distinguished alien ambassador who supposedly represented the ET side in Cooper's version of the "tech-for-flesh" deal at Edwards Air Force Base in 1954. The papers contained crucial information on the mysterious "Men in Black" (Krill called them "the silencers") and insect-like gray aliens from Zeta Reticuli ("insidious little fiends") who were responsible for many of the abductions.

"Bill was telling the host that the Krill Papers were real. He said he'd seen them when he was in Naval Intelligence," Lear recalled. "I pulled him aside and asked him what the hell he thought he was doing. I told him there was no way he could have read the Krill Papers in 1973 because I'd just written them along with John Grace only a few months before.

"At first I thought Bill had just gotten mixed up," Lear said. "But then he looked me in the eye and said that he definitely had seen the Krill Papers while in the Navy. That's when I knew he was afflicted." Cooper had UFO Disease, which Lear defined as "continuing to talk long after you have passed the point of what you actually know." After that, Lear said, "I knew I would have to carefully monitor my exposure to him."

Lear leaned back in his chair, thinking of his old confederate, Bill Cooper.

"When Bill got here, he said he could back up 50 percent of what I said. Then it became 150 percent. After that, he got mad, I can't remember about what. He couldn't say I worked for the CIA, because I really did work for the CIA. I never took it personally. I just thought, that's his deal, poor Bill Cooper."

Lear was on his feet now, moving slowly toward the piano he keeps in "Lear's Lair." The arthritis is a bitch, but he still likes to play, Lear said, knocking out a little Chopin and then a few bars of "Stardust." That was a nice touch. Cooper would have appreciated it. Louis Armstrong did a great version of the tune. Cooper sometimes played it on *The Hour of the Time.*

"Sure, I remember Bill Cooper," said Chris Carter when I rang him at his office in the winter of 2016. Creator and major domo of *The X-Files,* the preternaturally popular TV show, Carter had mentioned Cooper in an interview he did with *Rolling Stone* magazine in 1997.

"I get inspiration from paranoia," Carter said in the *Stone* piece, mentioning that at the moment he was reading *Behold a Pale Horse*. "You know, one of those books with all those CAPITAL LETTERS."

A native of suburban Bellflower who grew up listening to the Beach Boys and later spent thirteen years editing *Surfing Magazine*, Carter said "there's no paranoia like California paranoia."

It was about "the tension between opposites," the producer said, like sun-strewn streets and dark hearts from the mysteries of Raymond Chandler and Ross Macdonald. The dichotomy fit in with the paradoxical collision between the *X-Files'* twin taglines, "I Want to Believe" and "Trust No One." It was an interior conflict that proved an existential crisis for many who followed the show's overarching credo that "The Truth Is Out There."

More than any other popular culture vehicle, it was *The X-Files* that turned Roswell into "Roswell." The basic story, the strange landing, the cover-up, hidden alien-derived "black tech," the government conspiracy to protect the most compelling secret on Earth, all that has been canonized in *The X-Files* "mythology" shows.

Some in the ufology community protest that many of these concepts were originally developed during the furor over MJ-12 during the late 1980s and purloined by Carter to make his fortune. Many say they saw Carter lurking around lecture halls, taking notes.

Asked about this alleged cultural appropriation, Carter laughed. "I've got a BA in journalism. If I'm interested in something, I try to find out more about it. Did I pay attention to those UFO conventions and meetings back then? Of course I did! To me, a lot of the stuff people were talking about was like another kind of science fiction, which, if it's good, should have a predictive quality to it. If you want to make a show like *The X-Files,* that's what you need to know."

There have been numerous Cooper sightings in *The X-File* projects over the years. In one of the program's most famous episodes, "The Musings of a Cigarette Smoking Man" (season 4, episode 7), the unnamed MJ-12–like operative known as the Cigarette Smoking Man assassinates President Kennedy, shooting him from a storm-drain opening. It wasn't William Greer with a shellfish-toxin gun, but the motive was the same: Kennedy had to be killed before he blew the lid off the alien secret.

In *The X-Files: Fight the Future,* a movie written by Carter, the Cooper references are more specific. At one point, a character played by Martin Landau alludes to "Silent Weapons for Quiet Wars," the title of the most influential chapter in *Behold a Pale Horse.* There is a scene in which Agent Scully is stung by an infected bee. Agent Mulder calls for an ambulance, but when it arrives, the driver is not a medic but an assassin, shooting Mulder. When the ambulance pulls away, *Cooper* is spelled out on the back.

Cooper was well aware of these references. On October 24, 1998, he posted an item on his website noting that he'd watched a VHS tape of *The X-Files: Fight the Future.* "It was more than obvious to everyone present," Cooper wrote, "that a great deal of it came right out of my book, *Behold a Pale Horse.*"

His various vendettas against other ufologists aside, Cooper's days in the field were numbered anyway. They had been since the emergence of a rail-thin thirty-year-old scientist named Robert Lazar. In 1989, Lazar, his face obscured and using the pseudonym Dennis, appeared on television with local Vegas newsman George Knapp of KLAS-TV and said he'd been working on "several, actually nine, flying saucers, flying disks" secreted in a mountainside hangar near the remote, dry Groom Lake inside the secret base S-4, aka Area 51.

Lazar's story of "reverse engineering," anti-gravity machines, and the mysterious element 115, the alleged basis of the saucer propulsion fuel, created an entirely new UFO vocabulary, more suited to the Star Wars era. Next to Lazar's tales of sleek-hulled ships that entered and exited through hatches in mountainsides, Cooper's dusty twenty-year-old filing-cabinet apocrypha seemed like a Buck Rogers serial.

Not that it mattered to Bill Cooper anymore. The "ufoologists," as he now called them, could stew in their own bilious juices. He was moving on. One's own research can never stand still. And if there was one thing he had absolutely learned from his search for the truth about UFOs, it was that there was no such thing as flying saucers, not in 1947, not ever.

PART FOUR

Silent Weapons for Quiet Wars

9

Cooper said he'd begun to suspect flying saucers were not from outer space in late 1989, when a scientist of his acquaintance came to his hotel room late one night, carrying what the man called "a mysterious briefcase." Cooper described how when the scientist opened the briefcase, a miniature flying saucer rose out of it "under its own power, hovered briefly, and then vanished from sight."

The scientist told Cooper this was a man-made device, the product of Nazi anti-gravity technology brought to the USA by Third Reich physicists like Wernher von Braun during the post–World War Two "Operation Paperclip." It had not yet been ascertained what made the objects suddenly invisible or whether they disappeared into "the future or the past," but this was among the projects under study at Area 51. There were absolutely no aliens involved.

But what finally convinced Cooper that UFOs were "possibly the single greatest hoax in history" was his discovery of a 1917 speech given by psychologist and educator John Dewey. Considered, along with William James and Charles S. Peirce, to be the foremost champion of American progressivism, Dewey was arguably the leading public intellectual in the country at the time.

Dewey's 1917 speech took place in the ballroom of the opulent St. Regis Hotel in New York City at a dinner sponsored by the Carnegie Endowment for International Peace. The fête was in honor of Viscount Ishii, head of the visiting Japanese Imperial Mission who was touring the USA as a sign of friendship between the two rising powers of the early twentieth century.

The specter of crisis and world havoc hung over the evening. Within weeks, the "doughboys" of the American Expeditionary Forces under the command of General "Black Jack" Pershing would enter into World War One, a fresh hell of newly developed tanks, flamethrowers, bombs from the sky, and mustard gas. America's participation in the war was the issue of the day. To join the fighting would enter the country into the globalist realm. Abstention meant the country would remain relatively isolated, able to develop free of international influence.

After some initial hesitation, Dewey had come to support "the logic" of the nation's inclusion in the conflict. In an article published in the *New Republic* called "The Conscription of Thought," Dewey wrote, "The future of our civilization depends upon the widening spread and deepening hold of the scientific cast of mind." Given this premise, there was no choice but to join the war.

Dewey underscored these thoughts at the St. Regis dinner. "It is our problem and our duty . . . to turn our immediate and temporary relation for purposes of war into an enduring and solid connection for all of the sweet and constructive offices of that peace which must some day again dawn upon a wracked and troubled world," Dewey told the guests and Viscount Ishii, whose government would be dropping bombs on Americans less than a quarter century later at Pearl Harbor.

It was the usual scam, Cooper said, calling Dewey "the father of our failing disaster of an educational system." Setting up "phony utopias" as the end-product justifications of cataclysmic bloodletting was a standard New World Order technique. It was summed up in the phrase *ordo ab chao*, Latin for "order out of chaos." First create the chaos, then apply the order, that was the plan. The bigger the chaos, the bigger the order.

What struck Cooper was the opening line of Dewey's speech. "Some one remarked that the best way to unite all the nations on this globe would be an attack from some other planet," Dewey said. "In the face of such an alien enemy, people would respond with a sense of their unity of interest and purpose."

"When I read that," Cooper said, "I nearly fell out of my chair. . . . It hit me like a sledgehammer right between the eyes."

Now he knew. The "UFO distraction" was part of the longest-running conspiracy on Earth. It had been trotted out during the famous Orson Welles Mercury Theatre "War of the Worlds" broadcast that aired as a

Halloween special in 1938. It happened when President Ronald Reagan visited a Maryland high school in 1985. Recalling a meeting with his Soviet counterpart, Mikhail Gorbachev, Reagan said, "I couldn't help but say to him, just think how easy his task and mine might be . . . if suddenly there was a threat to this world from some other species, from another planet, outside in the universe. We'd forget all the little local differences that we have between our countries." Two years later, at the UN General Assembly of all places, Reagan, the supposed conservative, repeated the comment nearly verbatim.

The presence of UFOs from outer space was one more fear tactic, a trick to get a frightened public in line behind a one-world totalitarian government. The most infuriating aspect of the subterfuge, Cooper regretfully admitted, was that he had fallen for it.

Now he further understood why he'd gained access to so many top secret documents while in Naval Intelligence. It was because he was supposed to see them. They'd been left especially for him, him alone.

Cooper had thought he was fulfilling his duties as a messenger, warning of the impending alien danger, only to realize that he'd misled the very people to whom he wanted to bring the truth. Like in Vietnam, the string-pullers had played him for a sap yet again.

As he later told an interviewer, "At one time, I didn't believe the government would use me in that way. I had devoted my whole life to government service. There was no doubt of my loyalty. They knew I would never doubt what I saw as being real."

He felt a responsibility to own up to his mistake. "For many years," Cooper told audiences who came to see him speak, "I sincerely believed that an extraterrestrial threat existed and that it was the most important driving force behind world events. I was wrong and for that I most deeply and humbly apologize."

Yet even if Cooper had renounced ufology, chances are his life-changing book *Behold a Pale Horse* would never have been published without it. The story is told by Melody O'Ryin Swanson, owner of Light Technology Publishing, the one and only publisher *Behold a Pale Horse* has ever had.

"A metaphysical book publisher surrounded by auto repair shops. I think that is kind of perfect," said the silver-maned, seventyish Swanson, sporting tasteful turquoise jewelry as she sat in her tranquil office located in an industrial park off an I-40 exit in Flagstaff, Arizona.

Originally from a small town in South Dakota, Swanson, who often went by her middle name, O'Ryin, which most took to be "Orion," gravitated to the metaphysical world during the 1960s. For a time, she ran a spiritual center in Miami, hosting lectures by such luminaries as Ram Dass and Swami Muktananda. By the 1980s, she was in Sedona, Arizona, which had become the center of New Age thought and commerce.

"I wanted to become a spiritual teacher but wound up running a printing press, putting out business cards," Swanson said. She also staged a series of well-attended salons, which is where she first encountered Bill Cooper.

"We sponsored Bill's lecture in Sedona in September of 1989," Swanson told me when I visited her. "He was a good draw. A lot of people really wanted to know what he had to say.

"He was still talking about UFOs then. He seemed like a lot of people I met at that time: a guy in a pink sport shirt who wanted to shine a light on what was going on below the surface in the country. We were just starting our magazine, the *Sedona Journal of Emergence,* and used the transcript of Bill's speech in the one of our first issues."

At the time, Swanson had no idea Cooper was working on a book. "He didn't mention it and I didn't ask." She first heard about *Behold a Pale Horse* from her friend Janet McClure, a well-regarded spiritualist of the time.

"Janet was a founder of the Tibetan Foundation who primarily channeled Vywamus," said Swanson, mentioning an entity who devotees claim represents "the holographic higher-self aspect" of Sanat Kumara, son of Lord Krishna and head of the Spiritual Hierarchy of Shamballa.

"Janet told me that she had a session with Vywamus and he was very concerned how much humans were being controlled and manipulated. Vywamus was aware that Bill had written *Behold a Pale Horse.* He told Janet that it wasn't the greatest book in the world, but it would help people wake up to the danger.

"That's why I decided to publish it," said Swanson, adding that after a quarter of a century of publishing *Behold a Pale Horse,* she still hadn't read it, nor did she plan to. "Not my sort of thing," she said.

The role of Vywamus in the publishing of *Behold a Pale Horse* was somewhat ironic since Cooper was on record as hating channeling and almost everything associated with the "Light" side of the ET equation. Cooper had even once threatened to sue Gyeorgos Ceres Hatonn, a reputed nine-foot-tall "Space Brother" who presented himself as "the Commander in Chief, Earth Project Transition, Pleiades Sector Flight Command."

It was Cooper's contention that Hatonn, whose channeled revelations were printed in *The Phoenix Liberator*, a newsletter owned by right-wing millionaire George Green, had plagiarized sections of "The Secret Government."

Originally, Hatonn, speaking through his channel, Doris Ekker, a seventy-year-old grandmother from Tehachapi, California, derided Cooper as "a horrendous tool" who needed to realize that "he does not control the truth." But after the threatened suit, the Pleiadian sought reconciliation, offering to place Cooper "under the protection of the White Hats of the Cosmos, to stand forth in the test and discernment of the truth from Earth speakers."

Cooper was not mollified. "This channeling is complete bullshit and I am going to put a stop to it," he declared, saying he would take his suit to the Supreme Court, if need be.

Asked about this, Melody Swanson shrugged. She wasn't going to go into her sometimes fractious dealings with the author of *Behold a Pale Horse.*

Yes, Cooper's book had sold well over the years, the suddenly cagey Swanson said, but so had many others in the Light Technology catalog. *The Ancient Secret of the Flower of Life* by mystic Drunvalo Melchizedek far outsold Cooper's work. As for where all the money went from *Behold A Pale Horse*'s quarter-century-plus run of success, Swanson wasn't going to talk about that either, and she didn't have to. "Light Technology is a private company," she said.

Perhaps people did not realize that fact, Swanson said, but Light Technology, not Simon & Schuster, not Penguin, or any mainstream concern, was the perfect publishing house for *Behold a Pale Horse*. "I own the printing presses. They're in the back of the building. We just keep printing the titles." At Light Technology, no book ever went out of print.

But in the end, Swanson said, if *Behold a Pale Horse* was a publishing success, the real credit belonged to Vywamus. "He said Bill's book would open people's eyes. He turned out to be right about that."

Michael Barkun, author of *A Culture of Conspiracy: Apocalyptic Visions in Contemporary America*, the best of the many survey books on the subject, has said *Behold a Pale Horse* "has the look of a scrapbook kept by a not too tightly wrapped mind." At first glance, it is difficult to argue with that assessment.

The evocative book cover, painted by Joanna Heikens from a rough line drawing supplied by the author, is a mash-up of mythologic tropes, featuring four horses: two white, two black.

The first, a winged creature similar to the Greek Pegasus, ridden by a blond youth, charges through the air headed toward a glowing sun. But like Icarus before him, the youth will go nowhere. The tail of his winged horse is tethered to the long cape worn by the figure upon the pale horse below, astride the iron wheel of Hell. This rider is a smallish, gray-clad figure, reminiscent of the aliens who haunt the dreams of the abducted. The rider holds a skeletal, demonically smiling mask over his face. He is Death, forever restricting human striving.

Once opened, *Behold a Pale Horse* maintains this DIY scheme through to its seven appendices and thirty-five pages of ads for other Light Technology publications. A mélange of different typefaces are employed. The margins fill with undeleted handwritten scribbles. The words *top secret* appear at the bottom of each page.

The latter was perhaps a ham-fisted marketing ploy on Cooper's part, a reference to his Naval Intelligence background. Yet there is no classified material in the book, no Pentagon Papers or the sort of material that would later be released by citizen spies like Chelsea Manning and Edward Snowden. Here, rather, is the supposedly *verboten*, the stuff that is not supposed to be known by the ordinary citizen, the news from Pandora's Box that flew open inside Bill Cooper's head.

Selling books (thirty dollars for the hardback, twenty dollars for soft) as he traveled to and from lecture venues in his station wagon, Cooper told his prospective readers that *Behold a Pale Horse* offered "500 pages of the most well-researched collection of suppressed information in the history of the world. It is the only book that opens the door to the puzzles you have been baffled by."

For Cooper, truth and falsehood began with the document. Be it Dead Sea Scrolls, the Revelation of St. John, the Golden Plates of Joseph Smith, or a stack of papers found in a cabinet at Naval Intelligence, the secret document contained the seed to be worked into the ever-expanding concept, a meme, the kernel of a new belief system. In this manner, *Behold a Pale Horse* proved a most puissant vector.

For instance, "the FEMA camp" trope is a hardy perennial, in perpetual heavy rotation on the post-9/11 Alex Jones–style conspiracy mills. These are the Nazi-style concentration camps where freedom-loving Americans will be rounded up when the government inevitably declares martial law. The stateside Buchenwalds will be overseen by SS-like agents of the Federal Emergency Management Agency (FEMA).

Cooper devotes a full chapter to the concentration camp issue in *Behold a Pale Horse,* detailing the history of how FEMA came to be "an unelected government within the government" and "a tool that can be used to establish the police state."

Tracking the agency's development from its origin in the 1947 National Security Act, the chapter tells the history of the as-yet unnamed FEMA meme through a series of executive orders from the Kennedy administration to the 1980s. As with E.O. #10995, which, Cooper writes, "empowered the government to take control over the telecommunications industry in times of national emergency," each order further allows for the increase in federal power during times of stress. There are executive orders allowing for federal takeover of the electricity grid, the mass media, etc. Originally these powers were grouped under the Office of Emergency Management. Then, on July 20, 1979, President Carter (E.O. #12148) further concentrated, codified, and bureaucratized this structure with the creation of FEMA. By this time, Cooper contends in *Behold a Pale Horse,* so much emergency power had been ceded to the agency that "the HEAD OF FEMA, NOT THE PRESIDENT" will be making the decisions.

Little of what Cooper was saying about FEMA was new or original. Much of it is a reprint of a booklet that found its start in a lawsuit, "Complaint Against the Concentration Camp Program of the Department of Defense," filed in the Houston office of the United States

Attorney in 1976 by Dr. William R. Pabst. After the creation of FEMA in 1979, Pabst reworked his suit into a pamphlet entitled *Concentration Camp Plans for U.S. Citizens.*

Pabst's work was well within the tradition of activist literature produced by such disparate figures as John Milton, Voltaire, Frederick Douglass, Joseph Goebbels, and I. F. Stone as well as untold thousands of lesser-known religious and political tract writers, outsider punk fanzine graffitists, and, later, bloggers. It is a one-man polemicist/journalist school that includes both Bill Cooper and his great inspiration, Tom Paine.

Paine's 1776 pamphlet *The American Crisis* with its famous opening line, "These are the times that try men's souls," is the paragon. Indeed, Paine's oft-quoted fragment, "A long habit of not thinking a thing wrong, gives it the superficial appearance of being right," did much to foreshadow the two and a half centuries of American suspicion that continues to bulwark much of the so-called conspiracy thinking of today.

Pabst built on Paine's concept. Whether anyone took the time to realize what was staring them right in the face, the USA was about to be turned into a giant FEMA camp, Pabst warned in his booklet. More executive orders would soon be signed, dealing with "concurrent responsibility for prevention of escape from the United States," Pabst said. Other unilateral declarations by the executive branch would include "replenishing the stockpile of narcotics," "a national police force for correctional and penal institutions," and "the use of prisoners to augment manpower which would be slave labor."

With little to no corroboration, Pabst mentioned some sites where present or future FEMA camps were located. These included "the sleepy little village" of Allenwood, Pennsylvania, where, Pabst said, a minimum security prison could be "quickly refitted to house 12,000 people." Others could be found in Florence, Arizona; Tule Lake, California; Greenville, South Carolina; Montgomery, Alabama; Avon Park, Florida; and Elmendorf Air Force Base in Alaska.

In the early years of its existence, Pabst's pamphlet, now sporting a pale green cover marked with hand-drawn razor coil, was relegated to the sun-bleached shelves of flag-draped bookstores off the main highway. It would take Bill Cooper, in his role as Carl Sagan–like meme popularizer, to bring the FEMA camp notion to a larger audience by printing Pabst's booklet in its entirety in *Behold a Pale Horse*. Soon enough, the "FEMA camp" went viral in the right-wing patriot mind-set. It wasn't long before radio hosts were saying there were "at least six hundred" FEMA camps in the US. Any low-occupancy prison, abandoned airfield, or windowless factory building was considered a potential detention center.

As alarmist as these fears sounded, it was difficult to dismiss them after Hurricane Katrina hit New Orleans. Along with the National Guard and the hired armies of Blackwater, FEMA, now operating under the all-consuming umbrella of the Department of Homeland Security, hustled residents from their ruined neighborhoods, often at gunpoint, and shipped them off to the Superdome and motels across the country. It was then the FEMA camp meme was made flesh, so to speak.

A virtual greatest-hits repository of founding Truth Movement documents, *Behold a Pale Horse* also includes sections of the 1967 *Report from Iron Mountain*. Supposedly the minutes of a secret meeting of top military-industrial complex officials held inside a classified nuclear test site, "Iron Mountain" tells of the elite's quest to find "a political substitute for war." Among the means of effective societal control discussed is "environmental pollution on a global scale."

"It is true that the rate of pollution could be increased selectively for this purpose," the Iron Mountain report says. "In fact, the mere modifying of existing programs for the deterrence of pollution could speed up the process enough to make the threat credible much sooner."

The passage is cited as the origin of the worries about chem trails, which are allegedly poisoning the skies. It matters little that the *Report from Iron Mountain* was actually intended as a Strangelovian-style satire by its authors, Victor Navasky, longtime editor of the liberal *Nation* magazine, humorist Marvin Kitman, and Leonard Lewin. (E. L. Doctorow and economist John Kenneth Galbraith were also supposedly involved.) The prank misfired when the neofascist Liberty Lobby published it as genuine. Cries that it was a phony fell on deaf ears. Navasky said he spent decades trying to set the story straight, eventually deciding "to definitively throw my hands up in the air."

But the real news, at least in my neighborhood, was Cooper's decision to include the full text of the *Protocols of the Wise Men of Zion* in *Behold a Pale Horse*.

The most notorious anti-Semitic text of the twentieth century, the *Protocols* (alternatively called *The Protocols of the Meetings of the Learned Elders of Zion*) are reputed to be a verbatim record of a Jewish plan to overthrow Christian civilization and set up a worldwide Zionist state. The goals of the plotters, organized into twenty-four sections, or protocols, are expressed in a binary point of view. As the anonymous narrator, presumably the head rabbi of Paris, says in Protocol No. 1, "What I am going to set forth is our system from the two points of view—that of ourselves and that of the goyim."

A subject of hot debate, the provenance of the *Protocols* is shrouded in intrigue. Although many claim that the document dates back to Oliver Cromwell, mainstream chronology traces the *Protocols* to an 1846 play by Frenchman Maurice Joly entitled *The Dialogue in Hell between Machiavelli and Montesquieu*. It was after an interim of fifty years, in 1897, most scholars say, that sections of Joly's satire were lifted, sometimes word for word, by a committee of writers under the direction of Pyotr Rachkovsky, the Paris station chief of the Okhrana, Russian Czar Nicholas II's secret police.

After that, the document languished until it was first published in the wake of the Russian Revolution of 1905, appearing (again without much fanfare) in a book by Russian mystic Sergei Nilus titled *The Great within the Small and Antichrist an Imminent Political Possibility. Notes of an Orthodox Believer.*

It was only when the *Protocols* came to America that they would become widely known. It was the aftermath of the Great War, with the world turned upside down. The Bolsheviks were in power in Moscow, and the US was in the midst of the repressive Red Scare crackdown on labor, immigrants, and many others. During the accompanying Red Summer, deadly race riots racked thirty-three American cities, including Elaine, Arkansas, where white mobs killed more than 100 black citizens.

It was in the midst of this uproar, in May of 1920, that automaker Henry Ford published 500,000 copies of the *Protocols* in his weekly newspaper, *The Dearborn Independent*. Ford said, "The only statement I have to make about the *Protocols* is that they fit into what has gone on in the world situation these sixteen years. They fit it now."

Just as he had granted Americans their mobility with the invention of the Model T, Ford supplied many citizens with their first close view of the Jew—the *real* Jew—the one his paper proclaimed in its headline, "The International Jew: The World's Problem." This meant not only the hook-nosed, horny-headed plotters swaddled in their prayer shawls but the sleek bankers, too. These were the people *The New International Encyclopedia*, an early American answer to the *Britannica*, characterized as someone fond of "an Oriental love of display and a full appreciation of the power and pleasure of social position."

"Time was when Faith ruled . . . but now the power is Gold." These were the words of the head rabbi, as quoted in *The Dearborn Independent*.

In such conditions, the head rabbi continued, "any people attempting self-government can easily be turned into a disorganized mob." Once that happens, "everything is in our power," the Elder goes on, lauding the clever invention of false theories and principles like "Darwinism, Marxism, Nietzscheism," which have "a disintegrating importance upon the minds of the goyim."

For five years straight, Ford's paper reliably reprinted the *Protocols*. Then in 1927, a suddenly remorseful Ford apologized, saying "it is needless to add that the pamphlets which have been distributed throughout the country and in foreign lands will be withdrawn from circulation and that in every way possible I will make it known that they have my unqualified disapproval." Even the young Joseph Goebbels abandoned the *Protocols*. As the Reich minister wrote in his diary, "I believe that The Protocols of the Wise Men of Zion are a forgery."

After the end of the Second World War, the hoary old document, the object of attack by Jewish groups like the Anti-Defamation League (ADL), largely dropped from view, aside from the fulminations of George Lincoln Rockwell and a variety of backwoods haters.

That was until 1991, when Bill Cooper chose to reprint the *Protocols*, every word of it, in *Behold a Pale Horse* (at sixty-five pages, it takes up almost 15 percent of the book). Cooper offered the notorious text without comment, pro or con, save a small author's note: "Every aspect of this plan to subjugate the world has since become reality, validating the authenticity of conspiracy." To which Cooper added, "This has been written intentionally to deceive people. For clear understanding, the word 'Zion' should be 'Sion.' Any reference to 'Jews' should be replaced with the word 'Illuminati.' The word 'goyim' should be replaced with the word 'cattle.'" That was it, there was no further commentary.

This was, to say the least, an audacious stratagem. Yet, should one apply Cooper's seemingly disingenuous instructions and change "Wise Men of Zion" to "Wise Men of Sion," this shift of a single letter hurls the reputed nineteenth-century Czarist fakery into a wholly different realm of conspiratorial thinking. If the word *Zion* invoked a cascade of associations, *Sion* did the same.

For starters, *Sion* referred to the Priory of Sion, or Prieuré de Sion, the powerful secret society allegedly founded by Godfrey of Bouillon, Duke of Lower Lorraine, who laid siege to Jerusalem during the First Crusade, thereby winning the Holy City back from the Seljuk Turks in 1099. This event played a pivotal role in the creation of the now familiar mythos of the Merovingian dynasty that began with the union of the historical Jesus and Mary Magdalene.

Debunkers have long claimed that this saga is a hoax, invented in part by Pierre Plantard, a French ultranationalist who once wrote a letter to Field Marshal Philippe Pétain, offering his services as a clairvoyant to the Vichy government. But this did not stop authors like Michael Baigent, Richard Leigh, and Henry Lincoln from presenting the story as fact in their 1982 *Holy Blood, Holy Grail*. Twenty years later, author Dan Brown revisited similar terrain in his 2003 megahit, *The Da Vinci Code*.

This appeared to be Cooper's point. Deceptions abounded. You couldn't trust everything you read. You had to do your own research to ascertain what truth you were willing to accept. It also went to the question of whether documents like the *Protocols of the Wise Men of Zion* should be suppressed, as many believe they should be. As the simple switch of *Sion* for *Zion* demonstrated, the *Protocols* provided an elastic canvas adaptable to whatever group the authors wished to demean. It was a fill-in-the-blank libel, a masterpiece of the however disreputable form. You didn't ban that kind of document. Besides, doing so would be against the First Amendment.

10

C ooper reiterated his no-Jews-in-the-*Protocols-of-Zion* line many times. In an interview with a CNN reporter in 1993, a relaxed-looking Cooper said, "I get people who still come to me all the time and say, 'Bill, you're wrong. It's the Jews. The Jews are subverting the world.' And I tell them, 'Man, it's not the Jews. It's not the Jews, it's not the Catholics, it's not the blacks.'"

To understand the nature of domination, you had to envision the world as the Secret Government did, "the way they see it," Cooper said. The strategy of control laid out in the *Protocols of Zion* had run its course. Blame had its time constraints; there would always be someone new to accuse. The mounting anxieties of the modern world could not be laid at the doorstep of a single ethnicity or nation-state.

The emerging mass-consumer society required a regimen of control that excluded overt war. The process was too costly, the results unpredictable. A more easily managed, self-sustaining system was needed. Such a scheme already existed, Cooper told readers of *Behold a Pale Horse*.

Supposedly first announced at the initial meeting of the Bilderberg Group in Geneva, Switzerland, in 1954, the rudiments of the plan had recently surfaced in a top secret document bearing the unsettling name "Silent Weapons for Quiet Wars." "SWFQW" was nothing less, Cooper declared in *Behold a Pale Horse*, than "the Illuminati's declaration of War upon the People of America."

"This is their plan," Cooper often wrote on top of the dot matrix printouts of "SWFQW" he handed out on lecture tours. "Study it. Defeat it. God Bless You, William Cooper."

"This chapter could only come in the beginning," Cooper wrote in his author's notes accompanying the forty-four-page section that opened *Behold a Pale Horse*. "Your preconceived ideas had to be shattered in order for you to understand the rest of this book. In this chapter you can see every step that the elite have taken in their war to control this once great nation. You can see the steps that will be taken in the future. You can no longer pretend innocence."

Cooper said he had seen documents that "explained" the goals and workings of "Silent Weapons for Quiet Wars" while he was in Naval Intelligence. But it wasn't until July 7, 1986, that an actual copy of the document, dated May 1979, was "found in an IBM copier that had been purchased at a surplus sale."

First reaching the wider public in Cooper's book, "Silent Weapons for Quiet Wars" has become a classic of modern "conspiracy" literature, a staple on "truther" websites. It has been name-checked by hundreds of rappers. In 1997, Killarmy, a Wu-Tang Clan "affiliate," recorded an entire album entitled *Silent Weapons for Quiet Wars*. "I wield the silent weapon for this quiet war that's in store," the rapper says. His adrenaline revving like an engine, he's a ninja in camouflage, "avenging."

Reputedly an "introductory programming manual" for new employees of Operations Research, a creepily anonymous fearsome-sounding top secret military intelligence group, "SWFQW" opens with a hearty "Welcome Aboard." The document is said to mark "the 25th anniversary of the *Third World War*, called the 'Quiet War,' being conducted using subjective biological warfare, fought with 'silent weapons.'"

Written at the level of an undergrad paper in electrical engineering, "SWFQW" defines "a silent weapon" as differing from a conventional weapon in that "it shoots situations, instead of bullets; . . . originating from bits of data, instead of grains of gunpowder." It attacks "under the orders of a banking magnate, instead of a military general." Because the silent weapon "causes no obvious physical or mental injuries and does not obviously interfere with anyone's daily social life," the public cannot comprehend this weapon and therefore cannot believe that they are being attacked and subdued.

"The public might instinctively feel that something is wrong, but because of the technical nature of the silent weapon, they cannot express their feeling in a rational way. . . . They do not know how to cry for help, and do not know how to associate with others to defend themselves against it."

According to the document, the silent weapon is deployed like a time-release capsule, at modulated speeds and patterns, so the target audience "adjusts/adapts to its presence and learns to tolerate its encroachment on their lives." Inevitably, however, "the pressure (psychological via economic) becomes too great and they crack up."

It is the job of the programmer to control these "self-destructive oscillations." This is done through the application of data-driven "inputs" (living standards, social contacts, analysis of individual habits, self-indulgence, "methods of coping," etc.) to create successful "outputs," such as desirable levels of surveillance, the storage of information, legal functions, and health options, etc. Successfully regulated outputs are considered "controlled situations."

The resulting "atrophy of cognitive powers" is coupled with "unrelenting emotional affronts and attacks (mental and emotional rape) by way of a constant barrage of sex, violence, wars in the media." These are the building blocks of an American population that is "undisciplined," "confused," "disorganized," and "distracted."

Silent Weapon technology is designed as a self-perpetuating, self-modifying system but reserves the option to introduce "a shock test" to alter an unproductive pattern or simply to create a vehicle of chaos. "Shock tests" can be big or small, but a well-planned, efficiently run society need not require excessive police presence or employ more visible means of totalitarian control. Corrective change can be accomplished "by carefully selecting a staple commodity such as beef, coffee, gasoline, or sugar, and then causing a sudden change or shock in its price or availability."

The process can be said to be working effectively when "there is a measurable quantitative relationship between the price of gasoline and the probability that a person would experience a headache, feel a need to watch a violent movie, smoke a cigarette, or go to a tavern for a mug of beer."

Long before anyone was talking about the red and blue pills of *The Matrix*, Bill Cooper was warning of mass social engineering on the part of the New World Order. "In a study of mind control and psychological warfare, ladies and gentlemen," Cooper said, "it is not enough to simply review the latest technology of coercion, the most recent gadgetry of techno-junk littering the depths of government supply depots and so-called cults. Far more dangerous than these appliances is the praxis behind them. An ages-old underground current informs the modern project in this modern era; life in our modern era is little more than life in an open-air mind-control laboratory."

Who is "the modern man," Cooper asked. "He is the smartest, most advanced individual to ever strut the planet, the most relatively liberated being in history. He scoffs with great derision at the idea of the existence and operation of a technology of mass mind control emanating from the mass media and government. Modern man believes he is much too smart to believe in anything as superstitious as that. But the truth is, modern man is the ideal hypnotic subject."

For a long time, many assumed Cooper was the author of "SWFQW." After all, many of Cooper's signature lines, such as the uninformed public being nothing but "beasts of burden and steaks on the table by choice and consent," are quotes from the document.

In 2003, two years after his death, however, Cooper's authorship came into question. By then it was apparent that there was at least one more version of "SWFQW" out there. The text was similar to what appeared in *Behold a Pale Horse*, but the "new" copies included a number of electrical circuitry diagrams. With most digitized Internet users unfamiliar with such analogue material, the hand-drawn diagrams struck many as oddly occult symbols, filled with archaic meaning and dread.

This raised the eyebrows of "Joan d'Arc," then editor of *Paranoia* magazine. Acknowledging the august place of "SWFQW" in the literature, calling it "a dubious elite blueprint for control of the planet second only to The Protocols of Zion," Joan d'Arc thought the presence of "these sophisticated diagrams," absent from the *Behold a Pale Horse* version, cast doubt on the document's provenance.

"As far as I know, Bill Cooper was not a highly trained economist," Joan d'Arc wrote, suggesting the document might be the work of Unabomber Ted Kaczynski, or "the late anarcho-libertarian Murray Rothbard."

On December 17, 2003, *Paranoia* received a letter from Hartford Van Dyke, then a prisoner at the Federal Correctional Institution in Waseca, Minnesota. Van Dyke, sixty-three, had just begun serving an eight-year sentence after his conviction on conspiracy and counterfeiting charges.

"Dear Paranoia," Van Dyke wrote from his jail cell, claiming that he, not Bill Cooper, was responsible for the authorship of the legendary "Silent Weapons for Quiet Wars." He also took issue with Joan d'Arc's characterization of the document as "a paranoid manifesto."

"SWFQW" was not a work of paranoia but rather of "sociopathy," Van Dyke said. "It begins as a logical sociopathic work that ends as an emotional sociopathic work. Being as it is about war, the subject matter had to be sociopathic."

Van Dyke was far from unknown in the patriot/libertarian scene at the time. According to the Associated Press, Van Dyke and his codefendant, John S. Nolan, had attempted to pass more than $3 million of fake money, bills of their own design, many of which featured a picture of the queen of England rather than Andrew Jackson or Benjamin Franklin. In trouble for refusing to pay taxes, Van Dyke sent $600,000 of the phony notes to the IRS, saying he was sending "fake money to satisfy fake debts."

As for the authorship of "SWFQW," Van Dyke said he put the manuscript together, but "I am the author only in the sense that I compiled and linked the gems of other writers."

Foremost of these influences, Van Dyke wrote, was Harvard professor Wassily W. Leontief, winner of the 1973 Nobel Prize for Economic Sciences. Born into a bourgeois Jewish family in St. Petersburg in 1906, and having spent his early life on the run from the Russian and German secret police, Leontief invented the economic models of "in-puts" and "out-puts" supposedly adopted by the planners in "SWFQW."

"Silent Weapons for Quiet Wars," Van Dyke wrote to the *Paranoia* editor, was "a form of modern technological alchemy that produced gold for the few, dross for everyone else."

Van Dyke's letter also provided clues about the secret document's quirky path to its appearance in *Behold a Pale Horse*. He said he finished the "SWFQW" text in December of 1979, and printed "about 65 copies," intending to mail them out to "friends and organizations." Van Dyke said he had no idea what happened to these mailings but could "fairly well account" for what happened to one copy of the soon-to-be classic document.

Van Dyke tells of how he was driving on Interstate 5 sometime in 1980 when he picked up a hitchhiking soldier. "He was late for duty (or was going to be late), at McChord AFB in the state of Washington," Van Dyke wrote. "Even though I was traveling in my own locality, I drove him to McChord (a two-hour trip each way). On the way, I told him about "SWFQW," and when he stepped out of the car to go onto the base I handed him a copy."

Since McChord was not far from the auction site where the copy of "SWFQW" allegedly turned up on the IBM copier on July 7, 1986, Van Dyke surmised that it was the same document he'd handed to the soldier a few years before. Van Dyke said that very same copy later turned up in Phoenix, Arizona, where it came to the attention of Sheldon Emry, pastor of the Lord's Covenant Church. Emry, a former Army cryptographer and early adopter of the Christian Identity belief that the Anglo-Saxon peoples, not the Jews, were the true Chosen People of the Bible, published "SWFQW" in the November 1986 edition of his church newsletter, *America's Promise*. The document almost immediately resurfaced in the *American Sunbeam*, a four-page weekly paper published just outside the Ozark Mountain town of Seligman, Missouri.

Founded in 1881, the *Sunbeam* was once called the *Seligman Sunbeam*, in honor of Joseph Seligman. Eldest of ten children of a Jewish wool merchant from Baiersdorf, Germany, Seligman arrived in America at age eighteen during the 1830s. By 1861, the enterprising Seligman had prospered to the point where he was able to float a multimillion-dollar loan to support the Union cause in the Civil War. He also brought the railroad to the Ozarks, which is why locals named their town and newspaper after him.

The *Sunbeam*! The phrase itself connotes a newspaper that could be delivered by young boys with oversize baskets on their bicycles, be left open on lunch counters for the next customer to read, a chronicle of wedding announcements, grange meetings. Indeed the paper characterizes itself as

"A Bold Fearless, Energetic Newspaper" pledged to the defense of "The Union, The Constitution and the Enforcement of the Law."

After the railroad moved away, however, the town and paper went into deep decline. Then, in 1973, the *Sunbeam* was purchased by Edward Aloysius Roberts, aka the human manifestation of Delamer Duverus, the Sea of Truth, the City, the Mind of God.

The erstwhile Roberts (1910–1986), who grew up in the "gutters of New York City among the human animals," described his earliest encounter with "Silent Weapons" technology in his spiritual biography, *The Golden Reed*, published in 1973.

"It was the summer of 1947, immediately following World War Two. We were living in a rented stone cottage on the outskirts of a small town in the Hudson River Valley of New York State," wrote Roberts, then a struggling sculptor.

"We had survived the terrors and madness of war, and could not find the answer for the insanity of the event. Why, we asked. Why should humanity bathe in the blood of their species without any reason." It was then, Roberts wrote, that he was "suddenly, and unexpectantly, jolted loose by a power that filled our consciousness. It was as if a switch had been closed to send waves of pure energy through us. It was so great a power that coursed through us, it was unbearable." At first, Roberts thought he would be driven crazy by the electronic pulse, "but the intensity soon decreased to a tolerable flow."

It was during this event, Roberts wrote, that he gained insight into what he called "the first layer" of the deeper knowledge he suddenly felt compelled to explore. As he pored over each "impress of history," what he found was "contradictory to everything we'd ever been led to believe."

During the 1950s and 1960s, Roberts turned up among the southwestern UFO cults with a small band of followers. They lived communally in small towns throughout the southern states, moving often. During this time, Roberts, now calling himself Delamer Duverus, "an Atonga who speaks that which is given him to tell his people," came to the dying town of Seligman to revive the *Sunbeam*.

His work often appeared in the paper. In one essay, called "The Next Voice You Hear," Duverus wrote that while today's society had become a cacophony of useless noise, listening to the only sound that mattered was banned by the authorities. In the modern world, hearing voices in one's head was supposed to be a form of "mental disturbance," a trick by the Devil to delegitimize the voice of God's prophets, Duverus wrote.

But what really brought the *American Sunbeam* back to relevance was Duverus's political activism. In his FEMA concentration camp pamphlet, Dr. William Pabst thanks the *Sunbeam* for providing several locations for prospective detention centers. Along with some of the most scabrous racial and anti-Semitic material imaginable, Duverus also published a version of "Silent Weapons for Quiet Wars."

In *Behold a Pale Horse,* Cooper says he received his copy of "SWFQW" from "Mr. Tom Young, a fellow Warrior in the cause of Freedom," but he clearly had dealings with Duverus, who said the manuscript was delivered to the *Sunbeam* office by an "unknown person." In his introduction to the *Sunbeam* version of "SWFQW," the one that now circulates on the Internet with the oddly rendered circuit diagrams, Duverus thanks an anonymous gentleman "stationed in Hawaii," where he "held the highest security clearance in the Naval Intelligence."

Cooper reciprocated the gesture in the opening of *Behold a Pale Horse*, where he uses a full page to quote Delamer Duverus. Arranged on the page in the shape of a diamond (or a teardrop) the quote reads: "One basic truth can be used as a foundation for a mountain of lies, and if we dig down deep enough in the mountain of lies and bring out that truth, the entire mountain of lies will crumble under the weight of that one truth."

In 1991, Cooper appeared on the Staten Island, New York, public access TV show *Dimensions in Parapsychology*. Introduced by cohost Bryce Bond, a former soft jazz deejay, as "the Ralph Nader/Rambo of Revealing Secrets," Cooper was going to talk about "UFOs and the secret government," Bond said.

Cooper cheerfully complied, going through the motions of his 1966 sighting on the USS *Tiru*. But he soon started talking about the then-incipient American invasion of Kuwait.

What was about to happen in the Persian Gulf had nothing to do with evil aliens, the villainy of this year's boogeyman, Saddam Hussein, or even the price of oil, Cooper said. You had to look at history through the long lens, not the toilet tissue of lies issued by the mass media. The roots of Operation Desert Storm dated back at least six thousand years, possibly to Creation itself.

The first factor was the setting of the conflict. That's because Saddam's fiefdom wasn't really Iraq, some phony nation-state with borders sketched out on a blackboard by the victors of the First World War. It was Mesopotamia, the alluvial plain between the Tigris and Euphrates, the fertile crescent of biblical lore. It was Babylon, land of Sumer and Ur. It was here, amid the present-day targets of Basra and Baghdad, that the Brotherhood of the Snake, the first of the secret societies that continue to rule the world, came into existence.

Cooper first wrote about the Brotherhood of the Snake in his essay "Secret Societies and the New World Order": "History is replete with whispers of Secret Societies," Cooper began. "Accounts of elders or priests who guarded the forbidden knowledge of ancient peoples. Prominent men, meeting in secret, who directed the course of civilization are recorded in the writings of all people."

There were dozens of these groups, Cooper wrote in his essay. In a single paragraph, he named "the Order of the Quest, the Roshaniya, the Qabbalah, the Knights Templar, the Knights of Malta, the Knights of Columbus, the Jesuits, the Masons, the Ancient and Mystical Order of Rosae Crucis, the Illuminati, the Nazi Party, the Communist Party, the Executive Members of the Council on Foreign Relations, The Group, the Brotherhood of the Dragon, the Rosicrucians, the Royal Institute of International Affairs, the Trilateral Commission, the Bilderberg Group, the Open Friendly Secret Society (the Vatican), the Russell Trust, the Skull & Bones, the Scroll & Key."

Some of these societies catered to the blue bloods of Wall Street, others were made up of men in funny hats lined up for the early-bird special, but whether they knew it or not, they all could trace their origin to the Brotherhood of the Snake.

This was the real reason why Americans were about to enter harm's way in Iraq, Cooper told the increasingly slack-jawed hosts of *Dimensions in Parapsychology*.

"A half million of the most dedicated, most devout American patriots, people who have sworn to protect and defend the Constitution, are over there in the Middle East," Cooper said. They were in "a hostile environment where they can be killed very easily with chemical warfare." As he knew from his eleven-year stint in the military, Cooper said, "our troops have no protection in a desert situation against chemical weapons.

"Those men are dead," Cooper said, gauging the historical moment. After forty-four years, the Cold War that began in 1947 was at an end. The Berlin Wall, symbol of the divide between East and West, had toppled. Boris Yeltsin would soon be standing atop a T-72 tank to declare the end of the Soviet Union.

The joke of it all, Cooper told Bond, "was that the United States and the Soviet Union have been secretly allies for many, many years. We were never really enemies." All those sleepless nights, the enslavement of Eastern Europe, the proxy confrontations in Africa and Vietnam that killed millions, had been part of the plot.

Cooper had done his research on Cold War deception. He'd read *None Dare Call It Conspiracy* by Gary Allen, the John Birch Society spokesman and onetime George Wallace speechwriter. He'd gone through the work of Antony C. Sutton, books like the three-volume *Western Technology and Soviet Economical Development*, which makes the case that since US-financed Soviet manufacturing was the main source of supply for the North Vietnamese armies, American taxpayers were essentially footing the bill for both sides of the war.

The alleged "mutually assured destruction," eyeball-to-eyeball confrontation between the US and USSR was the ultimate "phony war." It wasn't a war at all but one more use of "the Hegelian conflict situation that was being artificially created to bring about the New World Order. It is called the Hegelian dialectic."

The reference came, of course, from Georg Wilhelm Friedrich Hegel (1770–1831), a titan of the Enlightenment who described the quest for truth as "an unquenchable, unhappy thirst that brooks no compromise." The process was a dialectic, Hegel said, hence the Hegelian dialectic.

First came the status quo, the accepted reality, the thesis. Then arose the antithesis, an opposing point of view, one that offered legitimate challenge to the veracity and utility of the current state of affairs. The thesis and the antithesis then engaged in dialectic combat that resulted in a new standard of truth, which was called the synthesis.

This was the way of the world, except the controllers of the New World Order had turned Hegel's dialectic on its head, Cooper said. "They determine the synthesis first, what they want, and then create the two forces to oppose each other, so they know what they have to do to bring about that synthesis, while everyone thinks it all happened by accident."

Manifested in bogus divide-and-conquer dichotomies like Democrats and Republicans, manipulation of the Hegelian dialectic was the main tool of the Secret Government, Cooper said. They'd used it to make the Cold War hum, and now that the US-USSR charade had run its course, another manufactured synthesis was getting ready to be born. Like a snake shedding its skin, the New World Order established in 1947 would soon be replaced by another.

The campaign had already been announced, Cooper told Bryce Bond, in a speech made by George H. W. Bush, the forty-first President of the United States, a few months before, on September 11, 1990.

Attired in his official custom-tailored blue suit and blood-red tie, Bush said, "Once again, Americans have stepped forward to share a tearful goodbye with their families before leaving for a strange and distant shore. At this very moment, they serve together with Arabs, Europeans, Asians, and Africans in defense of principle and the dream of a new world order."

"He said it. Everyone heard him say it," Cooper told his *Dimensions in Parapsychology* hosts. "He said it three times in his speech on September 11. Three times. On September 11."

11

can't possibly explain what my wife means to me," said Cooper during an *Hour of the Time* broadcast in celebration of Annie's birthday. "She's with me in everything I do," he said, dedicating the most cosmically romantic tunes on his playlist, *Smoke Gets in Your Eyes* by the Platters, and The Flamingos' *I Only Have Eyes for You*, to his wife as testaments of his "complete and total love."

The greatest thing in his life was Pooh, which is what Cooper called his daughter, Dorothy, after Winnie-the-Pooh, his favorite children's book character.

Cooper described Pooh's birth in *Behold a Pale Horse*. "It was a difficult labor, twelve hours before Annie was finally moved to the delivery room. She had taken no drugs. She had not been given a spinal tap. She did everything naturally. She was drained of energy and was experiencing great pain."

After a particularly hard push, Annie looked up "with all the innocence and trust of a little child" and asked, "'Did the baby come yet?' I had to tell her it hadn't."

A moment later, Annie "regained her composure. I could see the love in her eyes as she looked up at me. I squeezed her hand. She took a deep breath and pushed Pooh's little head out into the world. The doctor suctioned the baby's mouth, then Annie gave her all—a push that seemed to come from her very soul—and little Dorothy popped out, announcing her presence with a great cry.

"I am so proud of Annie. She is my hero. And Pooh is my always and forever friend," Cooper wrote.

Pooh was the fourth of Cooper's five children. He rarely talked about the others. One of the few clues to their existence was the dedication of *Behold a Pale Horse.* "To my children, Jenny, Tony, Jessica and little Dorothy. I love you every moment of every day."

Tony, the son Cooper had with Janice Pell, was only eleven when *Behold a Pale Horse* came out, but he recalled the situation vividly.

Now in his late thirties and living in the Silicon Valley area when we spoke on the phone, Tony said, "I always knew someone would come out of the blue and ask me about Bill Cooper. I guess that's you."

Tony said he understood from early on that Cooper was his biological father but did not think of him often, if at all. He had no recollection of ever laying eyes on the man.

"I was very young when my mother left him," Tony said. "Far as I know, he basically choked her out one night when he was drunk and that was it. The next morning we got in the car and drove to my aunt's house and lived there for a long while. I was lucky. My mom found a very loving relationship with my stepfather and I grew up in a normal, stable home."

Tony did speak to Cooper on the phone one time. "He called the house. He wanted to talk to me. He said he'd written a book and dedicated it to me. It was crazy. I didn't even really know who he was. He hadn't ever shown any interest in me, never called me on my birthday, any of that.

"We talked for a few minutes. It was pretty normal. He asked me how I was doing in school, if I liked sports. It was more like a job interview than talking to the father that disappeared from your life. I was eleven, I didn't know what to think.

"When I saw the book, I looked at the dedication and saw my name, along with these sisters I didn't know I had. That gave me chills."

Tony continued: "Over the years, sometimes I'd think back to that day and wonder, Why? Why did he call? What did he want? Was I supposed to be proud of him because he wrote a book? That was the only time in my life I remember talking to him."

Cooper and Pooh appear together in a remarkable picture he chose to publish in the foreword of *Behold a Pale Horse.* He sits in a chair beside the open blinds of a sun-flooded hospital waiting room, his huge, hairy forearms wrapped around his newborn daughter.

He looks sleepy, as new fathers usually do. He stares up at the camera, narrowed eyes accentuated by the bulb of his drinker's nose, his mouth crooked to a half smile or a sneer. The way he clutches tiny Pooh in his bearish grip, he seems to be saying "Mine!" Then again, he could have been holding on for dear life, to one last chance.

In *Behold a Pale Horse* Cooper wrote of how he and Annie had been constantly "followed and harassed. Death threats began showing up on our answering machine. . . . Government cars would park in front and well-dressed men watched the house. . . . The strangest people began to show up at our door, sometimes in the middle of the night."

One time Cooper pulled up into the driveway of where he and Annie were living, only to have "a government car" stop right behind him. Purporting to be a census taker, the driver asked Cooper his name. Telling the man to get off his property, Cooper asked Annie to fetch his gun.

"Now, many people would say I was paranoid in this instance," Cooper wrote in *Behold a Pale Horse*, "until they discover that census takers DO NOT DRIVE GOVERNMENT CARS." In response to "this constant harassment," Cooper bought Annie a .380 Taurus semiautomatic pistol and taught her how to use it. He had no doubt that if the situation arose, she'd shoot to kill.

Pooh's birth coincided with the Coopers' move to Arizona. "Bill said California was driving him nuts," said the late Jerry Etchey, a longtime member of the *HOTT* community. He'd met Cooper back in the saucer days and accompanied him to Area 51, where they sat in a trailer on Highway 395 filming lights in the sky and talking about music. After Cooper's death, Jerry stayed in the *HOTT* orbit, attending the Skills and Research conferences run by Doyel Shamley. It was at the 2014 edition of these deep woods camp-outs that I met Jerry, before his death the following year.

"Bill thought California was symbolic of what had gone wrong with the country," Jerry said. "California was supposed to be a paradise on Earth. The last chance to get away from the mess human beings had made of the world. Then you get there and it's the same crap.

"I remember him laughing, saying 'put up a parking lot,' like when in doubt, that was the answer for everything. Either that or jump in the ocean and start swimming. California was the end of the line, and everywhere you looked, there was someone saying 'You can't do that.' He decided to turn around."

Everything shoved into his big Buick, Cooper, Annie, and little Pooh made their way eastward. The first place they stopped was Camp Verde, Arizona, a former US Cavalry garrison town of about ten thousand, near the Mogollon Rim fifty miles south of Flagstaff.

It was from forts like Camp Verde that the forces of Manifest Destiny directed their assault on the resistant Apache Nation, which was led by famed guerilla fighters like Cochise and Geronimo. It was only when General George Crook, veteran of the Civil War bloodbath of Antietam, organized a contingent of Apache "scouts" that Geronimo's "raids" were brought to heel. Crook's tactic worked, even if many of the scouts eventually wound up dead, murdered for their collaboration.

Cooper finished *Behold a Pale Horse* in Camp Verde and then pushed east along Arizona Route 260, looking for a place to settle down. He and his little family went through the mountain resort of Payson, then to Show Low. They then went north to Taylor and east to St. John's before coming to Eagar, where Cooper found the place he would call home.

Cooper's notions of "home" were spelled out in an October 1982 letter he worte to Robert P. Jordan, director of special projects for the National Geographic Society. Residing at the time in Paramount, California, due east of Compton, aka the CPT, stomping ground of Ice Cube and Dr. Dre, who a few years later would be reading *Behold a Pale Horse,* Cooper pitched an article idea he hoped might be commissioned by *National Geographic.*

"Every day I see our way of life changing," Cooper wrote. "I see vast tracts of once proud buildings torn down to make way for new shopping centers and tall office buildings. I read of the independent farmer giving way to corporate agricultural conglomerates. Architecture of a past age is disappearing. Too precious few of these things are being preserved. I am afraid that many of the things that we, as Americans, once cherished will shortly be gone, lost forever.

"The schools, the neighborhoods, the family structure, homes with a swing upon the front porch, a white picket fence around the yard, trick-or-treating, and the old swimming hole are, in most cities, already gone." Soon enough, Cooper wrote, small-town America will "conform to the inevitability of change."

It didn't matter that he was a lowly photography student at the two-year Long Beach City College (he offered to supply samples of his work "on demand"), Cooper told the *National Geographic* editor that it was imperative for him to get started "as soon as possible," for "any delay would be disastrous to the project."

The story was so important, Cooper said, that even if the magazine decided "to assign it to someone else, I will be satisfied. However, I hope you will consider assigning the task to me. You will not be disappointed." The letter was signed "Sincerely, Milton W. Cooper."

Needless to say, Cooper did not get the assignment, but it might have been interesting to see what he came up with. He had almost no experience living in the America he proposed to document. Any trick-or-treating he might have done was limited to the officers' quarters on whatever base his father was stationed. As Sally Phillips, one of Cooper's former wives, said, "Bill's idea of daily America was what he saw in *Life* magazine and on TV."

Cooper's displacement from the land he loved could be poignant. "I've always envied those of you who have a hometown," he told his *Hour of the Time* listeners one night.

"I have always wanted to walk down a street and think, 'Oh, Mrs. Jones, she used to live over there. She taught me in the fourth grade. Oh, look, there's Jimmy Burns, we used to play football together.' . . . Almost everyone I ever met in my childhood has been scattered to the four corners of the globe."

As soon as he reached the Round Valley, which encompasses the twin towns of Eagar and Springerville, Cooper knew it was the right place to raise a family. At seven thousand feet, surrounded by the White Mountains, with ramrod-straight stands of ponderosa pine and juniper-pinyon, thick blankets of unsullied snow in the winter, great carpets of goldeneye in summer, you couldn't beat the countryside. He liked the people, too.

Of the two towns, Springerville, a mile to the north, carried the legacy of the Wild West. Named for Henry Springer, trading post owner and card shark, the town retained "an unenviable reputation for lawlessness and ruffianism," according to an article in the June 18, 1887, edition of the *Apache County Critic*.

Billy the Kid passed through here. So did Ike Clanton, on the run following the epic 1881 gunfight at the OK Corral in Tombstone, 270 miles south. Leader of "The Cowboys," a local band of petty thieves, Clanton claimed to have been set up by Wyatt and Virgil Earp, charging that the Earps and Doc Holliday were acting as a hit squad hired by the railroads to get rid of the locals. Soon after Clanton lost his suit, he was shot dead in a gun battle just west of Springerville in 1887 by J. V. Brighton, a member of the Apache County Sheriff's Office and part-time bounty hunter.

If Springerville retained a sliver of its cantankerousness, Eagar—on the other end of South Main Street—always was, and remains, the Mormon town, a comparative model of moral propriety and business sense. While Springerville was drinking and whoring, the Latter-day Saints were digging the Big Ditch, which was aimed at irrigating the higher elevations of the valley.

Possessing no dynamite, the pioneers lit giant fires to heat basalt rocks. Then they dumped buckets of cold water hauled from the Little Colorado River, which split the huge stones. When the clouds of steam dissipated, the Mormons carried the shattered boulders away. Eventually stretching nearly thirty miles in length, the Big Ditch proved largely ineffective as an irrigation tool, but served notice as to the lengths the LDS people would go to lay claim to the land.

Largely ignorant of this history at the time, Cooper first heard about the house on the hill at 96 North Clearview Circle while eating lunch in Springerville's Safire Restaurant. A young couple in the next booth were talking about how they'd just bought this wonderful place, only to find out that the husband was about to be transferred to another job location. They'd hardly moved in and now they were going to have to sell the place.

Cooper walked over to inquire about the house. He liked what he heard, but the couple said they couldn't show the place at the moment. No problem, Cooper said, telling them to finish their lunch while he went over to take a look at the exterior. He'd be back in ten minutes. Cooper drove up the steep rise, saw that the house sat on top of a hill overlooking the entire valley. There were no other homes around it. Never having set foot inside the place, Cooper drove back to the Safire and made an offer. At $130 grand, it was a steal.

In December of 1992, Cooper made a video to show off his new house. Everyone else—his mom, dad, brother Ronnie, sister Connie, and their spouses—would be spending Christmas at his parents' house in the Texas Gulf coast town of Port Isabel. Cooper said he'd love to be there, too, along with Annie and little Pooh, but, as always, money was tight. If he didn't show up, Cooper told his family members, the tape he was making "just might end up being your Christmas present."

The tape begins with a midrange shot of the two-story house, with the usual motor pool of aging classic cars in front. Everything is covered with the six inches of snow that fell the previous night.

"This is the front of the house," Cooper says, providing a tour-guide voice-over to the tape. "Right under the front porch, under that over-hang, is the kitchen and the rec room, and above that are the three bedrooms and the two bathrooms; the portion to the left is the living room, the fireplace." Then the camera, sitting on a tripod, begins to move. "Now I'll let you see our view.

"We have one of the most beautiful views in the world," Cooper said as he panned the camera across the open space. To the west was the Apache National Forest, which was full of "tall pines and aspen, deer and elk." There were also antelope and bear. To the east, over the tops of burned-out volcanic cones, was New Mexico. During the spring, every-thing was "green and beautiful." Now, with the wind whipping up, it was "a winter wonderland."

If Cooper sounded house-proud, it could be understood. "All Bill re-ally wanted was for his father to respect him," Sally Phillips told me. But there had been so many arguments, mishaps, disappointments. As Jack Cooper later told Doyel Shamley, he was "always having to bail Bill out of one screw-up or another."

There was no escaping the past. As Cooper photographed the south side of the house, he said he didn't want to go farther down the incline. With the snow and ice, it was "really slippery and I don't want to . . ." He stops then, lets out a deep sigh. "Oh, you know why," Cooper says.

It was his leg. There was no use going into it. When Jack Cooper heard his son Bill was claiming his motorcycle was run off the road by men-in-black minions of the CIA or worse, he was flabbergasted. As far as his father knew, drunk or not, Cooper had lost control of the bike all by himself. With the repeated attempts to reattach Cooper's leg, the accident proved costly, even with the government insurance.

Cooper wanted everyone to know that they didn't have to worry about him anymore. As his father told him, "Sometimes it takes a while for a man to find himself."

Cooper trained the camera on "the small town of Eagar" in the distance, pointing out the City Hall, the police station, and the grade school, where "you could see the kid stuff outside, the swings, things like that." Off in the distance was the lumber mill. "That's where everybody in this town works. At the mill," Cooper said. As he panned around, two boys came into view, one pulling a sled that carried the other.

"See the boys down there, sledding," Cooper said with a delighted laugh. "That's the road, the road that comes up our mountain." A more bucolic, all-American scene could not be imagined. Too bad Sugar Bear, Cooper's dog, wasn't there. Everyone loved Sugar Bear. But he had "a girlfriend" in town, Cooper said. "Yes," Cooper told his family, "Sugar Bear goes to town sometimes to see the elephant."

The tour over, Cooper told his family, "We love this house. We love this place. We love the people in the town. Everything is just wonderful."

"Next stop, balcony off the master bedroom," Cooper announced, like you haven't seen nothin' yet. And there they are: Annie, her black hair done up in a flattering bouffant, the two-and-a-half-year-old Pooh in her arms.

"Say Merry Christmas," Annie says in her heavily inflected but clear English.

"Merry Christmas," says Pooh, looking impossibly cute in her rainbow-striped sweater, baby-blue corduroy pants, and pink light-up sneakers.

"Merry Christmas," Annie repeats, then turns to Pooh. "Say Merry Christmas. Say hi, Grandma. Hi, Grandpa. Hi, Connie. Hi, Ron. Hi, Susie. Hi, Jennifer," Annie says, making certain to include Ron, the husband of Cooper's sister Connie, as well as his brother Ronnie's wife and daughter. Pooh runs through this list with aplomb and near impeccable diction.

At the end of the Christmas video, Cooper stands alone on the balcony, the Round Valley fanning out behind him. The late afternoon light on his face, he looks relaxed, genuinely content, a man who has caught a fleeting ray of hope.

"Hi, Mom, hi, Dad," he says, wishing everyone a great holiday.

"As you can see, we're having a beautiful white Christmas. Hope you guys have as nice a Christmas as we're gonna have."

PART FIVE

Mystery Babylon

The Tower of Babel by Pieter Bruegel the Elder

12

The Hour of the Time debuted on WWCR on January 4, 1993. Known as World Wide Country Radio before changing to World Wide Christian Radio, the Nashville-based station was the biggest thing in shortwave at the time. Its massive 100,000-watt signal was capable of reaching millions (the company's brochure says "nearly a billion") of listeners around the world. Renting a regularly scheduled slice of prime time on the WWCR's transmitter wasn't cheap, but if you were Bill Cooper, a messenger whose message needed to be heard, it was the place to be.

Cooper had done episodes of *The Hour of the Time* in the previous year, but at random times, intervals, and hookups. Those early shows still retained the laid-back, Khalil Gibran–quoting detachment of the FM stations he listened to in the 1970s. By the time he reached WWCR, however, Cooper was a nearly fully formed presence, able to escalate from folksy plain talk to full-blown Jonathan Edwards "Sinners in the Hands of an Angry God" mode at the drop of a hat. As with his *Radio Teen* days, when he spread the credo of rock and roll to the captive kids of Red China, he was a man on a mission, good and getting better. The very first song he played on his inaugural WWCR show was the Beach Boys' "Make It Big."

While Cooper had been able to crash the rinky-dink ufology party by sheer force of will, the "patriot" radio market was another kind of minefield. Even WWCR's mega-wattage was no guarantee of success. Here was a media with a history that included such figures as Father Charles Coughlin and the stem-winding priest from Royal Oak, Michigan, whose broadcasts endorsing the rising 1930s European fascism reached an astounding ninety million listeners per week. Mainstream conservative performers like Rush Limbaugh were attracting up to twenty million dittoheads a day.

Shortwave was the underground alternative, and like most sub-rosa scenes, the competition was fierce. WWCR already carried several "patriot" shows featuring off-grid stars like Chuck Harder and Tom Valentine. Cooper developed a healthy animus for both, especially Valentine, whose *Radio Free America* show occupied the prime 9–11 P.M. time slot and enjoyed the sponsorship of *The Spotlight,* the weekly newspaper of Willis Carto's powerful Liberty Lobby. Other competition included "celebrity" hosts like William Pierce, head of the racist National Alliance and author of the seminal novel *The Turner Diaries*; militiaman Mark Koernke, aka "Mark from Michigan"; and G. Gordon Liddy, Nixon's old Watergate plumber. The next time the feds come to your door, Liddy told his listenership of staunch Second Amendment supporters, "Go for a head shot; they're going to be wearing bulletproof vests. . . . Head shots! Head shots! Kill the sons of bitches!"

In the face of such opposition, Cooper proclaimed *The Hour of the Time* to be "not like any radio program you've ever heard." Cooper was his own man, totally independent. "There's nobody here who is afraid of anyone, or anybody, or anything," he told the audience on the debut show. "There are no vested interests in a career in radio, so if we get thrown off the air, it is not going to bother us one bit. We are not going to compromise anything we say no matter what pressure is put upon us. We're going straight through with it all the way."

During the nine-year run of *The Hour of the Time,* Cooper wildly exaggerated the size of the audience, regularly claiming listenership to be more than ten million. More likely, he topped out at five figures, often far less. Those who did tune in, however, remained deeply loyal.

A lot of it had to do with the nature of the shortwave experience. The cult of the ham radio hobbyist, the regular guy down the street with the big antenna on the roof, is one more American romance that has vanished in the Internet age. Cooper often lamented the ingress of faceless technology upon the self-esteem of the American male.

He told listeners about how he used to "take pride" in tuning up his car, adjusting the carburetor, "getting it to run a little rich the way I liked it." It was something he learned from his father, who wouldn't be caught dead in anything less than a V-8. Now, "just in my lifetime," Cooper told the audience, "I've gone from driving automobiles that I could take apart and put together blindfolded by myself as a teenager, to cars that I can lift the hood and not even recognize most of what I'm looking at, except that I know that it's an engine in there, some kind of system that ignites the fuel," Cooper bemoaned.

It was one more way the controllers separated you from the utility of your person. This was how Silent Weapons worked, how they stuck the dunce cap of helplessness on your head.

Shortwave cut against the trend. With its throwback crackle and thrilling blurts of feedback, it connected to another time when any Joe Blow could cuddle up with his Sky Buddy and send his call sign out into the wild blue, getting all goony because the person on the other side of the line was in Botswana or Brunei. It was tech from a time when a man could look a machine straight in the eye, on a level playing field.

Yet even with powerful frequencies like WWCR, things could go wrong. The signal might be interrupted by the weather, spots on the sun, or maybe that electric fence put up by the asshole next door. It could also be, as many Cooper listeners were often convinced, that the government was jamming the show to keep his message from getting out.

Rob Houghton, a Canadian listener who later worked with Doyel Shamley to transfer the *Complete Cooper* MP3 library to the *HOTT* website, recalled his early years as a member of the audience.

"I remember sitting there, in my room. Sometimes friends came over, but mostly by myself, getting ready for Bill's broadcast. I looked forward to it. I had my 'pen and pencil by my side at all times,' the way Bill always said I should because 'tonight's broadcast was going to contain important, very important information.' And then, the transmission would go out. You'd get static, dead air. Sometimes it came back, sometimes it didn't."

It was part of the experience. If Bill Cooper possessed even a thin hair of the truth, it should not be available on demand, summoned up with the half-thinking stab of an index finger on a dashboard preset. You should have to work for it, seek it out, be privileged to hear it.

Stanley Kubrick's monolith, *2001: A Space Odyssey*

Cooper covered the patriot waterfront, broadsiding the usual suspects, the Federal Reserve, the lying media, the fat-cat Monopoly-board plutocrat elites, etc., etc. He threw in some Wild West ruralism and hit the Second Amendment stuff hard. Claiming to have spent years in law libraries, he produced voluminous arguments questioning the legitimacy of federal agencies like the Internal Revenue Service and the Bureau of Alcohol, Tobacco and Firearms. He did a twelve-part series on "asset protection," offering seminars on how to draw up complex trusts to shield cash from federal overreach. Eighteen *HOTT* hours were spent reading a report prepared by his Citizens Agency for Joint Intelligence (CAJI) called "Treason," detailing unconstitutional acts committed on a daily basis by elements of the US government, elected and not.

"This is not conjecture, this is not guesswork, it is documented," Cooper said, channeling his inner Senator Joe McCarthy, to whom he bore an unmistakable facial resemblance. Here was the proof, he said, of treason by "every politician who has occupied any office since World War Two." Anyone thinking they could stop the report was wasting his time "coming out here to get it," Cooper said. As always, he had made 100 copies of the proof and sent them to trusted allies around the world.

There was no way to keep this information from getting into the hands of the American people, Cooper told the guilty. "It is too late for you. This is what will convict you."

The early days of *The Hour of the Time* were a remarkably fecund period for Cooper. Every day seemed to bring a new brainstorm, another avenue of investigation through which to lay bare the vast powers conspiring to enslave hardworking Americans. To the trolls who called him a fall-down drunk, he said, "In the past few years I wrote a book that became a bestseller. I put out a full-size newspaper. I made a dozen documentaries. I do a nightly radio show heard around the world. If I'm a drunken bum, what are you?"

When he was manic, he could work all night. As Doyel Shamley said, "You came into the kitchen and he'd be typing at the table with a pot of boiling water, spitting, on the stove right next to him. He'd never even look up."

But nothing in the *HOTT* catalog compares with *Mystery Babylon*, the massive forty-three-hour series that remains Cooper's most revered work. If "Silent Weapons for Quiet Wars" exposed the contemporary blueprint for the Iluminati's takeover of the planet, *Mystery Babylon* went far deeper, tracing the ontology of the organization back to its origins.

Like "Behold a pale horse," the phrase "Mystery Babylon" dated back to the key source material, the book of Revelations, specifically Rev. 17: 3–5, where the exiled John of Patmos offers his searing description of the most famous of all prostitutes.

The Prophet wrote: "And I saw a woman sit upon a scarlet colored beast, full of names of blasphemy, having seven heads and ten horns. And the woman was arrayed in purple and scarlet color, and decked with gold and precious stones and pearls, having a golden cup in her hand full of abominations and filthiness of her fornication. And upon her forehead was a name written, Mystery, Babylon the Great, the Mother of Harlots and Abominations of the Earth."

Mystery Babylon was nothing less than "the story of the entire human race, as seen by the Initiates and Adepts" of the hidden religion that ruled the world, Cooper said, placing the cosmology's origin not at the moment of Creation as described in Genesis, or the unheard Big Bang of five billion years ago. Instead, Cooper found *Mystery Babylon*'s beginning at a distinctly more modern source: Stanley Kubrick's film *2001: A Space Odyssey*.

Commencing the series' opening episode with the obligatory playing of Richard Strauss's *Also Sprach Zarathustra*, Cooper said: "When I saw *2001: A Space Odyssey*, I was amazed, awed, to say the least. . . . The entire scope of the movie was overpowering and, for most of the people of the world, completely baffling. Most people who saw that movie did not understand from beginning to end what it was that they had experienced, but they knew they had experienced something profound, that something had been communicated to the dark, deep recesses of their mind which they did not understand, that they were incapable of understanding."

Cooper wasn't the only one in awe of Kubrick's movie. As many members of the "baby boom" can attest, the overwhelming experience of watching *2001: A Space Odyssey* for the first time was in keeping with the tumult of the times. In New York, the film opened at the Loew's Capitol Theatre on April 4, 1968, the very day Martin Luther King Jr. was assassinated at the Lorraine Motel in Memphis. You walked mind-blown from Kubrick's movie to see the gut-punching news going by on a ribbon of blinking lights in the middle of Times Square.

Almost immediately, riots broke out in African American neighborhoods across the country. In Washington, the local police were overwhelmed, forcing President Lyndon Johnson to send in thirteen thousand federal troops to help quell the disturbances. In Chicago, Mayor Richard Daley deployed ten thousand cops to the South and West Side ghettos. "Shoot to kill any arsonist or anyone with a Molotov cocktail in his hand," Daley ordered. "Shoot to maim or cripple anyone looting any stores in our city."

While this was happening, my hippie friends and I kept watching *2001: A Space Odyssey*. We went four nights running. The first row wasn't close enough. It was better to lie down on the plush carpet that sloped gently upward to the curved, eighty-foot-wide Super Cinerama screen. We peered up and soaked it in: the monkeys and the monolith, the ballet of the spaceships, the odd, furtive bureaucratic chit-chat about cover stories and something being dug up on the moon.

Then came the battle between man and his creations, a story that reached back beyond *The Golem* and *Frankenstein* and will continue on, long past *Blade Runner, The Terminator, The Matrix*, and half a million more dystopian plots yet to come. For Kubrick and his collaborator, Arthur C. Clarke, the joke was that HAL, the plaintive-voiced computer who decides "the mission is too important" to be left in the hands of the astronauts, played by Keir Dullea and Gary Lockwood, who was the most human entity aboard the ship. Indeed, HAL's demise at the hands of Dullea's Dave Bowman is among the most excruciating death scenes in movie history.

"My mind is going, Dave," HAL tells the astronaut, who is unscrewing the computer's memory cells. "I can feel it . . . I can feel it . . ." Reduced to a second-grade learning level, HAL speaks of a tune he learned from his early programmer, Mr. Langley.

"It is called 'Daisy,'" HAL says, offering to sing it for his killer.

"Yeah, sing it for me, HAL," Dullea says, continuing his lobotomizing work.

"Daisy . . . Daisy . . . give me your answer, do," HAL sings, his voice slurring as he runs down. "I'm half . . . crazy over . . . the love of yoooou . . ." It was probably the last game of chess a human being would win against a computer.

After that was the "space gate" acid-test stuff, the strange room at the end of time, and the giant bug-eyed fetus floating in the cosmos. No one knew what was happening, but that was what made it great. All through life, at home, in school, on whatever stupid job, you always had to have an answer. Yes, sir, no, sir, fifty Hail Marys. If your answer was "correct," you got a check next to your name. *2001* freed you from that bondage. It flattened you to the floor with the joyful rush of no answer, of not knowing.

Risking his life on the Cua Viet in his PBR while me and my college-age buddies protested the rightness of his cause, Cooper missed the opening of *2001*. But once he saw the film, his "life was changed." He embarked on "many years of research," determined to make sense of the bewildering film. Then it came to him why most people found *2001* so confusing. That was because *2001* was not made for most people.

The movie wasn't for "the profane," slug hippies like me and my buddies, along with every other plebeian soul on the planet. Rather, it was for the Initiates and the Adepts of the ancient religion, those who could understand the "symbology" of the "Mystery Schools."

2001 was the key to "everything that has ever happened in the history of man, and everything that is happening now, and all that is to happen in the future," Cooper told those who tuned in to the first episode of *Mystery Babylon,* which, like the prologue of Kubrick's film, was called "Dawn of Man."

He told listeners to "go to their local video rental store and watch the movie again from beginning to end" because he was about to explain it all, crack the code. *2001* was a new kind of confidential document, Cooper told listeners. Secrets were no longer stashed away in filing cabinets, kept on snippets of microfiche, or written in invisible ink. No spy died rather than divulge a code word. "Eyes Only" documents were now splashed across the 70mm movie screens, yet remained as classified as anything Admiral Clarey ever handled.

That's because the keepers of Mysteries did not speak with a single voice. There were always two language systems at work. There was the "esoteric," the hidden tongue known only to the overlords, and there was the "exoteric," the vernacular of the everyman, what they allowed you to think and know. Such was the power and the arrogance of the Mystery Schools.

Those were the stakes with the *Mystery Babylon* series, Cooper told the audience. Through his now two decades of research, he had learned to recognize the true talk of the elites, which was their "symbology." He was going to crack open the encryption the Rulers had used for more than six thousand years.

People had been killed for doing less, Cooper told the audience. He understood the risks. "Those of you who are smart enough to know what is transpiring here will understand that these are historic broadcasts and by making them I have sealed my fate."

To understand the world from the beginning, it was necessary to start at the beginning. "Remember what happened in the Garden of Eden?" Cooper asked the audience.

"God told Adam and Eve to tend the Garden. Everything in Paradise was theirs" was the way Cooper told the story. "There was only one thing they couldn't do. They couldn't eat the fruit from the Tree of Knowledge of Good and Evil. God commanded them not to. He told them what would happen if they did. 'If ye do, ye will surely die.'

"Then Lucifer, through his agent Satan appearing as a serpent, seduced Eve by saying 'God lied to you. He is hiding from you your own true nature.' . . . Eve in turn seduced Adam." That was the story in the Bible, the Judeo-Christian version of God's expulsion of Man from Paradise, the Original Sin, the Fall. The serpent, the deceiver, was cursed by God to forever "go upon your belly and dust you shall eat."

But this was not how the Adepts of the Mystery Schools saw it, Cooper told the audience. To them, the snake was the hero. To them, eating from the Tree of the Knowledge of Good and Evil was the moment of liberation.

"You see, ladies and gentlemen, in the Mysteries they believe that Lucifer was good, and God, Jehovah, was the bad one. That's because the Garden wasn't a Garden at all but a prison where an unjust and vindictive deity was holding men enslaved, in the chains, the bonds of ignorance. . . . Lucifer set man free with the gift of intellect. And with the gift of intellect, Man could become God."

This was the story of *2001*, if you knew how to read the symbology, Cooper said. It was a retelling of the Garden of Eden story from the point of view of the Mystery Schools.

The film begins with a tribe of hairy apes milling around, surrounded by wild pigs and hyenas. This isn't Yahweh's Paradise or "the pleasant dwellings in gardens of perpetual residence" that Allah promised to believing men and women in the Koran. It is the Eden of Darwin, a grim utilitarian landscape described by Cooper as "a dark and gray and ugly world . . . with nothing growing, barren rocks, a barren desert."

These prehumans worshipped the light, Cooper said. The sun, which brought warmth and made things grow was their God. Yet every night, at sunset, their God died, sending them into darkness. Night was the enemy. At night they could be attacked by more powerful, more agile predators. They lived in fear until the morning, when the sun, their God, resurrected the Earth.

Then one night, as the tribe of early men slumbered in a cave, they were awoken by the "humming of bees, millions of bees." In the symbology of the Mysteries, Cooper said, "bees signify industry," but not the monotony of the assembly line that drove people like Richard Sharpe Shaver to hear the inner thoughts of his coworkers through factory welding machines. This was "industry working together in a societal form . . . the very basic rudiments of a new society."

And there it was: The Monolith, the sleek black slab Sir Arthur C. Clarke called The Sentinel in his 1948 short story of the same name. Where did it come from? Why does it suddenly appear here, among these monkeys? That's the Mystery, a thing unsaid.

In the movie, at first the apes are afraid, but their leader, called Moon-Watcher, approaches the towering stone. He reaches out a half-human palm to touch the impossibly smooth edge, but draws it back. He tries again, comes closer, his finger barely an inch from the sheer surface, the same distance Michelangelo left between the outstretched digits of Adam and the bearded Almighty on the ceiling of the Sistine Chapel.

For those of faith, this gap between man and God represented the unknowable wonder of the universe, but in the Mysteries, there is no separation between God and Man. As the ape places his palm upon the monolith, God, the warden of Paradise, melts out of existence like the Wicked Witch of the West. For all his power, the prison deity has now been subsumed into the birth of human consciousness, a world of the Mind, where Man is the measure of everything.

The *2001* "Dawn of Man" episode was the Garden of Eden story of Mysteries, as told by the adept Stanley Kubrick, the Bronx-born son of a Jewish doctor from the Grand Concourse, Cooper said, describing what happened next, one of the best-known sequences in the annals of cinema.

Moon-Watcher, now illumined by contact with the monolith, picks through the dry bones of a dead animal, looking for a not-yet-petrified morsel to eat. As *Also Sprach Zarathustra* swells once more on the soundtrack, the ape grabs a desiccated femur.

"He flops it from one side to another," Cooper said with proper understated suspense. "He hits another piece of rib bone that flies up into the air, and you could see the wheels turning in the mind of this individual."

It was at that point, Cooper said, "that monkey became the first priest of the Mystery Schools," because the next thing that happened with this new gift, this intellect and this original thought, was an attack on another group and "the killing of another primitive human being."

This is what illumination had brought to the mind of the first man, the unremitting narrative of mayhem and suffering. That much was clear when the ape-man exaltedly throws his murderous bone into the sky.

Higher and higher it flies until it turns into the spaceship carrying HAL, the inevitable product of the cult of the mind, which, given half a chance, sought to kill his human masters. It was an ellipse that took in all of history, Bill Cooper said.

This was a teaching that had survived the ages, passed from one roving band of hominids to the next until it was formalized six thousand years ago in the Mesopotamian kingdom of Babylon, the land of the famous tower, where King Nebuchadnezzar II brought the Hebrew prophets Ezekiel, Jeremiah, Daniel, and the rest into captivity after sacking Jerusalem in 587 BC. It was the same Babylon the exiled John of Patmos said was the home of the purple-and-scarlet whore, her golden cup full of abominations and filthiness of her fornication.

From this opening, *Mystery Babylon* traces the pathway of what Cooper called the Luciferian Philosophy. Reading from such texts as E. A. Wallis Budge's 1911 *Osiris and the Egyptian Resurrection* and Manly P. Hall's *Freemasonry of the Ancient Egyptians*, Cooper filled the audience in on how the Mystery Schools arose in Egypt, where the teachings were translated into myth. The story told of how King Osiris, symbol of the balance between order and disorder, was murdered by his jealous brother, Set, embodiment of violence and chaos.

Isis, both wife and sister of Osiris searches for her husband's body, which Set has torn into fourteen pieces, each part buried in a secret place. She finds the severed parts save one, Osiris's penis, which had been thrown into the Nile and eaten by a catfish. With the help of the wise Thoth, Isis replaces the phallus with a member of gold, raising Osiris to the physical plane just long enough for them to copulate, a union that produces Horus, who will avenge his father.

The way Cooper spins out the history, the Egyptian priestly class then organized the Mysteries into an intellectual hierarchy. It was considered essential that the knowledge passed through the ages remain circumspect, cloaked from the common man, who was considered too coarse to be trusted with the treasure of his own mind.

Greek scholars, acknowledging that Egypt was the center of human thought, came to Alexandria to study the forbidden wisdom. First was Pythagoras, who developed geometry, an abstract language unto its own. Plato then came to Alexandria, where he spent thirteen years studying the Mysteries before his initiation, which was performed, Cooper said, in one of the dark serpentine halls of the Great Pyramid.

According to Cooper, the Luciferian cult of "worshiping the intellect, or wisdom, or the mind" could be summed up in the philosophy of the Gnostics (from *gnosis*, Greek for "knowledge"), one of the many early Christian and Jewish sects that emerged following the crucifixion of Jesus Christ. Devoting an entire *Mystery Babylon* episode to gnosticism, Cooper made his feelings known by opening the program with a series of horror movie shrieks and playing the theme from Andrew Lloyd Webber's *The Phantom of the Opera*.

He then read from *A History of Secret Societies* published in 1961 by Arkon Daraul, the pen name of Idries Shah, a Sufi guru/sophisticate. A member of the Club of Rome, one of Cooper's most detested secret societies, Shah was also the founder of the London-based Institute for Cultural Research, where his friends and pupils included such writers as Robert Graves, Ted Hughes, Doris Lessing, and, most provocatively, J. D. Salinger, the reclusive author of the 1950s bastion of eastern US elitism, *The Catcher in the Rye*.

As Cooper read, "Gnostic belief is that there are two principles: that of good and that of evil. A balance must be struck between these forces; and the balance is in the hands of the Gnostic—*the Knower*—partly because nobody else can tell whether an action is for the eventual good of the individual or the community.

"There it is again," he exploded, issuing the cry of the so-called anti-intellectual strain that has run uninterrupted through 250 years of American heartland dissent: "*They know, you don't. Knowledge belongs to them.*

"They are looking to attain gnosis, through which they will receive apotheosis. And they believe that they are the only ones in the world who possess truly mature minds and, thus, the only ones in the world capable of ruling the rest of us, whom they refer to as cattle—*cattle.*"

Cooper then described how the Mysteries followed the path of history and conquest, from Greece to Rome and eventually throughout the empire. With each stop, like coats of paint on the Maltese Falcon, the gnosis acquired another layer of subterfuge. During the Crusades, groups like the Knights Templar brought the Mysteries to Western Europe. The Templars morphed into groups like the Freemasons, who covered the secrets with ever more ornate lore and ritual.

From there the saga enters the modern age, with the founding of the Bavarian Illuminati in Ingolstadt, Germany, on the iconic date of May 1, in the iconic year of 1776, two months before the signing of the Declaration of Independence. Led by Adam Weishaupt, a young professor and priest trained by Jesuits "to foment rebellion everywhere," the Illuminati fused the Mysteries with temporal politics.

What began as a freethinking humanist campaign intended, as Cooper said, "to topple the kings and queens of Europe who said they ruled by Divine Right," Weishaupt's Illuminati reputedly played major, if unnoticed, roles in both the American and French revolutions.

The ostensible goal remained the same as it had been in the Eden of *2001*, to free the human mind, to allow the full flowering of the species' dominance to take hold over the Earth. It was an irresistible romance, an ultimate hubris. It was Cooper's position that the utilitarian Illuminati had staged a virtual coup d'état within the Mysteries, their supposed progressive attitudes leading to the rise of capital, communism, and fascism. The notion of "imperfect men ruling imperfect men will never work," Cooper said, telling the audience it was not by chance that the last three episodes of *Mystery Babylon* centered on the occult history of the Third Reich. It is where the cult of Man as God always led, "to madness."

Running 280,550 words in transcription, *Mystery Babylon* represented Cooper's most formidable project to date. It took him a full hour-long episode just to read half the bibliography.

There was a personal angle to the story as well. As he noted in *Behold a Pale Horse*, Cooper had once been a member of a secret society himself, namely the Order of DeMolay, a Masonic organization for young men between twelve and twenty-one.

Founded in 1919 in Kansas City by local businessman and Masonic lodge leader Frank S. Land—later a trustee of Harry Truman's Presidential Library—the DeMolay Society was presented as an innocent fraternal organization stressing unaffected all-American virtues of courtesy, comradeship, and patriotism—a better sort of Boy Scout.

Joining the DeMolays was his father's idea, Cooper wrote in *Behold a Pale Horse*. As a young man who, he said, often found himself in trouble, Cooper felt his father thought joining the society "would give me something to do." As he would later find out, there was a lot more to the DeMolays than met the eye.

For one thing, the group was named for Jacques de Molay (1243–1314), the twenty-third and final grand master of the Knights Templar. By the time de Molay came to power in the late 1200s, the Templars, made fabulously wealthy through nonstop plunder, had transitioned from holy mercenaries to a supra nation-state. One of the first international banking cartels, the Templars accrued power by lending money to European monarchs, a practice later taken up by the house of Rothschild.

King Philip IV of France was not interested in paying the debt he owed the Templars. On Friday the thirteenth in October of 1307, he had de Molay arrested, torturing him until he falsely admitted heinous crimes. In 1314, when de Molay renounced his statement, he was burned at the stake in front of the Cathedral of Notre Dame in Paris. His reputed final words were often recited by the boys of the DeMolay Society: "The dreadful spectacle presented to me will not make me confirm one lie by another. Life offered me on such infamous terms, I abandon without regret."

Attending meetings of the society, Cooper became acquainted with the key rituals, including the Ceremony of Light, in which the young DeMolay member is taken into a darkened room lit only by seven burning candles placed at a sacred altar. Called "sentries," the candles symbolized "beacons in the darkness, lights to illuminate our pathway as we journey ever onward down the road of life." If the young DeMolays failed to achieve their goals, these flames would be extinguished, and the world would become muted in the shadows and darkness.

Throughout his life, Cooper talked a lot about the process of initiation, almost always in terms of trust. Whether it happens at boot camp, in a frat house, or joining the Mafia, the initiation process qualifies the candidate as someone who can be relied on, "one of us." In one episode of *Mystery Babylon*, Cooper says "initiation ceremonies of secret cults invariably involve tests, sometimes most severe ones. . . . It bonds members together in mysticism."

He talks about how much he treasured his experience as a young DeMolay in *Behold a Pale Horse*. "I loved the mystery and ritual," he writes. But he was never initiated. It is with obvious regret that he explains that, due to his father's shifting military obligations, his family soon "moved to a location out of reach of any lodge" and he became separated from the society. Still, the association was important, Cooper thought. In *Behold a Pale Horse* he writes that he believed it was his fleeting linkage with the DeMolay Society that gained him access to Admiral Cleary's files during his stay in Naval Intelligence. Every officer he met there was a Mason, Cooper wrote.

It was something to think about, now that he was a father again. *Mystery Babylon* was the ultimate conspiracy, a Luciferian plot dating back to the first glimmering of consciousness. The mystery priests of the mind were everywhere, enlisting young people with their ever more technologically sweet candy to suck on.

At the outset of *Mystery Babylon*, Cooper told the audience that as important as his words were, listening to the music he played during the narrative was equally essential. "Listen to the lyrics," Cooper advised the audience. "Research the title. Your age group is not the only age group listening, so it doesn't make any difference whether you like the music or not. It all has a message."

The *Mystery Babylon* series included many tunes, the Liza Minnelli version of "I Can See Clearly Now"; U2's "I Still Haven't Found What I'm Looking For"; "Long As I Can See the Light" by Creedence Clearwater Revival. But none of this music was as significant, or as troubling, as "When You Wish Upon a Star," which Cooper used to close the "Dawn of Man" episode.

Written by film music stalwarts Leigh Harline and Ned Washington, "When You Wish Upon a Star" was first performed in Walt Disney's

1940 animated feature *Pinocchio*. The tune won the Oscar for best original song. It had been covered by everyone from Rosemary Clooney to Sun Ra. It was an American classic, which was exactly Cooper's point.

How many parents had sung "When You Wish Upon a Star" to their beloved children before putting them to sleep? It was the theme song of *The Wonderful World of Disney*, which was one of Pooh's favorite TV programs.

It was part of Pooh's homeschooling, to be able to tell a good song from a bad one. And, of course, she was a quick study. One time when he was feeling giddy, Cooper did an entire show in the persona of Wolfman Jack, his all-time favorite deejay. Cooper went wild that night, screaming "Mr. Cooper, he gone" in the Wolfman's signature howl. Pooh loved it. Later, when she began to appear on the program along with him, Cooper used the Bill Haley line "See ya later, alligator." To which she replied, on cue, "After a while, crocodile."

"If you think your child is too young to learn, you're wrong," he told listeners. "Their brain is just waiting there. It's empty. It wants to be filled. A child is in a constant state of discovery and wonder, and whatever you want to teach them, they will soak it up like a dry sponge in a pan of water." That's the greatness of the human mind, but also the danger.

Case in point was "When You Wish Upon a Star," especially as sung by Jiminy Cricket, the top-hatted insect manservant of a wooden puppet best known for a nose that grew every time he lied.

How was Pooh to know that Jiminy Cricket's creator, Walt Disney, one of the greatest shapers of young minds in the history of the world, was a 33rd-degree Mason of the Scottish Rite? How was she to know that the morning star Jiminy wished upon was Lucifer?

13

Mystery Babylon was a hit. In early 1993, Cooper took it on the road, speaking at the Global Deception Conference held at the Wembley Arena in London.

"They're building their world right under our noses, and unfortunately, because they're right about us being cattle, those who don't use their brains, they're getting away with it," Cooper told UK fans.

Today's political crisis, the instinctive lack of trust for once beloved national institutions, went back to Adam Weishaupt himself, Cooper said, citing the illuminist as saying, "In reference to government leaders it is necessary to surround them with our members so the profane will have no access to them. . . . We must do our utmost to secure the advancement of all Illuminati in all civil offices. By this plan we shall direct mankind. To the profane these methods will appear illogical and contrived, so we may, in secret, influence all political interaction."

"That's why Franklin Roosevelt said nothing ever happens by accident, everything is planned," Cooper told the Wembley crowd, characterizing Illuminati goals as "the abolishment of private property, abolishment of patriotism and nationalism, abolishment of family life, abolishment of religion." Illuminati types were always talking about establishing Utopias. "A Utopia for *them*," Cooper told the Brits.

As lecture offers poured in, Cooper seemed well on his way. Someone was even making a movie of his life. According to a document dated September 19, 1992, Cooper entered into an agreement to option *Behold a Pale Horse* to Phillip Lambro, head of newly formed Trigram Films, "for the purposes of making a major motion picture production tentatively entitled *Cooper*."

While a novice movie producer, Lambro was not unknown in Hollywood. Son of Albanian immigrants, he grew up in Wellesley Hills, Massachusetts, where he showed early signs of being a musical prodigy. Propelled up the class ladder, he studied with Gyorgy Sandor, a protégé of Bela Bartok, and spent afternoons playing tennis with Sylvia Plath, whom he remembered as "immaculate in every way." By twenty-four, Lambro's symphonic pieces were being played by Leopold Stokowski and the Philadelphia Orchestra. Stokowski, who appears in Disney's *Fantasia*, praised Lambro's "talent" and "capacity."

As the music director and consultant at the United Nations from 1960 to 1964, Lambro was befriended by billionaire Huntington Hartford, who introduced him to many famous people, like Salvador Dalí, Jack Benny, John F. Kennedy, and Richard Nixon. By 1965, Lambro was in Hollywood ready to make a career as a film score composer. But rather than working for A-list directors, Lambro found himself doing background music for pictures like *Hannah, Queen of the Vampires* and spending evenings watching old films with Harold Lloyd at the silent movie star's mansion.

Lambro's luck appeared to change in 1974 when John Cassavetes introduced him to Roman Polanski. Polanski heard some of Lambro's modernist orchestral work and thought it might work for his next picture, a dark dream of Los Angeles called *Chinatown*. Lambro set to work. Polanski and producer Robert Evans loved the music, they said.

However, after a series of disastrous previews in which audiences singled out the score as "scratchy" and "distracting," Evans told Lambro his music was out. The new score, completed in ten days by Jerry Goldsmith, was credited with "saving" *Chinatown*, now universally regarded as one of the best of the post-studio-system American films. It was small comfort that Lambro's original music was kept for the film's trailer.

Lambro described this episode and many others in his 2007 memoir, *Close Encounters of the Worst Kind*, after the film by Steven Spielberg, an early Hollywood friend who, like almost everyone else, is roundly trashed in the book. The one person to get a favorable, if brief, mention is Bill Cooper.

"Bill Cooper was a friend of mine," Lambro told me when I called him in early 2015, only a few months before his death. "I went to see him speak at Hollywood High School," Lambro recalled. "He showed foot-age of the Kennedy assassination. I couldn't believe it. The driver shot the president.

"People told me, don't touch that story with a ten-foot pole. But I thought, 'I have to do this,'" recalled Lambro, who hired screenwriter Michael Vernon to work up what became a forty-two-page treatment for *Cooper*.

The prospective film opens with a title card, JANUARY 20, 1993, over a desolate, restricted landscape. From there the viewer finds himself in a labyrinthine underground base where, the treatment states, "a group of distinguished, but stoically threatening middle-aged men sit around an immense, glass-topped conference table." The men are watching a giant television screen that shows Bill Clinton taking the presidential oath of office.

One of the men at the table asks another, "What do you think, sir?" The other, clearly in charge, says, "No problem, Mr. Secretary. The tar-gets are ripe for the picking . . . the patriots ready for destruction."

"You're right, Mr. President," says another of those at the table, as Bill Clinton continues to be sworn in on the big screen.

The scene then shifts to a rural hospital delivery room where Annie Cooper is giving birth to Pooh. The delivery is difficult, as described in *Behold a Pale Horse*.

The camera settles on BILL COOPER, who is described as a "burly, rug-ged man in his late forties." The story goes on to follow Cooper's heroic struggle to get the truth out about what is happening in the country. The scene of Cooper being run off the road on his motorcycle by the un-known assailants is vividly depicted in flashback. But it is no use. Coo-per's message is perverted by the powerful. A prophet in his own land, Cooper is ignored.

The treatment ends with another birth scene. Except this time, the baby wears a "helmet covered with wires." A child being "programmed," the treatment says, "to easily do the bidding of others." This is the future, the world Bill Cooper was valiantly fighting to prevent. Asked why the movie never got made, Phillip Lambro said, "They screwed me. They always do."

One roasting-hot afternoon in July of 1993, Cooper returned to Area

51. He was there to present his *Mystery Babylon* material at the Little A'Le'Inn. One hundred miles northeast of Vegas, the Little A'Le'Inn, a café/bar/motel, was legendary in ufology circles as the only place to get plastered on a stretch of road known as the Extraterrestrial Highway.

Sitting on a barstool to the right of the video poker machines, Cooper pivoted on his good leg and pulled a dollar bill from his pocket. He asked everyone assembled to do likewise, saying, "If you don't have a dollar, borrow one from your neighbor. Don't worry about not paying it back. It isn't worth anything anyway."

It was a bitter joke. Because even if everyone at the Little A'Le'Inn knew that Federal Reserve Notes, backed by no gold or silver, had no value sans the government's say-so, they had no choice but to spend the majority of their waking hours slaving away for the worthless slips of paper. They woke up the next day and did it again; they would until they were dead.

The identity of those responsible for the outrage was printed right there on the greenback dollar itself, Cooper said, telling the crowd to turn the bill to the reverse side, where the Great Seal of the United States appeared. On the right side of the bill was the bald eagle, proud symbol of American sovereignty. Count the number of arrows in the bird's right talon and the olive branch leaves on the left, Cooper instructed. Add up the number of stars in the glory above the eagle's head. The answer in all cases was thirteen. There were even thirteen letters in the words *e pluribus unum*.

"What is thirteen doing all over our seal if it is such an unlucky number?" Cooper asked the crowd.

The fact was, Cooper said, "in the Mysteries, thirteen is the number of sacrifice and rebirth," the very traits the Illuminists associated with their true God, the light giver, Lucifer. Thirteen was also a memorial tribute to Jacques de Molay. King Philip imprisoned de Molay on October 13, 1307, the original Friday the thirteenth.

Then Cooper directed those assembled to look to the left of the bill, where the reverse side of the Great Seal appears. When the seal was first designed in 1782, perhaps it was possible to believe that the "All-Seeing Eye" that hovers over the pyramid represented the providence of the

Almighty. But now, everyone knew, it was the logo of the surveillance state, the unblinking orb of Lucifer himself.

Money, Cooper told those who had come to the desert to hear him speak, was not the root of all evil. It was evil itself. Cooper drew the audience's attention to the space between the floating "capstone" of the pyramid and the body of the structure below. Closing the space, finishing the job, was what those in the Mysteries called "The Great Work," Cooper said. Only when the Pyramid met the Eye would the task that began with the first illuminated ape-man be complete. And in case anyone lost sight of the goal of the Great Work, it was written right there on the base of the pyramid. The phrase came from Virgil, the fourth Eclogue, fifth Verse, *"Magnus ab integro seclorum nascitur ordo,"* or Novus Ordo Seclorum, which as Cooper translated it, was the "The New World Order."

As part of the Little A'Le'Inn program, Cooper showed his most recent video, *The Sacrificed King*, in which he revisited the Kennedy assassination. The film begins with a shot of a ten-cent picture postcard of Dealey Plaza in downtown Dallas. Like the Trinity site, like Disneyland and the ancient city of Babylon, "Dallas, Texas, is located on the 33rd parallel, the 33rd degree of latitude," Cooper narrated. To further make the point, the plaza was named for newspaperman George Bannerman Dealey, a 33rd-degree Mason.

The fact was, Cooper said, Dealey Plaza was a perfect example of the "esoteric" and "exoteric" at work. Thousands of motorists passed through the place every day, thinking about little but the traffic, but the Adepts knew the plaza was in reality "an outdoor Temple of the Sun."

Linchpin to the scenario was the obelisk at the corner of Main and Houston Streets. Constructed of fourteen separate stones, the same number of bodily pieces Isis used to reconstruct Osiris's dismembered body, the obelisk represented the reconstructed phallus, the life force of the Mysteries. As noted in *The Sacrificed King*, if seen from the correct angle, the top of the obelisk pointed directly at the sixth-story window of the Texas School Book Depository, from where Lee Harvey Oswald was supposed to have fired the fatal shots with his Mannlicher-Carcano rifle. This was how, Cooper said, the president's true assassins mocked the sheeple still crying over the demise of Camelot.

It was no mere coincidence that John Kennedy and Jacques de Molay both died on the same day, November 22, Cooper said. This correlation was important to many of Wild Bill Donovan's OSS men (Allen Dulles included), who traced their ancestry back to the Templars. Given these factors, Cooper's hypothesis was fairly straightforward: America's only Catholic president was killed as part of a centuries-old Luciferian revenge plot upon the Vatican.

This retelling of the Kennedy death was a creaky concoction, with nowhere near the simple audacity of the William Greer scenario, but it was worth a try. Cooper was a family man now, a breadwinner. Telling these stories, selling the videos, was how he kept things afloat.

To link the fates of de Molay and Kennedy, Cooper instructed the audience to "subtract 1307 from 1963. The answer you get is 666! And folks, *that is no accident.*"

If Cooper was aware that 1963 minus 1307 is actually 656, he wasn't going to let that stop him. He ended *The Sacrificed King* by showing a sequence from Oliver Stone's 1991 film, *JFK*. Kevin Costner, as the earnest truth-seeking New Orleans DA Jim Garrison, sits on a bench talking to Donald Sutherland, aka Mr. X. Behind them looms the Washington Monument, the great obelisk of the capital city's Masonic designers, a Moby Dick of a phallus jutting stiff into the sky.

Oswald, Ruby, Cuba, the Mafia are "just scenery for the public," Mr. X blathers on, obviously one more messenger of deception. "It prevents them from asking the most important question, Why? Why was Kennedy killed, who benefited, who has the power to cover it up? *Who?*"

"Who indeed?" Cooper asks on the soundtrack, freezing the action as Costner and Sutherland sit on the bench, dwarfed by the upward thrust of the lingamic monument.

"Oliver Stone is laughing at you, ladies and gentlemen," Cooper chortles, "because if you can't make the connection here, after hours of my instruction, if you don't understand who's behind it, what it means and what the symbology is—then I can't help you. You're beyond my help. You're beyond understanding.

"For those of you who are waking up and seeing the world as it really is for the first time, God bless you, I love you. My prayers are with you always. But as for the rest of you . . . You see that big tall thing on the video screen? You're going to get the shaft."

It was a living.

During this period, Cooper attended the PhenomiCon, an "Alternative Convention," in Atlanta, Georgia. A forerunner of the events like today's massive, deeply commercialized Comic "Cons," PhenomiCon dealt primarily with the as-yet unbranded cultural boomlet that arose at the end of the Cold War.

Staked to a sliver of zeitgeist-defining territory by such pioneering pop totems as William Gibson's cyberpunk *Neuromancer* and Nirvana's anthemic disaffection, the PhenomiCon drew from the DIY realms of fanzines, anarcho-veganism, Guerrilla Girl art feminism, 2600-era hackers, and followers of southern indie rockers like Dexter Romweber of the Flat Duo Jets, who was rumored to have spent a decade sleeping inside a coffin in his mother's backyard.

Here were people who had come of age in the aftermath of the Kennedy murder. What they knew of conspiracy came not from rightist sources like hoary old anti-Semites of the Eustace Mullins and Nesta Webster stripe. They'd grown up reading the work of left-leaning "assassinationologists," i.e., students of the Kennedy murder. A typical starting place was Mark Lane's relatively staid disputation of the Warren Report, *Rush to Judgment*. There was also Mae Brussell, daughter of a Beverly Hills rabbi who supposedly gave Rose Kennedy a note saying her son Bobby would be killed by the same people who killed Jack. Beyond that were sundry figures like A. J. Weberman, the "garbologist" who was caught red-handed trying to steal Bob Dylan's trash and wound up being stomped by the singer. Weberman did not fight back, he said, "because I knew I was wrong."

In search of perspective, I called up Paul Krassner, the much-revered editor of *The Realist* (1958–2001), the "magazine of social-political-religious criticism and satire" known for running "impolite" interviews with sixties heroes like Lenny Bruce, Dick Gregory, *Catch-22* author Joseph Heller, Norman Mailer, and Ken Kesey, along with then-not-un-PC articles like "Terry Southern Interviews a Faggot Male Nurse."

Krassner had been through the assassinationologist mill, so I asked when conspiracy moved from the ostensibly left-wing persuasion to the right.

"Ah, the bend in the river," said Krassner, who was then into his eighties and living in the California desert, but still talking like he hadn't stepped off the Brooklyn streets. This was a pretty deep question, Krassner said, but for sure it had something to do with "smoking dope."

Conspiracy was about connecting dots that seemed irrationally arrayed. Religion did it one way, but pot did it another, said the author of the 1981 *Realist* piece "My Acid Trip with Groucho Marx." THC was "a prime dot connector," Krassner said. A few puffs and suddenly the esoteric linkages became exoteric, and vice versa. If once marijuana was supposedly only for hippies and jazz musicians, use became far more inclusive over the years. Rednecks were just as likely to be chawing down on an edible as anyone else. They brought their own perspective with them, and had since the halcyon days of the Marshall Tucker Band. So, of course, they thought conspiratorially. Now that grass was increasingly legal in the US, one could only expect more paranoid-patterned thinking in the future, Krassner said, leaving me with the well-known quote from Charles Manson.

"Have you ever seen the coyote in the desert?" Manson asked in a 1970s interview in *Rolling Stone* magazine. "Watching, tuned in, completely aware. Christ on the cross, the coyote in the desert—it's the same thing, man. The coyote is beautiful. He moves through the desert delicately, aware of everything, looking around. He hears every sound, smells every smell, sees everything that moves. He's in a state of total paranoia, and total paranoia is total awareness."

Cooper was not without his fans at PhenomiCon. Kenn Thomas and Jim Keith, author of such syncretic stews as *Saucers of the Illuminati* and long discussions on then-canonical multi-reality texts like Philip K. Dick's *VALIS* (Vast Active Living Intelligence System), admired Cooper as something of a brilliant primitive. They loved Cooper's contention, as described in *Behold a Pale Horse,* that the Galileo probe recently launched by NASA to explore the moons of Jupiter would in fact set off a solar-system-wide cataclysm that will result in "a new star that has already been named LUCIFER." It was his ambition, said Keith, who died in 1999 after falling off a stage at Burning Man, "to become the hip Bill Cooper."

That said, it was a neat piece of synchronicity that landed Cooper on the same PhenomiCon panel as Robert Anton Wilson. Born in 1932 at Methodist Hospital in the Park Slope section of Brooklyn into a working-class Irish American family, RAW, as his many acolytes came to call him, was afflicted with polio at an early age, thereby affording him a lot of time to plow through the works of such authors as Ezra Pound, James Joyce, and H. P. Lovecraft, along with huge stacks of 1950s sci-fi of the fantasy-tinged Theodore Sturgeon variety.

This reading proved to be an early aid in short-circuiting the concrete hustle designed to make Brooklyn boys lose their souls. By age eighteen, according to RAW's semi-autobiographical *The Cosmic Trigger*, which comes equipped with an introduction by Timothy Leary, he had "a strange experience of coming unstuck in time like Billy Pilgrim in Kurt Vonnegut's *Slaughterhouse-Five*. . . . I had a kind of spontaneous Satori, a sudden awakening to the immanent divinity of all things," RAW wrote.

By 1962, at the age of thirty, Wilson began to experiment with mind-altering drugs, i.e., "psychedelics" or, as dolphin researcher John Lilly put it, "metaprogramming substances" that would enable the human mind to reach "a new state" in which "we can reorganize or re-imprint our nervous system for higher functioning."

This was part of entering what Wilson described as "the door to Chapel Perilous," defined as a realm of experience that "cannot be located in the space-time continuum; it is weightless, odorless, tasteless and undetectable by ordinary instruments."

For Wilson, the practical side of this portal opened while in the employ of Hugh Hefner, who charged him with the task of running the Playboy Forum, a faux-philosophical discussion center with a pile of frat-boy sex talk thrown in. As legend has it, it was the odder inquiries Wilson and his coeditor, Robert Shea, received that gave them the notion to create the eight-hundred-plus-page *The Illuminatus! Trilogy*, first published in 1975.

According to Wilson, all his work (he wrote thirty-five books altogether) is to one degree or another an exercise in "guerilla ontology" in which the author "mixes the elements of each book [so] that the reader must decide on each page 'How much of this is real and how much is a put-on.'"

No doubt this was the plan for *The Illuminatus! Trilogy*, in which

Wilson and Shea trace their cartoon noir characters from Vegas lounges to dusty back alleys of Atlantis and on to the inner circle of Adam Weishaupt's Bavarian Illuminati. Forty years later, *The Illuminatus! Trilogy*, considered by its authors to be a "fairy tale for paranoids," remains exhaustingly entertaining, with the sequence of gunmen representing every major assassination scenario firing at the president at the same time at least as funny as anything to be found in similarly themed efforts by literary stars like Thomas Pynchon and Don DeLillo.

It tickled Wilson that many of the details and concepts trotted out in his *Illuminatus!* books, "real" or "put-on," eventually found their way into widely believed conspiracies that emerged during the 1980s and '90s, Bill Cooper's work included. As RAW commented, anyone seriously "researching occult conspiracies that have taken over the world" will eventually reach "a crossroads of mythic proportions" from which the seeker would emerge "either stone paranoid or an agnostic; there is no third way." For his part, RAW said, he became "an agnostic," a knower of and believer in nothing. As for everyone else, he wished them the best of luck.

Cooper was certainly familiar with Wilson's work at the time of their meeting. A number of RAW's books, including *Cosmic Trigger*, were found in Cooper's storage units after his demise. Cooper also owned a copy of the *Principia Discordia*, which Wilson freely acknowledged as a main inspiration for many of his works. He dedicated *The Illuminatus! Trilogy* to *Principia* authors Greg Hill and Kerry Thornley.

Thornley's sad tale deserves mention here since he was almost certainly the first Kennedy assassinationologist to write about Lee Harvey Oswald. Thornley met Oswald in the Marines when they were both stationed at the El Toro base in Santa Ana, California, during the late 1950s. When Oswald defected to the Soviet Union in 1959, Thornley decided to make him a major character in the novel he was writing, *The Idle Warriors*. After the book was finished in 1962, Thornley lost the original typed manuscript but still wound up getting subpoenaed by the Warren Commission.

Later, Thornley, strung out and living a down-and-out life in the New Orleans French Quarter, began to claim that he was actually a would-be assassin himself, a virtual physical double for Oswald (whom he looked nothing like), "in competition" with his former Marine buddy to see which one of them would wind up shooting Kennedy first.

Despite their stretch of shared conspiratorial ground, Cooper and Wilson did not hit it off. By the early nineties, RAW was content to play the counterculture's last man standing, a Mr. Natural figure for third-generation Grateful Dead fans. He was on record as saying that while Cooper and Lear's MJ-12 notions made for a "wonderful metaphor," taking such "bad 1950s science-fiction B-movie plots" seriously was akin to believing in "Snow White and the Seven Dwarfs or the Easter Bunny."

One of the tropes most associated with Wilson is Operation Mind-fuck (OM). A central tenet of discordianism, Operation Mindfuck usually takes the form of a practical joke, or "situationist prank," aimed at shocking a person or group of people out of their overly rigid worldview, known as a "reality tunnel."

At the Atlanta PhenomiCon, as Cooper sat close by, Wilson proposed an Operation Mindfuck to ascertain what percentage of the population could be convinced "beyond a shadow of doubt to attribute all national calamities, assassinations, or conspiracies to the Illuminati." It would be a ton of fun, Wilson said.

What happened next is recalled in a 2001 Internet post following Cooper's death. It came from "the Reverend Ivan Stang," the "sacred scribe" of the discordianesque Church of the SubGenius, a parody religion alleged to have been founded in 1953 by Ward Cleaver look-alike J. R. "Bob" Dobbs. The SubGenius Church was at the PhenomiCon to stage what they called a "Swingin' Love Corpses and Devival," a sort of open-mic "prayer meeting," said Rev. Stang, who accompanied Wilson— the honorary "Pope Bob" of the SubGenius cult—to the panel discussion where Cooper was present.

"It was the WEIRDEST scene!" wrote Rev. Stang on the alt.slack Usenet site, describing how he, Wilson, UFO researcher Donald Keyhoe, and "a string of little old ladies who were New Age seers or such hocus pocus" were arrayed around a large table.

"Then there was BILL COOPER, a great big guy, all florid and red faced, partly from acne scars. He was MAD AS HELL. He immediately started to 'take command' of the panel by denouncing these NEFARIOUS

people on the right end of the room—me and Pope Bob—who had TRIV-
IALIZED and MOCKED the very serious subjects that this convention
was all about, and that we were TRAITORS TO AMERICA just as bad
as the Feds. . . . Pope Bob and I just sort of looked at each other, like, damn,
busted."

Some yelling and screaming ensued, after which Cooper got up and
left, reportedly nearly smacking his head on the door as he went. "You
think everything is a joke, don't you," Cooper said, training his gaze on
an eternally amused RAW.

"Laugh all you want," Cooper screamed at the coauthor of *The Illuminatus! Trilogy*. "You'll see soon enough how funny it is."

14

Doyel Shamley hiking at the 2014 Skills and
Research Conference

Doyel Shamley and I were riding west on Arizona 260 in his pickup
with the battering ram attached to the front bumper, when he told
me about his "epiphany," one of many he had while he was fighting for
his country as a member of the Third Armored Division during Operation Desert Storm.

"We were moving fifty, sixty miles a day. No army ever went that fast, because of our technology. We were blowing shit off the map, busting up these T-72s, the supposed invincible 'battle tank of Mother Russia.' We'd just blow them up and paint upside-down V's on them, like a calling card. We'd take them for joyrides, play bumper cars. Half the turrets didn't even turn . . . It was incredible to me. I'd read that we had really built up the Soviet military, taking over truck factories to make tanks. Now I get inside the T-72 and I see the data plate—every tank's got one—and its in English. Not Russian, not Arabic. English. All you can say is 'holy shit.'

"We were heading for Basra in the south. They'd been telling us about the Revolutionary Guard, who were supposed to be Saddam's elite forces, badass, for real. Everyone in there had been fighting for ten years, against Iran and whoever else. Here they are, seasoned, in their own backyard, while we had to get acclimated, and we're just cleaning their asses. We killed like twenty-six thousand the first day and lost maybe forty men.

"We knew from our briefings that Saddam had three bunkers. Two of them had already been cleared; the only one left was Basra. We were the spearhead of the ground war; we wanted to get there first.

"Then, we're fifty miles outside the city, moving through these Bedouin villages with the heat rising off the sand, and we hear there's a cease-fire. No one believed it. We thought it was one of those Tokyo Rose deals, so we're still killing the fuck out of these poor bastards. Everyone was doing it, right up to colonel level, that was our training.

"It was a fucking mess. All these dead bodies. Huge black clouds. You have to remember I was pretty well read. I'm looking around, firing at these fucks, and thinking of *The Divine Comedy*, the Inferno portion, because I'd actually read these works, unlike most GIs.

"Then these generals started flying in, putting down in the middle of nowhere in Black Hawk helicopters, threatening individual units with court-martials. That's when we knew they were serious.

"So we're just sitting there, pondering. We were supposed to get this bad guy, we're fifty miles from his last bunker, and they're calling off the war?

"Nobody knew what happened. Even when I got home, my dad was saying: *What the hell?* You hear all these explanations, like how Saddam wouldn't go along with the IMF and the World Bank, so that was the reason for the invasion . . . there are plenty of stories.

"But we weren't thinking anything like that back in the desert. We just looked at each other and we knew. 'We're going to be back here again,' someone said. Ten years later, there we were again, with a whole bunch of new recruits.

"After I came home, it was hard for me to concentrate," Doyel said. "I tried picking up the cello again, but I didn't have the patience for it. I thought about going to school, but I didn't want to do that either. I stayed in the military, in the reserves. But mostly it was a lot of nothing."

Doyel had always been up on the patriot literature, starting off with Gary Allen's *None Dare Call It Conspiracy.* "I saw it and my father said, 'Oh yeah, that's a classic.' From there I read the whole library. I read through *Tragedy and Hope* by Carroll Quigley, which has got something like twelve hundred pages, in like a day. I collected all this stuff about the Brotherhood of the Snake. I also did a lot of sitting around listening to the radio.

"It was the heyday of what was called the Patriot Radio Wars. There were a lot of shows on. I listened to WWCR, picked up Joyce Riley, Tom Valentine, there were a lot of them." By the middle 1990s, Doyel was running a patriot lecture series at the VFW hall in his Portersville, California, hometown. "My dad told me it was getting so I was to the right of Attila the Hun, but it was kind of fun. We had a lot of speakers. Colonel Bo Gritz, Fritz Springmeier. We had John Quade several times. He was an actor, always playing the bad biker in Clint Eastwood movies. He became pretty militant. Then it came up that we should have Bill.

"People said 'you can't just call up Bill Cooper,' like he was such a big deal. He had a reputation for being hard to deal with. A real prima donna. Fuck that, I said. I called him and made him an offer. He was charging so much by then, he'd just about priced himself out of the market. He wanted crazy percentages of the door. But we came to an agreement.

"Then I said, 'Okay, that's good, but you can't act like a complete asshole.'

"'Who said I was an asshole?' Cooper demanded to know.

"'Just about everyone I ever talked to. It's pretty much common knowledge if you don't know' . . . I suppose he could have hung up right there. But he just laughed because he knew it was true."

Cooper hated to fly. It made him break out into sweats, not that he let on. He said he didn't fly because he never knew when his enemies would try to take him out. If they blew up his plane, then he'd be endangering the lives of innocent passengers, he said. So he drove the seven hundred miles from Eagar with Annie and the kids and gave a presentation that lasted nearly eleven straight hours. The whole speech, given the summer of 1997, remains available on *HOTT* under the title "Bill Cooper in California—The Porterville Presentation."

"Bill always said it was his best work," Doyel remarked, and aside from the lighting miscues that render Cooper's head a featureless silhouette for long stretches, it might be. It includes one of Cooper's more striking riffs. A few hours into the lecture, Cooper was trashing global warming, not yet to the point of division it would become. Not only wasn't the Earth heating up, Cooper said, but the fact was "an ice age is on the way, and it will occur quickly."

Then Cooper turned to the fate of the nation.

"A lot of Americans have been spending a lot of time trying to figure out who in the hell is destroying this country," Cooper said. "Well, if you've been spending all that time—what's your answer? The answer is you still don't know, isn't that correct? You look around for the enemy, but you can't find the enemy."

Cooper paused a moment. "You know, ladies and gentlemen, I have spent my entire life trying to find the Devil." This was so. Cooper had sought the Evil One in outer space, tried to track him down in the priestly sanctums of secret religions, searched the endless corridors of government. "But now I've finally found him. You know where he is?"

Cooper thumped his palm on his beefy chest. "Right here. He doesn't exist anywhere else."

That's what it came down to, Cooper told the Portersville audience, the Devil was inside you. "I can let him take over or I can cast him out." Everyone had that choice.

Doyel and Cooper hit it off. "We just got into these long conversations. We'd argue all the time, but we knew what side we were on."

"I just made up my mind. I was a staff sergeant and had a chance of making sergeant major, highest you could go as an enlisted man. Officers don't say boo to sergeant majors. But I'd had it. I didn't want to be in the Army anymore. I didn't want to be in California. I walked into my CO's office, resigned my commission, turned in my stuff, and went down to Arizona. A couple of days later I moved in with Bill and his family in Eagar."

We were driving on Arizona 373, heading toward Greer, a small mountain resort town. Cubby, Doyel's black, curly-haired Lhasa Apso had his front paws up on the dashboard, peering out the gravel-pocked windshield like a watchful sentry. Barely a foot long, Cubby is Doyel's "service dog." When people think it's funny that he has an eight-pound service dog, Doyel smiles and says, "You have no idea how many people's lives have been saved because of this dog."

We hadn't gone very far before the dead, burned-out trees began appearing, charred stumps halfway up the mountain on either side of the road. This was the site of the Wallow Fire, which began in May 2011 and raged out of control for weeks, burning 538,000 acres, the biggest, most-destructive blaze in Arizona history. Several local towns had to be evacuated, Eagar and Springerville among them.

Along with most every able person in the area, Doyel volunteered to fight the fire, working twelve-hour shifts, sometimes around the clock. It was an exhausting, wrenching job, not all that different from Desert Storm, with giant DC-10 VLATs (for Very Large Air Tankers) flying in at low altitude and dropping great plumes of orange-colored fire retardant on the burning treetops.

Three years later, new growth had come up, big swaths of goldenrods and a few spindly aspens shooting up among the blackened spikes of Douglas fir and ponderosa pine. Eventually, the two idiots who didn't stamp out their campfire were hit with a $3.7 million judgment, but Doyel, along with many like-minded locals, knew who the real culprits were.

"The feds, Forest Service, National Fish and Wildlife, all of them," Doyel said. It wasn't just the 538,000 acres. "It was the seven million animals killed, the birds, the elk, bears, deer, antelopes, snails, frogs, and fish. The entire watershed. You could just feel the place dying around you." For Doyel, Wallow was another epiphany. It was something he used to talk about with Cooper, a kind of obsession. Everything was about jurisdiction. Who has power over what? Who owns what? Who has responsibility to decide what's best for the community? When he had some time, Doyel said, he was planning on writing a book called *Jurisdiction for Dummies*; he was certain it would sell.

The federal government and the environmental movement failed the people of Apache County long before the Wallow Fire, Doyel said, ticking off the instances of alleged mismanagement and sheer arrogance. The Feds' one-size-fits-all notions of preservation apparently did not include maintaining the forest road system that would have helped firefighters get around. Worse was the refusal to thin the forest, or even clear away the dead, fallen trees that provided the fuel for huge blazes. Often, the Christmas tree for the federal building in Phoenix comes from the White Mountain area. After the Wallow Fire, several Round Valley residents brought another tree to the state capital: It was the burned trunk of a giant pine. It seemed a fitting gesture.

"Do you have any idea how much of New York State is owned by the federal government?" Doyel asked. "Less than 1 percent." The feds owned barely 4 percent east of the Mississippi River. Out here, it was different. The feds controlled 38 percent of Arizona; in Idaho it was 60 percent; Nevada was over 80 percent. There were a lot of reasons for that, mostly owing to the sheer size of western space. But what if you lived next door to a federal land holding, say the 2.76-million-acre portion of the Apache-Sitgreaves National Forest, where much of the Wallow Fire took place? The national forest was a fiefdom that lived by its own rules, enforced by its own cops, which might be fine until your own little paradise got burned down.

Then there was the spotted owl. With a decided soft spot for the sharp-eyed, proficient predators of nature's great scheme, Doyel had nothing against owls. Except that the spotted owl was no longer flesh and feathers. It was a pawn in the great game of land-use rights. If the spotted owl needed protecting, well, who could be trusted to do that? Certainly not the untidy rednecks of eastern Arizona. Only a Washington bureaucrat could do that. It insulted your intelligence, Doyel said.

"Man is supposed to be steward of the land. Their stewardship of the forest was totally fucked. What kind of habitat protection is that, wiping out the entire forest?" Doyel said, adding the sad moral of the tale: "They loved the spotted owl. They loved it to death."

. . .

"Bet you can't do this back in Brooklyn," Doyel said, after placing a tight bunching of .223 bullets into a plastic laundry detergent bottle about 100 yards away.

That was right. In Brooklyn you couldn't get in your truck, drive a couple miles down the highway, pull into a cinder pit, and exercise your Second Amendment rights by blowing the fuck out of the first thing you saw. In Brooklyn, you were going to jail for touching any gun, much less this arsenal, which today included a Sig Sauer 9mm, a .22 also by Sig, a Beretta 9mm, a shotgun, and a variety of AR-style "black guns" Doyel made himself back in his workshop, which he calls Shamley Arms.

It was another of those lifestyle things. Outside of BB guns at camp, I'd made it through nearly seven decades of life without ever firing a rifle or pistol. In Eagar-Springerville, nine-year-olds get .22s for Christmas.

Doyel approached our session with the stern air of a longtime shooting instructor. We started off with the M14 US Army battle rifle. Doyel thought I might be interested in firing it because it was the closest thing to the M1 Garand that my father carried during the winter of 1944 as a member of the 133rd Combat Engineers under General George Patton.

I was always proud of that, my dad, just a New York City junior high school teacher, taking on Hitler's Wehrmacht, marching into the Nazi *Vaterland*, saving the world. It never occurred to me to ask him about the rifle he carried, the caliber of shell it shot, and whether he found it easy to use the open sights. Back in Flushing, Queens, it never came up.

"It should have," Doyel said. "That M1 might be the only reason you ever got born."

He took back the M14 and gave me an M16. There was a certain symbology to it, since the M16 was the gun that replaced the M14 before the Vietnam War because Defense Secretary Robert McNamara wanted a new weapon for a new war, something sleeker, with more horsepower. Unfortunately, the M16, reputedly never fully combat tested before it was deployed, proved unreliable in the eyes of many soldiers, especially in comparison with the AK-47 the NVA and Vietcong used. I knew this about the M16 because, as Dad carried his M1, the M16 was supposed to be my gun for my war, the thing I'd carry if I was dumb enough to lose my 2-S student draft classification and end up in the soup like Bill Cooper.

It is a standard question for many men in my generation: How'd you get out? It was the smart move, the best move. No question. The war was wrong. Yet, with each passing year, I find myself increasingly emotional about what happened back then, the way so many got sent over there and wound up dead. Sometimes I can't even talk about it. I just start weeping.

I discharged a magazine or two before Doyel took back the M16 and gave me one of his black guns, the homemade jobs built in his workshop, according to his personal specs. Like any good teacher, he was calm, genuinely pleased when I showed progress. When I pumped a few shells into a battered Frisbee nailed to the canyon wall a hundred feet away, he sounded his approval.

"You're doing phenomenal! Keep doing like that and we'll get you signed up for the JDL," he said.

That was when Doyel brought out the pièce de résistance: Bill Cooper's personal .45.

During my first days in Eagar, I'd viewed the original manuscript of *Behold a Pale Horse,* complete with editor's marks. I'd seen Cooper's raised copper bust of John Kennedy, which, no matter how many times Cooper moved, was always given prominent wall space. There was plenty of memorabilia inside the storage unit Doyel still kept: Cooper's medals, his old microphone, the Wu-Tang Clan–brand stereo system someone sent him.

But when it came to artifacts, nothing quite equaled Cooper's 1911 Springfield Armory Silver Chief .45. Emblematic of his status as a free man, the gun never left his side, Cooper often told the *Hour of the Time* listeners. When and if the jackbooted minions of the New World Order stormed his mountaintop outpost, he expected the tension of his finger on the pistol's trigger to be his final sensation.

I let the gun's weight rest on my palm. Cooper had had a lot of work done on the 1911, Doyel said. He'd added a competition metal trigger mechanism, fancy grips, inlays on the body and barrel.

"You know, it looks okay now," Doyel put in. "But after Bill died, I found it lying around all gummed up with lint and hair, like something you'd find in a pool of Coca-Cola at the bottom of a cupholder. My dad and I had to soak it in kerosene just to get it to working order."

Not that it mattered. "Bill really couldn't shoot for shit anyhow."

PART SIX

Across 125th Street
aka
Knowledge, Wisdom, Equality Path

Boondocks comic strip

15

Nowadays you can buy a copy of *Behold a Pale Horse* from Walmart, $14.50, with two-day shipping, but if you want to know how Cooper's book came to Harlem, the fastest way is still the A train to 125th Street. From there, walk east to between Frederick Douglass and Adam Clayton Powell Jr. Boulevards, which is where, if he's in the mood, you can find Bro. Nova at his sidewalk table across from the world-famous Apollo Theater, where James Brown used to tear it up on a regular basis.

All varieties of items can be bought from street vendors on 125th Street: vats of shea butter, aphrodisiac tinctures, copies of old Bruce Lee and Pam Grier movies, T-shirts with iron-ons of rainbow-hued marijuana leaves, twelve-dollar Louis Vuitton pocketbooks made in Shenzhen. But even though he's spent more than half his life as a 125th Street merchant, Bro. Nova, a tall and sleek man now in what looks to be his early forties, has always stuck with books.

It is a matter of continuity, Nova said, because, "In the Beginning there was The Word and long after all this shit has been washed to the sea, there will still be The Word."

Gentrification was a hell of a drug, Nova said with a laugh, casting a wary gaze at the as-yet unpurchased air rights hovering over the two-story Jimmy Jazz urban wear store. Everywhere you looked, a condo was going up, glass middle fingers spiking across the sky, junior one-bedrooms starting at a million two. Once upon a time, many of Harlem's best-known brands were stamped on tiny glassine bags: KICK ASS, TOO STRONG, BLUE MAGIC. Now there is Red Lobster, Banana Republic, and T.J.Maxx.

The 125th Street booksellers took their cue from people like Lewis Michaux, who ran his famous store at the corner of 125th Street and

Seventh Avenue for nearly forty years. According to a sign outside, Michaux's store contained nothing less than WORLD HISTORY ON 2,000,000,000 (TWO BILLION) AFRICANS AND NON-WHITE PEOPLES. Hot-selling volumes were touted with ads reading "*The God Dam White Man* is the title of this Book. Read it!" Part store, part library, part debating society, Michaux's was, as another sign read, THE HOUSE OF COMMON SENSE, HOME OF PROPER PROPAGANDA.

Bro. Nova and his fellow merchants carry on in this tradition. On their tables are the classics, books by Ralph Ellison, Richard Wright, James Baldwin, Toni Morrison, a hard-boiled Donald Goines, *The Autobiography of Malcolm X, The New Jim Crow*. Also present are hard-to-find pan-African analyses like *Yurugu: An African-Centered Critique of European Cultural Thought and Behavior* by Marimba Ani, *How Europe Underdeveloped Africa* by Walter Rodney, and *Thomas Sankara Speaks*, a collection of speeches and essays by the anointed "African Che," revolutionary leader of Burkina Faso who was assassinated in the capital, Ouagadougou, in 1987. There is also a heavy cache of books from Dr. Malachi Z. York aka Imperial Grand Potentate Noble: Rev. Dr. Malachi Z. York 33°/720° aka Dwight York. Former singer in the disco band Passion, founder and leader of the Nuwaubian Nation, current federal prisoner, York authored *Are the Caucasians Edomites?*, which is prominently displayed on Bro. Nova's table.

It might seem a reach to find *Behold a Pale Horse* in this company but bookmen like Bro. Nova have been selling Cooper's work since the early 1990s.

In fact, Cooper's name recognition is probably higher on 125th Street than anywhere else in the physical world. I'd done my own research on that, walking up and down Main Street of what used to be called the Capital of Black America. The survey wasn't very scientific, but I did ask a range of individuals, men and women, old and young. Fifteen years after his death, approximately one person in three over twenty-five who identified themselves as longtime Harlem residents was aware of Bill Cooper and/or his book.

"Most people, anyone who once thought of themselves as radical in any way back in the 1990s, knows William Cooper," said one dapper-looking man standing under the marquee of the Apollo. "*Behold a Pale*

Horse, it was something you had to read. We used to just call it 'The Book.'" People also recalled talks given by the late Steve Cokely, a 1990s African American independent researcher/street speaker who occasionally referenced Cooper. In the middle of a presentation, Cokely would pick up a copy of *Behold a Pale Horse* and say, "Let's see what the white boy has to say about this."

Financially speaking, *Behold a Pale Horse* had been very good to the 125th Street bookseller. An older seller next to Bro. Nova estimated he'd personally sold "maybe one thousand copies" over the years. Everyone agreed, the book's early 1990s rise in popularity came out of the state prison system. In Attica, they were reading Bill Cooper. In Clinton-Dannemora, Green Haven, Sing Sing, it was the same. Cooper's book was big, too, at east Jersey's Rahway, as well as in joints down to Baltimore and Washington.

One bookseller summed it up this way: "One in four black men winds up in jail one time or another. The incarcerated African American is the most legitimately paranoid man in the world. When you get to William Cooper, he is one paranoid white man, he speaks the same language."

"He helped wake me up," Bro. Nova said with a smile. "And you know, out here, you got to *stay woke*."

The narrative of how Bill Cooper's *Behold a Pale Horse* jumped the seemingly unbridgeable racial divide to land on Bro. Nova's table is long and winding but worth knowing. On the temporal plane it dates back at least to a bright Fourth of July morning in 1930, which is when a mysterious stranger calling himself W. D. Fard appeared in the Paradise Valley section of Detroit, Michigan.

It was the Great Migration. As many as six million people of African descent had fled the slavery grounds of the rural south to the great industrial cities of the north. They came on segregated bus lines and trains, and in rickety automobiles packed high with belongings, to what was being touted as the Promised Land.

The dream of a better life, if it was ever attainable, was delayed by the stock market crash in 1929 and the Depression years that followed. No one had money, least of all the residents of Paradise Valley. So it seemed odd when Fard (pronounced Far-rad), a slightly built man in his middle forties, wearing a well-cut suit, began going door-to-door selling silk cloth.

It was true his wares were expensive, but this was to be expected, Fard told his prospective customers. These were not ordinary silks, the cheap fabrics piled high in bargain stores. The design harkened back to the ancient Shabazz, a society of black people who first inhabited the Earth 66 trillion years ago.

The world of the Shabazz, or the Original Man, was the most brilliant society ever seen on the planet, Fard said. This was the true Eden, not the fairy story of Adam and Eve in the Bible. The Shabazz lived in complete harmony with their surroundings, pursued the highest goals of the mind. Black astronomers scanned the heavens. Black mathematicians calculated the order of things. Best of all, there were no white people.

This was the way it stayed through the eons, until 6,600 years ago, when a brilliant but willful young prince arose in Mecca. Known as Yacub, the "Big Head Scientist," the prince was already famous by the age of six for his establishment of the laws of magnetic attraction and repulsion. Now Yacub left Mecca with 59,999 of his followers and moved to the Aegean island of Patmos, where 4,000 years later the exiled Saint John would set down his visions in what would become the Book of Revelation.

While on Patmos, Yacub conducted a monumental Mendelian cross-breeding project. Isolating a "black germ" and a "brown germ" from the tissue of the Original Man, Yacub produced progressively lighter-skinned offspring. Eventually, Yacub's "bleaching" process created whites, a race Fard called "blue-eyed devils." These ghost-colored Frankensteins came to oppress the Original Man, making them slaves, submitting them to an endless cycle of humiliation and hardship.

W. D. Fard told this story as he unrolled bolts of dazzling Shabazz silks for his customers' inspection. To those who doubted his word, Fard bade them to take a look around. Here they were, in a place called Paradise Valley in what was supposed be the Promised Land. Yet what did they see? A shabby apartment, freezing cold in the winter, without even an indoor toilet. They worked at meaningless jobs for small wages at factories owned by whites who could fire them on a whim.

In what way was this alleged Promised Land superior to the tenant farms they'd left in Mississippi and Louisiana? This was the "tricknology" of the White Man. He told you things that were not true, kept the offspring of the sublime Shabazz in the bondage of ignorance through the primitive violence and lies of what Fard called "the spook civilization."

Now, however, Fard said, there was good news. The reign of the devils was coming to an end. In World War One, the whites had fought among themselves and almost destroyed the planet. Their recklessness and cruelty could no longer be tolerated. This was why he had chosen the present moment to appear in their midst, Fard told the people of Paradise Valley. It was time for the Original Man to rise up.

"The Original Man is the Asiatic Black Man," Fard declared. It was the Original Man who was "the Maker, the Owner, the Cream of the Planet Earth, the Father of Civilization, the God of the Universe." The seemingly lowly and despised people of Paradise Valley were His children.

For the descendants of the Shabazz to return to the real Paradise, it was essential that they accept Islam, the religion of the Original Man, Fard said, and he opened the Allah Temple of Islam on Hastings Street. This was a neighborhood of churches. Only a short walk away was New Bethel Baptist Church, soon to be pastored by C. L. Franklin, father of Aretha. Followers of evangelical stars like Sweet Daddy Grace and Father Divine abounded.

All this so-called Christian piety was precisely the problem, Master Fard, as he now called himself, wrote in his study guide, *The Supreme Wisdom Lessons*. The Christian religion was a plot of the Devil, Fard said.

Also included in *The Supreme Wisdom Lessons* were the "Actual Facts," which each congregationalist had to commit to memory. These included such items as "The total area of the land and water of the planet Earth is 196,940,000 square miles," "The circumference of the planet Earth is 24,896 miles," and "The Earth is 93,000,000 miles from the sun."

There was nothing secret in these "Actual Facts"; they could be found in any world almanac and likely were. But they existed far beyond the realm of their exactitude. To people whose immediate forebears had grown up in a society of enforced illiteracy, the simple idea that it was possible to accurately measure the distance between the sun and the

Earth was astounding in itself. The idea that these miraculous facts and figures were the product of an ancient black civilization was even more so.

To the powerless, nothing could be taken for granted. You were the captive of an enforced alien reality. Every day, they could tell you something different and you had no choice but to accept the rules, however unjust. If the descendants of the Original Man were going to reclaim their rightful place, they would have to begin at the beginning, cast out the devils' brainwashing, come to a piece of solid ground. In that context a single *actual*, unchanging fact seemed a holy thing.

In 1923, the man who became Master Fard's greatest disciple came to Paradise Valley. Elijah Poole, the twenty-six-year-old, five-foot-five son of a Georgia sharecropper, had high hopes of economic success for his young family. Yet, in eight difficult years of scraping to get by, working odd jobs, including sometime employment on the Chevrolet assembly line, Poole lost faith in the supposed Promised Land of the American Negro. He'd been considering booking passage on one of Marcus Garvey's Black Star Liners to return to the Motherland, when his wife suggested he see Fard speak at the Allah Temple.

In his 1965 book, *Message to the Blackman in America*, Elijah Poole, then known as the Honorable Elijah Muhammad, writes about that first meeting. He recounts the rage he felt as Fard explained "how we were made slaves." But he is impressed by how his heart soared when Fard said that God "loved us, the so-called Negroes, his lost and found, so well that he would eat rattlesnakes to free us if necessary, for he has power over all things."

After the sermon, Elijah approached Fard and asked, "Who are you and what is your real name?"

Fard said, "I am the one that the world has been expecting for the past two thousand years. . . . My name is Mahdi; I am God, I came to guide you into the right path." That moment, Elijah became Fard's apostle, spending the next three years learning the theology and practical teachings of the Lost-Found Nation.

On December 7, 1934, after a series of encounters with the authorities (there was talk of a "human sacrifice" at the Allah Temple), Fard was put on a train to Chicago, never to be seen again. After a protracted power struggle, Elijah Muhammad became the leader of the Lost-Found Nation of Islam, the "Last Messenger of Allah."

Elijah Muhammad served as leader of the Nation of Islam, aka the Black Muslims, for nearly forty years, until his death in February of 1975. It was a tumultuous reign that produced such outsize figures as Malcolm X and enabled the transformation of Muhammad Ali from a brash, talented prizefighter to a world icon. Possessed of a third-grade education, Elijah transformed Fard's ragtag Lost-Found Nation of Islam into one of the most culturally significant political/religious movements of the American century.

Along with a genius for organization, Elijah Muhammad displayed a flair for situational cosmology. He sharpened Fard's opium dream of the Original Man into a searing, tightly plotted racial revenge saga. Central to this was the spectacular Mother Plane, which touched on a number of ontological concepts that would later become familiar to fellow cosmologists like Bill Cooper.

As Elijah Muhammad describes it, the first recorded sighting of the Mother Plane appears in chapter one, verse 16 of the Book of Ezekiel, the most visually imaginative of Hebrew scribes held prisoner during the Babylonian Captivity.

"The appearance of the wheels and their work was like the color of a beryl: and they four had one likeness: and their appearance and their work was as it were a wheel in the middle of a wheel," the prophet Ezekiel said.

Elijah Muhammad's description of the famous "Wheel in the Sky" is more specific. "The present wheel-shaped plane known as the Mother of Planes," Elijah wrote in *Message to the Blackman*, "is one-half mile by a half mile and is the largest mechanical man-made object in the sky. It is a small human planet made for the purpose of destroying the present world of the enemies of Allah. The cost to build such a plane is staggering! The finest brains were used to build it. It is capable of staying in outer space six to twelve months at a time without coming into the earth's gravity."

Going on, Elijah further described the Mother Plane's attributes, saying that "at a given signal, the belly of the Plane is set to open, loosing 1500 bombers, small circular planes called flying saucers, which are so much talked (about) or being seen . . . Each one of the saucers are piloted by Black men who have been trained since the age of six to do a special job." These fliers will be "able to hit any spot in America, blindfolded, as the Devil will soon see. . . . Do not think of trying to attack it. That would be suicide."

This colossus was not the product of some highly advanced alien technology that could be reverse-engineered by the likes of Bob Lazar. It wasn't from outer space at all. The Mother Plane was constructed on Earth by the scientists of the Shabazz 66 trillion years ago. In all that time, the Mother Plane had flown through the far reaches of space. But now, the Last Messenger said, the great craft was being called upon to perform the one and only task it had been built to accomplish, "to destroy the world."

In chapter 118 of *Message to the Blackman,* entitled "America Is Falling, Her Doom Is Sealed," Elijah Muhammad identifies the Mother Plane's target. "I compare the fall of America with the fall of ancient Babylon. Her wickedness (sins) is the same as history shows of ancient Babylon."

Then like Bill Cooper in the "Dawn of Man" episode, Elijah Muhammad invoked the words of St. John of Patmos. "'Mystery Babylon, the Great' is none other than America. Mystery Babylon is full of riches, hatred, filth, fornication, adultery, drunkenness, murder of the innocent and idol worship."

The Mother Plane versus Mystery Babylon—that was the match-up for the Final Battle, the true Armageddon, Elijah Muhammad said. He lived for the moment when he could gleefully unleash his Fruit of Islam saucermen to set flame to the corrupt capital of the White Man.

It was during the 1950s, as Elijah's teachings were first beginning to gain a foothold in the New York area, that a third-generation figure instrumental in bringing *Behold a Pale Horse* to 125th Street appeared on the scene. This was Clarence Edward Smith, aka Clarence 13X, and eventually Father Allah.

Born in the harshly segregationist town of Danville, Virginia, on February 22, 1928, the future Father Allah soon moved with his family to Harlem (which he later renamed Mecca), where he worked as a bootblack and developed a zeal for gambling, occasionally running numbers for several local criminal entrepreneurs, including, it is rumored, the Ur-Harlem gangster, Bumpy Johnson.

In his early twenties, Smith was drafted into the Army and sent to fight in the Korean War, where he saw a good deal of combat and was awarded a Bronze Service Star among other citations. Discharged in 1954 with the rank of private first class, Smith returned to Harlem possessed by a remarkable epiphany he claimed to have had while fighting the North Koreans: He was a god, a supreme being on the Earth.

Sure that people would think him mad, Smith did not speak of his insight. It wasn't until he joined the Nation of Islam Mosque #7 on 116th Street near Lenox Avenue, then headed by Malcolm X, that he began to understand the nature of his godhead. Now calling himself Clarence 13X and teaching karate to the temple's paramilitary unit, Fruit of Islam, he believed he'd found a flaw in Elijah Muhammad's interpretation of Fard's *Supreme Wisdom*. By this time, Fard had been formally declared by Elijah Muhammad to be the Mahdi, or God, a being apart from all others. To Clarence 13X, this made Fard "a Mystery God."

The so-called Mystery God, an unknowable deity who lives in the sky, was one of the Devil's greatest tricks. The rulers often used the Creator's supposed will to cover their criminal tracks. The issue was addressed in the Q and A call-and-response section of *The Supreme Wisdom*.

"Who is that Mystery God?" the group leader asks.

"There is not a Mystery God," is the answer.

"So why does the Devil teach that?"

"Because he desires to make slaves out of all he can so he can rob them and live in luxury."

By claiming Fard was a Mystery God, Elijah Muhammad had proved himself a hypocrite, Clarence 13X said. In 1967, two years after Malcolm X's murder at the Audubon Ballroom, this was the sort of talk that could get you killed in Harlem. As it was, along with allegations that he'd been drinking, gambling, and philandering, Clarence 13X was kicked out of the Lost-Found Nation of Islam.

His expulsion conjured up the revelation Clarence 13X first glimpsed as he hunkered down in the frozen killing fields of Korea. God was not a mystery. God dwelled within the heart and mind of every black man; it was a race of gods. The mystery was in how to find Him, how to reach the Most High within yourself.

Yet if all black men were potential gods, why weren't more people aware of it? The answer, Clarence 13X felt, was in *The Supreme Wisdom*, lessons 14–16, where Fard breaks humanity into three categories. By far the largest segment was "the 85% . . . the uncivilized people; poison animal eaters; slaves from mental death and power." These were the sleeping dead-in-the-heads, the *dunya*-dwelling cattle. Then there was "the 10%." These were "the rich; the slave-makers . . . The Blood-Suckers Of The Poor."

This left "the 5%," whom *The Supreme Wisdom* defines as "the poor, righteous Teachers . . . the all-wise," those who understand and teach "Freedom, Justice and Equality to all the human family of the planet Earth. Otherwise known as: The Civilized People."

These were the children of Clarence 13X, who now was called Father Allah, patriarch of a race of born Allahs that came to be called the Five Percent Nation. To accompany these male urban gods were their female counterparts, the Earths, the humble nurturers of the royal male seed, hence the Nation of Gods and Earths.

For his Gods and Earths, Father Allah invented esoteric concepts like the Supreme Alphabet and the Supreme Mathematics, with each number and letter assigned a hidden attribute. Number one was "knowledge," two meant "wisdom," three was "understanding." Hence the simple rote learning of 1 + 2 = 3 morphed into Knowledge plus Wisdom equals Understanding, simple arithmetic transformed to a whole other plane of self-realization.

In the end, Father Allah taught, the ultimate attribute was the Word. Word was bond, Father Allah said. Gods needed to become lyrical assassins because what was the use of a couple of Uzis and MAC 10s when the other side had tanks? The tongue was the sword, Father Allah said, and properly sharpened, it could "take more heads than any army with machine guns could ever do."

For a time thrown into a mental institution by authorities who claimed he was a paranoid schizophrenic, Father Allah was shot to death by an anonymous assailant in the elevator of a West 115th Street housing project in 1969. But there were plenty of gods to pick up the Word in his absence.

16

The names of Five Percenter–identified rappers who have mentioned Bill Cooper and/or *Behold a Pale Horse* in their rhymes, interviews, or videos include Big Daddy Kane, Busta Rhymes, Tupac Shakur, Talib Kweli, Mobb Deep, Nas, Rakim (of Eric B. & Rakim), Poor Righteous Teachers, Gang Starr, Goodie Mob, Suicideboys, Boogiemonsters, Wise Intelligent, Public Enemy ("pass the Ol' Gold / Behold a Pale Horse"), Miz MAF, Aslan, Lord Allah, Ras Kass, and the Lost Children of Babylon, who tell their listeners to prepare to meet your fate "like William Cooper . . . when the storm troopers breach your gate."

Not every reference is complimentary. In his 2013 rap "The Wormhole," Talib Kweli ruefully rhymes about his youthful infatuation with Cooper's work. Saying he was a "hoarder" at Borders, Kweli mentions "Behold the Pale Horse or the New World Order," but concludes you really don't know what you're reading if you "don't know the author."

That said, Cooper has shown remarkable staying power in the idiom. Just the other day, I put the phrase "Behold a Pale Horse" into the Sound-Cloud player and 312 entries came up. One, by an MC Pale Horse, talks about how, since he is about to "clue you" to his prophetic visions, you should "light up a blunt and call up the voice of William Cooper." Groups with names like Lizzard Frequency and the Harlequins of Eden don't talk specifically of Cooper but pick up a sound byte of him reading about the last of the Four Horsemen of the Apocalypse, to whom "power was given unto them over the fourth part of the earth, to kill with sword, and with hunger, and with death and with the beasts of the earth."

As Ol' Dirty Bastard told me when we talked in 2003, Bill Cooper was "curriculum." You ignored him at your own risk. It was a theme he speaks about in a vintage YouTube video he did with Method Man.

"They are brainwashing our people with the mind control theory," Dirty says. You could tell that, he said, by how "they play the same song over and over again on the radio." Fake hip-hop, spread by "the government," was taking over. ODB was against it. His purpose on the planet was to make sure things stayed "dirty, dirty, dirty."

Hearing this, Method Man looks over his shoulder with mock alarm. "I love the government," he said. "CIA, FBI, I love all you niggas, don't come knocking on my fucking door." ODB, seemingly taking the hint, said, "I love them, too, they all my children."

There was a reason people started reading the book in jail, Bro. Nova, the 125th Street bookseller, told me. "Where else were they gonna read it? Back then, everyone was in jail. Or dead."

This had the ring of truth. In the year 1990, 2,605 people were murdered in New York City; 2,571 were killed in 1991, by far the highest two-year total in the city's history. In the black community, a good deal of this mayhem was due to the so-called crack epidemic, the influx of the highly addictive "rock" cocaine. To listen to the news, every day brought a new slew of "crack babies," their innocence stolen at birth. It was one more crisis, a plague that required the presence of griots, and a next generation of Father Allah's "lyrical assassins" stepped up.

"It was like a holocaust, man. Know what I'm saying? Every day someone you knew was dying," said the rapper Prodigy (born Albert Johnson), who along with his partner, Kejuan Muchita, aka Havoc, made up the classic NYC hip-hop duo Mobb Deep.

We were in a café in Manhattan in the summer of 2014, getting ready to drive across the river to the Queensbridge projects, where Mobb Deep was due to appear in a "homecoming concert." Along with fellow Cooper acolyte Nas, Mobb Deep has always been identified with Queensbridge, built in 1939 and still the largest single public housing development in the country. Prodigy and Havoc had traveled around the world, made millions with their streetwise raps, but hadn't played "the QB" since they were fourteen years old, trading verses behind the buildings at Twenty-First Street and Fortieth Avenue.

Killing time before the show, I asked Prodigy if it was true, as he'd said on a hip-hop website, that he had read *Behold a Pale Horse* four times when he was younger. "No, man," the diminutive rapper replied, "that's a misquote. I read it *six* times. I needed to get that shit right and exact before I went out there.

"The book was kind of incredible because William Cooper wrote these things that everyone kind of knew. Everyone believed the CIA was running dope, but you never saw it written down. AIDS being made up in a test tube at Fort Detrick, MKUltra and that shit: It was all ways to wipe out people they didn't want around. Back then, if you were like sixteen years old and your friend just got shot, it was hard not to believe it."

Prodigy was never the typical hood rapper. He was the great-great-great-grandson of William Jefferson White, founder of Morehouse College, where Martin Luther King Jr. (and Spike Lee) graduated. He was the grandson of Budd Johnson, a tenor saxophonist in the Kansas City style, who'd made his debut with Louis Armstrong and performed with Duke Ellington, Count Basie, and Billie Holiday. Prodigy's mother, Frances Collins, was in the Crystals in the post–Phil Spector days, singing "Da Doo Ron Ron" on a nightly basis.

A more salient factor, at least in the street-cred section of the vitae, was that despite Mobb Deep's Queensbridge identity, Prodigy was not from there. He lived in Hempstead, Long Island, until he was twelve, then moved to LeFrak City, a massive middle-class apartment complex on the Long Island Expressway built by Sam LeFrak, father of current owner Richard LeFrak, childhood chum and golfing buddy of fellow Queens real estate *macher*, Donald Trump.

Some people held this pedigree against Prodigy, but it is hard to deny the urban menace in the group's great masterpiece "Shook Ones (Part II)," the sonic distillation of what it feels like to find oneself walking down the wrong street at the wrong time.

It was Prodigy who helped bring Cooper's obsessions to a larger audience. He did it in a single verse, in the 1995 video for the remix of LL Cool J's "I Shot Ya." Filmed in dramatic black and white, a very young-looking version of the former Albert Johnson stands in a crowded alley with assorted hood types and raps: "The Illuminati want my mind, soul and my body." Secret societies, Prodigy rapped, were "trying to keep they eye on me."

Here was an astonishing new kind of 411. As many teenage hip-hop fans of the moment will attest, this was the first time they'd heard of the term *Illuminati* or knew that there was such a thing as a "secret society" that Prodigy said kept an "eye on" you. When Prodigy's Illuminati verse was in turn sampled by Jay-Z on his 1996 debut album *Reasonable Doubt*, the meme predictably blew up.

It wasn't long before everyone was talking about the Illuminati, what it was, how it ran the world, and which rappers had been co-opted to disperse its malign symbology. Professor Griff of Public Enemy did about "a hundred videos on it," Prodigy said. Half of Brooklyn knew if you inverted Blue Ivy, the name of Jay-Z and Beyoncé's daughter, and made it Ivy Blue, it came out to "Illuminati's Very Youngest Born Living under Evil."

A lot of that began with Cooper, Prodigy said. "We were seventeen. We weren't learning nothing in school, so we'd cut out and go to the Brooklyn library on Eastern Parkway, and we'd read books, the works of Dr. Malachi Z. York, stuff like that. *Behold a Pale Horse* was the first place I heard of the Illuminati." It was right there, in the first chapter, "Silent Weapons for Quiet Wars."

Many years later, when Prodigy was sentenced to three and a half years on gun charges (2008–2011), he was surprised to find "lots of guys inside there were still reading *Pale Horse*.

"You'd think it would go out of fashion. There are like a million books about secret societies now. But I go in and people are still reading it. It was like, that's the deal, when you are in prison, you read *Behold a Pale Horse*."

Now, like ODB and so many of Father Allah's verbal assassins, Prodigy was dead, passing away in June of 2017 from complications of sickle-cell anemia, a disease so painful that it made him "hate God." Still, it wasn't as if Prodigy ever totally left Bill Cooper. The last record he made before his death, a piece of work that he called "my magnum opus, where all the seeds I planted over the years come up," is titled *Hegelian Dialectic (The Book of Revelation)*.

Rappers William Cooper and Killah Priest in
Brooklyn (aka Medina), 2016

If Prodigy was one generation of Cooper-influenced rapper, Andrew
Kissel, a Newark, New Jersey, MC who started performing under the
name William Cooper in the middle 2000s, was the next.

The name kept coming up in the Google searches I was doing for Bill
Cooper. The first item that jumped out was a video William Cooper
made for his 2009 debut album *Beware of the Pale Horse.* Called "American Gangsters," the tune made reference to the then-recent Hollywood
picture *American Gangster,* in which Denzel Washington plays Frank
Lucas, a particularly rapacious Superfly-style Harlem heroin dealer of the
1970s. I was acquainted with the subject matter since I'd spent many
hours with the intermittently collegial Mr. Lucas, writing the magazine
piece the movie was based on.

Animated in brutalist digital style, the "American Gangsters" video
begins with menacing plinking of a child's music box. Then comes the
voice of William Cooper. Set against an image of barbed wire twisted

into the pattern of a double helix, the rapper begins with an all-inclusive *j'accuse*: "The CIA wants my DNA wiped off the planet!"

Loud staccato, not to be denied, William Cooper next turns his attention to the smoking World Trade Center. "9/11 terrorism," he declares. "The Secret Government planning. Gave birth to the recession. Now the world's in a panic. Another amber alert got the sheeple running frantic."

This is followed by the fingering of suspects, usual and not. J. Edgar Hoover and a roster of Bilderbergers, C. D. Jackson, Richard Perle, Kissinger, Lawrence Summers are picked out of the lineup. These are mixed with shout-outs to heroes Huey P. Newton and Malcolm X. There are warnings to "beware the bar code, that's the fingerprints of Lucifer" and anthemic exhortations to "break free from the Matrix, follow my lead."

Then William Cooper's "American Gangsters" fixes on a single image. Like the POV of shooter video games, the viewer is positioned at the beginning of a long alleyway lined by shadowy, towering housing-project buildings. At the end of the gauntlet, in a tiny pool of light, is an American flag.

As William Cooper raps that he won't live on his knees, he's breaking free, got "tricks up my sleeve," the POV rushes toward the flag, which is torn and battered, full of holes. It grows to take up most of the frame.

Shouting out an RIP to his namesake ("Rest in Peace, William Cooper!"), the rapper says he and his crew are on top of the plot, "the puppet masters pulling strings for the microchip future." They're not going to be deluded by the criminal romance offered by crooks and killers like Frank Lucas. They've been studying, learning new ways to stay sane in a world programmed to drive you mad.

I reached William Cooper through his YouTube account and made an appointment to see him out in Amityville, Long Island, "the home of the Horror," where he was making his new album in what he called "the studio."

William Cooper turned out to be a large, interior lineman–sized white guy in his middle thirties, wearing a long yellow T-shirt over knee-length cutoff jeans, who'd been raised in a lower-middle-class family in Bloomfield, New Jersey, under the name Andrew Kissel. The "studio" he mentioned was a three-foot-square closet in the apartment where he works with his good friend and longtime producer, who never takes off his sunglasses and is known only as BP.

"No echo in here," William Cooper told me, displaying the confines of the tiny recording chamber. Then he pointed to a long list of autographs that adorned the closet door. These were rappers who'd recorded here, some from as far away as Philly.

"Some of the best in the game been in the Box," William Cooper remarked.

Big as he was, William Cooper could barely fit inside the closet. During the summer, after fifteen minutes, the sweat would be pouring down his chest. But that was the way William Cooper preferred it. This was the way "real" hip-hop was made, or should be made, he said. "In a closet, off the grid, out of the way, saying what you to have to say. Guerilla style."

It was the rapper Killah Priest who named him William Cooper, Kissel said. That was back in '04 or '05, when he began working with the Black Market Militia, a Wu-Tang Clan satellite group. It was something for a young white guy to be surrounded by such semi-legends as Timbo King, Hell Razah, 60 Second Assassin, and Tragedy Khadafi, a Queensbridge Five Percenter who used to call himself Intelligent Hoodlum. But it was the presence of Walter Reed, aka Killah Priest—a name taken from a character in the Clan's founding text, the 1983 Hong Kong kung fu movie, *Shaolin and Wu-Tang*—whom Kissel most held in awe.

An older head, born in 1970 in Brooklyn, which Father Allah called Medina (as opposed to Harlem's Mecca), Killah Priest had grown up "thick in the Brownsville shit," during which time he faced off in many back-alley rap battles where only the strong survived. Best known as the author of "B.I.B.L.E." (in the Supreme Alphabet "backronym" rubric, it stands for "Basic Instructions Before Leaving Earth"), which appears on GZA's classic 1995 album *Cold World* Killah Priest surprised Kissel one day when he said, "You should be William Cooper. You should rap under William Cooper."

"I didn't know what he was talking about. I had a name. I was Booth, of Booth and Ozwald, a little group I started with my friend Mike Sims. We wanted to make money, you know, *dead presidents*. We asked what makes dead presidents, so we became Booth and Ozwald. I never heard of William Cooper. Then Priest said, go to the bookstore, get a copy of *Behold a Pale Horse,* read it, and come back and tell me if I'm right or wrong."

Kissel read through *Behold a Pale Horse* with interest. "The way he explained who he was, his background. It was firsthand, he went into depth. All that stuff about Vietnam. I knew a lot of people in my parents' generation who had been in Vietnam. The way he put it seemed honest. He wasn't putting himself on a pedestal. He was saying, this is me, warts and all. This is what I've got to say."

Killah Priest had told him to pay close attention to "Silent Weapons for Quiet Wars"; it was full of jewels. "When I read that, I felt like the future had already happened," William Cooper said. "Like the plan was already in place. We were living inside it."

William Cooper listened to Killarmy's *SWFQW* album, but nothing touched him like Killah Priest's version, the song "Quiet Weapons for Silent Wars," recorded with the Sunz of Man in 1996 but never formally released.

When I ran into him in front of a Williamsburg club in 2016, Killah Priest, now edging toward fifty, his hair flecked with gray, remembered the lyrics of his take on "Silent Weapons."

"Data, data, alpha, omega / breaker, breaker," Priest recited, standing on the sidewalk on North Sixth Street, once a totally deserted stretch of warehouse buildings but now among the highest-rent districts in New York. "Every eye watches the clock / waiting for the ball to drop / tick tock."

"Silent Weapons for Quiet Wars" was "giant" to him when he first read it, said Killah Priest. "I got this idea it was a blueprint for extinction. . . . It was like looking at a technological Book of Revelation."

Kissel dutifully read through some of the murkier precincts of *Behold a Pale Horse,* which he had to allow was "pretty obscure." But what really struck him was *The Hour of the Time.* This was new. The first generation of Gods and Earths knew Bill Cooper exclusively from *Behold a Pale Horse.* Shortwave wasn't a thing in Green Haven or Attica. Even now, many older readers of the book don't know Cooper ever had a radio show.

But Andrew Kissel, the next generation, did. He downloaded plenty of episodes from *The Complete Cooper.* "I can sit there and listen to him for hours, just zone out on his voice. It can put you into a meditative state, when he's not screaming," said William Cooper. He loved the opener, the blaring sirens, the barking dogs, the tramping feet, the screams in the night. It was like downtown Newark, right outside his window.

"To me, that intro, that's like Bill Cooper's entrance. Here he is, the champion, coming into the ring to defend his title, carrying his belts above his head," Kissel said.

So Andrew Kissel told Killah Priest, yeah, okay, he'd be William Cooper. Ten years later, even his mother calls him Cooper. As for Bill Cooper, he's called Milton William Cooper so no one gets mixed up. It was a lot better than naming yourself after some drug dealer like Noreaga or Rick Ross, Kissel thought.

"He was a patriot," William Cooper said, "which I like, because I am a patriot. I am a proud American. This country was supposed to have been built to question authority, to hold the people in power account-able. Not to bite your tongue. Just to put it out there, right or wrong, let everyone else decide."

Killah Priest told him, "If the world's a prison, then Bill Cooper is a jailhouse lawyer." Kissel said, "I liked that because I thought, that's what a rapper should be. You get up before the court and plead your case. Point a finger at the guilty."

Kissel was back in the Box now, doing a little work on the last few numbers of the disc he was finishing, *God's Will*. It was an ambitious effort that had taken more than four years to complete, requiring many commutes from Newark to the far reaches of Long Island. The tracks include "Something Ain't Right," "True-N-Livin' Nightmares," "Verbal Checkmate" (featuring Killah Priest), and "Holy Mountain," in which he rhymes "no easy Jesus" with "the pyramids of Giza."

William Cooper thought "every single song could be a hit," but he held out special hope for "Secrets of Oz," which retells the L. Frank Baum story from the conspiratorial view, and holds that Glinda the Good Witch, in league with the hated Woodrow Wilson, is the villain and that the whole thing is about the creation of the Federal Reserve System. William Cooper thought that one could "really take off."

A few months later, when William Cooper gave a listening party for the *God's Will* debut at New York's Quad Studios, "Secrets of Oz" was one of the favorites. Famous as the spot where Tupac Shakur was shot in 1994, the Quad offers a boffo view of the Times Square hubbub from its tenth-floor window. On this night the tourist business-as-usual was interrupted by a protest over the then-recent death of Freddie Gray in the back of a Baltimore police van. Watching the crowds rage through the streets, William Cooper pronounced the scene to be "an omen," even if he didn't know what kind.

17

There was no fucking way he would be William Cooper if Bill Cooper was a racist, Andrew Kissel told me. He'd done his research, satisfied himself. There was nothing in *Behold a Pale Horse*, nothing he'd ever heard on *The Hour of the Time*, that led him to suspect that Cooper was a racist.

It was something to think about, the sum total of Bill Cooper's many views on the subject of race. Long before the phrase came into common usage, he hated identity politics. Americans should be Americans, he said. Obsessing over ethnicity was a danger to the Republic. If Jews cared more about Israel than the US, they should go live there. "Make your dream come true there. Fight there. If you have to, die there." If black people insisted on calling themselves African Americans, they might as well "go back to Africa," Cooper was heard to say. He screamed the same thing about Italian Americans, the Chinese, and the Irish, too. But still, it is piercing to hear the phrase "go back to Africa," when said by a white man.

On the other hand, it is unlikely that another patriot shortwave radio host would have created an episode like "Vomit from the Sheeple." As usual, Cooper was in the midst of lambasting the audience's lack of commitment to the restoration of republican constitutional government. The patriot audience was nothing but a bunch of "couch-potato, do-nothing, never-contribute-to-anything, what-can-I-do-I'm-just-one-lonely-human-being" complainers, Cooper said. It made him sick, like he was going to barf.

Cooper made a loud chundering sound, a deep, phlegmy "Blulafff!"

Then he taunted, "Come on people, get real," and put on a 1929 recording of the Louis Armstrong orchestra's rousing performance of

"St. Louis Blues." When the tune was done, Cooper, as hep as any cat on Fifty-Second Street, said, "All right, *Louis!*"

Armstrong didn't wait around for anyone to pay for his trumpet lessons, said Cooper, who had just started playing the instrument again after a long hiatus. "He just got a horn and played it better than anyone else ever had or will." It was no surprise that Armstrong's birthday was the Fourth of July, Cooper noted. He was an American, a real one.

For as many times as he'd play Lee Greenwood's gummy version of "God Bless America," Cooper's musical choices often seemed to be an assault upon the resolutely square and know-nothing portions of his listenership. One time he played George Clinton's 1982 hit, "Atomic Dog," with its exaggerated heavy-breathing funk and the eternal question of why the singer always felt the need to chase the cat. "Just the dog in me," Clinton concluded.

"I know most of you people out there don't like this kind of music," Cooper addressed the funkless portion of the audience. "But this is *good* music."

Probably the most sustained statement Cooper made about race relations in America came in a pre-WWCR broadcast pertaining to the riots following the verdict in the Rodney King case.

"Ah, it's May 6, 1992," Cooper began. "It's my birthday, folks, and I'm going to do a show that I don't want to do but it's got to be done by somebody and I'm the one to do it."

In the past week and a half, hundreds of buildings had been burned to the ground, Cooper said. Forty people, "more than in the Watts Riots" had been killed, seven hundred arrested, and "an entire economic community was destroyed."

It was a special kind of American nightmare, to be sitting in the safety of one's home, munching on some chips, watching the truck driver Reginald Denny, a white man, yanked from the cab of his vehicle and beaten senseless on the ground. "He got up . . . he tried to get away, and a black woman came up to him and asked, 'Can you see?' He said, 'No.' She said, 'I'll be your eyes.' . . . Such were the scenes we watched," Cooper said. "And we were torn between understanding and loathing. Hatred, love, and shame."

Cooper's broadcast then moved to a clip of Rodney King talking.

"What's it like to be a black person in America?" King said in an interview. "It's like being in hell, if you can visualize that. Like being in a living hell."

It wasn't anything Cooper was about to dispute. On the ground, unable to defend himself, King had been hit "fifty-six times in eighty seconds," Cooper reported. Filmed by a bystander, it was hard to come to grips with the violence on display. There seemed no way the cops could get off. But they did, acquitted of all charges.

"It was an incredible verdict," Cooper said, adding that he knew there were people who would defend it. "Cops might say it was okay because of the stress on the job. Most people might throw up their hands and think, 'What can you do?' Then there were those who thought, 'If Rodney King caught a beating, well . . . he must have done *something.*'" There were always those kind of people, Cooper said.

"Those people are racist. In a country where to be a black person is to struggle from the moment of birth to the moment of death," Cooper said, the very unremarkableness of the incident was the real outrage. For black people, "it was as if they had already been thrown into the cesspool of life and someone had come along and dumped another cesspool on top of them," Cooper said, looking for the right metaphors.

"It took all the hope away from these people," Cooper said, adding that "it also took some of the hope away from me because I have been predicting this for a long, long time."

It was so simple, so elementally inevitable. Rodney King and Reginald Denny, one black, one white, both beaten to a pulp by people conditioned to lash out, were only two victims in what was "a perpetual, around-the-clock beating."

Cooper blamed the listeners. "When you sit in front of your television on Friday and Saturday night and watch *Cops, Top Cops, Lady Cops, 911 Cops, Swat Cops, Detective Cops, Grandma Cops* . . . you watch them break down doors without identifying themselves, without a search warrant, without a court order, rip people's mattresses apart, throw away their clothes; if they don't find anything, all they have to do is drop a little bag of white powder . . .

"You sit there cheering them on, 'Get those scummy so-and-sos.' And the reason you do it is because you're watching it happen to blacks, to minorities, poor white trash. Puerto Ricans. Everyone who is a threat to you."

This was the way the game was being run, Cooper said. Did they really think it was an accident that a judge, "a Masonic judge," changed the venue from Los Angeles to one of the wealthiest counties in the state of California, "a county in which over two thousand police officers reside, where less than two percent of the population is black"?

What other verdict could come from Simi Valley? And what was likely to happen once that verdict was announced? It was preordained, reinforced by thousands of years of divisive programming, the inevitable result of which could be found in the burning heart of South Central LA, where it would take years to return to anything like normal life, if it ever did.

"We're being propelled toward a police state," Cooper said. That was obvious in the King case, when the judge, "another Mason," ruled that the cops "could not be found guilty if they acted in accordance with their training."

"Fifty-six blows in eighty seconds!" Cooper said, allowing the terrorizing numbers to sink in. This was their training?

Rodney King and Reginald Denny were two sides of the coin, a matched pair. As blacks were horrified by what they saw on the King video, whites were equally dismayed by the assault on Denny. Cooper then addressed the people of South Central. His heart broke at the sight of the destruction, the random death, the foul burden of history they labored under. But by rioting, "you've been very stupid . . . you've played right into the hands of those who would oppress us."

As for the whites' reaction to the Denny beating, Cooper said, "They were scared. They'll never forget the scenes they saw on that television set," which was the exact reason the media kept playing the tape, over and over again. Race was the most effective methodology of the Hegelian Dialectic, the perfect clashing opposites that produced the maximum hate and fear. It was something Cooper hoped to change one day.

It wasn't until August of 1994 that Cooper heard that black people were reading *Behold a Pale Horse*. The news came from his fellow conspiracy theorist, filmmaker, and record producer Anthony J. Hilder.

"Bill and I were very close before they shot him," Hilder told me as we talked in the summer of 2015 at a picnic table on the Pacific Palisades in Santa Monica.

I'd heard that Hilder had acted as something of a mentor to Cooper. Hilder waved that aside. "He was *my* mentor. He still is. Bill Cooper was a genius. I have heard everyone on the radio and he was one of the best. No one could touch him when he was on."

Turning eighty, but still handsome in a ravaged Johnny Cash way, his hair dyed to a black sheen, Hilder's once formidable motor mouth had been slowed considerably by the effects of a 2012 stroke. But his impeccable résumé as a primo princeling/hustler of the mid-twentieth-century Southern California variety preceded him.

Born in LA in 1935, Hilder was the stepson of the Hollywood character actress Dorothy Granger, a regular in the Mack Sennett stable, playing opposite such stars as W. C. Fields and Harry Langdon (later Abbott and Costello and the Three Stooges). By the late 1950s, Hilder was a handsome young man about town, getting parts in cheapo pictures like *The Hideous Sun Demon,* billed as Tony Hilder.

"I knew a lot of the young stars then," Hilder said. "Brando was a friend of mine. We used to hang out together at Ruby Lui's with Wally Peepers [Wally Cox] arguing about Aleister Crowley. I started wearing black leather jackets because Brando looked so great in *The Wild One.*" Brando introduced Hilder to Lee Marvin, who put him in some episodes of the TV show *M Squad.* "I was always the heel," Hilder recalled. "Lee would show up and stomp me. What a great guy."

The acting was really more of a sideline, Hilder said. His big thing was producing surf music. "I had the Revels. They did 'Church Key'; that was a hit. Quentin Tarantino used 'Comanche' in *Pulp Fiction* . . . I had my own labels." During this time, Hilder often crossed paths with the greatest of surf bands, the Beach Boys. Brian Wilson was "brilliant but he had this really bad breath. Colossal bad breath," Hilder recalled.

Hilder was also deeply involved in the particular right-wing politics of the American West. He was in the Stars for Barry, a group of Hollywood actors supporting Senator Barry Goldwater's 1964 campaign. "That's when I met Hitlery," Hilder said brightly, referring to Hillary Clinton, the former "Goldwater Girl."

I asked how far to the right Hilder was at the time. Was he into the Young Americans for Freedom?

Hilder rolled his eyes at this unthinkable characterization. "Further to the right," he said.

"How far?"

"Far, very far," Hilder said, recalling how, when Bob Dylan put out a tune called "Talkin' John Birch Paranoid Blues," he convinced one of his surf party bands to record an answer song, "John Birch, American."

In the following years, through the political maelstrom of the 1960s and early seventies, Hilder was known as a right-wing "dirty tricks" operative. Saying he was "a professional-level hypnotist," Hilder was accused of placing convicted assassin Sirhan Sirhan in a trance as part of a CIA mind control program. Hilder still vehemently denies the charges. "I even wrote a book to dispute it," he said, referring to *The Man, The Myth, and The Murder*, in which he claimed that RFK was really killed by members of Helena Blavatsky's Theosophy movement.

Without doubt, Hilder's most important contribution to the current conspiracy world was his 1967 recording of the three-LP spoken-word album *The Illuminati and the Council on Foreign Relations* by Myron Coureval Fagan (1887–1972).

Beginning his career in 1907 on the New York stage as a playwright and actor working with the likes of Douglas Fairbanks and John Barrymore, Fagan moved to Hollywood in the 1930s but found little success. This changed when he turned his attention to the Red Menace supposedly infecting Tinseltown during the late 1940s and early fifties. Forming the Cinema Educational Guild, Fagan set about turning out numerous pamphlets describing what he called the "Red Conspiracy in Hollywood."

It was a new career that would provide Fagan with his most resonant stage moment. Putting on his anti-Communist play *Thieves' Paradise* at LA's El Patio Theater in April of 1948, Fagan appeared onstage after the conclusion of the show. Two years before Joe McCarthy would use the same ploy, Fagan raised a piece of paper over his head.

"Here in my hand I hold a list of names," the playwright said. Everyone on the list was an "outright red," Fagan said, then proceeded to read the names, which he arranged alphabetically "just so that they won't feel slighted by the billing." Starting with Larry Adler, the list went through

Burt Lancaster, Vincent Price, Frank Sinatra, Orson Welles, to Jane Wyatt. Now a far more powerful Hollywood figure than he'd ever been as a writer or producer, Fagan became a go-to source for the House Un-American Activities probe into the entertainment industry.

"I met Myron Fagan in 1967 at a party at Mae West's house," Anthony Hilder told me as a line of scantily clad roller skaters passed by on the Pacific Palisades. "Mae and I were great friends for years. . . . She used to tell me to stay in school, that the sex education was simple, only the homework was hard." Hilder chuckled.

By the Summer of Love, Myron Fagan, past eighty, his work now unabashedly racist and anti-Semitic—in a 1965 tract, *How Greatest White Nations Were Mongrelized, then Negroized!*, he continually referred to "Martin Lucifer King Jr."—was a largely despised relic of the plague years. But Hilder didn't see it that way. "To me, he was a historical figure. He had a lot of knowledge, unique experience. I thought it should be preserved."

Hilder convinced Fagan, whom he described as being "like nails," to come over to his surf music studio to record his views for posterity. The result was the aforementioned three-LP package, *The Illuminati and the Council on Foreign Relations.* Spread over six sides and more than two and a half hours, Fagan, his voice like a blackboard screech, unveils the history of the Illuminati from its start, tracing how Adam Weishaupt, "born a Jew" turned "Jesuit-trained professor," came to embrace "the Luciferian Conspiracy."

It is all there, deception by deception, one stab in the back after another, up to the present day. What is surprising about Fagan's history is how little it has changed over the past half century. Myron Fagan's story of the Illuminati is *the story*, the version that has been feverishly cut-and-pasted on the net since the invention of the PC, the same version you can hear among booksellers of 125th Street where the old LPs can still be found. It was the same story accepted both by Prodigy and by Bill Cooper (who called Fagan's work "monumental"), the one that remains posted on the *Hour of the Time* website to this day.

Asked about the odd staying power of his 1967 recording, Anthony Hilder, whose other work includes videos *Illuminazi 9-11* and *Malthusian-Minded Men of the New World Order*, said, "There is no revisionism in truth."

By the early 1990s, when everyone in creation was listening to Dr. Dre's *The Chronic* on a near-permanent loop, Hilder, still in the recording business, was looking to get into rap music. He was cutting items like "Ordo Ab Chao," which is Latin for "Order Out of Chaos," the motto of 33rd-degree Scottish Rite Freemasonry. "Depression, inflation. Create the panic, then rape the nation," Hilder rapped, at least as good as Warren Beatty in *Bulworth*.

"I was with this this guy, Afrika Islam . . . I don't remember his real name," Hilder recalled, speaking of the former Charles Glenn, one of the more illustrious of New York's early hip-hop figures. Beginning as a ten-year-old rapper with Harlem's Rock Steady Crew and then moving over to Afrika Bambaataa's Soulsonic Force, Afrika Islam was producing Ice-T's records by the time he was twenty, including the controversial "Cop Killer."

"Afrika Islam and I," Hilder said. "We went to this club downtown. The Grand Slam . . . I think Prince owned a piece of it . . . I look around, and there's this big picture with the cover of Bill Cooper's book . . . *Behold a Pale Horse*! It was hanging on the wall, like in a museum. Fourteen feet high. I was floored. I told Bill about it, called him while he was on the air."

"It was amazing, Bill," the pre-stroke Hilder told Cooper excitedly. "You look at the walls and there are pictures, slide projections, of the cover of *Behold a Pale Horse*. Your book, Bill—it is popular among Muslims, black Muslims. They hate whitey . . . they're reading your book."

He told Cooper about a visit to the Moulin Rouge Hotel in Vegas. "A black hotel. I went up with Afrika Islam and John Henderson, who was a member of the Crips." Two years before, Henderson was out on the street "looting and robbing," selling dope on the corner since he was nine. "I asked him what turned him around; he said reading *Behold a Pale Horse*."

Did Cooper realize what this meant, Hilder wanted to know. "We are now getting together for the first time. It is happening, now. We're seeing a turnaround." All black people wanted, Hilder told Cooper, was "what everyone did, to be respected, have authority over their lives, gain their place in the sun, which they deserve."

Now, however, Hilder said, by reading *Behold a Pale Horse*, blacks were beginning to realize that it wasn't "The White Man" they hated. It was "white men, *particular white men*—the same white men who were the enemy of all people, black or white." The news couldn't get any bigger than that.

"Bill . . . you are becoming a cult figure," Hilder said.

Cooper stopped Hilder there. "Don't use the word *cult*." He laughed, clearly trying to play down Hilder's accolades.

"I'm serious. You shouldn't be embarrassed about this, Bill," Hilder implored. "Your book is becoming a household word, a sort of Bible of the New World Order investigators in the black community. Farrakhan is putting it out."

Cooper interrupted. "Do you think this is a flash in the pan?" Hilder didn't think so. It was real.

Cooper was amazed, thrilled at the part *Behold a Pale Horse* was playing in what could be the key to exorcising the demons of race that had set the nation against itself, that still ravaged the society.

"Are people finally beginning to realize how much we've been manipulated?" Cooper asked Hilder. "Are people finally coming around to the fact that we don't have to hate each other?"

PART SEVEN

Patriots

18

Life would take a turn for Bill Cooper on the Sunday morning of February 28, 1993. That was when, shortly after dawn, a column of government vehicles stretching nearly a half mile began to move across the Brazos River country of central Texas. A collection of military equipment that would eventually grow to include seven Bradley armored personnel carriers, four fifty-four-ton Combat Engineer Vehicles, two M1 Abrams battle tanks, and numerous Black Hawk helicopters. This convoy was headed up by two large cattle trailers.

Inside each of the cattle trailers, concealed by a plastic tarp, were approximately eighty agents of the federal Bureau of Alcohol, Tobacco and Firearms (BATF), outfitted in SWAT team gear. The BATF group was heading to the Mount Carmel Center, in Waco, Texas, where 125 Branch Davidians, 43 of them children, lived along with their leader, the thirty-three-year-old David Koresh.

Under the rubric of what usually qualifies as an apocalyptic religious cult, the Branch Davidians presented a convincing pedigree. The group traced its roots to the Millerites of upstate New York, part of the Second Great Awakening that swept through nineteenth-century America. After much biblical calculation, the pastor William Miller and his associates set October 22, 1844, as the likely date for the Second Coming. Thousands gathered in Miller's camp to await the dawn of the good news. When the appointed day passed without incident—known as "The Great Disappointment"—the Millerites split into many factions. Among these were the Seventh-day Adventists, who established a formidable presence under the leadership of their prophetess, Ellen G. White. In 1929, Victor Houteff, a Bulgarian immigrant who had been "disfellowshipped" by the

Adventists over doctrinal issues, moved with his followers to Waco, Texas, where they established the Mount Carmel Center.

Now calling for the reestablishment of the "Davidic Kingdom," the group renamed themselves the Davidian Seventh-day Adventist Church, attracting as many as 100,000 adherents over the years. When the church splintered in 1959 following an incorrect prediction of the world's end by Victor Houteff's widow, Florence, the Mount Carmel Center fell into the control of Benjamin Roden, a former Oklahoma oil-field worker, who called his new church the Branch Davidians.

Vernon Wayne Howell, who would become David Koresh, arrived at Mount Carmel in 1982. Born to a fourteen-year-old mother, beaten by his alcoholic stepfather, handed off to grandparents at age four, sexually assaulted at age eight, Howell, a dyslexic high school dropout, at twenty-two, took up with Benjamin Roden's widow, Lois, then in her midsixties, who'd become the Branch Davidian prophetess after her husband's death in 1978.

It was during this relationship that Lois Roden, a strong believer in the equality of the sexes, who described the Holy Spirit as "a silver angel, shimmering in the night. It was a feminine representation of this angel," decided that Howell was the long-awaited "seventh angel" of Branch Davidian doctrine, the king who would produce a generation of chosen children who would lead the members of the sect to heaven.

This prophecy was disputed by Roden's aggrieved, violence-prone son, George. It was bad enough that a vagabond hustler like Howell was screwing his mother, but now she was handing the interloper the spiritual leadership of the group, a mantle George believed was rightly his. The two men clashed, setting off a near-decade-long, often bloody feud. For a period of time, Howell and his supporters were routed from the Mount Carmel Center, the axis mundi of the Branch Davidian universe. Likening themselves to the Jews in Babylonian exile, for two years Howell and his small flock lived in tents, cooking on camp stoves, in and around Palestine, Texas.

After gathering new followers, largely from the United Kingdom and the Caribbean, Howell attempted to reclaim Mount Carmel. In response, George Roden challenged him to a test of spiritual power. He dug up a twenty-year-old corpse and placed it in a casket inside the Mount Carmel chapel. A true holy man should be able to raise the dead, Roden said, challenging his rival to do so. Declining this challenge, Howell instead called the Waco police in an attempt to get Roden arrested for disturbing the dead. When this failed, Howell, along with eight of his followers, attacked Roden's group, leading to a forty-five-minute gun battle. Even though the only injury was a bullet wound to one of Roden's fingers, Howell was arrested on attempted murder charges. The case resulted in a mistrial. It was only after Roden's subsequent conviction on an unrelated murder charge that Howell, now calling himself David Koresh, was able to gain full control of the seventy-seven-acre Mount Carmel property.

This was one side of the Waco incident. On the other was the federal Bureau of Alcohol, Tobacco, and Firearms.

The BATF lives in the minds of many as the armed collection agency of the US Treasury Department, descendants of flinty-eyed revenuers who busted up hillbilly stills. Once they were Eliot Ness's Untouchables, jailing bootleggers and mobsters; now they just came for your guns.

In early 1993, the BATF said there was a big problem over at Mount Carmel. The Branch Davidians were in violation of firearms laws. The church, which supported itself by buying and selling weapons at gun shows, had allegedly received a number of M16 carbine "kits" capable of modifying consumer-grade AR-15 semiautomatic rifles into fully automatic machine guns. This was against the law.

The gun charges were part of a lengthy search warrant that also alleged the Davidians were harboring illegal aliens. Most shocking, however, were accounts from former members of the group who claimed that Koresh had gone insane with spiritual entitlement and had "married" several underage women, some as young as eleven, which made him guilty of serial statutory rape.

The feds could likely have picked up Koresh during his solitary jogs along the Double Ee Ranch Road, but the agency had decided to go big, enacting what they called a "dynamic entry" at the Mount Carmel compound. Seeking favorable coverage, the BATF leaked information about their plan, which they called Operation Showtime, to the local news media.

This stratagem backfired when Jim Peeler, a cameraman for Waco's KWTX-TV, got lost on his way to cover the scene. By chance, Peeler stopped David Jones, a US mail carrier, to ask for directions. "Something" was going to happen with a "religious group" over at Mount Carmel, Peeler told Jones as the two men heard the distant rumble of helicopter engines.

"Are those helicopters?" a suddenly agitated Jones asked before jumping in his car and driving away. Jones, it turned out, was David Koresh's brother-in-law and went immediately to Mount Carmel, where he warned of the feds' approach. Jones would never leave the compound, perishing in the fatal fire.

Despite realizing they'd lost the essential element of surprise, the BATF commanders decided to go ahead with their plan regardless, a decision a Treasury Department report on the matter called "flawed."

It has never been established who fired the first shot. According to the BATF, the Branch Davidians fired through the compound's front door at them as soon as they approached the building. The church members told a different story. They said that the BATF agents first killed their dogs, and when Koresh himself appeared in the doorway, shouting, "We have women and children in here; let's talk," he was met with a volley of bullets.

The battle began after that, at about 9:45 A.M. It continued for the better part of the next two hours, the longest mass shoot-out in American law enforcement history. When a cease-fire was finally negotiated shortly before noon, ten people—four BATF officers and six Branch Davidians—were dead. Another twenty federal agents had been wounded, along with an unknown number of Branch Davidians, including Koresh, who was shot in the left hip and wrist.

That was the beginning of the fifty-one-day siege of Waco, an event that for many, Bill Cooper included, would signal a state of war between the American government and its people.

Days went by before Cooper commented on the Waco situation. Even as the feds shut off the Branch Davidians' heat and electricity, blasted Nancy Sinatra's "These Boots Are Made for Walking," and shined floodlights into the windows of the compound all night long, Cooper was silent. Instead of offering commentary on an event that became a key symbol in the coalescing worldview of much of his listenership, Cooper continued the rollout of his *Mystery Babylon* series, airing hours of lectures on

Knights Templar banking practices and the rise of European Freemasonry.

When Cooper finally addressed Waco on March 25, the twenty-sixth
day of the siege, he said, "We have refrained from commenting on the
debacle in Waco, Texas, until tonight. . . . We knew the federal government was lying. We knew the FBI was lying. We knew the BATF was
lying. We were waiting for facts."

Now, Cooper said, "we've got some things to give you on Waco,
Texas, ladies and gentlemen. Some things that are going to make you
sick, things that are going to jar you awake, because if you're one of those
people who said, 'Oh, that *cult* . . . they probably deserve exactly what
they're getting . . . they should all be shot,' then you should be ashamed.
You should hide from the rest of the world because you were wrong. You
were a stupid, stupid, miserable sheeple. Just as you will always be when
you make judgments like that about other people."

Grimly, Cooper recounted what had "really happened" when the
BATF arrived at the door of the Mount Carmel Center on the morning of
February 28. "Three buses pulled up to the compound during a religious
service; children were in the nursery," Cooper narrated. "These three buses
had over one hundred members of SWAT teams, anti-terrorist units of the
BATF crouched, hiding on the floors." It was true, Cooper said, that the
feds could have gotten Koresh anytime. "He came into Waco every week,
sat at the same table.

"But that's not what they wanted, folks, not at all," Cooper said, telling how the SWAT teams rushed out from the buses "and stormed the
compound. . . . They threw a gas grenade in the children's nursery, then
fired blindly and killed a two-year-old child. *Killed a two-year-old
child!* . . . Then they opened fire with a machine gun and literally cut a
six-year-old child in half." This information came "from people directly
on the scene . . . You will not hear this from the regular media, or from
anybody else."

The events at Mount Carmel were "abhorrent, disgusting," Cooper
said, disclosing how machine-gun-carrying BATF men approaching the
Branch Davidian nursery were stopped by a pair of seventy-year-old
women who defended the babies by shooting back, wounding two of the
agency cops.

"Two old women, scared to death!" Cooper exclaimed. "These cowardly creeps, these traitors who are supposed to be protecting us, these *brave government men* who thought they were going to take this place by storm, were beaten back by two seventy-year-old women.

"Then they call for a truce to gather up their dead and wounded. And these so-called terrorists, these cultists inside the church, let them do it. But when the church members asked for medical supplies to treat their own wounded—guess what. *They were denied!* They were told no medical treatment for you. No medical supplies. No food. No water. No nothing."

The media coverage was an exercise in robotic sensationalism; the "cult" needed to be stopped, period. But anyone who bothered to do his research knew that this attack was part of a long chain of events, with roots that stretched back centuries. This was why it was a shame he hadn't been able to play the entire *Mystery Babylon* series before the siege began, Cooper told the audience. You could never understand the present unless you knew the past.

The immediate antecedent was clear to anyone who remembered Ruby Ridge. The story began in the middle 1980s when Randy Weaver, a former Vietnam-era Special Forces officer, looked up from his job assembling John Deere tractors, each exactly like the others, and wondered exactly what the hell he was doing with his life. Weaver's wife, Vicki, was deeply impressed by Hal Lindsey's best-selling Christian end-of-the-world book, *The Late Great Planet Earth,* and felt they should move away from the corrupted world of their Iowa upbringing.

The Weavers found direction in Mark 13:14, in which the apostle quotes Jesus Christ as saying, "When ye shall see the abomination of desolation . . . let them that be in Judaea flee to the mountains." They took all their savings, about $5,000, traded in their truck, and bought twenty acres of land, where they built their own home on the sweetly named Ruby Ridge in a remote section of northern Idaho favored by survivalists, homeschoolers, tax protesters, "sovereign citizens," neo-Nazis, and Klansmen. The first time Vicki saw the property, she said it was "just what the Lord showed."

The trouble began in 1989, after Weaver sold some illegally modified shotguns to a biker named Gus Magisano, whom he'd met at a rally for the white supremacist Aryan Nations group. Magisano turned out to be Ken Fadeley, a BATF informant. Given the choice of facing charges or acting as a government snitch in the local militia scene, Weaver refused to cooperate. Feeling he could not get a fair shake in the federal justice system, he took refuge in his home on Ruby Ridge.

Cooper picked up the narrative from there on *The Hour of the Time,* describing how one afternoon, Weaver, his fourteen-year-old son, Samuel, and friend Kevin Harris heard the dogs barking. "The dogs set off through the woods, yapping and baying as if they were chasing a deer or elk. Being poor people, that sounded like food on the table to them," Cooper said with a *Boys' Life* tone, which quickly darkened.

As Samuel Weaver went into woods he knew and trusted, Cooper said, "He ran into some men in camouflage dress, no insignias, no badges, no nothing. These men starting shooting the dogs. Randy Weaver's son screamed, 'You're shooting my dogs. You're *killing my dogs.*' He shot at the men, because he didn't know if he was next.

"The men returned fire," Cooper continued, describing how the first bullet nearly ripped Randy Weaver's son's arm from its socket. Then the boy was fatally hit in the spine. "A fourteen-year-old boy, shot in the back."

Cooper continued, telling how "five hundred agents of the federal government" massed around Randy Weaver's cabin, the way FBI sniper Lon Horiuchi shot Vicki Weaver "right between the eyes" as she held her "eight-month-old baby in her arms."

"That was life for Randy Weaver in the next week," Cooper said: holed up in his cabin, refusing to give in, his dead wife lying on the floor, his dead son out in the yard, his young daughters by his side. Even after all that, the feds were not satisfied, Cooper said. They flew a helicopter over the cabin, attempting to "drop a fuel bladder on Randy Weaver's home and burn everyone inside to a crisp."

And what had Randy Weaver done to deserve such treatment? Cooper demanded to know. He'd sold a gun that was too short. That was a misdemeanor as far as he knew, Cooper said. "We don't kill people for misdemeanors in this country . . . at least until now." Ruby Ridge was "a shock test" for what was happening now at Waco. "They needed to see if they could get away with it," Cooper said. "To see if anybody would care, if anyone would do anything to stop it."

For those who didn't know what a shock test was, Cooper told them to get a copy of *Behold a Pale Horse*. It was right there in the first chapter, "Silent Weapons for Quiet Wars." A shock test was meant to determine exactly how much stress a person, a group, a whole society could take before cracking, what they were willing to put up with to maintain the delusion that everything was normal, basically okay.

Randy Weaver was a marginal, easily expendable individual, just one more fundamentalist gun nut in the boonies. No one, at least no one who "counted," cared about Randy Weaver. You weren't going to hear a great "rising voice" of outrage about what happened to Randy Weaver and his family, Cooper said.

Waco was the logical next step, a raising of the ante. Here was a bunch of antisocial marginalists, a sagebrush version of the black radical group MOVE, which was firebombed by the police in Philadelphia in 1985.

Cooper had a bad feeling about what was going to happen at Waco. The first hint was the media chatter about potential mass suicide, as if Koresh and his people had entered into some death pact. It was the old Kool-Aid narrative, the way the crazed Jim Jones and 909 members of his Peoples Temple had killed themselves in the Guyana jungle in 1978.

Fifteen years later, the memory was still fresh. There were some similarities: Like Jones's group, Mount Carmel was an integrated congregation; more than a third of the members were of African descent. Others were from England, Australia, and New Zealand. They spoke several different languages, like the doomed believers in the Guyanese jungle.

Once the word *cult* came into the story, the fix was in. "That's what we're hearing about, ladies and gentlemen," Cooper said during his first Waco broadcast. "That this *cult* is getting ready to commit *mass suicide*. This is what they're telling us. In the newspapers, on the six o'clock news. Dan Rather said it: 'These people are going to commit *mass suicide*.'"

Cooper belittled the idea. "Well, folks, even if these people are planning on committing mass suicide, there's nothing in federal law that prevents it," he said. Suicide was not under federal jurisdiction. If the feds truly believed in such a possibility, Cooper said, "they should have notified the local authorities, who would have sent down the local district attorney or the chief of police, or maybe just a patrol car, who would have dropped by and asked, 'Hey, fellas. What are you guys up to? We heard you're going to commit *mass suicide*. That true?'

"Ladies and gentlemen. Ask yourself. If they were going to commit mass suicide, why haven't they done it yet? Especially in face of what's happening to them now? They have the weapons in there that they need to do it. If they were going to poison themselves, they have that, too."

The fact was, Cooper said, the Branch Davidians were not planning on committing mass suicide. That was the last thing they wanted to do. They were doing something that the federal government and the elite mass media never imagined a bunch of religious nuts way out in the sticks could ever do, Cooper said. "They are acting on *principle*.

"This is about religion, belief, about Christians who own weapons and who are prepared to oppose the New World Order," Cooper declared. "The people inside that compound are not stupid; they don't have to listen to my radio show to know something like this might happen to them. . . . They *knew* this day would come because of who they are.

"That is the plan, ladies and gentlemen," Cooper told the audience, explaining how each successful "shock test" would lead to another, each bigger than the last, with more people murdered just the way Vicki and Samuel Weaver had been. "Soon, government agents are not going to be content to lay siege and wait for the people to come out. They will literally destroy the compound and everyone in it. Wipe them all out because that's really what they would like to do . . . *massacre them*."

That was it, the frightful conclusion Cooper's research had revealed to him. It was going to happen, sooner or later. The fact that no one else could see what was about to transpire at Waco pushed Cooper into a palpable anguish.

"I don't know why I am fighting this battle for so many people who are so stupid that they can't put two and two together and come up with four on a consistent basis," he despaired. "It makes me want to stop. It makes me want to take my family somewhere away from all of you and all of this and have the best time we possibly can in the time we have remaining. I get so angry, emotion swells up in my chest—and then I'm interrupted by my little daughter. She crawls up into my lap, wanting to know, what's wrong, Poppy? Then, it all goes away and I find myself right back here at this console again. . . .

"These people are going to become heroes and martyrs, folks," Cooper said. "*Heroes and martyrs.* For they are the only ones who, knowing they are within their rights and having broken no laws, have had the guts to stand up to the encroaching powers of the despotic socialist totalitarian New World Order. And this is just the beginning . . . *just the beginning.*"

After that, eight hundred miles from Waco in his Arizona studio, Cooper spoke directly to the Branch Davidians in their blood-splattered church, where they were tending to their wounded children in the dark, heatless bunker.

"If you are listening, those of you held prisoner, surrounded by agents of the BATF, the FBI, military units in armored vehicles . . . if you are listening, you are an inspiration to millions of Americans. You may have not been told that, but you are hearing it tonight."

And then, like a lone deejay in the wilderness, Cooper said, "For the church known as the Branch Davidian, this is for you," and played "Amazing Grace."

With the FBI now in charge at Waco, replacing the overmatched BATF, Cooper continued to cover the events on *The Hour of the Time.* He'd quickly consolidated his talking points. Now the church people, who had "committed no crime and broken no law," were officially installed as "a small group of Americans exercising their First and Second Amendments rights to free speech, freedom of religion, and to bear arms."

In his role as the director of the Citizens Agency for Joint Intelligence, Cooper continued to anchor the *Hour of the Time* coverage from his Arizona studio, doing extensive phone interviews with patriot-friendly correspondents on the scene. One of these was Gary Hunt, a land surveyor from Orange County, Florida, who had temporarily shut his business to chronicle the Waco siege for his newsletter, *The Outpost of Freedom.* Asked why he was in Waco, Hunt said, "because I felt something that would significantly alter the course of American history for some time was under way."

Together, Cooper and Hunt attempted to suss out the governmental thinking behind the BATF attack. "They probably picked Sunday morning because they knew everyone would be in a prayer meeting or Bible reading," Hunt said. As for why the assault was so elaborate, he continued, "the only logical conclusion I can come to is that this was a training exercise for what they intend to be doing all over the country." The presence of 100 to 120 troops amounted to "one giant on-the-job training experience, how to break down doors and arrest a large amount of people with a massive force."

Agreeing with Cooper's shock-test analysis, Hunt said, "Ruby Ridge was about a small family; it was lost in the press." But Waco was different. It was on the scale of Lexington and Concord in 1775. "The British have come. And the defenders are standing there," Hunt said.

"I firmly believe," Cooper said, "that if two or three million real Americans encircle the compound, stand there very quietly and unarmed, the siege would be lifted." But Gandhi-like civil disobedience was not the American way, even if you could get so-called patriots to do anything real when they could just gas off on talk shows.

Hunt agreed. Soon after first learning about what was going on in Waco, he'd heard there were "two to five hundred" patriots on the scene. But when he got there, there were fewer than a hundred. A proposal to pitch tents in between the feds and the Mount Carmel defenders would have sent a strong patriot message, Hunt said. Originally "about twenty people" were for it. But when the number dropped to "two or three," the plan was abandoned.

Cooper sighed. That was the way it was when it came to "the real nitty-gritty." So many sheeple were "willing to send their sons and daughters off to die in the Sahara Desert or some such place in the Middle East, so George Bush and all the other oil people can keep getting rich. But when it comes to standing up and defending the nation for real, they melt into the night."

For the duration of the siege, the "facts" turned up by Cooper's crack CAJI team proved a mixed bag. One account had the feds sending in containers of milk for the Branch Davidian children to drink. It was supposed to be a goodwill measure, but like the smallpox-infected blankets given to the Native Americans by European invaders, much of this milk was poisoned, Cooper said. Two church youngsters had died from drinking it. There was no truth to this claim, but Cooper kept repeating it.

Cooper was also off target when he said that David Koresh, was "a Christian. . . . He believes in having only one wife, in a monogamous marriage. He has two children from that one wife." All the craziness about Koresh having "six or seven wives and twenty-three or twenty-four children . . . that is a lie," Cooper assured listeners. "He has one wife and two children and does not, *does not,* play around on his wife."

While it was technically true that Koresh had only one legal wife, Rachel Jones, whom he married in 1984, he did have multiple spouses, perhaps as many as twenty. Koresh's polygamy started in 1986, at the Branch Davidian celebration of Passover, when he took Karen Doyle, thirteen years old at the time, as his second wife. In 1986, he married two more women, Rachel Jones's younger sister, Michele, and Robyn Bunds, both of them underage.

This was in accordance with Koresh's "New Light Revelation" announced in 1989. Koresh, a spindly, stringy-haired man usually pictured wearing aviator-style glasses, declared that *all* women in the group were his "spiritual wives" and would bear only his children. Koresh was now the lone male in the group who was allowed to have sex. All the other men, their marriages dissolved by Koresh, were to take an oath of celibacy.

Koresh justified this grotesque setup (many of the Branch Davidian males left during this period, which might have been the intention to begin with) by citing his vaunted ability to interpret the Bible, which he viewed as a puzzle of infinite pieces, the singular truth of which could be "decoded" only through the mix and match of seemingly unrelated passages.

For the New Light Revelation, Koresh paired Psalm 45, verses 14–16, which describes how "thy fathers shall be thy children . . . princes in all the earth," with Revelation 14: 1–4, John's account of seeing "the Lamb, standing on Mount Zion, and with him 144,000 who had his name and his Father's name written on their foreheads."

Herein lay the path to heaven, Koresh contended. It was only through his seed as the "seventh angel" appointed by Lois Roden that Branch Davidians could find the "twenty-four princes on the twenty-four thrones" who would produce the 144,000 people who would ascend to the Kingdom of Heaven.

"There's only one hard-on in this whole universe that really loves you," Koresh reportedly said as he separated the other Branch Davidian children from his own. His were "the first fruit" or "God's grandchildren," said Koresh, who enjoyed taking his brides for a spin in his beloved Camaro, which the feds would smash flat with their M-1 Abrams battle tanks.

In the first days of the siege, twenty-one children left the compound even though their parents remained inside. When asked to send out the rest of the kids, Koresh refused. "We're dealing with *my* children now . . . my biological children . . . my children are different than the other children."

Now a devoted husband and father, Cooper was appalled by Koresh's scheme to repopulate the planet with his own Noah-like seed, but talking-point-wise, this took a back seat to the Branch Davidians' status as modern-day American freedom fighters.

In the struggle against *Mystery Babylon*, David Koresh cut an odd but compelling figure. For starters, there was his *nom de guerre spirituelle*, Koresh. Described in the Book of Isaiah 45:1 as "his anointed one" or "messiah," Koresh was Hebrew for Cyrus the Great, King of Persia, whose armies had defeated the Babylonians at the Battle of Opis in 539 BC. The victory signaled the end of the Jews' decades-long Babylonian Captivity during which many of their leaders and scholars had been taken prisoner following the destruction of Jerusalem and Solomon's Temple by King Nebuchadnezzar II.

In his Bible classes, some of which went as long as eighteen hours, David Koresh often centered on the major prophets of the Babylonian Captivity—Daniel, Ezekiel, Jeremiah, and Isaiah—whose voices represent an apex of scriptural literature. Emphasis on the exiled prophets was in the tradition of the earlier Davidians. Both Victor Houteff and Lois Roden placed great importance upon Ezekiel's ninth chapter, in which the prophet tells the story of Jerusalem's fall and the subsequent enslavement of God's Chosen People.

In Ezekiel's account, the defeat of the Jews has little to do with Nebuchadnezzar's military superiority; the real drama is about the covenant between the Jewish people and their God. Yet again, Yahweh has been angered by the failure of the Jews to keep his faith, charging that many of the Chosen People have fallen into "abominations." As Hasidic rabbis would later say about the Nazi holocaust, the Babylonian army was portrayed as merely the tool of God's vengeance upon his wayward people.

As federal forces surrounded Mount Carmel in what Bill Cooper described as "Mystery Babylon laying siege to America," David Koresh often read from the writings of Jeremiah, who is known as "the weeping prophet," in no small part due to his apparent reluctance to carry God's message.

It is Jeremiah (*jeremiad* is derived from his name) alone who has the temerity to question the Lord of the universe. In Jeremiah 19–20, passages often cited by Koresh, the prophet, after despairing at the Lord's delight in bringing "such disaster upon this place that the ears of everyone who hears it will tingle," offers this stunning rebuke: "O Lord, thou hast deceived me, and I was deceived. Thou art stronger than I, and hast prevailed: I am in derision daily, every one mocketh me. . . . I cried violence and spoil; because the word of the Lord was made a reproach unto me, and a derision, daily." Yet Jeremiah's complaint will come to nothing. Like all men, he longs for freedom but cannot achieve it. Just as there is no escape from God, it is equally impossible to toss off the burden of being His prophet. As Jeremiah says, the Lord's work lives in his heart as if it were "a burning fire shut up in my bones" (Jeremiah 20:9).

Jeremiah is the most modern of the Captivity prophets in that he feels the terror of the moment on a personal level as opposed to a communal one. He is in many ways a contemporary paranoiac, which may be why his work is often more vivid in more recent versions of the Bible, i.e., the kind they used to advertise on late-night TV.

Rather than the poetics of the King James Version, Jeremiah's key complaint (Jeremiah 20:10) gets a more straightforward translation in the Tree of Life Version (published 2005 in Rome, Georgia): "For I heard the whispering of many. '"Terror on every side." Denounce him! Let's denounce him!' Even all my close friends are watching for my fall: 'Perhaps he may be deceived, so we'll get the better of him and we'll get our revenge on him.'"

Here is the prophet's persecution complex at work, the gnawing distrust of the inmate serving a life sentence in a global panopticon where the harsh deity sees everything and everyone with his all-seeing, unforgiving eye. It is also the lament of the exile, a man apart from his roots. Indeed, few works evoke the sorrow of homesickness as well as Psalm 137 in the Septuagint, the Greek translation of the Old Testament, which is signed "for David, by Jeremiah, the Captivity."

Psalm 137 wasn't anything David Koresh had to open a Bible to find. He knew of it from his itinerant teenage years, being passed from home to home, flophouse to flophouse, taking solace practicing Black Sabbath riffs on his guitar, back when he believed being a rock star, preferably in Spandex, would be his true ministry. By his late teens, Koresh was a Bob Marley fan, with more than passing interest in the singer's Rastafarian faith, which he later discussed with Livingston Malcolm, a Jamaica-born Branch Davidian (killed in the fire) who was a nephew of Cedella Booker, Marley's mother.

To the Rastas, "Mystery Babylon" was not just a biblical reference. "Babylon" was an all-consuming modern metaphor for the cancer eating away at the soul of the planet. The Rastaman says there are two main states of being: "I-tal" is the state of spiritual harmony, the realm of the good. All the rest is, as put by Peter Tosh, Marley's onetime bandmate, "the Babylon Shit-stem." The tourist board called their island a vacation paradise, but they knew the truth. The palm trees, the turquoise waters, were merely an illusion of the Devil. In reality they were in jail, a deep and dark dungeon far from their true home.

The most eloquent reading of Psalm 137 comes from the Melodians, a Rastafarian trio who recorded the piece as "Rivers of Babylon" in 1970. Produced by the Chinese-Jamaican Leslie Kong, the Melodians' tune was a hit in the hothouse Kingston "sound system" scene and went worldwide after its inclusion in the score of the epochal 1973 Jamaican gangster drama, *The Harder They Come*. The song basically quotes Jeremiah's psalm, describing the lot of the captives trapped in Babylon, weeping for their home in Zion. When their overseers insist they sing, they ask, "How can we sing King Alpha's song in a strange land?"

A version of the song turns up on David Koresh's self-recorded album, *Songs for Grandpa* (the record, available on YouTube, also includes the tune "Mad Man in Waco"). Koresh's rendition, sung in his reedy voice accompanied by elliptical guitar stylings, is in many ways the opposite of the gospel sound expected from someone willing to die for the

Lord. But the essentials are there, the mournfulness of the cosmic chain gang, the melancholy chant of displacement.

As Cooper predicted, time was running out for David Koresh and his Branch Davidians. Following a number of unfulfilled promises from Koresh to lead his flock out of the compound, FBI patience had worn thin. Janet Reno, the first female US Attorney General, who had only been confirmed in the job in mid-March, after the beginning of the siege, was being pushed hard to give the go-ahead to remove the Branch Davidians from Mount Carmel.

Koresh dug in. In a video made by Branch Davidians, he sits on the floor in a bloody T-shirt. "I don't care who they are. Nobody is going to come to my home, with my babies around, shaking guns around without getting a gun back in their face. That's just the American way," he said.

Then, on April 14, the forty-fifth day of the siege, Koresh sent the FBI a message. He'd been waiting for instructions from God before acting. Now that message had been received. His plan was audacious, the act of a spiritual Houdini. Koresh was going to unlock the Seven Seals of Revelation, crack open the code of the most secret of documents. When the contents of the Seals were first revealed to John of Patmos, they were represented as events that "must shortly come to pass." That time had finally arrived. This was what the Lord had told him, Koresh said. As the namesake of Cyrus, conqueror of Babylon, he was being given "permission" to peek beyond the Seals' cover.

For weeks, as the feds had bombarded them with one torment after another, the Branch Davidians had remained calm, even oddly joyful. They called their embattled home "Rancho Apocalypse" (outside, the national media, under the impression that "nothing" was happening, called the press pen "Camp Boredom"). The alleged cultists playfully hung a series of gallows-humor banners outside the compound's second-story windows.

There was: THE MEDIA AND FBI DON'T KNOW THE TRUTH, THEY CAN'T HANDLE THE TRUTH. Also: BATF KILLED MY FAMILY AND FRIENDS, CAN WE STILL HAVE A FEW BEERS? And the particularly trenchant: RODNEY KING, WE UNDERSTAND.

The topic of the Seven Seals had come up in a phone interview Cooper did with Rita Riddle, a Branch Davidian who had survived the initial BAFT attack "by lying on the floor and holding the babies." Riddle said that back home in Asheville, North Carolina, when the topic of the Seven Seals came up, the preachers said, "That's not for us to know." What David Koresh said was, "It *is* for us to know," Riddle told Cooper.

Now that the Lord had authorized Koresh to expose the Seven Seals to the light of day, the Branch Davidians rejoiced. The horsemen would ride, the trumpets would blow, and Mystery Babylon would fall. The siege would be lifted, the BATF, the FBI, and the rest of the unclean world would disappear, their misguided molecules scattered away in the East Texas wind. The church members, faithful candidates for inclusion in the 144,000 bound for heaven, would walk out of Mount Carmel as totally free people.

Outside the walls, the State used other metrics to elucidate the standoff that had already cost several lives and untold dollars. As they saw it, Koresh, a punk-ass con man and child raper, had embarrassed them long enough. Now he was saying he wasn't bringing his deluded followers out until he opened the Seven Seals, which hadn't been opened for two thousand years, if ever. When the feds, many of them steady churchgoers, inquired when Koresh might finish his Seals exegesis, Steve Schneider, Mount Carmel's second-in-command, eschewed deadlines. "It might take six weeks, might take six years," Schneider said. That wasn't going to fly.

Like many Americans, Cooper watched the horror unfold on television. He saw the FBI's forty-eight-ton armored Combat Engineer Vehicles punch holes in the side of the Mount Carmel church, watched the authorities shoot 40mm CS grenades into the building, sat uncomprehending as the Branch Davidians unfurled one last plaintive demand from their second-story window. As Mystery Babylon's massive machinery crashed against Mount Carmel's walls, just as Nebuchadnezzar's evil horde once smashed the ramparts of Jerusalem, their banner read, WE WANT OUR PHONE FIXED.

The fire started around noon, on the far right side of the building. In the fresh wind, the place went up fast. The church burned to the ground in less than an hour, which is just about the time it took two trucks from the Waco Fire Department to finally arrive on the scene. Many of the bodies were found melted together in the concrete tornado bunker the Branch Davidians had used to store their gardening supplies.

Watching the fire left Cooper feeling "so angry, so upset, so emotionally distraught." The kicker was a statement by Bob Ricks, the FBI assistant special agent in charge. "David Koresh, we believe, gave the order to commit suicide, and they all followed the order," Ricks said.

Again, Cooper had been right, called it from the beginning. "Mass suicide" really meant "mass murder." And if anyone needed more proof that this was the next stage in a series of New World Order shock tests as described in "Silent Weapons for Quiet Wars," the FBI had brought in Lon Horiuchi, the same sniper who shot Vicki Weaver dead as she held her baby on Ruby Ridge.

Cooper wasn't about to gloat about his prediction. It made him sick. He could barely get out of bed. Truth be told, it is no great trick for a conspiracist like Bill Cooper to hit on a high number of predictions. Unlike the detective on the beat, tasked with finding the culprit, the conspiracist always knows who did it from the start. The Illuminati, the government, the CIA; there are any number of "theys" to pick from. The only hard part was figuring out who was going to be set up to take the blame.

Waco didn't fall into that category. It was too raw, too personal. All those children killed. And for what? Because their parents were sweetly dim enough to follow a loony horndog who made them an offer they could not refuse: to escape the humdrum of the work-unto-death existence offered by the system for an opportunity to live out a real-life Bible story, to ride the whirlwind of Revelation. It was too sad for words. These poor souls went with Koresh because he sold them heaven. Instead, Mystery Babylon gave them hell.

When he returned to *The Hour of the Time* on April 22, his first show after the fire, Cooper opened by saying, "America the Beautiful is no more . . . the second battle of the second American revolution just ended—and, folks—*we lost*."

During the siege, even before the fire, the unfolding disaster left Cooper frustrated and angry, but it also renewed his determination. Contrary to news reports, David Koresh never claimed to be the Second Coming of Christ. He was merely God's tool, a conduit between man and the heavens, a messenger. Cooper felt that he, too, was a kind of messenger, responsible to his flock. As such, it was imperative that he provide an answer, some insight, some background into the horrible events.

During that time, Cooper twice replayed the broadcast called "Creator-Endowed Rights." Recorded in 1992, the show is listed as the second *Hour of the Time* program in *The Complete Cooper*, following his WWCR debut. The program documents Cooper's central inquiry into what it means to be a free American. For Cooper, his long hours of research, plowing through Locke, de Tocqueville, Adam Smith, and the writings of the framers of the US Constitution, could be distilled to a few words found in the Declaration of Independence: the self-evident truth that all men are created equal, *endowed by their Creator with certain unalienable Rights* . . .

"Creator-endowed unalienable rights" was the unique idea that "changed the history of the world and made America great," Cooper explained to listeners. For thousands of years the head of state, be it "the king, the queen, the emperor, the sultan, the emir, or whoever happened to be sitting on the throne, claimed the divine right to rule," a status that essentially gave them "ownership of the subjects . . . the subjects being the people."

Creator-endowed unalienable rights were rights owed to the individual simply by virtue of being alive and doing no harm to his fellow citizen. "Unalienable rights are rights that cannot be alienable from man," Cooper told the audience. "He cannot contract to give them away, cannot sell them, cannot brush them aside or discard them . . . for they are given by the Creator and so cannot be taken away, *not even by yourself.*"

This was the genius of the Founding Fathers, the original makers of America, Cooper said. They declared divine right not to be simply for the king and queen but for the people at large. This is what made the American citizen "the first person to ever walk completely free on the face of this earth . . . a sovereign king in his own right, with the government as his servant."

It was so simple. The beauty of Creator-endowed unalienable rights was that you didn't have to believe in Yahweh, the Buddha, the Father, the Son, or the Seven Seals. You could believe in none of them. You could believe in all of them. As far as he was concerned, Cooper said, he was "a Christian." He believed in the words of Jesus Christ "written in red" in the Bible one might find in a motel room drawer. But as for what others believed, that was none of his business.

But there was one thing you had to do. You had to accept the idea that there was something in the universe that transcended the imperfections of man, and that this force, by its very existence, had conferred upon human beings rights that were unalienable. Against the humanist cult of Mystery Babylon, Creator-endowed unalienable rights were your only protection in a world that was out to get you at every turn. Without these rights, Cooper told the audience, "you are no better than the cockroach that scurries beneath your sink when you turn on the light at midnight."

In this context, the Waco situation was best illustrated in a much-told tale about Benjamin Franklin. As first recorded in the diary of James McHenry, a delegate from Maryland, the story went back to the final day of the Constitutional Convention in 1787. A crowd had gathered, anxious to hear the Founding Fathers' vision for the new nation. As Franklin, one of the most recognizable men in the country, was walking down the stairs of Independence Hall, he was approached by "a gentlewoman" by the name of Mrs. Powel.

"So, doctor," Mrs. Powel inquired of the great polymath of the Enlightenment, "what kind of government do we have?"

Franklin turned to Mrs. Powel and replied, "A Republic, if you can keep it."

It was a marvelous, yet endlessly vexing answer. The Republic, the government of laws, not the twisted will of flawed, power-mad people, was the exacting Ideal. The chances of maintaining the Republic were so slim that it is difficult to take Franklin's acerbic retort as anything but a dare. Indeed, considering that Benjamin Franklin was, as Cooper said, a deist, Freemason, and noted libertine who "only acted like a pious Christian when he was in the colonies," there was every chance that the notion of the Republic, along with the Constitution itself, was one more trick of the Devil, who loved to set impossible tasks for humanity just to watch them fail.

But that didn't mean a man couldn't try, it didn't mean the people who lived in the country shouldn't at least *attempt* to be Americans. To be an American was a crown of civilization, something everyone should strive for. The smoking ruins of Waco only proved, yet again, how difficult saving the Republic would be.

It certainly wasn't going to happen sitting on your ass, not at this late hour. It was going to take sacrifice, possibly even the ultimate sacrifice. Cooper knew where to place the blame for the debacle. It wasn't the Branch Davidians' fault. They had broken no constitutional laws. You couldn't even put it on the cops; they were just tools. Cooper's fury was mainly reserved for "the American people." Through sheer "laziness and stupidity," they'd done their best to give away the Republic, even tried to divorce themselves of their Creator-endowed rights, allowing the devils of Babylon to take over by default.

"You might fool yourself," Cooper snarled at the audience. "But you can never fool me. . . . Never, ever, try to get me to believe your fantasies and rationalizations. You are responsible." When the listeners found themselves enslaved by the One World Totalitarian Socialist Government, they'd better not come crying to him, Cooper seethed. "Because I will laugh at you. I will laugh right in your face."

Before the fire, Cooper said, he had been trying to arrange for a helicopter pilot "with balls" to fly him into Mount Carmel so he could interview the Branch Davidians. Now, after the disaster, he traveled to Waco with Annie and Pooh to see what, if anything, was left.

It was a dispiriting experience, Cooper reported somberly on his April 26 *Hour of the Time* broadcast. The Waco townspeople, another pathetic crew of Good Germans, were "not sad those people are dead. They just go about their business every day as if nothing has happened. They don't give a damn."

Cooper spoke of how he'd sat at Kelly's Bar, where the FBI and BATF thugs liked to drink. They were all there, "strutting around like little roosters . . . arrogant braggarts, proud of what they'd done," Cooper told the audience. Throughout the siege, the Branch Davidians had flown their royal blue flag over Mount Carmel. Now that everything was done, the BATF had raised the agency's standard over the ruins like a conquering army.

The politicians were no better, Cooper said, playing a tape of a speech by Pete Domenici, US senator from New Mexico. Koresh was "crazy," said Domenici, who was slated to sit on a congressional committee looking into the government conduct at Waco.

What happened at Mount Carmel was "not a suicide. Koresh and his gang committed murder," Domenici said, like the impartial arbiter he proposed to be. Bill Clinton, the Illuminati wonder boy himself, chimed in. Anyone who was considering joining a cult like the Branch Davidians should take what happened in Waco "as a warning," Cooper reported the president as saying.

Cooper told the audience about driving out to the Mount Carmel site. During the day, cops were everywhere; there were roadblocks at the intersection of farm road 2491 and the 340 Loop. The place was packed with sightseers and vendors selling buttons and bumper stickers.

"Everyone wants to see where the evil Jesus met his death," Cooper said. He called it "despicable, a carnival. . . . The rest of the world, I know, they're just shaking their heads at these stupid Americans."

At night, however, after the hucksters dispersed and the cops went home to their families, it was possible to get nearer the compound site, "close enough to take pictures with a strobe." The first thing that hits you, Cooper said, was something he remembered from his days on the Cua Viet River, "the smell of death . . . a sweet, sticky smell."

19

In the months following the Waco fire, Cooper often spoke about the looming conflict between the patriots who truly cared about the future of America and the Mystery Babylon cabal in charge of the United States government. Cooper wasn't spoiling for battle. He'd seen war, knew what it did to people, even the ones who imagined they'd come home in one piece.

To hear the loose talk bandied about in some of the so-called patriot groups, it was as if nothing had been learned from the shoot-outs of the 1980s. Among the most racist, violence-prone of these groups was CSA— the Covenant, the Sword, and the Arm of the Lord. Hunkered down in their Ozark "Combat City," hoarding apartheid-era gold Krugerrands and denouncing non-Aryan "mud people" and the Zionist Occupied Government (ZOG), CSA's membership included the infamous Richard Wayne Snell (1930–1995).

On November 3, 1983, Snell, son of a Church of the Nazarene pastor, walked into a Texarkana, Arkansas, pawn shop and killed the proprietor, William Stumpp, whom he incorrectly believed to be Jewish. Six months later, in De Queen, Arkansas, Snell murdered Louis P. Bryant, an African American state trooper who had stopped him for a minor infraction.

Snell also had the distinction of being among the first to research the alleged criminal lives of Bill and Hillary Clinton. Having heard that the CIA was using the Mena Intermountain Municipal Airport south of Fort Smith, Arkansas, as a drop point for illicit drugs, Snell surreptitiously filmed the airport traffic. He claimed to have footage of then-governor Bill Clinton and his wife, Hillary, standing on the tarmac overseeing the shipments. Long before the alleged murder of deputy

White House counsel Vince Foster, Whitewater, Pizzagate, and the rest, it was the first widely circulated Clinton conspiracy.

The most apocalyptic of the eighties "patriot" groups, however, was the Order, aka the Brüder Schweigen, or Silent Brotherhood. Their lead player was Robert Jay Mathews (1953–1984), who grew up in the Mormon Church and joined the John Birch Society at age eleven. By nineteen, he was leading militia-style training exercises in the Arizona desert. Further radicalized by reading works like Oswald Spengler's *The Decline of the West*, and *The Turner Diaries,* William Pierce's 1978 fever dream of Caucasian race salvation, Mathews sought to establish a separatist "White American Bastion" in the Pacific Northwest.

Separatism was a matter of racial survival, Mathews said in a speech delivered at the general conference of William Pierce's National Alliance in Arlington, Virginia, on September 4, 1983. The time had come to stand up against "the filthy lying Jews and their parasitical usury system," Mathews said. He then recited Ralph Waldo Emerson's *Concord Hymn*: "By the rude bridge that arched the flood, / Their flag to April's breeze unfurled, / Here once the embattled farmers stood / And fired the shot heard round the world."

Mathews told those assembled that he dreamed of the day Emerson's words would be rewritten to say: "Out of the valleys, out of the fields, poured the Aryan yeoman horde / Their flag to April's breeze unfurled / Thence the Aryan farmer came / And removed the Jew forever, forever from this world."

The resurrection of the yeoman farmer as "a living monument to American masculinity" would not be easy, Mathews said. "TV satellite dishes are springing up like poisonous mushrooms across the domain of the tillers of the soil. The electronic Jew is slithering into the living rooms of even the most remote farms and ranches. . . .

"I think that deep within the breast of our Aryan yeomanry lies a long-dormant seed," Mathews railed, attempting to rally the slumbering *Volk*. "The seed of a racial awakening. The seed of resurgence, the seed of anger, and the seed of the will to act."

Declaring themselves "the legions of the damned, the army of the already dead," the Order's year of helter-skelter began in October of 1983, when they stole $369 from an XXX adult bookstore in Spokane,

Washington. Soon they were knocking off banks and payroll offices. In Seattle, they robbed an armored car in a shopping mall, getting away with half a million in checks and cash. They used the proceeds to set up a nationwide counterfeiting ring.

The Order planned to assassinate Jewish show-business figures, whom they regarded as mind controllers, as dangerous as plutocrats like Paul Warburg and Jacob Schiff had ever been. The hit list reputedly included Jerry Lewis (née Levitch) and Norman Lear, producer of *All in The Family.* Colorado radio talk-show host Alan Berg did not have the fame of the other targets, but he was a Jewish loudmouth who delighted in ribbing white nationalists. He was also easy to locate. On June 18, 1984, Order members waited for Berg to return home from a trip to the supermarket and shot him dead in his driveway with a MAC-10 submachine gun.

A month later, Order members stopped a Brinks truck near Ukiah, California. They held up a sign that read GET OUT OR DIE and made off with more than $3.6 million, one of the largest such heists in history. Mathews gave $300,000 to the White Aryan Resistance and $50,000 to William Pierce to finance the writing of *Hunter,* a sequel to *The Turner Diaries.*

In November, set up by a supposedly trustworthy former Klansman, Mathews was ambushed by authorities at the Capri Motel in Portland, Oregon. Wounded, he managed to escape, retreating to a house he'd rented in the Puget Sound town of Freeland, Washington. On Pearl Harbor Day, 1984, seventy-five feds surrounded his house, demanding Mathews surrender. He refused, setting off a thirty-five-hour gun battle during which the Order leader fired more than a thousand rounds before the authorities set the house on fire with three M-79 Starburst flares. Mathews's body was found with his Brüder Schweigen medallion melted into his chest.

The Order's legacy was carried on by David Eden Lane (1938–2007). While serving a 190-year sentence for the Alan Berg murder, Lane became the Order's scribe/prophet, creator of the Fourteen Words, a neo-Nazi sacrament. Memorized by racists throughout the country, the less-than-poetic fourteen words are "We Must Secure the Existence of Our People and a Future for White Children." Lane also came up with the exhaustive 88 Precepts (88 = HH, as in *H*eil *H*itler), a spiritual framework for a pure racialist society that might well have sprung from the pen of Heinrich Himmler. When you hear someone say "14–88," they are quoting David Eden Lane.

Cooper made it clear from the start that he had no use for such hateful mayhem. People like Richard Wayne Snell and Robert Jay Mathews were exactly the opposite of patriots. They were madmen, killers, just the kind of plants the government would use to discredit any attempt to restore the constitutional republic. Likewise, Cooper had only contempt for figures like Robert G. Millar, who lived with twenty-five of his thirty-four grandchildren in Elohim City on the Arkansas–Oklahoma border. Millar and his group were believers in British Israelism, which is basic to the dogma of many so-called Christian Identity groups. As related by Cooper in a two-part show on *The Hour of the Time,* the British Israelites believed they were descended not from the primates of Africa or Abrahamic Jews, but rather from Seth, who, they said, was the only surviving white child of Adam and Eve, born as a replacement for Abel after he was murdered by Cain. Contrary to the account given in Genesis 4:9, Cain and Abel were not really brothers, the British Israelites preached. They were half brothers, Cain being the black child produced by a liaison between Eve and the serpent.

Seth was the true progenitor of the Israelites, who existed not, as commonly thought, in the Middle East but in northern Europe. They migrated to the British Isles, where they founded the House of David, eventually passing on this pure bloodline to the dynastic English kings. This fable of Empire, foisted on the conquered peoples of Africa and India by British colonizers back to Sir Francis Drake, was adopted by the backwoodsmen of Elohim City, who imagined themselves to be the fullest flower of God's people.

That story, Cooper told the audience, was "the biggest bunch of hogwash I ever heard in my entire life. These people are racist, completely mental," he told the audience, saying Christian Identity groups "might call themselves patriots, but they are not. They have no interest in restoring constitutional government. They are liars, lying to us."

Cooper was not a racist, nor was he anti-Semitic, he told the audience. One of his most famous broadcasts involved a thirty-five-year-old follower of William Pierce's National Alliance, who called in to bemoan the country's having been "taken over by the Jews." Young people had been fed "a lot of politically correct garbage by the Jewish-controlled media, all this crap about diversity and how we all have to come together and listen to rap music and have miscegenation," the caller complained. Didn't it bother Cooper that whites were an endangered species in the US? How did Cooper feel about his great-grandchildren having "dark skin and nappy hair"?

Cooper replied that he was married "to a Chinese woman from Taiwan." His children had Native American, English, Scotch, Irish, and Chinese blood in them. These were genetics he was going to be "very happy to send into the future." Little by little he wore the Nazi down, appealed to a better side of the guy that he possibly didn't even know existed. By the end, the separatist was subdued, thanking Cooper for giving him a whole new outlook on life. Cooper won the Nazi over.

Did this sound like the actions of an anti-Semite? Bill Cooper didn't think so. But that's what some people were calling him, tarring him as a Jew hater. It drove him crazy that supposedly liberal-minded groups like the Anti-Defamation League of B'nai B'rith and the Southern Poverty Law Center continued to lump him in with the Robert G. Millars of the world.

"The smear campaign," as Cooper called it, started when he had the temerity to include the *Protocols of the Wise Men of Zion* in *Behold a Pale Horse.* Now it was continuing, Cooper said, in the pages of *Omni* magazine, the now-defunct Bob Guccione (of *Penthouse*) compendium of sci-fi and futuristic tech reporting. This was particularly annoying because, according to Cooper's ex-wife Sally Phillips, *Omni* was Cooper's favorite magazine. "When it came in the mail, Bill sat down and read it cover to cover."

The article in question, published in the magazine's July 1993 edition, was a discussion of alleged anti-Semitism in the UFO community. The piece included the old Theosophist huckster/contactee George Adamski's description of riding in spaceships piloted by marvelous "Nordics," a handsome race of Aryan aliens. Then the *Omni* piece turned to a familiar figure, the nine-foot-tall "Risen Master," Gyeorgos Ceres Hatonn, the Commander in Chief, Earth Project Transition of Pleiades Flight Sector, whom Cooper had once threatened to sue for allegedly plagiarizing his

"MajestyTwelve" piece. From his vantage point above the firmament, Hatonn could tell that "the so-called Jews" were not the children of Israel but rather a band of imposters, "descendants of Khazars, a Mongolian nomadic tribe."

The reference to Cooper in the article was brief and relatively mild, basically just repeating the Protocols incident. Nonetheless, it was enough to provoke a typically outsize counterattack.

Opening his next show with Ray Charles's song "Don't Set Me Free," Cooper, his feelings clearly bruised, began by citing two newspaper articles, one each from the *New York Post* and *New York Daily News*. Stating, erroneously, that tabloids were "owned by Jews, published by Jews, and edited by Jews," Cooper quoted from one article noting that while officials of the victorious Red Army had once claimed that four million Jews had been killed at Auschwitz, the death count was now thought to be closer to a million and a half. The second article, from 1993, further revised the toll, saying "nearly a million" had been killed.

"First it's six million, then four million, then *nearly* a million," Cooper exclaimed, saying he was "sick and tired of having the Holocaust thrown in my face all the time." It wasn't his fault. He wasn't even born until 1943. He'd never knowingly hurt any Jew and certainly wasn't going to have "a big guilt complex" about what the Germans did.

Who appointed the Jews, this self-anointed Chosen People, as the arbiters of morality, anyway? "They didn't give a damn about Cambodia, where six million were killed," Cooper railed. They didn't care about the starving millions in Africa, or the genocide in Bosnia. He didn't see any Jews saving anyone during the siege at Waco.

Before the Jews started attacking him, they ought to put their own house in order, Cooper said, imploring the audience to write letters to *Omni* magazine. "Write until your fingers ache from writing. Tell them the truth about Bill Cooper."

Did these comments make Bill Cooper an anti-Semite? Possibly, but not any more so than when he claimed that the aliens who had fleeced Dwight D. Eisenhower in the tech-for-flesh deal were known as the long-nosed Grays, star travelers taxonomically distinguished by "huge hooked noses that came out of their head to a bump." Cooper's line drawing of three Big-Nosed Grays appears in noted ufologist Linda Moulton Howe's

1989 book, *An Alien Harvest*. Supposedly a re-creation of a photo Cooper saw while in Naval Intelligence, the aliens resemble a trio of mighty-honkered Shylocks.

After that, Cooper kept up the pressure, in 1994 launching into a multi-part series called "The Ugly Truth about the Anti-Defamation League."

"Folks, tonight I'm going to embark on a course from which there is no return," Cooper told the audience before the first anti-ADL show. He wanted to make one thing clear at the outset: "I am not talking about Jews. *This has nothing to do with Jews.*"

The fact was the B'nai B'rith, founded by immigrants in 1843 on the Lower East Side of New York City, was "not a Jewish organization at all but rather a branch of the Illuminati," Cooper said, exploring the group's connections to Albert Pike, the Fort Smith, Arkansas–based Ku Klux Klan member and founder of the Scottish Rite of the Southern Jurisdiction of Freemasonry.

As far as Cooper was concerned, the cornpone Aryans of Christian Identity and the double-dealing Illuminatists of the ADL were really one and the same; they were both the enemies of the restoration of the constitutional republic, groups with "an agenda."

Not that Cooper would be rewarded for this even-handedness. As the ADL and the Southern Poverty Law Center continued to brand him a right-wing loon, neo-Nazi mouthpieces lambasted him as a Jew lover. In later years, *The Daily Stormer*, a hard-line Trump-era alt-right site, savaged Cooper's reputation among a whole new crew of Aryan wannabes. Cooper was nothing but "an obese, 'its-not-the-Jews' shill," *The Daily Stormer* said.

If there was one last-ditch protector of republican government, it was the Second Amendment, Cooper said. Every target shooter swore they'd go to the mat for their Second Amendment rights, but, as usual, they had never taken the time or energy to research the topic. They did not understand the meaning of the words: "A well-regulated Militia, being necessary to the security of a free State, the right of the people to keep and bear Arms, shall not be infringed."

The militia was the true soul of the Second Amendment, "not, as some absurdly would suggest, concerns with hunting and sporting rights," Cooper said, going on to attack the National Rifle Association. "The NRA is not your friend," Cooper told the audience. If you wanted to let Big Brother know everything about you and the guns you owned, joining the NRA, filling out their forms, paying your dues, sticking their decals on your truck window was a very efficient way to do that.

The Second Amendment wasn't about freedom to spend your last dime to engorge the bottom line of the Smith and Wesson, Colt, and Winchester companies. It wasn't about having one hundred weapons locked up in the steel-reinforced safe screwed into your garage floor.

What the Second Amendment was about, Cooper said, is "that the government is the servant of an armed citizenry, and the tyrant over an unarmed citizenry."

In the Founding Fathers' time, Cooper told the audience, the men of the militia "met upon the Village Green to select their officers and train." Artists of the time produced many detailed images of the exercises: men in tri-cornered hats carrying bayoneted muskets, practicing classic tactics of assault and retreat. No one paid much attention. Why should they? Militia training was part of everyday life.

Over the years, the militia, the independent, armed contingent of the citizenry, was slated for extinction. After all, where was the Village Green in this version of the United States? In some crime-infested city park of a decaying downtown? In the parking lot of a shopping mall by the interstate? Who needed a militia when every municipality had their own, ever more militarized police force, and cameras mounted on every available telephone pole and rooftop?

The militia was intended to be the people's response to the ever-present temptation by those in power to impose governmental tyranny, Cooper told the audience. Now, if a community tried to exercise its right to protect itself from an unjust government, as was their constitutional right, the SWAT teams and black helicopters would not be far behind, in the name of public safety.

Times change, but Creator-endowed rights do not. While the cops in even midsize US cities were riding around in Bradley Fighting Vehicles, the militia, if it could even be called that, was still mainly composed of race-hating British Israelite skinheads back in the boonies who imagined themselves engaged in a perpetual game of chicken with Armageddon. What was needed was another kind of militia, one that looked toward the future.

The Second Continental Army of the Republic (SCAR) was this new militia, Cooper announced during the November 21, 1994, broadcast of *The Hour of the Time.* He'd been expecting the orders for some time, he said, and they had finally arrived from what he called the "General Command Staff." The statement had been coded on computer disk, he said. "It was keyed, and I am the only one in the world who has that key." He then began reading the decoded file.

"The indications are as follows," Cooper briefed the listeners. "Mock American cities" had been built on several Army and Marine bases. FEMA, the National Guard, and elite Special Forces were using the facilities to practice "breaking, entering, and house-to-house search-and-seizure tactics . . . foreign pilots, including Germans, are being trained by Central Intelligence Agency proprietary companies to identify areas from the air by terrain recognition." Unidentified helicopters "of different colors, but primarily black" had appeared in recent months.

It was clear, the General Command Staff Statement indicated, that "an incident is being planned . . . a large-scale terror event." The purpose of the attack was to ensure the passage of the murderous Clinton administration's Omnibus Counterterrorism Act. Sponsored by congressional "traitors" like Joe Biden, Arlen Specter, and Charles Schumer, the counterterrorism bill was poised to take advantage of then-emerging technologies and databases to give federal agencies like the NSA, the FBI, and the IRS previously unimagined power to spy on the American citizen. Among other tyrannies, Clinton's counterterrorism bill would "allot an additional $27 billion to build new penitentiaries" as well as "mandating the death penalty for fifty-seven crimes not previously punishable by death."

All that was needed to make the bill the law of the land was "an excuse," Cooper said, continuing to read the secret memo. Whatever that excuse was, it was coming soon. Given the circumstances in the country following the Waco massacre, it was the opinion of the SCAR General Command that patriots should be ready "mentally and spiritually to fight the war to reinstate the Constitution of the United States to its legal and lawful place as the Supreme Law of the land *within six months*."

The secret message was signed by the commanding general of the Second Continental Army of the Republic. "Forgive me if I do not mention his name," Cooper said.

Seeking a nonviolent alternative to what he imagined to be an inevitable armed clash between government forces and the patriot community, Cooper first suggested a financial takeover, "hostile or not," of the publicly traded Gannett media corporation. Owners of *USA Today*, then the largest-circulation newspaper in the country, Gannett also owned dozens of radio stations and most of the highway billboards in the country. The company was just the kind of "proverbial gorilla . . . that thinks it can sit anywhere it wants and take a crap all over you and tell you to think whatever it wants you to think," Cooper said.

The plan was for patriots to buy the company a share at a time. When they took over, Cooper said, they were "going to print the *real* truth and the *real* news, in the newspapers, on the television sets, and on the radios, and use those billboards for *constructive* purposes." But with the Gannett shares then going for sixty dollars apiece, few were willing to put up the money. Cooper's takeover bid failed.

Then one summer evening in 1994, Cooper took to the air to proclaim, "America is no longer a two-party country, ladies and gentlemen." He was announcing the formation of the Constitution Party. Throwing heart and soul into a political party was a "difficult decision for me to make," Cooper said. But given the circumstances, it was a chance every peace-loving patriot was obligated to take.

Cooper had learned of the Constitution Party a few months before when he met Aaron Russo (1943–2007), a well-known entertainment industry figure at the time. A Sephardic Jew from Long Island, Russo had worked in his father's lingerie business, a stint during which, he told Cooper in an *Hour of the Time* interview, he "invented the bikini panty." By the late 1960s, Russo was in the rock-and-roll business, opening the Kinetic Playground on North Clark Street in Chicago, a Midwest version of Bill Graham's Fillmore auditoriums. The Doors, Jimi Hendrix, the Who, and Led Zeppelin, among many others, played there. Russo also formed a long-lasting relationship with Bette Midler, then a smash as the Divine Miss M, star of the Continental Baths, a famous gay hangout on upper Broadway in New York City.

Russo and Midler went to Hollywood, where they scored an immediate triumph with *The Rose,* a pop-rock-era remake of *A Star Is Born.* Midler played the Judy Garland role, with Russo getting the producer credit. When Russo followed with the successful *Trading Places,* starring Eddie Murphy and Dan Aykroyd, he seemed on his way to being a major showbiz player. But Russo soon had a change of fortune. His pictures' grosses decreased and he was having trouble with the IRS, which eventually placed more than two million dollars worth of liens on his property. Feeling persecuted by an outrageous authoritarian system, Russo declared himself "Mad as Hell" and embraced rightist libertarian politics, writing a platform for a proposed third party.

Hearing this, Cooper suggested they work together. If Russo's third party was going to gain any traction, a conduit to the grassroots patriot community that listened to *The Hour of the Time* was essential, Cooper told Russo. The two men spent time brainstorming the idea, Russo turning Cooper's head by taking him to pricey Hollywood restaurants and introducing him around town. Soon, Cooper became the shortwave voice of the Constitution Party, which, he was telling the audience, was "the last-ditch chance to avoid bloodshed in this country."

In the summer of 1994, after reciting the introduction of *Behold a Pale Horse* as if to demonstrate the importance of the occasion, Cooper read the full platform of the Constitution Party, as written by his "good friend Aaron Russo," on the air.

"We, the founders of the Constitution Party, hold that our federal government has consistently violated the Constitution of the United States," Cooper read. The fifteen party planks emphasized the elimination of prosecution for "victimless crimes," the reinstatement of "sound money," and a curtailment of the IRS, along with positions against public school entitlement programs, national health care, and the UN.

While standing behind these principles, Cooper was not sure how parts of the platform would go over with sections of the *Hour of the Time* listenership. "Let's see what kind of flak we're going to get on this,"

Cooper said. "Because I'll tell you, folks, everyone believes in the right of free speech, until someone says something they don't agree with. . . . Then those other people have to be silenced. They have to be *shut up*."

Two party positions were already "creating dissension," Cooper said. The first was plank number five, which read: "Regarding abortion, the government has no right making laws dictating to a woman what to do with her body." On this, Cooper told the audience, "we are firm, ladies and gentlemen. God put us here to make choices, and the moral choice is the woman's and if she fries in what some of you would call Hell for eternity, that is her choice, for it is she who will fry. But it is not the business of the state to say yes, no, maybe, or anything else."

The second problematic plank pertained to "the right to be homosexual." This point was important to Russo, who in 1977 had produced an evening at the Hollywood Bowl entitled "A Star Spangled Night for Rights." While the gathering was advertised as an across-the-board call for human liberty, discrimination against gay people appeared to take precedence. At least this was the way it seemed to one of the evening's headliners, comedian Richard Pryor. After mentioning some humorous bisexual events he'd witnessed, and even participated in, while growing up in a Peoria, Illinois, whorehouse, Pryor's mood turned angry.

Sure, gay people should have their rights, the comic said, "but where were you when they were burning Watts? You were doing what you wanted to do down on Hollywood Boulevard. . . . This is an evening for human rights? Well, I am a human being, too. . . . Kiss my rich, happy black ass." Pryor's comments proved so incendiary that Russo never released the tapes of the event.

"I am not a homosexual," Cooper told the audience listening to him on World Wide Christian Radio. "I cannot even imagine myself engaging in any homosexual acts. But homosexuals have lived among us since the beginning of time. You're not going to wipe them out today or tomorrow. . . . The most that you can ever hope to do is force them back into the closet so that you cannot see them . . . and then you will be living a lie, just as we have been living lies throughout our history. And lies must stop."

From mid-1994 into 1995, Cooper devoted himself to building the Constitution Party. *The Hour of the Time* became the party's nerve center. There were announcements of party-building gatherings in Days Inn meeting rooms across the country, which Cooper hyped on the radio. The goal was clear: Stop the New World Order in its tracks. To this end, Cooper rallied support against the recently enacted North American Free Trade Agreement, a blatant undermining of American economic sovereignty by the Clintons, another step in the march toward "one-world socialist totalitarian government."

Just when Cooper was positive the Constitution Party was about to take off, Russo pulled out. He told Cooper he could help the cause in other ways. Several of his Hollywood projects were beginning to cook. There was a TV talk show from the Constitution Party slant that perhaps Cooper wouldn't mind hosting. Russo was also developing a feature film touting the need for constitutional restoration. Meryl Streep, then not too far removed from her role as activist Karen Silkwood, loved the script, Russo said. But, as Cooper later learned, these were all lies. There was no TV show, no movie, no money, no Meryl Streep.

Cooper had spent hour after hour on the radio, calling Russo the Founding Father of the Constitution Party. Now the man had shown his true colors. There were accusations that Russo had embezzled money from the party. Cooper was heartsick and furious, telling Russo off during a radio interview. The Constitution Party was dead and the country was one step closer to disaster.

Meanwhile, Cooper had to keep making a living. Dumping money into his many projects, keeping the Constitution Party going, he'd taken advances against royalties on *Behold a Pale Horse*. The book was blowing up, the Nation of Islam ordering bulk copies, but he had to get by on his weekly stipend, worked out years before with Light Technology. Cooper was allowed to sell the book on *The Hour of the Time*, but he had to purchase the copies from the publisher at the author's rate. By the time the shipping and handling was done, his take was pennies.

He did, however, pick up a sponsor for *The Hour of the Time*, the Phoenix-based Swiss America Trading Corporation, a dealer in precious metals, primarily gold and silver coins. These "hard assets" were popular among patriots who hadn't trusted US currency since America went off the gold standard. For years, Cooper ran "The Metal Report" as a regular *Hour of the Time* feature, keeping patriots apprised of any price fluctuations. After a while, "The Metal Report" evolved into a commentary on other markets, a running account of how Mystery Babylon bankers were fixing the exchanges to ensure maximum profit for themselves and financial ruin for everyone else. With the markets subject to such cynical manipulation, the lone patriot needed protection. This was the selling point of Swiss America Trading's products, as Cooper's ad copy reflected.

"Hi, this is William Cooper for Swiss America Trading," a typical Cooper commercial began. After alluding to the double-digit inflation of the Jimmy Carter era and reminding the audience that the country had just elected another southern liberal governor as president, Cooper said, "Well, folks, if you feel that paper assets will be safer than gold and silver in the coming times of high-interest rates, possible currency recall, and financial collapse—*Relax!* You've got nothing to worry about! If you feel the government is looking out for your best interests—*no problem!* Don't call! . . . But if you're like me and know the true purpose of the Federal Reserve and the Internal Revenue Service, then call Swiss America Trading. *Tell them Bill Cooper sent you!*"

The sponsorship helped, as did selling discounted survival rations guaranteed to get a family of four through the roughest nuclear winter. For a while he sold herbal teas. But there were always piles of unpaid bills. Rates on the WWCR signal kept increasing. The house needed repairs. Totally exposed atop the hill, baking in the summer, battered by howling winds all winter long, the house's upkeep was expensive.

Luckily, he had Annie to help him. "In the job I have chosen for myself—or maybe was foisted upon me—as a messenger, I can no more stop doing what I'm doing than I can stop breathing." He wouldn't have blamed Annie if she'd done as almost any other "modern woman" might have and "sought the comfort of the court." But she had not. She had never failed to be "loyal, trustworthy, and more loving than anyone I have ever known."

She was integral to the mission, his bookkeeper and treasurer. As he told the audience, when *Hour of the Time* fans sent in their hard-earned money for their CAJI memberships or bought a videotape, it was Annie who filled the orders. She stayed up so late "duplicating those tapes like a mad priest at midnight" that Cooper feared for her health.

In the past, Cooper had always used personal appearances to generate cash. A quick trip to Atlanta or a symposium in Los Angeles, bargaining hard for the lion's share of the door, pushing the merch to the faithful, could gross four or five thousand bucks. Recently, however, he had become increasingly reluctant to leave his home on Cooper Hill.

Some of this uneasiness stemmed from an incident that took place during a family trip Cooper, Annie, and then-four-year-old Pooh took to Phoenix in the late summer of 1994. Booked into an Embassy Suites, the Coopers went out to eat at a nearby restaurant. Cooper soon got into an argument with people at the next table. Voices were raised, pushing ensued. Someone called the cops.

Not interested in waiting for the arrival of the police, Cooper and his family went back to the hotel room. They weren't there long before Cooper became convinced that a toxic gas was being pumped into their room through the ventilating system. Waking up Pooh and Annie, Cooper said they were being poisoned and had to get out of the room. But once in the hallway, he heard loud voices. Certain it was the cops after him because of the restaurant encounter, Cooper rushed Annie and Pooh back into the hotel room, wrapping wet towels around their faces to protect against the invisible gas still supposedly pouring into the room. He tried to contact the front desk, but there was no answer.

It was an impossible situation. Leaving the room would land the Coopers in the hands of the police, but staying risked asphyxiation. Cooper started calling friends, telling them to tape the conversations as evidence if anything happened to him. A few days later, he played tapes of the calls on an *Hour of the Time* episode called "Motel from Hell." Cooper is heard talking in a voice muffled by the towel across his face. "No way we're leaving this room unless we're accompanied by Arizona patriots," he says.

When the Coopers finally left the hotel, half a dozen police cruisers, called by worried friends, were outside. After some back-and-forth with cops, Cooper was arrested. But as he told the audience a few nights later, "They didn't take me to a normal cell in the Maricopa County jail. They drove me to an abandoned building, with nobody around whatsoever. It was dark, they had to unlock the door and turn on the light. They put me in a little bitty cell." When he protested, the cops said, "Tell it to the FBI." This proved, Cooper told the listeners, that the feds were in on it, too.

The experience shook Cooper up. As he often told the audience, he learned what it was like to be responsible for the lives of others when he was a boat captain on the Cua Viet. But that was nothing compared to what a man owed his family. He'd give his life for his family. And now that Annie was pregnant with their second child, it was a responsibility that would only grow.

By late 1994, Cooper was operating out of his Research Center in St. Johns, the Apache County seat thirty miles north of Eagar on Highway 191. He moved his studio and vast library into a former drugstore on Commercial Street, next door to Surplus and Stuff, a gun shop owned by his patriot friend and erstwhile town policeman, Tim Lesperance. Beside that was Katy's Kountry Kitchen, a breakfast place run by Lesperance's wife, Katy. Cooper started doing *Hour of the Time* broadcasts out of the Research Center, which, he often bragged, had more books than most town libraries. It was also here Cooper first put out *Veritas,* his self-published national newspaper.

Cooper had been talking about starting a newspaper since the days he was running the Absolute Image Photo Gallery in Long Beach back in 1981. As Sally Phillips said, "Bill always wanted to run a newspaper." A 13 x 20-inch broadsheet, or roughly the same size as *The New York Times, Veritas,* like *Behold a Pale Horse* and *Mystery Babylon* before it, was nothing if not ambitious. The idea was to create a nationwide paper for patriots, based on the reporting of what Cooper called "a worldwide community of citizen journalists," that would replace the fraudulent media now under the total control of the New World Order.

From the outset, *Veritas* was a formidable effort, with a number of contributors across the country, editorials and several other features attributed to the CAJI News Service. There was a health and nutrition column and a regular feature on *Mystery Babylon* symbology. In the first issue, Cooper established the tone with a four-thousand-word autobiographical "Open Letter to the People of St. Johns, Arizona."

His new neighbors might have heard things about him, Cooper wrote in his letter, calling attention to the recent libelous press he'd gotten in an *Arizona Republic* (known to him as the *Arizona Repulsive*) piece on the militia movement. The article was "yellow journalism of the worst kind," an all-out attempt to demonize him, Cooper wrote. He didn't "fear black helicopters" or cower under his bed, imagining that "foreign UN troops" were marching down every street. The people of St. Johns should know that about him. Those who didn't, those who just believed whatever they read in the government press, Cooper said, "you should be thoroughly ashamed of yourselves."

The front-page banner of Cooper's paper carried an image of "nude Veritas," the Roman goddess of truth, with the paper's name spelled out in blue letters. The color printing cost more, Cooper told the *Hour of the Time* audience, but since "blue is the color of truth," it was worth it. The first issue had a print run of 2,000, but at $3 per copy ($50 for twenty-four copies), rapid growth was expected. Cooper bragged it would not be long before *Veritas* surpassed Willis Carto's *Spotlight,* the flagship publication of the ultraconservative Liberty Lobby.

"Everyone in Washington, DC, is going to get this paper in their mailbox, every single issue," Cooper said on *The Hour of the Time.* "The president, the vice president, the cabinet, the Joint Chiefs of Staff, Supreme Court justices, each and every congressman, they're all going to get it and they're going to read it."

The first issue's most popular feature was "From the Horse's Mouth," a five-page chronology of quotes from *Mystery Babylon*'s main players, proving in their own words that the New World Order was not a hoax, not just some stupid conspiracy made up by Bill Cooper. There were 161 quotes altogether, fully annotated, from Adam Weishaupt's 1776 comment, "It is necessary to establish a universal regime and empire over the whole world," to Henry Kissinger's 1994 comment, "It (the New World Order) cannot happen without US participation, as we are the most significant single component."

This was Cooper's "standard admonition" at work, the fruit of decades of determined autodidactism. There was no such thing as peer review, because there were no peers. Truth was singular and personal. In a world that could not be trusted, where school systems were suspect and everyone was trying to sell you everything you didn't need and didn't want, self-education was the best defense. Right or wrong, at least it was yours.

To hear Cooper tell it, he was working on the very first issue of *Veritas* when the two guys arrived at the Research Center. One was tall and lanky with a close-cropped military haircut. He looked like a soldier, mind-blown, with that far-off stare Cooper could pick out in a crowd anywhere. The other was shorter, stocky, wearing a black cap. They were traveling east on I-40 from Kingman, they said, when they turned off at Sanders and drove down old Route 666 to see Tim Lesperance at Surplus and Stuff. Lesperance asked them if they had ever heard of Bill Cooper. Sure they had, the two men said. Bill Cooper was their favorite. They listened to him all the time. "Then come on, he's right in here," Lesperance told the men, leading them into the Research Center.

At the time, Cooper's presence in St. Johns was on the QT. He never mentioned that he was in St. Johns in his broadcasts. The post office box he used was in Show Low, an hour's drive to the west. It was just a chance meeting, or so it seemed.

Cooper later described the encounter on *The Hour of the Time*. The shorter man, the one with the hat, did nearly all the talking. If the taller one said "twenty words, that was a lot," Cooper remembered. There were some other people there, around that time, working on *Veritas*: Bart Chow, Michael Apante, and Apante's wife, Sharon. In their early twenties, they'd quit their jobs and come in from California to help put out the paper. They believed in Cooper and his message. They wanted to help out, make a difference, save the country.

The guy with the hat started talking about how they "were going to do something to get things back on track," Cooper recalled. They wondered if Cooper, whom they respected, could offer some words of wisdom.

"Well, that depends on what you guys are going to do," Cooper responded.

"Can't tell you that," said the shorter guy.

"If you can't tell us," Cooper replied, "then we can't help you."

They continued chatting and the shorter man asked Cooper if he knew where to sell objects that were signed by George Washington. Suspicious now, Cooper said no, he didn't know anything about that. If it was really signed by George Washington, it probably belonged in a museum.

Finally, the taller man, the one with the crewcut and the far-off look, spoke up. Other than hello, he hadn't said a word. In a quiet voice, he asked Cooper what to do if he was stopped by a police officer.

Cooper was nonplussed. It seemed like a strange question. "For what?"

The man shrugged. "You know, like a ticket."

"Do you have any warrants out on you?" Cooper asked. The man shook his head no.

"Then just take your ticket and go on your way."

"You don't think I should shoot him?" the man asked.

"Shoot him?" Cooper replied, taken aback. "Why would you shoot someone over a ticket?"

The man took this in like he was making a mental note, and thanked Cooper for "the advice."

The men said they had to get going and Cooper got up to see them off.

"They were driving a big green station wagon with a puke-yellow interior and a big television set in the back seat," Cooper said. The taller guy opened the tailgate and Cooper could see that the cargo area was filled with copies of William Pierce's *The Turner Diaries*. The skinny guy offered Cooper a copy. Cooper said, "I told him I already had a copy of that book." But they left it anyway.

The men got in their car. As they were pulling away, the shorter one yelled back, "*Watch Oklahoma City.*"

20

Shortly after 9:00 A.M. on April 19, 1995, Michele Marie Moore, a forty-one-year-old ballet instructor and member of the Intelligence Service of the Second Continental Army of the Republic (SCAR) was at home having her morning coffee, when a friend called and told her to turn on her television. Something terrible had happened.

Moore put on the set to find the Alfred P. Murrah Federal Building in downtown Oklahoma City, a short drive from her home in Norman, had been blown apart by a massive explosion. The entire front of the nine-story building was missing. No one knew how many were dead yet, but it was going to be bad. Six hundred people worked in that building every day. There was a day care center on the first floor. The kids, many of them under the age of five, had already arrived for the day when the bomb—if that's what it was—went off.

As Moore later wrote in her book *Oklahoma City: Day One*, the first thing she did was "telephone a report to my commanding officer, William Cooper." It was 7:00 A.M. in Arizona, and Cooper's wife, Annie, answered the phone. Apologizing for calling so early, Moore identified herself as an officer of the Intelligence Service and said it was an emergency.

When a sleepy-sounding Cooper came on the line, Moore, an ardent *Hour of the Time* listener, suddenly found it difficult to speak. "Thousands of possible imminent scenarios were passing through my mind," Moore wrote. "Indecisiveness had a paralyzing effect upon my thinking."

Calmly taking matters in hand, Cooper told Moore to get a grip. Now was not the time to get rattled. To succumb to the manufactured atmosphere of shock and confusion, the so-called Fog of War, was exactly what the enemy counted on. It bought them the time they needed to cement the final details of the "official story" into place.

After Moore told him what she knew so far, Cooper explained what was going to happen. First would come the stretch of yellow police tape, the line that declared state ownership of the evidence, real and doctored. Next would be the news media, stenographers with good hair whose job it was to disseminate the "breaking news" as doled out by the FBI special agent in charge—Bob Ricks, recycled from Waco. The circle of deceit would be drawn further as media arrived to fill in the details of the story they'd been hired to tell. This was freedom of the press according to the New World Order.

The task of the Intelligence Service, the aboveground arm of the SCAR, was to combat this procedure, to expose the "official story" as the lies it was.

Michele Moore was perfect for that. Throughout her life, long before she heard of Bill Cooper, she had done her own research. While growing up in Tulsa, where she played the harp in church, many of her friends were content to sit in front of the television set, but she was a voracious reader, and a fine writer, with a gift for poetic language.

Moore liked what Cooper had to say about the value of freedom, and how most people seemed only too determined to give it away. So she sent in her money, got her stack of Intelligence Service stationery, her press credentials. In the presence of a notary, she signed the Oath of Allegiance required of all officers of the Intelligence Service: to "gather by any and all legal and lawful means information from all sources . . . [to] provide for the free flow of information to the whole of the People, the Militia of the several States of the Union." With "a firm reliance on the protection of Divine Providence," Moore pledged "my life, my Fortune, and my Sacred Honor." In return she was commissioned as a second lieutenant of the Intelligence Corps, with a certificate signed by the "director of intelligence," William Cooper, along with the "general of the army," who was listed as George Washington.

Appointed Oklahoma City's "station chief," Moore got her marching orders from Cooper. She was to get as close as she could to the Murrah Building, talk not only to those who were at the scene but also to those miles away who had experienced the event in real time. In addition, she was to monitor police scanners, follow the rescue workers. That was one part of the job. The second involved recording every TV and radio report, both national and local, and cataloging statements made by government officials, municipal, state, and federal.

This dual accounting was part of the standard operating procedure of the Intelligence Service. "There are at all times two records being compiled simultaneously," Moore wrote. "Into one is fit all of the pieces that can be documented as the true account or state of whatever is being investigated. Into the second is fit all of the documentable pieces of the deception, if there is one. These two jigsaw puzzles are in various states of completion. Between them sit all the pieces . . . that do not yet fit into either category. There they remain until they can be placed with surety into either the record of truth or the record of deception."

Moore's husband, also a member of the Intelligence Service, was assigned to keep track of the media and government reports. To this end, Moore wrote, "Every available audio cassette deck was in use. Every boombox was recording. . . . The video recorder was rolling tape." The machines had to be isolated in bedrooms, closets, and bathrooms to keep the soundtracks from overlapping.

Moore took to the streets, collecting testimony, attending briefings, crisscrossing the shaken heartland city. One discrepancy between the personal reporting and what was coming out of the media was how many explosions there had been. Several people she spoke to described hearing two separate explosions, seconds apart. Brett Wooley, working on his car in his front yard at the time, heard "two very loud 'staccato-like' explosions" five to eight seconds apart. Michael Hinton, who lived at the YCMA a half block from the Murrah Building, said he had just gotten onto a bus to go to work when "I heard this very violent rumble under the bus. . . . About six or seven seconds later, another one which was more violent than the first . . . I thought the second time the bus was going to turn over." At the Geological Survey on the University of Oklahoma's Norman campus, seismic records showed evidence of two distinct blasts.

This "two explosion" hypothesis was quickly shot down by authorities. From the start, they were locked on their scenario. There was only one blast and that had come from the detonation of two and a half tons

of ammonium nitrate drenched in diesel fuel stashed in the back of a
Ryder rental truck parked in front of the Murrah Building. Like the
Warren Report, like the lie that the Branch Davidians had fired first, this
was the official story of Oklahoma City: one Ryder truck, one fertilizer
bomb, signed, sealed, delivered, nonnegotiable.

As Moore drove around, she was overwhelmed by what had happened. The middle of April, Moore wrote, was when a resident of central
Oklahoma could wake up and feel "the first vibrant blush of wild prairie
spring." It was usually a time "both tranquil and fragrant." Now, instead,
there was this.

That evening, Moore, dead tired, came home and, in compliance
with her duties as Intelligence Service station chief, "put together the
snippets of paper" on which she had written her notes. She typed them
out as quickly as possible, faxing the manuscript to her commanding
officer, Bill Cooper. The report arrived just in time, just a few moments
before that night's edition of *The Hour of the Time*. Like any good reporter, Moore made her deadline.

"Today is the second anniversary of the Waco massacre," Cooper
began that evening's program. "I don't want anyone out there to forget
that, ever." A thousand years from now, any real American patriot should
still be remembering April 19, 1993, he said. "Unfortunately," Cooper
went on, his voice souring, "someone is using this anniversary to pro-
mote an *agenda*.

"As usual, the Intelligence Service has all the facts that are available at
this time, facts that have not been reported in their entirety anywhere else
in the world," Cooper told the audience in somber, even tones. "The body
count is expected to go up, but as of 4:30 P.M., twenty-two have been confirmed dead, seventeen of them children from the day care center," Cooper
read verbatim from Moore's notes.

Darkness was beginning to fall, the temperature dropping through
the 40s. "Huge floodlights have been brought in by an oil-field equipment company," Cooper read. "Large heaters are also being provided to
the scene as rescue work continues into the cold of the night." Two hundred adult-size body bags had just arrived.

"The majority of rescue workers are completely stressed out. . . . They are liable to say anything. You can hear it in every word on the scanner," Cooper continued, reading from Moore's report. In the middle of the show, when Cooper took his break, the musical interlude was a long section of Bernard Herrmann's score from Alfred Hitchcock's *Psycho*.

When he returned, Cooper addressed an item in Moore's report about four men of "Middle Eastern appearance" being sought. This was to be expected, Cooper said. He predicted Muslims would be the first suspects. The official story was developing. They'd even flown in Connie Chung, CBS-TV's replacement for Walter Cronkite, the erstwhile "most trusted man in America." Enraging the locals by arriving at the death scene in a limousine, the stylishly coiffed Chung told her millions of viewers that the bombing had "Middle East terrorism written all over it."

There was a small population of Muslims in the OKC area, many of them university students, but in this case, Cooper knew the Islamic terrorism scenario was merely a feint. The symbology was way out of line.

"Hezbollah has no truck with April 19!" Cooper shouted on *The Hour of the Time* that night, exhorting his listeners not to fall for the bogus Islamic connection. Clearly, however, if someone wanted to blow up a federal building, killing kids in a day care center, and pin it on the patriot movement, April 19 would be the day to do it.

April 19 wasn't only the second anniversary of Waco. The significance of the date went back to 1775, to Lexington and Concord and the original Patriots' Day. More recently, April 19, 1984, was the day Robert Jay Mathews and the Order arrived in Seattle to stage one of their biggest armored-car heists. A year later, on April 19, 1985, the feds shot it out with the Covenant, the Sword, and the Arm of the Lord in the lakeside town of Elijah, Missouri.

Exactly a decade later, following extensive appeals in the Stumpp and Bryant cases, April 19, 1995, was the date set for the execution of Richard Wayne Snell. The feds could have killed him any day, but April 19 was the one they chose. On the morning of the nineteenth, according to the Arkansas state prison "death watch log," Snell, scheduled to be executed at 9:00 P.M., passed a few hours "smiling and chuckling" as he watched the coverage of the OKC bombing on TV. The synchronicity of the situation likely amused Snell, who, after his arrest, had told police that he'd once intended to blow up the Murrah Building himself, spending several days casing the area. Snell's plan to set off a giant fertilizer bomb inside a parked rental truck sounded remarkably familiar.

As he was being led away for his lethal injection, Snell had a bit of advice for Arkansas governor Jim Guy Tucker, Bill Clinton's successor, who was present for the execution. "Look over your shoulder," the murderer said. "Justice is coming. I wouldn't trade places with you or any of your cronies. Hell has its victories. I am at peace."

This sort of stuff was not supposed to happen in places like Oklahoma. America's heartland was home to good, honest folk like Michele Marie Moore. It was here that Cooper's own people had come when they first went west. Now it was just another terror zone, a target like Iraq or Palestine.

"What happened in Oklahoma City only too conveniently overshadows Waco," Cooper closed his broadcast on April 19, 1995. Then he played a recording of a large explosion. *Boom!*

"Memorize that sound, ladies and gentlemen," Cooper said. "You will be hearing it more and more in America."

In the epilogue of her 640-page book, Moore wrote that "some might find it strange" to read so large a work (seven appendices, including the complete text of the Omnibus Counterterrorism Act) "and find no mention of Timothy McVeigh." This was by design, Moore said. The title, *Oklahoma City: Day One,* meant just that, an account of April 19, 1995, nothing else.

The tale of Tim McVeigh, his role in the bombing, "the evidence deliberately fabricated against militia groups," and the media's nonstop demonization of the patriot movement would have to wait until Volume Two of the OKC saga, Moore wrote. These were the orders of her commanding officer and director of the Intelligence Service, Bill Cooper. In recognition of her tireless work, Cooper promoted Moore from lieutenant to major, which made her Major Michele Marie Moore.

The publishing schedule was a business decision on Cooper's part. He had poured a fair amount of resources into the project, much of it his own money. He knew that if *Oklahoma City: Day One* was going to be the debut volume in a new Modern Library of true citizens' journalism, it would have to look the part. It couldn't be another *Behold a Pale Horse,* with its hippie cover, outbreaks of CAPITAL LETTERS, and thirty pages of ads for O'Ryin Swanson's Light Technology books on channeling and crystals.

With its stark black jacket featuring a finely wrought lithograph of a rose springing from a heart-shaped fire, *Oklahoma City: Day One* was a book made for posterity, a volume to be pulled with reverence from a mahogany shelf by a dedicated researcher one hundred years hence. It was a unique sort of history, the chronicle of duplicity, the step-by-step assembly of a cover story. There have been many books refuting so-called "official stories," but never one constructed in real time, certainly not in the detail Moore and editor Cooper employ.

The chapter heads, taken from quotes of famous writers and thinkers, indicated the scope and seriousness of the effort. The chapter title "Putting Things in Order" came from the phrase from Denis Diderot, "Putting things in order always means getting other people under your control." The Arthur Miller quote for chapter 5, "The Structure of the Play," came from the comment "The structure of the play is always the story of how the birds came home to roost."

Convinced he was on the verge of publishing a sea-changing work, Cooper decided on a classy initial offering of five hundred copies of *Oklahoma City: Day One*, each signed by Moore and himself, priced at sixty dollars apiece. It was an unheard-of sum for patriots who were used to smudgy, offset newsletters. Cooper handled much of the promotion himself. He ran house ads in *Veritas*, and even read the entire six-hundred-page book during a four-hour segment of *The Hour of the Time*.

But *Oklahoma City: Day One* was not a bestseller like *Behold a Pale Horse*. It barely sold at all; no one was quoting lines from it in rap songs. Years later, Doyel Shamley still had several untouched boxes of the "limited and signed First Edition" piled up in Cooper's old storage unit.

On April 21, 1995, Timothy McVeigh was announced as a prime suspect in the OKC bombing. Yet another other shoe had dropped. The face of the new Manchurian Candidate had been revealed, this time in a police sketch labeled JOHN DOE #1 that depicted the suspect as a youngish man with a nearly triangular face, smallish, alien-like mouth, blank eyes, and a forbidding close-cropped military flattop.

The picture was prepared with the aid of the staff of the Ryder rental agency in Junction City, Kansas, where McVeigh leased the vehicle with a cheap-quality fake driver's license, made out in the name of Robert Kling, D.O.B. April 19, 1972. (McVeigh's actual birthday was April 23, 1968.) A half-blind barroom bouncer would have recognized the phony license in a second, yet the rental people made no fuss.

The sketch was immediately confirmed as accurate by Lea McGown, manager of the Dreamland Motel off I-70, where McVeigh, using his real name, had rented room 25 from April 13 to 17, 1995. McVeigh had made an impression by haggling over the room price, getting it from twenty-eight dollars down to twenty dollars a night, as if those eight dollars really mattered in the scope of what he planned to do. The address he gave was the Decker, Michigan, home of James Nichols, brother of Terry Nichols, who was later convicted as an accomplice in the bombing. Later, the feds claimed that the accuracy of the McVeigh sketch proved essential in cracking the case so quickly.

This was so much crap, Cooper told the audience that night. The "police sketch" of John Doe #1 and the face of Timothy McVeigh were a dead match because it was not a police sketch at all; it was "a copy of a photograph." It had clearly been prepared well in advance.

If you were looking for someone to play the patsy for the largest act of domestic terrorism in American history, even the most cynical of FBI profilers couldn't have scoured up anyone better than Tim McVeigh. He checked every box on the spectrum. He grew up amid the diminishing expectations of the 1970s in Pendleton, New York, a rust belt suburb of Buffalo. His parents divorced when he was twelve. His mother took his two sisters and moved to Florida, leaving young Tim with his father, a depressed assembly line worker at a downsizing General Motors radiator plant. Called Noodle because he was so skinny, painfully shy, he passed his days playing Space Invaders on his Commodore 64, stopping only to arrange his comic book collection. If he ever had a girlfriend, no one knew about it. Outside of hookers, there was every chance he died a virgin. Later, after a distinguished stint in Desert Storm, McVeigh surprisingly washed out of Special Forces training. He left the Army and bummed around the country in his beater Chevrolet "Road Warrior," turning up at the Waco siege.

Plenty of people saw him there, selling bumper stickers reading BAN GUNS—MAKE THE STREETS SAFE FOR GOVERNMENT TAKEOVER, and posing for pictures as he sat on the hood of his car.

Even before McVeigh was arrested, Cooper was on the air, saying "You're starting to hear the words, ladies and gentlemen . . . 'white supremacist,' 'religious fundamentalist,' 'constitutionalist,' 'patriot groups.' . . . You can be certain that whoever is arrested will first be proclaimed a racist, and later a militia connection will be fabricated," Cooper predicted. Now, exactly on cue, the feds were wheeling out twenty-seven-year-old Timothy McVeigh.

Cooper read a communication from the general staff of SCAR. "All militias are to remain on full alert," he intoned. "Militia commanders are to maintain discipline of their units. Every unit is to protect their leadership. Under no circumstances are you to allow the militia to be broken as a result of the propaganda campaign being waged against the legitimate, legal militia of the several states and the United States of America."

From OKC, station chief Michele Moore reported that McVeigh was being held at Tinker Air Force Base, where Cooper's father had once been stationed. A federal judge had been flown in to arraign him. Ordinarily, they would have run him through the process at the old State Courthouse, but the building had been damaged in the blast. Besides, Cooper said, there was no way the feds were going to risk losing jurisdiction over this particular suspect.

The hysteria was ramping up, just as he knew it would, Cooper said, announcing the results of a poll taken by a Shreveport, Louisiana, newspaper. Citizens were asked if they would be willing to give up "some, most, or all" of their personal freedom in exchange for protection and security; 74 percent of the people said they would. This meant, Cooper said, with bitter resignation, "that 74 percent of those people regard their freedom as a negotiable instrument to be traded for a small amount of security—security to be meted out by our flawed, Marxist-controlled government.

"Timothy McVeigh is the Lee Harvey Oswald of the American Reichstag!" Cooper exclaimed, pointing out that no real patriot could have attacked the United States of America. "We know who did it! *You know in your heart who did it.* If I have to tell you what is coming, then you're as blind as a bat and just as stupid."

It was not until 2001 that Cooper spoke publicly at any length about the two strangers who'd visited him at the St. Johns Research Center with a stack of *The Turner Diaries* in the back of their big green station wagon with the puke-yellow interior, the men who'd told him to "watch Oklahoma City!"

His reticence was understandable. For years he'd imagined himself in the crosshairs of the enemy. They'd run him off the road, taken his leg, nearly driven him crazy. Now he was looking at this guy on television in an orange jumpsuit, surrounded by federal agents: Timothy McVeigh, John Doe #1, a man who bore a very strong resemblance to one of those guys who'd dropped by St. Johns, saying what big fans they were of *The Hour of the Time.*

It was as if his audience had come out of the darkest part of the woodwork and it was Timothy McVeigh, soon to be the most hated man in the country.

Since Waco, Cooper had hoped to avoid *Pale Horse* and the hell it brought with it. Trapped in a world of homicidal maniacs and nice church ladies who read the terrors of Revelation and prayed for them to commence, Cooper never wanted bloodshed. He'd tried to take over Gannett, put up with phonies like Aaron Russo to avoid it. But the illuminists defeated him.

They sent out McVeigh, one more perfect human zombie in a seemingly endless assembly line of them, to do their bidding. Now 168 people were dead, twice as many as at Waco; who knew how many would die in the next "terrorist attack"? For a family man anxious to watch his children grow up, it was fearsome arithmetic.

Besides, the feds already knew about the St. Johns visit. In fact, they probably staged it. For Cooper, it was something to worry about, the way his name kept coming up in the McVeigh case, as if the feds were tightening their noose around his neck.

In early 1996, James Nichols had testified in federal court that he, his brother Terry, and McVeigh listened to Cooper as often as they could get a clear signal. In August 1995, Michael Fortier, who met McVeigh and Nichols in basic training at Fort Benning, Georgia, did an interview with *The Outpost of Freedom*, the newsletter run by Cooper's old Waco correspondent, Gary Hunt.

"What led to the bombing?" Hunt asked Fortier, who had backed out of the Murrah Building plot halfway through and later served as the State's star witness against his former compatriots.

"Well," Fortier sighed. "I can't say a whole lot, but we heard lots of tapes and saw videos and read things. There is this guy with a radio station in Arizona, Bill Cooper. He keeps calling people 'sheeple' and was mad that they ain't doing anything to change things. Well, we got to thinking that's right, *things need to change.* Tim really responded to that."

In September of 1996, the FBI got a tip that McVeigh and a friend had visited Cooper in St. Johns. Special Agent Steve Fillerup was sent to investigate. An experienced operative who had spent a number of years in the hectic Phoenix office, working cases along the Mexican border and on Indian reservations, Fillerup, then in his early forties, had recently taken over the Bureau's sleepy Lakeside-Pinetop office in the Arizona White Mountains. Being the head of a one-man office in the middle of nowhere suited Agent Fillerup.

"After the bombing, the agency went a little overboard on the domestic terrorism front," Fillerup, now retired from the FBI, told me when I called him at his current place of business, the Nebo Peaks Process Service in Elk Ridge, Utah.

"We knew that McVeigh and the Nichols brothers used to listen to Cooper on the shortwave," Fillerup said. "Then we got this tip. 'Okay,' I said, 'I'll go check it out.'" An account of his meeting with Cooper appears in Fillerup's 2014 autobiography, *Heaven's Hammers*, in which the FBI man writes about balancing the choices he had to make as a law enforcement agent with his deeply held Mormon faith.

After a few tries, Fillerup finally reached Cooper on the phone. "Am I a suspect?" Cooper wanted to know. Assuring him that he wasn't, Fillerup tried to set up a face-to-face meeting, but Cooper balked. He didn't want Fillerup coming up to North Clearview Circle, and he wasn't about to drive all the way to Pinetop. After some negotiating, the two men agreed to meet at a turnout on Highway 191, a few mile markers north of Springerville.

Cooper's pickup was waiting for him when he pulled up, Fillerup writes. "Bill was wearing a shoulder holster that contained a large pistol. 'Well,' he said, 'you can see I'm armed. I'm carrying a .45-caliber.'"

"I see that, Bill. I'm armed, too. I've got a Glock .40-caliber," Fillerup replied, patting the bulge under his shirt.

"Where's your backup, Steve?" Cooper asked.

"I have no backup, Bill. I just came to talk to you and get this lead covered that was sent to me."

Not taking Fillerup's word for this, Cooper "pointedly looked north and south on the highway, and after seeing nothing, he even looked up in the skies."

According to *Heaven's Hammers*, Cooper then told Fillerup that "some months before the bombing, McVeigh and another man had looked him up while they were passing through Arizona. There was no discussion of the bombing plot, and Cooper had no contact with McVeigh since that encounter." Satisfied with this, Fillerup thanked Cooper for his time and drove back to his office.

Cooper had a reputation for being difficult to deal with, but things had gone fairly well, Fillerup concluded in *Heaven's Hammers*, adding that some time after their meeting, the radio host "actually provided me with an unsolicited tip on a man, a political zealot whom Cooper considered dangerous." The tip, stating that a member of the Lee County, Florida, militia was planning an OKC-type hit, was mailed to Fillerup on Intelligence Service stationery and signed by Cooper. It is included in Cooper's FBI file.

Cooper's longest, and most emotional, account of the McVeigh meeting came on June 11, 2001, the day the OKC bomber was executed by lethal injection at the federal facility in Terre Haute, Indiana. McVeigh was thirty-three years old at the time, the same age as David Koresh when he was burned alive.

Cooper was in a particularly foul mood that day, steamed about an article that appeared in the *"Arizona Repulsive,"* a rehash of the old news about how McVeigh was a fervent *Hour of the Time* fan. Again, Cooper was being placed in the same bag with the backwoods racists and Jew-hating end-of-days types. He was sick of it, he said, playing "Armageddon

Days Are Here (Again)" from an album called *Mind Bomb* by the British synth band The The.

During the St. Johns visit, the shorter man, whom Cooper had long ago identified as Michael Brescia and believed to be the brains of the operation, said that he and McVeigh were "on a mission for the Army," Cooper told the audience. The Army knew everything he and McVeigh did, Brescia said, because they were being tracked with some kind of computer chips implanted under their skin. Brescia pointed to a spot below his left shoulder, bidding Cooper to touch it.

"I felt it," Cooper told the audience. "There was something under his skin. It was hard, and square."

Then the withdrawn McVeigh spoke up, plaintively. He also had a computer chip implanted in his body, he said. Cooper could touch it if he wanted to. It was in his right butt cheek.

"He really wanted me to confirm it was there. I declined for obvious reasons," Cooper said, suddenly turning sympathetic to the executed bomber. "But I wish to this day that I had not been so squeamish and had personally checked his buttock to see if there was something there."

There was also McVeigh's strange question about what to do if he was pulled over by a policeman. Should he just take the ticket or shoot the cop? McVeigh had asked Cooper.

The odd query now seemed more significant in light of what had happened about two hours after the Murrah bombing. Attired in a T-shirt on which was written Thomas Jefferson's words THE TREE OF LIBERTY MUST BE REFRESHED FROM TIME TO TIME WITH THE BLOOD OF PATRIOTS AND TYRANTS, McVeigh was making his getaway in his $300 Mercury Marquis northbound on I-35. Passing the small town of Perry, not far from the Kansas line, McVeigh was pulled over by Highway Patrolman Charlie Hanger. Did McVeigh know his car had no license plate? Hangar asked.

McVeigh could certainly have shot Hanger as Richard Wayne Snell did State Trooper Louis P. Bryant. He'd already killed 168 people—what was one more? But McVeigh chose to follow Bill Cooper's advice and simply take his ticket. By then, however, Hanger noticed the pistol in McVeigh's shoulder holster.

Hanger then put his pistol to McVeigh's head and pulled him out of the car. McVeigh was taken to the county jail, where he stayed for the next thirty-six hours. Just as the county sheriff was about to let him go, the police sketch landed on his desk. After that, McVeigh was on the fast track to being convicted as the main player in the most horrific act of terrorism yet seen on American soil.

Throughout his incarceration and trial, McVeigh rarely spoke. Then, at his sentencing he rose and said: "I wish to use the words of Justice Brandeis dissenting in Olmstead to speak for me. He wrote, 'Our government is the potent, the omnipresent teacher. For good or for ill, it teaches the whole people by its example.' That's all I have."

In the McVeigh biography *American Terrorist,* authors Lou Michel and Dan Herbeck tell how, when asked if he felt any remorse, especially considering how many children died, McVeigh replied that Harry Truman, the signer of the 1947 National Security Act, never expressed any remorse about dropping atom bombs on an already defeated Japan, killing 200,000 people, many of them children. Truman didn't have to say he was sorry, because it was an act of war.

As far as McVeigh was concerned, OKC was war, too. As he told his biographers, "I chose to bomb a federal building because such an action served more purposes than other options." The bombing was "a retaliatory strike," a counterattack for federal actions that grew "increasingly militaristic and violent, to the point where, at Waco, our government— like the Chinese—was deploying tanks against its own citizens."

Whatever the truth of the OKC bombing, it resulted in a huge boost for Cooper's standing in the patriot radio wars. Being Tim McVeigh's favorite talk-show host had its upside. It came in the form of a news flash, announced over the air by no less than the king of conservative radio, Rush Limbaugh, right in drive time: "I'm holding in my hands a memo from the White House written by President Bill Clinton," Limbaugh told his massive audience. "The memo says 'William Cooper is the most dangerous radio host in America,'" Limbaugh said, adding with feigned relief, "So, folks, you see it is not me. It is William Cooper, Bill Cooper, broadcasting from a storefront in Arizona."

"*William Cooper Is the Most Dangerous Radio Host in America!!!*— William Jefferson Clinton, President of the United States." It was a heck of a blurb, the best kind of compliment. "I must be doing something right," Cooper said.

With that acclaim, however, came increased scrutiny, a bigger target on his back. At the time, Cooper was playing a lot of Leonard Cohen songs on his show. One of his favorites was the looming, insinuating "Everybody Knows," which opens with the lyrics "Everybody knows that the dice are loaded . . ." For Bill Cooper, the stakes had been raised.

21

Cooper announced the birth of his daughter Allyson Dovie Cooper, his fifth child, during the August 18, 1995, broadcast of *The Hour of the Time*. It had been a wild day, Cooper told the audience, and he was "just fried."

He'd been tinkering around at the house in Eagar, "defragmenting a hard drive and loading in new facts." Cooper noticed that Annie seemed to be pacing around, but she said she was fine, so he kept working. A few minutes later, she came back in the room and said it was time to go to the hospital.

The hospital was in Show Low, west along Highway 260. It was a two-hour round trip, but Cooper, ever cautious, thought it best to maintain a post office box in the town. It was part of Annie's duties to drive over on a near-daily basis to pick up the orders for broadcast tapes and other *Hour of the Time* merchandise. In fact, Annie and Pooh had just returned from the run, which, on this day, included a stop in Taylor, a small mountain town where Cooper also kept an address. It was while in Taylor that Annie's water broke, but she hadn't said anything about it upon her return to Eagar.

It was "fifty miles to the hospital on winding country mountain roads," Cooper regaled the *HOTT* audience, telling them how "every police car in Arizona has radar, so I hooked up the ECM, the electronic countermeasure, and loaded Annie and Pooh into the Bronco." Then they were back on 260 headed to Show Low.

"Annie's having contractions every five minutes," Cooper continued, "and poor Pooh was beside herself, wanting to comfort her mother and not even really knowing what was wrong." In the high-country twilight, it was hard to see, Cooper said. You could corner a mountain curve and find "a two-thousand-pound elk standing right in the middle of the highway . . . or a whole herd of antelope." When they got stuck behind a slow-moving construction crew, Cooper said it was "possible that that baby was going to be born on that road." He recalled the last time he participated in the birth of a baby. "It was in Vietnam a million years ago, and to tell you the truth, I don't even remember what I did."

When Pooh was born, the delivery had been difficult. Annie was in labor for twelve hours. "The screams were primal," Cooper told the audience. "They came from somewhere I can't touch, so it touched me deeply." In contrast, the birth of Allyson Dovie Cooper was progressing fast, much faster than anyone had anticipated, Cooper told listeners.

Always the radio man, in the background, Cooper had added a nearly imperceptible drum-and-guitar track with a steady, hypnotic heartbeat, building the suspense. They got to the hospital just in time, Annie giving birth shortly after.

Later that night, after making it perfectly clear to hospital officials that there was not going to be any signing of a birth certificate, or applying for a Social Security number, or any of that government tracking nonsense, Cooper heard the baby crying. Annie had drifted off. "I knew Allyson needed somebody to hold her," Cooper said.

"Everybody was so busy that finally I asked the nurse if she could get the baby, and she did. She brought her over, and, folks, I held that baby in my arms and she stopped crying instantly and just opened her eyes. I know that babies can't see at that point, but she had the biggest, beautiful brown eyes and just appeared to be looking at me."

The next morning Cooper got into a squabble with the hospital officials, who said they wanted to keep Allyson in the hospital for ten days. Her white blood cell count was too high, they said. She needed a regimen of antibiotics. "As you can imagine," Cooper told listeners, "I wasn't going to go for that." Declaring that "the medical profession is full of people who sometimes think they are God," Cooper said the only reason for Allyson to stay in the hospital "was to put more money in the doctors' pockets." A second blood test proved him correct, Cooper said. The baby was fine. So Allyson Dovie Cooper came home to 96 North Clearview Circle.

That night, *The Hour of the Time* featured Pooh as the cohost. She'd made her formal debut as an on-air member of the team a couple of years before. "Ladies and gentlemen," Cooper said that night, "this little four-year-old girl surprised me the other day as we were driving home from Los Angeles. Annie was falling asleep in the back seat, when I heard something wonderful. . . . Pooh asked me if she could demonstrate what it was that we heard from the back seat of the Bronco. So without further ado, here's Pooh."

Pooh stepped up to her daddy's microphone and happily recited the Pledge of Allegiance. It was a flawlessly cute, little-girl, pink version of the Pledge, yet delivered with the resolve of a fearless princess, hand over her heart. When she was done, Cooper was choked up. "Folks," he said, "I don't know where she learned that, but I am so pleased and so proud of my daughter Pooh."

Pooh became a regular on the *HOTT* broadcasts, part of the gang at the St. Johns Research Center. She was a natural-born radio raconteur. It wasn't long before she started to take over whole segments of the show, choosing which records to play. When it was time for her to go to bed, she'd sign off with flair. "Good night, folks. See you when the moon turns green and the cows come home!"

Cooper had fathered three children and "lost" them all. That was how he put it: "lost." He never mentioned the drunken rages, the wife beatings, the fact that the mothers of his older children had all run away from him; those things were edited out of the story. As Sally Phillips, mother of Jessica, said, "Bill had a lot of love in him. But you could never be sure what he'd do next. The other side was always in there."

Pooh seemed to have changed that. Pooh was Cooper's girl, a chip off the old block. From what can be heard during the *Hour of the Time* episodes, they were always together, taking rides in the country, walking the playful Sugar Bear, who would become Pooh's dog, especially after Cooper got Crusher, the attack-trained Rottweiler. On the air they were a team, playing records by Sam Cooke, who they agreed was the greatest singer of all time. "Cupid" was Pooh's favorite, especially its opening lines, "Cupid, draw back your bow, and let your arrow go . . ."

Cooper's love for his daughter was "complete," he said, telling the audience how when Pooh was just a little baby, he'd come in from doing the show around midnight. Annie always had dinner waiting for him. He'd eat it and then let Annie go off to sleep. "I'd spend the night holding Pooh and singing to her, talking to her and holding her and rocking her and throwing her up in the air and everything you can think of," Cooper told the audience.

"We developed a pretty good friendship back then, didn't we?" Cooper asked Pooh on the air the night Allyson was born. It was true, Pooh said.

"Pals to the end?" Cooper asked his daughter.

"Pals to the end!" she replied.

Cooper worried about how Allyson's birth might affect Pooh. He said that he and Annie "had not been expecting another addition to the family. . . . In fact, I think Pooh kind of thought she was going to be the only one for a while. And her mother and father did, too." Still, Cooper said, he had wished in his "heart of hearts for another child, so that Pooh would not have to be alone a lot of the time."

It was not easy being the child of a messenger, Cooper told the audience during the broadcast. When he and Annie traveled to lectures and events, "it's usually adults who attend these functions, and so Pooh doesn't get to meet a whole bunch of other children. And, of course, we live up here on the mountaintop. There are no next-door neighbors, so her greatest playmates are her father and her dog, and when mother's not too busy, her mother, too."

It would be different if Pooh attended school, he said. There were several public schools in the Round Valley area, but Cooper wasn't about to send his daughter to one. "When you hear the word 'public,' it really means 'Socialist,'" he often said. Instead he chose to homeschool, at least as much as time permitted. Father and daughter talked about it on that evening's *Hour of the Time,* when Cooper asked Pooh what she had done that day.

She said she didn't really remember "because yesterday, I mean, I did the same thing and I did the same thing today, too! Because I just pretend I went to school and I did a lot of things really good. Because I *like* going to school. It's a lot of fun."

Cooper, coaxing, replied, "When you say you're just pretending, that's because you really don't ever go to a school. You learn here at home, huh?"

"Yeah. Because it's not really a school, it's just my room."

Cooper then addressed the audience. "It's a room, but it's got a lot of stuff in it, and boy, she learns to read with the real phonics, folks. She doesn't get into this baloney that has so many illiterate people running around today."

Cooper was happy that Pooh had been there the day Allyson was born, so she'd know her sister from the very beginning. On the way to the hospital, he'd looked into the back seat of the Bronco and seen Pooh sitting there "looking like a ghost." At the hospital he lost track of her for a moment, only to find her in the recovery room, staring at her sister, simply taking in the scene, the change of the order of things.

Recalling the moment, Cooper told the audience, "I think she was deeply impressed and has a better understanding of what life is about than she did before."

The little family was growing. It wouldn't be the way it had been, those drives up and back from St. Johns, just Poppy and Pooh, pals forever. But it was life, life, and life only. Pooh, so wise beyond her years, seemed to know that. "Boy," she said to Cooper, "I really like the show tonight because I love my family. I love you, I love Mommy, and I love little Allyson."

Then, with the logical rigor of a budding mathematical mind, Pooh analyzed the bonds of the new family unit. "I wouldn't leave without you and Mommy and Allyson, and you wouldn't leave me and Mommy and Allyson, and Allyson wouldn't leave without me and Mommy and Poppy, and Mommy wouldn't leave without me and Poppy and Allyson."

"That's absolutely right," Cooper told his daughter. "And I'm glad you understand that, because you don't have to feel insecure ever."

If the government strategy had been to set up McVeigh to destroy the patriot movement that had been rekindled on Ruby Ridge, they had succeeded. At the time of the OKC bombing, there were over eight hundred militia groups with a membership that numbered somewhere between 50,000 and 200,000, depending on who you believed. After

McVeigh's conviction, this number dropped steadily, bottoming out at perhaps 15,000 by the mid-2000s, before the huge rebirth that accompanied the election of the first black president in 2008.

Much of the early decline was due to increased and redirected police activity against what was now called domestic terrorism. The FBI hired 570 new agents within a year of the Murrah Building bombing. More significantly, as Danny Defenbaugh, who headed the FBI's post-OKC investigation, said, "We were allowed to range more freely."

Meanwhile, Cooper and Michele Moore continued to develop their OKC research. As the feds continued to lay the blame solely on McVeigh and the Nichols brothers, Cooper expanded his list of John Doe coconspirators. By the end of 1996, he was up to seven, having added the Elohim City Christian Identity pastor, Robert G. Millar.

Cooper competed on the John Doe front with such patriot commentators as Mike Vanderboegh, the self-identified commander of the First Alabama Cavalry Regiment. Editor/publisher of *The John Doe Times*, an often wry, gossipy chronicle of OKC lore, Vanderboegh attacked Cooper in a piece called "Oklahoma City Squirrels and Militia Looney-Toons: Michele Moore and Wild Bill Cooper Work Themselves into a Frenzy."

As "a militia unit commander myself," Vanderboegh said, he took exception to a secret communication from SCAR headquarters that Cooper read on *The Hour of the Time*. The commanding general, Cooper said, had ordered all militias of the United States to assume Red Alert status until further notice.

"Pray tell, Mr. Napoleonic Cooper, who gave you authority to issue orders to me and mine?" Vanderboegh replied, snarkily reminding *John Doe Times* readers that Cooper was the same guy who once "engaged in laser battles with Martians on behalf of Uncle Sam."

Cooper's response was to add Vanderboegh to his John Doe list, making him #8. This was not an empty gesture, as Gary Hunt of *The Outpost of Freedom* told me. "I don't know why Cooper got mad at me, but he made me John Doe #4," Hunt said. "Someone was supposed to have seen me walking past the Murrah Building a few minutes before the explosion. But I was in Orlando at the time. I could prove it. But a lot of people still believed Cooper. It took me years to shake that John Doe #4 label."

Cooper's biggest ally at the time was frequent *Hour of the Time* guest Linda Thompson, an Indianapolis lawyer and one of the very few significant female voices in the patriot scene. Author of the pamphlet *The Clinton Body Count: Coincidence or the Kiss of Death?*, Thompson caused a sensation with her 1993 film *Waco: The Big Lie*. Along with some very interesting footage supporting the Branch Davidian side of the initial BAFT gunfight, *The Big Lie* purported to show the feds setting fire to the Mount Carmel compound.

"The following footage proves beyond any doubt that the tanks intentionally set the house on fire," says Thompson, narrating the film. "It proves that the Branch Davidians were murdered." The video is murky, but Thompson directs the audience's attention to a tank, which she says has "a gas jet on the front that shoots fire." And there it is: an orange triangle that appears to be a flame close to the front of the tank. The fire leaps toward the compound building, which appears to combust. The vehicle pulls back and advances again, shooting what looks to be more fire.

Waco: The Big Lie had a profound impact on many horrified by what happened at Mount Carmel. Among them was the comedian Bill Hicks (1961–1994), whose reaction can be seen in two Waco-related YouTube videos. In the first, Hicks is goofing around near the "Camp Boredom" press area. He mocks the Branch Davidians' name, referring to them as "the church of the Latter Day Saints of Jaw-Way."

The second video shows Hicks, whom many regard as perhaps the foremost social comic after Lenny Bruce, doing a stand-up gig. It starts with some jokes. David Koresh had no choice but to change his name from Vernon Howell, Hicks says. "You got to call yourself Jesus, that's part of the Messiah deal," Hicks says. "What are you going to say, 'Vernon speaketh, and He saith, we're gonna stop and go for beef jerky'?"

Then, interrupting his own flow, a palpable anger overcomes Hicks. "I have seen footage that has never aired on network television," he says, referring to Thompson's film, "footage of Bradley tanks shooting fire into the compound. The Branch Davidians did not start that fire. They were murdered in cold blood by the pussies, the liars, the scumbags, the ATF."

The feds knew Koresh was "really trying to finish that Seven Seals horseshit he was doing," continues Hicks, already suffering with the pancreatic cancer that would kill him within a year. "They burned those people alive because the message they want to convey to you is, State power will always win. . . . We'll say any lie we want over our propaganda machine, the mainstream media, and we'll burn you and your children in your fucking homes."

Another person buying into Thompson's version of the Waco fire was Timothy McVeigh. He insisted the movie be played at his trial so everyone would see the motivation for his actions. The problem was that, according to most observers, however criminally the feds might have acted at Mount Carmel, their Bradley tanks almost certainly did not, as Thompson said, "shoot fire." Jim Pate, who covered Waco for the now-defunct *Soldier of Fortune* magazine, said, "When you look at the unedited video, it's obvious when the vehicle backs out, that it [the flame] was debris being reflected in the sunlight. The question then became, does Linda Thompson believe this, or did she know better but edited it to pander to paranoia?"

In many ways Thompson's fire-shooting tank, a quirk of the visual record that occurred at a decisive moment, recalled Cooper's contention that William Greer shot President Kennedy with a shellfish-toxin pellet gun. It opened a plausible portal through which the true believer could see exactly what they wanted to see. Perhaps recognizing a kindred spirit, Cooper remained a Thompson supporter long after most patriots deserted her.

In late 1996, Cooper abruptly left WWCR. He'd done 944 broadcasts under the station's call letters, reaching what he claimed to be ten million listeners. Now he was doing his last program, saying that the station's call letters really stood for "World Wide Christian Hypocrite Radio."

The problem began when Cooper asked to change his time slot. He was paying for the 11:00 P.M. to 12:00 midnight time slot, which meant his show didn't end until 1:00 A.M. on the East Coast, too late for many fans. Cooper claimed he'd been promised by WWCR general manager George McClintock that if an earlier time period opened up on the evening schedule, he'd get it. Cooper especially coveted the two-hour slot held by the venerable right-wing radio figure Tom Valentine and his powerful sponsor, Willis Carto's *Spotlight* newspaper. Cooper began targeting Valentine, producing "proof" that Valentine was actually an Illuminati mole and a high priest of the Mystery Schools, and he referred to Valentine's program, *Radio Free America*, as *Radio Free Masonry.*

When Valentine eventually did leave his time slot, Cooper called McClintock to remind him of his promise. Yet, to hear Cooper tell it, McClintock reneged. "He told me *The Hour of the Time* was *too controversial* on a Christian broadcasting station to put on any earlier."

Cooper hit the ceiling, pointing out that if WWCR was so pious, why did they carry a program called *The Anti-Christ* that was hosted by a man who actually claimed to be the Anti-Christ. Cooper told listeners he'd given WWCR operations manager Adam Locke thirty days' notice. He had no intention of staying at a radio station that was capable of such "blatant dishonesty and manipulation," Cooper told the manager. He and his listenership, which Cooper was then touting to be as large as "twenty-five to thirty million," were leaving. It was meant to be a bluff, but Cooper had overplayed his hand. A few days later, when he attempted to smooth things out with Locke, the WWCR boss said, sorry, the station had taken Cooper's thirty-day notice seriously and was already closing a deal to rent his transmitter time to another host.

Cooper found himself in the radio wilderness. Nothing in shortwave matched the strength of the WWCR signal; it was the top of the line and Cooper had tossed it away. Trying to put the best face on the situation, Cooper told the audience it was time to "take back the airwaves." He would set up his own far-flung satellite network "completely free of obstacles like establishment-controlled media and people like George McClintock." It was a big vision that would require huge sacrifices of "time, effort, and money." He urged patriots who were really committed to saving the Constitution to open their wallets and "get in on the ground floor of this new network."

But now, instead of cuddling up to your Sky Buddy shortwave radio to hear Bill Cooper's planetarium-style readings of great tales of the Knights Templar and the mendacity of the secret lodges of Mystery Babylon, you had to have an Orbitron SX-7 dish, a Pansat 3500 receiver, 100 feet of RG6 coax cable, and who knew what else. Cooper was selling the full kit for $485, plus $10 for handling. It was the cheapest price possible, but still beyond many budgets. Installation could be a hassle; the instruction manuals were an inch thick. While many followed Cooper to satellite, most did not. His audience dwindled.

It was around this time that Cooper's tax problem flared up. The IRS claimed Cooper and Annie were in arrears. This was a lie, Cooper said. He and Annie had always paid "all legal and required tax." This did not mean, Cooper said, that he was "a taxpayer." Paying legitimate taxes did not make you a "taxpayer." That only happened when you signed your name on the 1040 form on the line where it said "taxpayer." That's what cemented your contract with the bill collectors who had seized control of the government. It was a trick, Cooper told listeners, he had no intention of falling for, ever again.

The fact, Cooper pointed out, was the nation itself was based on tax protest. Eight years before the famous Boston Tea Party of 1773, the British attempted to raise money to finance their imperial presence in the New World with passage of the Stamp Act of 1765, which placed a tax on the issuance of commercial and legal papers. John Adams and Patrick Henry were among those who opposed the new laws.

After the Revolution, however, the shoe was on the other foot. In 1791, now in power, the newborn American central government levied its first federal tax, on the production of distilled beverages. Farmers from western Pennsylvania, Ohio, and Virginia who raised the grains to run the stills protested, setting up an angry confrontation that was labeled the Whiskey Rebellion.

It was a critical moment; how would the former Revolutionary leaders who now made up the new federal government react to local political and economic concerns? George Washington provided the answer when, in full regalia and astride a white horse, he personally led a column of thirteen thousand fully outfitted troops to quell the insurrection of about five hundred farmers with pitchforks. The precedent for federal power was set.

The most literary of American tax protesters was Henry David Thoreau, who in 1848 went to jail for refusing to pay taxes to support the Mexican and Indian Wars as well as the continued tolerance of slavery. When Ralph Waldo Emerson came to bail out his friend, he asked, "Henry, what are you doing in there?" Thoreau replied, "Ralph, what are you doing out there?"

More than sixty years prior to the passage of the Sixteenth Amendment, which created the Bureau of Internal Revenue in the fateful year 1913, Thoreau, a nineteenth-century survivalist, had already written the lines that would become key talking points for modern-day tax protesters like Gordon Kahl of the Posse Comitatus, the Montana Freemen, and untold numbers of militiamen and women, Bill Cooper included.

Thoreau said: "If I deny the authority of the State when it presents my tax bill, it will soon take and waste all my property, and so harass me and my children without end. This is hard, this makes it impossible for a man to live honestly, and at the same time comfortably, in outward respects." He also said, "When I meet a government which says to me, 'Your money or your life,' why should I be in haste to give it my money?"

Cooper advanced his own tax protest position during *HOTT* broadcast #28 (2/28/93) entitled "Income Taxes Are Voluntary." The reason paying taxes was voluntary, Cooper told listeners, was not, as many ill-informed patriots believed, because "the Sixteenth Amendment to the Constitution was improperly ratified." Nor was it "because of the definitions of wages or incomes, *or* because form 1040s don't have an OMB number, *or* because the IRS is a corporation, *or* because you're free, white, and twenty-one, *or* because in 1933 the United States went into bankruptcy, *or* because the Victory Tax was repealed in 1944, *or* because you signed documents with UCC-217 above your name."

No, Cooper said, paying federal income tax was voluntary because the law said so. It was as simple as that. The proof was right there in Title 26 of the Code of Federal Regulations 31.3402(p)-1 under the heading "Voluntary Withholding Agreements." In the very first sentence, it said an employee and his employer "may enter" into an agreement under 3402(p)(3)(A). It was Cooper's contention that since the money was not going to the employer but rather to the government, the phrases "voluntary" and "may enter" carried legal significance.

Understanding tax law wasn't that hard if you were willing to do your research, Cooper told his listeners. All you really needed "was a copy of *Black's Law Dictionary*, a good brain, and a few hours."

Then, acknowledging that even tax-aware patriots sometimes require assistance, Cooper went into selling mode, suggesting every red-blooded American get in touch with the Pilot Connection Society, a Stockton,

California, firm offering the "Untax Package." Selling for $2,100, "or 10 percent of your existing tax problem (if any), whichever is higher," the Untax Package came with Pilot Connection founder Phil Marsh's book, *The Compleat Patriot*, a copy of the Constitution, a text of Psalm 91, and a picture of Marsh and his wife, Marjorie, "suitable for framing." If there was any problem with the Pilot Connection services, Cooper said, listeners could call him and he'd get "in touch with Phil Marsh directly" to sort it out.

Two years later, in 1995, Cooper offered more tax-avoidance information in the article "BATF/IRS—Criminal Fraud," which ran in the September 1995 issue of *Veritas*, and continues to show up online. While most citizens believed the BATF and the IRS to be legitimate agencies within the Department of the Treasury, this was not the case, Cooper explained. The truth was that both agencies owed their very existence "to a broad, premeditated conspiracy to defraud the citizens of the United States of America.

"Magic is the art of illusion. Those who practice magic are called Magi," Cooper wrote. It is the job of these Magi to create "obfuscation and confusion in the law." These Magicians had "frightened" Americans "into filing and paying 'income taxes.' . . . Millions of lives have been ruined. Hundreds of thousands of innocent people have been imprisoned on the pretense they violated laws that do not exist. Some have been driven to suicide. Marriages have been destroyed. Property has been confiscated to pay taxes that were never owed."

The IRS was a front, something that didn't actually exist, Cooper said. It was "a fiction, a legal fiction." He had done his research on this, spent weeks going through the IRS deception, from the Lincoln-era "war tax" through the alleged passage of the Sixteenth Amendment. He'd studied reams of the *Congressional Record*, searched through the entire United States Tax Code. Nowhere did he find a single reference to an entity called the Internal Revenue Service. The fact was people paid taxes to the IRS because they were afraid not to. It was the biggest protection racket in the history of the world. It was time to wake up to that fact. Taxes were nothing but a tribute. "A tribute paid by slaves to their masters."

It mattered little that Wayne Bentson, with whom Cooper wrote the BAFT/IRS article wound up in jail for following his own text remedies, as did Phil Marsh of the Pilot Connection and Hartford Van Dyke before him. "Successful use of this material requires a lot of study and an excellent understanding of the legal system," Cooper wrote in *Veritas*. "It is not enough to discover this information. You must know it inside out, backward and forward, like you know the smell of your own breath."

It is not clear when Cooper, in his words, "had the guts to stop" filing his income tax returns, but a September 30, 1996, letter he sent to Janet Napolitano, then US Attorney for the District of Arizona, is tagged "re: Proposed Cooper criminal prosecution." On *The Hour of the Time*, Cooper railed at Napolitano, who would go on to become Arizona governor and Barack Obama's head of Homeland Security. She was "the puppet of Phoenix, a slave in the service of the murdering Janet Reno," Cooper told listeners. His personal correspondence with Napolitano, however, took a more moderate approach.

Referring to previous communications in which he had enumerated "various reasons why I should not be indicted for federal income tax crimes," Cooper's letter to Napolitano discusses the elements of his case. There are a lot of code citations and references, including a discussion of the Paperwork Reduction Act of 1980. Even though the stationery letterhead was hand-typed ("From the desk of M. William Cooper"), it's clear that the author intended the correspondence as an exchange between equals: Citizen Cooper to Citizen Napolitano. In a more perfect union, one where The People truly had representation and access to legitimate government, this might have worked.

But this was not the world envisioned by the Founding Fathers. This was 1996. This was the middle of a blood struggle over whatever was left of the nation. Napolitano was a politician on the make, Cooper was an economically stressed father living on a hilltop in the poorest county in Arizona. The idea that he would be taken seriously in the quarters of power was a naive pipe dream.

As 1997 turned to 1998, Cooper suffered repeated financial setbacks. He complained that he was making "nothing" from the ongoing sales of *Behold a Pale Horse*. His dream of establishing his own satellite network was in tatters. *The Hour of the Time* could still be heard over some shortwave stations, including WRNO and WRMI, but their reach was nothing like WWCR. Outages were common, signals intermittent.

A tired-sounding Cooper talked about his growing money problems during a 1998 show. He said that he and Annie had "exhausted ourselves, we've exhausted our resources. We don't have nice furniture and things. You guys look up here on the hill, if you live in the Round Valley, and you think this is a wonderful house up here. Well, we do have a wonderful view, but everything is falling apart. The furniture all has holes in it. Annie and I have had one vacation in about ten years."

The financial failure of *Oklahoma City: Day One*, and the out-of-pocket expenses incurred by the Constitution Party boondoggle, had taken their toll. Cooper wanted to keep publishing *Veritas* as a full-size newspaper, but it was difficult. Months would go by without an issue. Faced with such obstacles, "most people would have declared bankruptcy," Cooper told the audience one evening. "They would have taken the money and run." There was no way he was doing that, Cooper said.

During this period, Cooper finished his last major essay, the 15,000-word reworking of his earlier "MajestyTwelve" piece. Published in the May 1998 edition of *Veritas* and later appearing in an expanded version on the *HOTT* website, the deeply pessimistic "MajestyTwelve" attempts to update the various strands of Cooper's thought over the previous decade.

"The following is fact. It is not a theory, it is a genuine conspiracy," Cooper began, citing the Admiral Cleary documents certifying "the following information is true and correct to the best of my memory and the research that I have accomplished. I will swear to it in any court of Law."

The cache of secret papers that once seemed to reveal the alien presence on Earth and then the ongoing takeover by "a One World Totalitarian Socialist Government" had now taken on a religious tenor, predicting the rise of an Anti-Christ-like *benevolent dictator*, who "will be presented as the *Messiah*."

The long-running mind control programs were nearing full strength, Cooper wrote. Soon no one would either know or care that the Constitution and the Bill of Rights had disappeared. Anyone who even remembered the days of individual rights would be considered crazy. It would be a state where only a relatively small "internal police force" carrying only "minimum weapons [would be] needed to maintain internal order."

When this process is completed, "the human race will be shackled to a computer in a never-ending cycle of debt. No action or movement will ever again be private."

For a preview of this new world, Cooper suggested readers "see the movie *They Live*," a cheapo 1988 film made by *Halloween* director John Carpenter that stars former wrestler Rowdy Roddy Piper. The well-cast Piper arrives in a near-future, dystopian town that has been taken over by an alien/satanic race. The evil interlopers remain invisible and undetected until Piper's character, a good-hearted drifter with primo fighting skills, finds a pair of sunglasses that enable him to see the demonic truth behind the everyday facade. Justly lauded for Piper's signature line, "I'm here to kick ass and chew bubble gum, and I'm all out of bubble gum," *They Live* became a cult movie for the newly paranoid after the 9/11 attacks, but, of course, Bill Cooper, his sunglasses always on, was there first.

On June 18, 1998, Cooper and Annie were indicted on tax evasion and bank fraud charges, the latter stemming from some alleged misstatements on a loan application. Now, Cooper was watching as a federal marshal started walking up the hill toward 96 North Clearview Circle with papers in his hand.

On that night's episode of *The Hour of the Time*, Cooper described the encounter. It was all about knowing the law, he told listeners. "You can't give up jurisdiction voluntarily. . . . When the federal marshal came to my home, I could have invited him in and allowed him to do whatever he wanted to do, if I was a sheeple. Instead, I understood his lack of jurisdiction and I told him so. Most people would have volunteered to be served, to go to jail, to be tried, and all the other things that happen to people unlawfully in this country every single day."

Cooper reported that the marshal stood in the middle of the road looking like a little child having a tantrum. "He said, '*I do have jurisdiction! I do have authority!*' I said, 'No, you don't, you're trespassing. Get off my property now.' He had no answer. He held up the papers and asked, 'What am I supposed to do with this?' I told him those papers were made out to a legal fiction. To be served in a fictional jurisdiction. Which did not exist." Cooper told the marshal to serve his fictional papers in that fictional jurisdiction.

The frustrated marshal yelled at Cooper from the road. "He told me we were being summoned to appear in federal court in Phoenix, Arizona, on July 1, 1998. He said that if we did not appear, a warrant would be issued for our arrest.

"Well," Cooper told the audience, "they can issue whatever they want to and we will not appear, because the court has no jurisdiction or authority over us. We will stand and fight. We will not be like the Jews of Europe, or the Gypsies, or the Poles and gather our little belongings and march off, peacefully, to the boxcars."

Cooper felt he had won the first skirmish, but the battle wasn't even close to being over; it had barely started. On July 2, 1998, one day after Annie and Cooper chose not to appear in federal court, another representative of the federal government appeared on North Clearview Circle. This time it wasn't some faceless marshal, a lackey IRS delivery boy. Cooper recognized the visitor immediately.

It was Special Agent Steve Fillerup of the Federal Bureau of Investigation, who, two years earlier, had met Cooper on Highway 191 to ask about Timothy McVeigh.

Cooper described his second meeting with Special Agent Fillerup this way: "He approached the bottom of the hill and honked his horn. He attempted to entice us to accept a document that he held in his hand. We refused the document and refused to enter into discussion with him. I told him he was out of his jurisdiction and cited the documentation and Supreme Court cases to that effect which we have in our possession. I told him to inform his traitor supervisors that they 'stepped on their dicks this time.' He replied, 'I think we probably did.' He got back in his Blazer and drove away."

Fillerup confirmed Cooper's account, more or less. In *Heaven's Hammers*, the retired agent writes that he thought Cooper was right. "We, the feds, 'had stepped on our dicks,'" but not necessarily for the reasons Cooper thought. Fillerup thought it was outrageous that the IRS hadn't bothered to advise the Marshals Service "that Bill Cooper was not an ordinary citizen who had fallen behind on his taxes."

As Fillerup told me in 2016, "When I first met Bill during the McVeigh investigation, I got the impression that no matter what he said on the radio, he got some kind of thrill out of talking to a real G-man."

The Bill Cooper he encountered only two years later was "a different man," Fillerup said.

"The truth was I hadn't come to arrest him. I felt the Bureau had suckered ourselves into incidents like Ruby Ridge and Waco by acting like tough guys. No one wanted anything like that again. I just wanted to talk to him, to open the conversation. Since we knew each other I thought I could be effective that way.

"But he wasn't going to listen. When you have been in law enforcement as long as I was, you get a sense about people. I looked at Bill up there on the hill and thought, here is a guy who could take it to the grave."

Fillerup's impression resonated a couple days later, on July 6, 1998, when Cooper issued "A Public Notice" on his website.

"WARNING!!" Cooper's notice read. "Any attempt by the federal government or anyone else to execute the unconstitutional and unlawful arrest warrants will be met with armed resistance. Any person who attempts to kidnap our children will be shot upon discovery. We are formed as the Constitutional and Lawful unorganized Militia of the State of Arizona and the United States of America and have made many public statements to that effect since 1990. All of these statements are on record on tapes of our lectures and broadcasts. These tapes are dispersed in the hands of Americans across the nation.

"Therefore a STATE OF WAR exists between the Citizens of the Union States and the corporate United States. We will be Free under Constitutional Republican government guaranteed to us by the organic Constitution for the United States of America or we will be dead.

"This is the land of the free and the home of the brave. We have drawn our line in the sand."

PART EIGHT

Armed and Dangerous

22

W ell, it's official, ladies and gentlemen," Cooper told the audience. "We just got a call from a reporter on Channel Five News. . . . The court has issued a bench warrant for the arrest of myself and my wife."

He had a message for people like Special Agent Steve Fillerup and the rest of the "good Germans" who kept telling themselves they were "only following orders."

"I've spent my time being stupid," Cooper reiterated. He'd fought a phony war in Vietnam. But now he was "*really* fighting for freedom. *In this country!* That makes me feel *damn* good."

Cooper opened another line of communication to the audience during the standoff, posting daily diary entries entitled "The Cooper Family Update" on his new website, theharvest-trust.org.

On June 24, 1998, even before his no-show in federal court, the Update announced to the audience that "reinforcements" had arrived on Cooper Hill. "All are experienced hard-core combat veterans. We keep out of sight so as not to reveal our numbers."

By July 4, Independence Day, the Update reported that the family had received "hundreds of offers to respond with arms if we are attacked." Four different state militias had promised to deploy. "Armed patrols" were operating in the surrounding neighborhoods "accompanied by a trained attack dog (Crusher loves it)."

The July 10 Update announced that a message had arrived "by courier" from the commanding general of the Second Continental Army of the Republic (Militia). The defense of Cooper Hill was as "good a time, and as good a cause as any" to begin the uprising that would restore constitutional republican government to the nation. "If the government will not enforce the laws of the union, it falls incumbent upon the Militia to chase the tyrants from the halls of government," Cooper quoted the commanding general as saying.

Other "Cooper Family Updates" included exhortatory biblical verses sent in from *HOTT* listeners, along with long sections of dialogue from *Casablanca*, which Cooper called his favorite movie. There were days of excitement. An early August Update reported that "at 09:40 hours," the "civilian sky patrol" spotted a military helicopter entering Round Valley air space. "We immediately activated helicopter traps and recalled all personnel from outside positions to protected heavy rifle positions. Women and children were ordered to shelter, to prepare the medical facility for treatment of wounded." It was only after the craft left the Round Valley vicinity that "the militia was ordered to stand down." Most of the time, tedium ruled. Great stretches of the updates were denoted with a single word: *uneventful.*

Nonetheless, the running account of the family standoff proved popular with the audience, or so Cooper said. In the month of July 1998 alone, he claimed the "Update" had been accessed 565,110 times on the net. In late August, Cooper boasted the site was averaging an astounding "25,000 hits a day."

"The Cooper Family Update" wasn't the only running account of the standoff at 96 North Clearview Circle. On June 29, 1998, the Phoenix office of the FBI opened a file on Cooper. The report eventually grew to hundreds of pages, including hand-drawn maps and aerial surveillance photographs of Cooper Hill.

"Cooper seems to be relishing the role he has created for himself in defying the FBI and the federal government," the file's first entry read, with stolid bureaucratic pique. "While the US Marshals will probably end up with the unpleasant task of apprehending Cooper, the Phoenix Division will most likely be involved in one way or another. Therefore, it is recommended a preliminary inquiry be opened."

While the expectation on Cooper Hill was that an attack was imminent, the authorities were taking a different tack. Representatives from the US Attorney's Office, the US Marshals Service, the IRS, and Agent Fillerup met to discuss their options. They agreed that there would be "no immediate action taken to arrest" the Coopers. Given that the family house "sits on a high ridge overlooking a quiet residential area," the group acceded to Fillerup's view that "it was better to not initiate overt or provocative action."

The feds decided they could wait "for a year and half, if necessary" before taking action. They felt this would give Cooper plenty of time "to cool off." Sooner or later, "cabin fever" would set in on Cooper Hill. As one person close to the case was quoted in the file as saying, "How long can you eat MREs?"

Cooper anticipated this strategy on the feds' part, writing that "Special Agent Steve Fillerup of the FBI is very carefully planting the idea with people whom he knows will communicate his words back to us that the government will not attempt to attack us or come to our domicile and arrest us."

Due to Fillerup's "blatant efforts to plant a false sense of security, we have checked and double checked our perimeter alarm system, increased our state of alert, and have doubled our patrols. Unlike others, we have learned the lessons of Ruby Ridge and the Waco Massacre."

In response, the feds characterized the Coopers as "ARMED AND DANGEROUS."

The production schedule of *The Hour of the Time* became erratic. Aside from a two-part series that took its name from Thomas Paine's Revolutionary newsletter, "The American Crisis," Cooper played many reruns. At one point, there were nearly ten straight weeks of previously broadcast programing.

Regular *HOTT* listeners were already accustomed to reruns. Programs were often re-aired when Cooper was away on lecture tours or decided to take vacations. Later, spates of reruns were taken by listeners to indicate illness, depression, or, as many came to believe, extended benders.

"You'd settle in, ready to listen to Bill, and have it be a repeat. It could be a letdown," said Robert Houghton, the Ottawa *Hour of the Time* archivist. But Cooper had never gone this long without doing a live show. Listeners worried about him, fearing the worst had happened.

When Cooper finally returned to the air for a live show on September

21, he had new call letters, WBCQ, aka The Planet, operating over the shortwave frequency 7.415 mHz. In Allan Weiner, owner of WBCQ, he had found a formidable ally.

WBCQ was not WWCR, but it had decided advantages. For one thing, Weiner (born 1953) had the right attitude. The best-known state-side figure in what was called pirate radio, Weiner had been running unregistered radio stations since he was in grammar school, when he'd put his "tower" on the roof of his parents' home in Yonkers, New York. Crazy for the broadcast voice, Weiner was one of those kids who spent weekends haunting "Radio Row," the dusty old tube and tuner stores in Lower Manhattan that were swept away to make room for the building of the ill-fated World Trade Center. Continuing to build his own "stations," and deejaying the tunes of the day from suburban basements, Weiner was still in high school when he began to run afoul of the Federal Communications Commission, which shut him down for operating without a license.

Convinced that the airwaves should be free of government control, in 1987, Weiner came into possession of a Japanese fishing boat, which he named MV *Sarah* after an old girlfriend. Outfitted with a towering transmitter, the *Sarah* dropped anchor four miles off Jones Beach on the Long Island, New York, coastline and began broadcasting under the self-assigned call letters WRNI for Radio NewYork International. The first tune the station played was "Come on Down to My Boat, Baby," a number 6 *Billboard* hit for Every Mother's Son in 1967.

RNI was in operation for less than a week when Coast Guard and FCC agents boarded the *Sarah* at dawn. Weiner, his fellow deejays, crew members, and *Village Voice* reporter R. J. Smith were handcuffed on the deck, where they sat in the summer sun as the authorities dismantled the transmitter tower and hauled it away for "evidence."

A few years after that, Weiner went relatively straight, founding the shortwave station WBCQ based in remote Aroostook County, Maine, on the edge of the Canadian border.

"Bill Cooper was exactly the sort of person I wanted to get on the air," Weiner told me when I reached him as he vacationed in Florida during the globally warmed winter of 2015. "I liked his style, what he stood for. He grew up listening to radio, he really loved it.

"For his type of thing, I'd put Bill Cooper up against any talk-show host ever," Weiner said. "He could be difficult but nothing he said ever bothered me. The only First Amendment right I'm against is being boring. Great radio takes an original mind and the ability to get it across. Bill had that. He was a natural.

"Plus, how could you beat the situation?" Weiner went on. "Bill was a federal fugitive the entire time he was on WBCQ. Just think of it! The one lone voice in the wilderness, on top of a mountain, surrounded by FBI agents. Bill and his microphone against the full power of the government . . . And it's *real . . . it's really happening!*"

The effect that the ongoing siege was having on Annie and the kids was a topic of conversation both in the Round Valley and in law enforcement circles. On August 9, the "Cooper Family Update" carried an item saying the word was out that FBI agent Steve Fillerup had been in the Round Valley doing interviews and telling people that he was "really concerned about Cooper's children."

"We think it's very funny that Fillerup (and the government as a whole) were never worried about our children until our family came under the threat of mass murder by the United States," Cooper wrote in the Update.

In his early "Public Notices," Cooper had expressed hard-line defiance concerning what might happen if the FBI were to move against his family. "Our children will remain with us," Cooper replied angrily to suggestions that he was using Pooh and Allyson as "shields" to prevent his capture. "Our children are not shields any more than children have been shields for families which have been attacked by despotism throughout history. Allowing our children to disappear into the immoral and destructive government child care and foster home industry run by the mind-controlling bogus psychology profession only to be abused and sexually assaulted for many years is a fate worse than death, and we simply will not allow such a thing to happen to our precious little girls. . . . No one takes my children but over my dead body," Cooper said.

Six weeks into the standoff, however, Cooper offered a more measured, almost plaintive response. "We LOVE our children," he wrote in the "Update" on August 9. "They are happier than most children you will ever meet. They are better educated than any child their age who attends any Public School. They have never been abused, beaten, hungry, or without shelter in their lives. I have taught them about Freedom, the great Principles and Ideals which have made their country great, and of the Constitution of the United States of America for which we fight.

"Their mother comes from a People (Taiwan) and a family (Pang) that has fought socialism and communism for many decades. They have been taught by their mother the deceptions and dangers of socialism and communism. . . . Our children are not now and never will be in danger from me or their mother."

It was one family against the world up on the hill. Cooper expected nothing from his birth family. He hadn't talked to them in years. In a February 1999 entry, the FBI file describes an interview with Cooper's brother and sister, Ronnie and Connie. Even though their older brother had been holing up for months, neither sibling seemed to know about it. But, as the file recounts, "they replied they were not at all surprised."

While Cooper's siblings described him as "very eloquent and articulate," someone with "a voracious appetite for information" and "the ability to hold someone's attention" on a variety of topics, they'd resolved never to visit their brother again, following a family get-together five years before.

According to Cooper's brother and sister (whose names are redacted in the FBI report), Cooper "continually attempted to engage them in debate or conversations on various conspiracy theories." If anyone disagreed with him, he "became belligerent so the smart solution was to simply agree with him." His "heavy binge drinking only made him more aggressive." Cooper would occasionally be "friendly and supportive," the file quotes the siblings as saying, "but when he speaks or has an opinion on a subject, he cannot tolerate dissension. He will become argumentative and irrational, thereby becoming very unpleasant company."

The FBI said Cooper's family described him as someone who "needed to be dominant in any relationship." They did not know whether physical abuse was part of his current marriage, but they were "confident that he mentally abused (redacted) if just by his personality." Cooper's FBI file mirrored this analysis, using terms like "personality disorder," "paranoia," "says government tried to shut him up," and "delusional" in the report, many of the notations underlined two and three times.

When I called up Cooper's younger brother, Ron, in 2015, his feelings appeared unchanged. Ron Cooper said he wasn't interested in talking about Bill. "I have nothing to tell you," he said. "He was a couple of years ahead of me and he went off on a different tangent. . . . He put our family through a lot. I don't want to have anything to do with anything that is going to glorify him. Nothing that is going to bring attention to him." Then he wished me good day and hung up.

Five months into the standoff, on Thanksgiving Day morning, Cooper made a video to show how the family was bearing up. Called *Cooking with Cooper* and available for sale on the *HOTT* site, the video documented the preparation of the holiday meal.

No celebration of Norman Rockwell–style Turkey Day excess, the video instead harkened back to the true essence of the first American holiday. The pilgrims came to find freedom in a new land. The bounty of the countryside provided assurance of God's blessing of their venture. Now the Coopers were celebrating something similar up on 96 North Clearview Circle. To sit down to a Thanksgiving Day meal with all the trimmings even as the enemy of those freedoms was deployed about their home was an assertion of human liberty, an act of ultimate defiance.

Shot in the manner of a single-angle live-audience 1950s TV show with a camcorder on a tripod framing the family kitchen, *Cooking with Cooper* begins as the man of the house, attired in a striped, short-sleeve shirt, places the handsome, golden-brown turkey on the counter. As Annie stands with her back to the camera, washing the dishes, the kids— Pooh, now eight and sporting a regal ponytail, and Allyson, cute as a button—sit by as Cooper begins to carve. The kids hadn't been off Cooper Hill for months, which was difficult for everyone, but today was a special day.

"This isn't good skin, this is *great* skin," Cooper says, giving the girls a piece of the bird. However, as Cooper removes one of the drumsticks, he frowns. The turkey isn't cooked all the way through. He calls Annie over.

Six years earlier, in the Christmas video Cooper made shortly after moving into the hill house, Annie was a sparkling presence in her shiny ski jacket, her hair done up in a fetching bouffant shag. Her thick accent and rudimentary English only added to the charm as she stood on the porch, waving to Cooper's mom and dad, his brother and sister. Now, dressed in layers of drab-colored flannel to protect her against the late-November drafts that often swept through the house insulation, Cooper's wife looked tired, stressed, fed up.

Looking at the bird, Annie agrees that the turkey, made according to Cooper's secret recipe, is not done. It is raw in spots. It will have to be cooked some more. But the oven door is a problem; it doesn't shut properly. "It's broken," Annie says, sourly. demonstrating by opening and closing the door, which makes a metal-on-metal creak as it moves.

Cooper stands there a moment, before walking over to the stove and kicking the oven door hard with his prosthetic leg. "Now it's okay," he says sharply. Cooper stands there staring balefully at the truncated remains of his once perfect bird. "That makes me so angry," he says.

That night, Cooper did not appear on *The Hour of the Time*. Pooh did the show instead. She was a semi-regular on the broadcast by then. She'd cohosted shows with Doyel. But she'd never gone solo before, not for a whole program. Her dad was "tired, lying down," so she wanted to give him "a Thanksgiving Day present by doing the show," Pooh, a trouper, told the audience. Barely tall enough to reach Cooper's treasured antique 1920s RCA 44-BX microphone, Pooh calmly said that since it was Thanksgiving, she wanted the listeners to call in to tell "what you're thankful for."

"I'm thankful for the loving watch and care of our Heavenly Father," said "Granny from St. Johns," a dyed-in-the-wool *Hour of the Time* listener who was one of the people Cooper said was present the day Tim McVeigh stopped by the Research Center. Granny was also thankful for Bill Cooper, Annie, and for Pooh herself. By remaining steadfast atop Cooper Hill, the Cooper family was "taking a stand for the Lord and [the] United States of America, the greatest country there is, even if these people are trying to tear it down as fast as they can."

Thanking Granny for this sentiment, Pooh answered that she was also thankful to God. It was God and his angels that had made "all the animals," she said. "He did good work. I'm proud of Him." Pooh went through the entire program with the same cheerful manner, with nary a smidge of dead air. Like her dad, she was a natural.

There were further signs of stress on Cooper Hill. The FBI file tells of one instance of a listener who said that Cooper "did not sound well" and, fearing he "might have suffered a heart attack," drove over to the hill to see if everything was all right.

Despite Cooper's frequent claims of tight security, the witness experienced "no defensive measures taken regarding the arrival of his car." He entered Cooper's residence to find himself in the middle of "a free-for-all." Cooper was yelling at someone whose name is redacted but is clearly Annie. There was "a lot of tension and hostility," as Cooper told (redacted) that she should "pack up and go." The respondent goes on to say that he "lost a lot of respect for Bill from what he saw last night."

Some hours later, according to the FBI file, "on the early morning of 9/11," an Eagar policeman followed "a white Bronco leaving the Cooper house . . . to the local Super 8 Motel." The (redacted) went into the motel but "didn't get a room, probably it was too late to get a desk manager." After leaving the Super 8, the file reports the Bronco "headed west on Highway 60 towards Show Low." A few days later the white Bronco was once again back at 96 North Clearview Circle.

However many times Cooper had been married before, his life with Annie was different. He didn't stay out all night, he wasn't a bipolar time bomb. To look at the many pictures they took together, Cooper had approached a degree of happiness in his life on Clearview Circle. Once, Cooper marketed a video called *Cooper in Hawaii*. Fans who expected to see a filmed lecture were surprised to find only home movies of Cooper, Annie, and the kids wearing colorful shirts and eating in tiki-themed restaurants.

"I was living up there then," said Doyel Shamley. "I spent a lot of time with the kids; I'm good at it from my cousins and whatnot. I worked them on sums. How to make change, things like that. Bill and Annie would argue, but I didn't pay that much attention. It was none of my business. Except one day I was with Annie and she says, 'Sometimes I think about putting a bullet in his head.'"

The siege that wasn't really a siege had taken its toll. For weeks, Annie had been stashing the kids' stuff in the trunk of the 1957 Chevy Biscayne. A classic nexus of form and function, the Chevy was an icon of American mid-century creative dominance. Cooper loved it, but it didn't run, so it became sort of a rotting museum piece, which made it a perfect hiding place.

Then, one morning, in the spring of 1999, quite by chance, Cooper saw Annie closing the Biscayne trunk. Thinking something was up, he went to investigate. Everything was in there: his childrens' clothes, their favorite toys, the birth certificates and official papers he'd often told the audience the kids didn't have, would never have, in order to avoid being branded, bar-coded, and owned by the New World Order.

Cooper was horrified. For so many years he'd beaten back the demon. He'd cut down on his drinking, at least for the most part, kept his temper in check. Certainly, there were many unpaid bills, stuff bought on time. Rare was a day that mail from a collection agency didn't arrive, stuff Cooper filed in the trash. But he'd managed to keep it together, more or less. He'd been a good dad. His children loved him. Now Annie was leaving, taking them with her.

What happened next was an awful thing. Cooper and Annie stood screaming at each other on opposite sides of the gravel driveway in front of the house. If Annie wanted to go, that was her right, Cooper reportedly said. But the kids were the light of his life. If he ever truly loved anyone, it was them. He and Pooh were pals, pals forever. Stay with me, Cooper begged Pooh. Don't go. It was a lot to ask of a nine-year-old.

Harsh words were spoken, things that Cooper would regret saying. Pooh grabbed her mother's hand and started to cry. After that, Annie and the girls got in the Bronco and drove away from Cooper Hill for the last time, never to return.

When Cooper next went on the air it was April 20, 1999, the day of the mass shooting at Columbine High School.

"I don't want to do this broadcast tonight," he said. "I hate these kinds of things. My heart just goes out to those parents who will never see their children again. I've lost children. I know what it feels like. It is a grief that you can't imagine. It never, ever, goes away."

Cooper then started talking about April 19, day of patriot dismay. Six years past the Mount Carmel fire, four years beyond Oklahoma City, it had been proven, he said, that horrible things happened in the days around April 19. You could trace it back to Mystery Babylon. The spring was the time of human sacrifice in the early incarnation of the Mystery Schools, a rite of "Ishtar, Moloch, and the rest of the terrible Gods."

Now there was Columbine, so many more children dead, and Cooper could not cope, pausing several times before continuing.

"This is awful for me, because I knew this was going to happen. I've known it for years. *I told you that.*" In *Behold a Pale Horse* he'd predicted an increase in school shootings. A society that couldn't take the responsibility to raise its children without hours of television and piles of drugs so they could act "normal" would inevitably breed a population of teenage maniacs, Cooper predicted. And he'd been right, just like he always was.

"I've spent most of my life trying to stop this shit," Cooper said, now openly sobbing. He was "just overcome with the sadness and the terrible waste. . . . I wish with all my heart that there was something I could do to make it all go away. To turn back the clock and make it like it had not happened."

It wasn't until several months later that Cooper made a statement about Annie, Pooh, and Allyson's departure from the hill. The disclosure occurred during a heated discussion on the message board of the misc .activism.militia group on the Radio Free Vermont website. Michael Pardo, an original member of the *Veritas* staff who had fallen out with Cooper claimed that his former boss had been trying to deceive *HOTT* listeners as to the whereabouts of his family.

Pardo charged that Cooper must have been "drinking or smoking doobies again," since he was using "taped material" to make it seem that his family was "still with him up on the mountain when they were not." Replying that Pardo was an "atheist homosexual and liar" who had been "discharged" from *Veritas* and SCAR on "mental incompatibility grounds," Cooper nonetheless allowed his family had gone.

It was true. Annie, Pooh, and Allyson were not on Cooper Hill anymore. He'd sent them away. "I made them pack, put them in the car, and forced them to go." It was "the hardest thing I ever had to do," Cooper wrote, but he saw no other way.

Sooner or later the feds were going to storm the hill. There was no reason for his beloved family to be around when this happened. Vicky

Weaver and her son were killed on Ruby Ridge. All those babies had died at Waco. The sacrifice was enough. If Cooper had deceived the audience by keeping his family's escape secret, he was sorry, but Annie, Pooh, and Allyson needed a head start on their journey to safety, which, he told the audience, might take two or three months.

"They are no longer in this country," Cooper told the audience, saying he would stay at his post, broadcasting the truth as he saw it. From that point on, Cooper ended his *The Hour of the Time* broadcast by saying, "Good night, Annie, Pooh, and Allyson, I love you."

23

It was not until July 29, 1999, that the FBI file made mention of the departure of Annie, Pooh, and Allyson from Cooper Hill. According to the file, the Lakeside agent (Fillerup's name is again redacted) had received word from an IRS representative saying "that (redacted) of Bill Cooper" had been located in California. The information came to the IRS from members of the Los Angeles County Sheriff's Office (LACSO) who had discovered Annie and the kids while investigating a crime in the same house.

When Annie's identity as a federal fugitive came to light, the FBI file said, the authorities suggested she would likely "receive favorable treatment from the prosecutor and the court if she assists investigators." As the agent writing the report said, the absence of Annie and the kids "may allow for more and better options to apprehend Bill, while minimizing risks to federal agents, Cooper's associates, and Cooper himself."

On November 22, 1999, Cooper opened his broadcast with more bad news about his family. His beloved mother, whom he described in *Behold a Pale Horse* as "the kindest, gentlest woman that I have ever known," had suffered a stroke. She was in a hospital in Harlingen, Texas, not far from his parents' Gulf Coast retirement home in Port Isabel.

"She can't do anything. She can't brush her teeth, she can't brush her hair, can't talk, can't walk. She's trapped. It must be horrible for her." He didn't see "a good outcome," Cooper despaired, adding that "this is the worst year of my entire life. I don't know if the stars are turned upside down or someone put a curse on me, or what."

The really maddening part, Cooper told the audience, was that his father, brother, and sister were giving him "a lot of flack because I'm not there."

As usual, his family didn't understand the situation. "There's a federal warrant for my arrest," Cooper wailed. He couldn't even leave his house, much less come to Texas. To do so would be to walk right into a trap. It was one of the "favorite tricks" of the "Nazi jackbooted KGB thugs," Cooper said. "They keep tabs on your relatives and when one of them gets sick or dies, they're at the funeral, or the hospital, waiting for you to show up."

His family couldn't "get that through their heads," Cooper said. All he got from them was an endless whine. "*If you really loved your mother you'd be here*," they said. Asking the audience to keep his mother in their prayers, Cooper said that he would provide updates on her condition, "as depressing as it is." Then he put on one of Dovie Cooper's favorite songs, Willie Nelson's version of "Stardust." He hoped the song would give her "some comfort," Cooper said.

That was "pretty much the end between Bill and his family," Doyel said as we sat chowing down on plates of "chicken-fried chicken," a specialty of the house at the Safire Restaurant in Springerville.

Asked why he'd stayed, Doyel said he wasn't going to leave a friend like that any more than he'd leave a fellow soldier on the battlefield. In retrospect, given the grim circumstances, much of his life on Cooper Hill sounded funny.

"Here I was, a trained combat veteran, in Desert Storm. And I was marching up and down in full body armor guarding Bill Cooper's backyard," Doyel said, cackling at the absurdity of the memory.

"We had a bunch of Radio Shack motion sensors that we stuck in the ground around the house. It was a waste of money because jackrabbits kept setting them off," Doyel reported. "A few days later, I heard Bill bragging to the *HOTT* audience that the compound was so secure that a jackrabbit can't twitch its nose without us knowing about it.

"I had a routine. In the mornings and early afternoons, Bill and I prepared that night's broadcast. Then I'd go pick up the mail, go shopping. I'd go into the supermarket and there would be someone on the government dime snapping a picture of me buying a head of lettuce. That sort of thing."

There was still the show to put on, but for the most part, he and

Cooper passed the days quietly, Doyel said with a touch of nostalgia. "We'd go run the dogs, hang around the back porch barbecuing. . . . I'd find these giant puffball mushrooms, big as a dinner plate; we'd cut them up and put them on the grill. We had secret knocks and code words. I'd whistle a certain way so he knew it was me. . . . We would sit there on the porch in the summertime listening to Art Bell's *Coast to Coast AM* show. Bill would refute everything he said, point for point.

"Bill was so used to thinking he was the smartest person in the room, he just ran over people," Doyel recalled. "'Do your own research,' that was his big advice, except he didn't follow it. After a while he decided he knew everything worth knowing. Mention a topic and he already knew all about it.

"That wasn't going to work with me. We had some incredible arguments, about history, religion. They'd go on for days. I kind of miss that, because I could usually trip him up one way or another. But I'd be lying to say I didn't learn things from him, just on the age difference alone.

"One time we decided we were going to sneak down the mountain and go to Belize. We even got passport pictures taken. Another time we were going to travel to Europe and join the Knights of Malta. 'They'll be happy to see us,' Bill said, 'we already know their secrets.'

"We had a pact from the beginning that if they killed me first, Bill would get all my research and writings and if they got him, I would carry on with his work," Doyel said.

Then one day, a young Cooper acolyte who'd helped with the start-up of *Veritas* drove in from LA with some friends. "This woman, someone's girlfriend, came over to me," Doyel recalled. "She smiled and said, 'So you're Bill's new *nigger*.'

"I think it was supposed to be a joke, but it really stuck with me. It was more than just the word. At the time, I was working as a lineman for the cable company, doing all kinds of overtime. I was basically supporting the whole *Hour of the Time* operation.

"Meanwhile, Bill was sitting on his ass ordering this stuff online. Once he realized he could buy stuff without leaving the house, he went hard on that. He bought camera equipment, stamp collections, old '78s, model airplanes. One time he bought a bunch of clocks from decommissioned Russian battleships. The UPS guy was coming all the time; we made him call from the road because we didn't want just anyone dropping by.

"The stuff piled up. There were some packages Bill never bothered to open. I'd scream at him, like what are you going to do with this shit? How was this going to help restore the Constitution?

"Then there was this day when I noticed that Bill's name wasn't mentioned on the website with the federal fugitives. In the beginning, he'd been right up there, in the top ten. Now he wasn't there at all. I thought he'd be happy they dropped him off the list. 'Bill, you won,' I said.

"He got mad. He said this was a trick, some way to get him to give up. One day he said he wasn't sure if he could trust me anymore. Now I was an agent like everyone else. That was it. I'd been up, taking care of him, basically being his caretaker, fucking popping these gross pustules he got on his back, helping him with his leg, and he's saying he can't trust me."

After that, even though he continued to help prepare the *Hour of the Time* broadcasts, Doyel left the hill, moving down into the flatlands below. "Even then, I'd get home from work and then like three minutes later the telephone rang. It was Bill. He could see my house from his window. He was up there with binoculars, watching, waiting for me to get back.

"Sometimes he'd call in the middle of the night, saying he saw headlights on the road. I'd get my clothes on and go up there. But there was nothing. He was just lonely. He'd go into that business about how we were brothers, that we should stick together. You know, what are you going to do? I had a lot of love for the guy, no matter how he acted. So I said, yeah. I'll come up. Like old times.

"Then he'd say, 'Hey, Doyel, mind picking up a bottle of Jack on the way?'"

As always, even as he felt his eyesight was going, Cooper continued to work in manic spurts, putting out new issues of *Veritas*, updating the website (which now had a chat room), and broadcasting on WBCQ. In July 2000, as members of the audience continued to pray for him and support his stand by sending him homemade cookies and Laser Mind energy pills to keep his brain sharp, Cooper predicted the return of the Bush family to power.

Cooper saw the Mystery Babylon machinations at work in the Ralph Nader candidacy. It was the Perot gambit in reverse, except this time to sway votes from Democrats. The election was going to be close, so Nader didn't have to get a lot of votes, just enough "to make George Bush Jr. the führer-to-be."

Then, in mid-June, Cooper opened his show by saying he'd received an e-mail that "had changed my entire life." It was from Jessica Dovie Cooper, the daughter he had with Sally Phillips in 1980. He hadn't seen her since she was a little kid.

"Hi," Cooper read from Jessica's e-mail on the air. "I'm not sure what to say, or how to start this. I guess just, I am your daughter. I've been looking for you for so many years that I'd almost given up. I got this website from Aunt Connie; Grandpa told me she contacted you on it when Grandma had her stroke.

"I feel there is one thing I should make clear from the start; I have no ill will toward you. I don't hate or resent you. I'm not looking for some perfect father figure to enter my life as if he was always there. I don't even want money. I just want you.

"I look in the mirror and see a stranger's face. A bit of my mother, of course. But then there are those characteristics that are just, sort of there. I want to see the face of my father in my own but I can't. I've never seen the face of my father at all. I have some old black-and-white photos that Grandma sent me, but they are small and from a long time ago. I met my brother, your son Anthony, and my sister Jennifer a few years back. I am slightly calmed by the fact that you were nice and receptive to Tony. Jenny said you were nice as well. I can only dream that you will show the same loving kindness to me as well.

"Please e-mail me as soon as you can. Respectfully yours, Jessica D. Cooper."

When he first read the e-mail, Cooper told listeners, "I couldn't believe it. I thought someone was messing around with my head. I started to get very emotional. I read it again, and again. I must have read it forty or fifty times.

"Believe me, I was scared, but at the same time I had this incredible hope. All this love for a little girl that had left when she was four years old," Cooper said, clarifying that he didn't really leave Jessica.

"She was taken away from me," he said. According to Cooper, he had "done everything I could do to hold that family together." But it wasn't to be. His wife Sally "met another man and fell in love with him."

He still loved Sally, Cooper said. She was brilliantly intelligent, witty and sharp and fun. When she walked into a room, every eye looked at her. "When we fought, we fought 'tooth and nail.'" But when they loved, it was "one of the greatest loves in the history of the earth."

This was the cauldron of passion from which Jessica emerged, Cooper said. When Sally decided to leave, he found himself faced with "two choices." He could "resort to violence and snatch her. Or I could move on. I moved on."

This didn't jibe with Sally's version of their marriage, the one that had Cooper kicking her and Jessica out of the car in Long Beach. Sally said she felt bad for leaving Bill while he was in the VA hospital after his breakdown, but that was the best chance for her and Jessica to get away.

None of that changed the urgency of Jessica's e-mail. Not knowing what to do, leery of a cruel deception on the part of feds, Cooper called Doyel, asked him to stop by the Safeway and pick up a bottle of scotch. He needed a stiff drink.

"Please be my little Jessica," Cooper wrote back, recalling the times "I changed your little diapers, sang to you, pushed you in your stroller." He'd taken many pictures of her, Cooper wrote, "some of which were very good." But he didn't have them anymore, Maybe Sally did. A few hours later, Jessica replied.

"Daddy!" she wrote.

"Daddy, *exclamation point*," Cooper told listeners. "That stopped me right in my tracks. Daddy, with an exclamation point . . . When I saw that, I knew I had struck gold, the kind of gold that is really hard to come by."

He went back to reading Jessica's second e-mail. "I heard from Tony that you had written a book. I wanted to get a copy but I didn't know the name," she wrote. "I have looked for you for so long, almost five years now. I went to lengths you wouldn't believe. I never had money for an investigation. And now here you are, on the net. In print. I want to know everything about you, and selfishly, the part of you when there was me. Father's Day is coming up soon—"

Cooper stopped. He couldn't get the words out. "Father's Day . . . Father's Day . . . is coming soon . . ."

It was "a day that is always sad and very hard for me," Cooper read, audibly weeping. "I am exhilarated that now I really have a father for the Day. Perfect timing, huh? I have so much to say. . . . This is the most important day of my twenty little years so far, thank you, your old daughter, Jessica."

Cooper composed himself. "And now she wants to come to see me," he told the audience. "*Boy*. Won't that be something? That might cause a flood here in Eagar. So you better start building your dikes right now. But we need the water, real bad. So I don't think anyone will complain."

Three weeks later, instead of the usual sirens and snarling dogs, Cooper began his show with the 1930s standard "I Miss You So," the original 1937 version by slick Chicago crooners the Cats and the Fiddle. "I Miss You So" had been "in the back of my head without me even knowing it" ever since he lost Jessica, Cooper said. Now he could finally play it.

Cooper provided a little exposition, saying how he'd asked Doyel to drive the four hours to Phoenix to meet Jessica at the airport. Cooper spent the time fixing up Jessica's room and scrubbing out the bathroom so it was "spotless."

When the truck finally arrived on Cooper Hill, Doyel parked in "a different place than he ever parked before." The doors didn't open for a long time but when they did, "out stepped this very tall, very beautiful young woman and she just rushed into my arms."

Now, a few days later, Jessica was sitting right beside him, sharing the *Hour of the Time* microphone. "Let me paint a picture of her for you," Cooper said. "She's five foot nine. She's got beautiful long brown hair, and the most beautiful smile I think I have ever seen in my life. No, that's not true because it's her mother's smile. But also much her own, too." He went on, singing his daughter's praises, talking about her great intelligence, her grace, her sense of humor, but Jessica soon interrupted.

"He's lying," she said, with a perfectly deadpan delivery. That made them both laugh, a special laugh that fathers and daughters have with each other. Five minutes into the show, they were already a team.

Cooper opened the phones. There was Joe from North Carolina, Danny from Texas, Bob from Long Island, regulars like "Captain Audio."

Everyone wanted to welcome Jessica. Many had been praying for Cooper in his standoff against Mystery Babylon and its federal hired guns. Those prayers were answered. If God had seen fit to take Annie, Pooh, and Allyson away, He'd seen fit to bring Jessica home.

After a while the phones went still. Cooper was about to sign off when he said, "Do you like to dance, Jess?"

"Ohhh," she replied noncommittally.

"Would you dance with me?"

Then, because he already had it cued up, Cooper played Leonard Cohen's "Dance Me to the End of Love." Perhaps it was the title that caught his attention, or that he liked the tune's muted gypsy swing, but it was an unsettling selection on Cooper's part. Cohen himself said the song was inspired by the string quartets who played at Nazi death camps, "beside the crematoria, pressed into performance while this horror was going on."

Still, an author's intention and the listener's reaction need not be the same. So, in the tiny radio station on the besieged hill, Cooper and Jessica danced together, into the night.

If you wanted to write a book about Bill Cooper, she was as good a person to talk to as any, said Jessica, now Jessica Caulboy, when we spoke fifteen years after her visit to Eagar in the summer of 2000.

This was because, she said, "I'm exactly like my dad. I'm a violent alcoholic."

The statement was borne out by the thirty-four-year-old Jessica's current residence, which was the Coffee Creek Correctional Facility in Wilsonville, Oregon, ninety-five miles up I-5 from her home in Eugene.

Her incarceration stemmed from an August 2011 incident in which the Lane County Sheriff's Office responded to a domestic-violence call to find three people—Jessica, her live-in boyfriend, and a neighbor—all bleeding from stab wounds. According to the cops, Jessica and her boyfriend had gotten into an argument and when a friend, attempted to intervene, he wound up being stabbed in the chest with a kitchen knife.

Well into her second year (of three) at Coffee Creek, Jessica wasn't denying the charges. "We'd been drinking. This really big guy, six foot two, 340 pounds, pushed me against a wall. I got knocked out cold. When I came to, I lost it, went spider monkey all over him, completely destroyed the house, trashed a computer. I don't like to fight but when I do, I want to fuck you up. Every aspect of my life has been full of this sort of craziness."

Like many of his ideas, Bill Cooper's genetics have staying power. Jessica bears a facial resemblance to him, as does his older daughter, Jennifer. According to Janice Pell, her son Tony not only sounded like Cooper but also used similar expressions, stuff she'd never heard anyone else say.

"Tony doesn't remember ever seeing Bill in the flesh," Janice Pell said. "But sometimes, I'd look at him and just see Bill. It was a strange way to feel. It was like Bill was still there, haunting me after all these years."

Jessica and I had an arrangement. I put money into her phone account and she called me at 1:00 P.M. every day she felt like it. We'd chat for the State-allotted thirty minutes until the computer voice said to stop and the call went dead.

Sometimes she couldn't get on the line. There were 140 inmates in her "dorm" and phone time was tight. There would often be a racket in the background that made conversation difficult. "There are so many lunatic bitches in here, watching these idiot TV shows, fighting to get over to 'beauty bar' so they can put this shit on their faces like they're going anywhere," Jessica said. She had some friends in the joint, but in jail you couldn't really trust anyone. Everyone was a potential enemy.

That much and a lot more was going to be in the book she was writing about her incarceration, tentatively called *Everything I Know I Learned in Prison.* It was a "part diary, part *Don't Sweat the Small Stuff,* AA-type thing; a do-and-don't about how not to get killed in a hellhole like this," she said. "People who say the world would be better if it were run by loving, caring women have never spent any time in a women's prison, that is for sure."

When asked if by writing a book in jail she was carrying on the Cooper literary tradition of *Behold a Pale Horse,* the classic prison book, Jessica laughed. The reputation of her father's book lived on at Coffee Creek, she said. "The older inmates know it. Some of the younger ones, too, because their dad or boyfriends had it."

On the outside, people sometimes asked about her father. She recalled one time she was working as a waitress around Eugene when "this young guy asked me if I was Bill Cooper's daughter. I said I was and he looks me right in the eye and says, 'I'd take a bullet for you.'"

In jail, though, she tried to avoid such interactions. It was a recommendation she was going to include in her prison book. "If anyone comes up to you that you don't know or don't want to talk to, just start crying. Big tears. A lot of muffled shrieks. That usually stops them in their tracks."

Getting thrown into the hole was a relief. For one thing, Jessica said, "they give you better treatment in solitary because they're nervous you'll commit suicide, which is a drag for them, paperwork-wise. At least it's quiet, so you can actually think. I like to read these long romantic poems in the hole. Emily Dickinson. Lord Byron. Edgar Allan Poe. I just got his complete works . . . anything as long as it's downbeat and heartbroken."

The problem with the hole was no phone privileges, which prevented her from talking to her then two-year-old son, who was living with his father. Every night that she could, she got on the phone to read her son a bedtime story, sing him a song. He loved it, but that was no way to grow up, with a mom who was "a woman in a cage, a voice singing on the phone."

While not denying responsibility for her bad actions, she pointed out the DNA of the situation. It was one of the complaints she had against her mother.

"I love my mother but she has problems. She's a hoarder. When I was about five, after we left my dad, she decided that the best thing for us to do was ride around in a Greyhound bus for months, sleeping in these crazy places like hippies. There were all these stepfathers I never connected with. She wasn't a bad mother, just a little careless. There's a lot of rainbows and unicorns in my mother's world. But she married my father, who was mentally ill. That's how they came up with me."

Recalling her visit to Eagar, Jessica said, "My dad sent me the ticket. I was supposed to stay fifteen days. But I only stayed a week. One week. That's how long I got to spend with my father.

"I was twenty. I'd never been anywhere like Arizona. I knew he was in trouble with feds, but no one told me about what the scene was. All I heard was my mother telling my father, 'Don't let her drink.'

"Doyel came to meet me at the airport in Phoenix. It took us a while to find each other because I didn't know what he was supposed to look like. It was like 115 degrees and his truck had no air-conditioning. From the beginning I could tell he didn't like me but at least he was polite about it.

"Then I saw my father and he just looked so incredibly happy to see me, I jumped into his arms. I was really anxious but then I saw his room. His bed, his fake leg. It seemed like a normal person's bed. This messy, cluttered, normal person's bed. He used Old Spice. That seemed so perfect. Old Spice. *Like that was what a father was supposed to smell like.* It was an amazing feeling.

"He'd tried to clean up but the place was a wreck. But Pooh and Allyson's room, that was just how they left it. All their toys were still there, their teddy bears. That got to me. When I first found out about my father on the Internet, he was always talking about Pooh and Allyson. He never mentioned me or Tony or Jennifer. I thought, 'I'm his kid, too.' I was bitter about it.

"But now my heart went out to him. When Annie and the kids left, they didn't take anything, just the clothes on their back. It was so sad. Me, him, them. All of us together. One of Allyson's little tiny shoes was on the coffee table in the living room, like my dad had been looking at it. That's still vivid to me. *Allyson's shoe.* That's what I remember most."

As for how things turned out during her Eagar trip, Jessica said, it was "upsetting to think about." Since Cooper couldn't go out for fear of capture, father and daughter spent hours in front of the TV, watching movies.

"My father really liked these old movies. Black-and-white, Humphrey Bogart, John Wayne. I wanted to see something newer." They were watching the Spike Lee film *School Daze* and he said, "How can you keep watching this propaganda?" "I said he didn't understand modern society. He started making this big speech. I don't really remember the details, but I wasn't in the mood. I said, 'Can't we just watch the movie?'"

This seemed to set Cooper off, Jessica said. The argument over the movie quickly escalated to long-suppressed resentments. Jessica got up in the middle, went into her room, and locked the door. Then Cooper was outside, banging on the door, telling her to open up.

"I started to get scared," Jessica told me. "There was so much pent-up feelings and we were trying to pretend like everything was so magical. It kills me just to think about it. He yelled, 'You're just like your mother!'" I screamed back, 'Of course I am! She raised me, not you!' . . . That's when I freaked out and called 9-1-1. I just had to get out of there."

According to an Eagar police report, at 10:24 P.M. on July 19, 2000, local officers Crowe and Czarnyszka responded to what was called "a domestic disturbance" on Cooper Hill. What officers found is summed up in a fax from Eagar police chief Scott Garms to FBI Special Agent Steve Fillerup under the subject line "Another Cooper Report."

Garms's account said "everything had been going okay, but they were drinking that night and watching movies. Cooper flipped out for no reason and scared Jessica to death. She refused to go back into the house. She abandoned all her property there and we took her to a motel with nothing but her pajamas."

The next day, Garms wrote, "My secretary got Jessica some new clothes and drove her to Show Low so she could take a bus back to Phoenix." Garms's note added that "Jessica's mother Sally Phillips called the next day to check on her status. She described Bill as someone with some very good qualities; however, he has gone off the deep end with the UFO stuff and she thinks he has a mental illness."

"I felt pretty numb after the whole thing," Jessica told me from Coffee Creek. "My father kept calling to try to talk to me. Finally my mother put me on the phone with him. He told me he loved me. He was so, so sorry. He wanted me to come back. Nothing like that would happen again."

Shortly thereafter, Jessica said, some men from the US Marshals office came to see her. "They'd been watching me. They knew everything about me. They wanted me to help them make a map of my dad's house and tell them where all the guns he had were. They told me that my father was going to get arrested sooner or later and they didn't want anyone, including him, to get hurt. So I told them there were a lot of guns. There was hardly any place where the guns weren't. I was a twenty-year-old girl; I didn't want my father to get shot."

The feds told Jessica they had a plan. She was to go back to Eagar accompanied by "a really handsome" US Marshal pretending to be her boyfriend. The two of them would convince Cooper to leave his house to go eat in Los Dos Molinos, a Springerville Mexican restaurant he liked.

"It was supposed to a normal night but in reality everyone in the place would be agents pretending to be normal customers," Jessica recounted. "At some signal I was supposed to go to the bathroom and then they'd arrest him. No one would get hurt. The agent playing my boyfriend wouldn't break his cover, so Dad would never know I was in on it. This was like the dumbest plan ever. Really stupid.

"I couldn't believe it. I said, 'You want me to rat out my own father? You got to be kidding.'" Then, Jessica said, the feds started bargaining. "They wanted to give me five hundred dollars and an apartment so I could move out from my mother. They wanted me to sell out my dad for five hundred dollars and an apartment."

Jessica called Cooper to tell him about the meeting. That night Cooper responded with a broadcast called "Something to Die For." The show, somewhat mysteriously, does not appear in the roster of *The Complete Cooper* but rather can be found on the web in an intermittently audible bootleg version. Cooper collector Graceful Watchman posted it on YouTube. Cosmic089 also put it up, adding that "Something to Die For" was the most prophetic show William Cooper ever made. "He KNEW how his life would end," cosmic089 wrote.

"I am very upset tonight. I'm very angry, on the verge of . . . I'm not even going to mention what I am on the verge of," Cooper began his program, sounding drunk and impossibly weary. "I talked to my daughter Jessica earlier this evening. . . . She said the United States Marshals are after her in an attempt to make her betray me. They want her to tell them all about my house. All about the rooms and what's in the rooms and how many weapons are here . . . and how I am going to defend myself should they come after me."

The Marshals Service had "intimidated" Jessica, Cooper said. "In fact, they *terrorized* her. They told her if she did not cooperate, she might go to prison. *She's twenty years old!* She's never known me or seen me in her whole life until recently, when she came and spent some time with me."

Cooper then went off on Eagar Police Chief Garms. He was nothing but a "stinking little shit," a "federal rat." Didn't he know that he had been elected to protect and serve the people of Eagar, not to spy on residents and report back to the feds? Garms, the Eagar Police, on up to county and state officials, the US Marshals, the FBI, and BATF were one and the same, Cooper said. They weren't working for the United States government. They were working "for Satan, for deception, for lies." They were "puke-faced, lying, threatening, despicable, dishonest, unethical, blackmailing, suck-ass, immoral bastards" who would rather pick on a twenty-year-old girl than come up Cooper Hill and face him.

It went on like this for nearly fifty minutes without stop. He didn't care what the FAA or FCC had to say. He was "an American patriot, an American fighting man" and if need be, he was "going to come off this mountain and personally start the restoration of the constitutional republic" all by himself. If Garms or anyone else threatened his daughter, his family, or his friends ever again, he would "lay a path across this nation that no one will ever forget."

"Come on, come on," he kept shouting. "Find your balls! Come on up here. Chickenshit bastards!"

More than a decade before, in the introduction to *Behold a Pale Horse*, Cooper wrote, "I believe with all my heart that God put me in places and in positions throughout my life so that I would be able to deliver this warning to His people. I pray that I have been worthy and that I have done my job."

That was when he set down what he called MY CREED, where he lists the four things that he stood inviolately behind. First, Cooper wrote, "I believe in God, the same God in which my ancestors believed." Second, "I believe in the Constitution of the Republic of the United States of America, without interpretation, as it was written and meant to work." Third, "I believe in the family unit and, in particular, my family unit." Fourth, and last, Cooper said, "I believe that any man without principles that he is ready and willing to die for at any given moment is already dead and is of no use or consequence whatsoever."

So much had been lost over the years. God remained silent in Cooper's struggle with the Devil. The Constitution had been victimized out of sheer neglect, proving once and for all time that Ben Franklin had been right when he doubted humanity's ability to live up to the document's intentions. Cooper's family was gone. There was nothing left but the fourth tenet of his Creed, the resolve not to give in.

Some weeks after Jessica's departure from Cooper Hill, Doyel came up to visit. "I came up to work on a couple of broadcasts. Bill was in a funny sort of mood. We were standing in front of the house, by the cars. Then he turned to me and said he figured it out, decided what he was going to do now."

"Well," Cooper told Doyel, "I can always be a martyr."

24

For years the kids of Eagar-Springerville looked forward to riding their bikes on what used to be called R.V. Hill. It was the highest place around and, before the town's modest sprawl, out on the edge of things. A boy could ride to the top and feast his young eyes upon the delightsome land the Heavenly Father had provided for his Saints in which to dwell. Then, having offered thanks to Creation, that same boy could ride down the hill as fast and wild as he wanted, front wheels rimming six-inch-deep rain ruts in the unpaved road, no helmet on, chancing fate with every unseen stone.

Scott Hamblin, who grew up in the Round Valley, was one of those boys back in the seventies and eighties. Now Dr. Scott Reynolds Hamblin, he felt a sweet continuity when he opened his own practice in Eagar. He'd fulfilled his outreach ministry, graduated medical school, done his residency. He opened his medical practice on North Main Street. He was a cherished and indispensable member of the community. He was home.

On July 11, 2001, Dr. Hamblin, wife, Deanna, and their young daughters went out for a run at Water Canyon near Big Lake in the Apache-Sitgreaves National Forest. It was beautiful up there on the early summer evenings, a decade before the Wallow Fire burned everything to the ground. Driving back to Eagar in their van, the Hamblins stopped off at the Dairy Queen for ice cream cones. A thunderstorm was rolling in. They decided it'd be fun to drive over to the old R.V. Hill road to watch the lightning streak across the sky.

What happened next was a "most bizarre occurrence," Dr. Hamblin wrote in the statement he filed with the Eagar Police Department the next morning.

After about ten minutes, "the kids were ready to go home, so we started back," Hamblin's report read. "As we turned down the hill, a vehicle pulled up very close behind us with brights on. He followed us VERY closely till the bottom of the hill. At the stop sign he was within inches of our van."

The truck continued to tailgate the Hamblins' vehicle to their home on East Second Street, about a mile away, pulling into their driveway right behind them. Hamblin remembered "a premonition" he had earlier about the hill where he played as a boy. He'd heard there was a man up there "who was in some way connected to Timothy McVeigh." Now, looking at the pickup idling ominously in his driveway, he wondered if he should have taken the feeling more seriously.

Hamblin told Deanna to get the kids inside.

He took a few steps toward the truck when the driver got out and yelled, "Stay the f— off my hill!"

Hamblin told the man, whom he did not recognize, that he and his family hadn't meant to go on his property. They just wanted to watch the lightning.

"I know what the hell you were doing up there!" the man shouted. "You were spying on me!"

"I don't even know who you are," Dr. Hamblin replied. The man then approached and stuck his index finger hard into the doctor's chest. "Then you better *find out* who I am," he said.

According to his statement, Hamblin grabbed the man's finger and bent it back "forcefully." After that, the driver "stepped back to his pickup, leaned over, and picked up a small, squarish handgun. He pointed it within one foot of my face and charged it." Glaring at Dr. Hamblin, the man said, "Don't you EVER come up my hill again." Then he got in his truck and drove away.

Soon after filing their complaint, Dr. Hamblin and his wife were asked to look at a police photo array of potential suspects. They both immediately pointed to picture number 3. To the surprise of no one, it was Bill Cooper.

Cooper had been involved in several such incidents since declaring himself at war with the federal government. In December 1999, he'd run off the coach of the beloved Elks, the Round Valley High School football team.

Cooper was ordering people off property he did not own. The lot where his house sat was the extent of his holdings. He justified these actions by saying he was only performing his duties as the duly registered captain of the Neighborhood Watch program. "We're the only ones up here, so we're the neighborhood," Cooper told listeners.

Cooper's attempt to control his privacy perimeter was further complicated by the hill's long-established status as the town's lover's lane. Round Valley residents had been groping one another in the back seats of cars in the vicinity of North Clearview Circle long before Bill Cooper declared the hill the last bastion of constitutional law in the country.

"They think this is the Blueberry Hill of Eagar, Arizona," Cooper complained on *The Hour of the Time,* saying he was sick of cleaning up the used condoms and beer cans. Cooper's intervention with time-honored Round Valley rites of passage sparked some resentment at the high school and in bars over in Springerville. Driving up to Cooper Hill and making a racket became a town dare. If you got "old man Cooper" to come raging out of his house on his fake leg with his gun and killer dog, you were a winner.

"I could barely see the driver the whole time he was following us. I only saw the grille of the truck. Even that looked angry," Dr. Hamblin told me when I visited him at his pleasant Eagar home in 2016. In his early fifties, Hamblin and his family had thrived in the years since their run-in with Cooper. The doctor's practice, where he specializes in hospice and palliative care, was doing well and he had helped many people.

Friendly and accommodating, the doctor drove over from his office to meet me at his house for lunch. He wife, Deanna, had prepared a lovely spread. In retrospect, it was "fascinating and scary" to revisit the fifteen-year-old incident, Hamblin said. It wasn't every day that "someone points a gun in your face in front of your house."

The memories came tumbling back. "One thing I recall," Hamblin told me. "When I pulled back his finger, it was cold, there was no resistance at all. Like clay." But the main thing Hamblin took away from the incident, he said with a sharp laugh, was that "*I didn't die*. I didn't die that night."

Deanna was proud of how her husband handled himself. "I'm a person with a strong faith," she said. "I probably should have been petrified but I wasn't. I was with my children and family. That's where I was supposed to be, so I felt things would work the way they were supposed to.

"Being with our family, I think that's what saved Scott," Deanna went on. "He was a man with a family and he was protecting his family. He wasn't backing down, even with a gun cocked in his face. I think that he . . . Mr. Cooper . . . realized that."

Deanna turned to her husband. "I think that's why you're still here," she said.

What most bothered Hamblin in the immediate aftermath of the encounter was what he then took to be inaction on the part of the Eagar police. "After I filed the report, I thought they would arrest him. But they didn't seem to be doing anything."

Hamblin became more adamant that something be done about Cooper. He understood that Cooper was a federal fugitive and it was the FBI that was largely calling the shots. Yet it was intolerable that someone could put his family in danger in his hometown without any repercussions from the local officials, many of whom were his friends and patients.

"At the time, I thought they were afraid to go up the hill. To tell you the truth, I thought they were cowards," Hamblin told me over lunch. The inaction was surprising. After all, it wasn't as if the Hamblins were nobodies in the Round Valley.

Across southern Apache County, certain names come up over and over again. The Lees, the Browns, the Burkes, the Crosbys, the Udalls, and the Romneys are but a few. These are the descendants of the "pioneer families," Mormon believers who settled the Little Colorado basin during the 1870s and 1880s. These were the people who built the Big Ditch, people whose descendants continue to make up much of the Round Valley establishment. However, few family names inspire the same kind of reverence as Hamblin. To get to Dr. Hamblin's house from Highway 260, it is best to make a right on Hamblin Street. As of this writing, the mayor of Eagar is Bryce Hamblin.

The prestige of the name derives in no small part from the defining role played by Jacob Vernon Hamblin in the early days of the LDS Church's singular place in the epic of the American West. Born into an Ohio farming family in 1819, Jacob Hamblin went west with Brigham Young after the death of the Mormon prophet Joseph Smith at the hands of an angry mob in Carthage, Illinois, in 1844.

A member of the feared Mormon militias, Hamblin was widely rumored to have been involved in the infamous 1857 Mountain Meadows Massacre in which 120 members of a California-bound wagon train were allegedly killed in a Mormon ambush. Hamblin's main task, however, was to defend the Saints against the Lamanites, as the Native Americans were called.

It was a struggle predicated on scripture, part of the prehistory of the continent as described in the Golden Plates, one of the most significant of American secret documents. Found in the same upstate New York area that gave birth to the Millerites and translated from the "reformed Egyptian" language by the prophet Joseph Smith with help from the Angel Moroni, the Book of Mormon offered a history of the early American races, including the "delightsome" light-skinned Nephites and the Lamanites, whose rebelliousness against God caused them to bear the curse of dark skin. By 420 AD, the warlike Lamanites had wiped out the Nephites. But with Joseph Smith's discovery of the plates, the descendants of Nephites, the resurrected Latter-day Saints of Jesus Christ, had returned to reclaim their ordained place in the New World holy land.

Then, as the story went, Jacob Hamblin found himself face-to-face with a formidable member of the Lamanites. The Lamanite shot his arrow as Hamblin fired his gun. Neither was hurt in any way. For Hamblin, it was a revelation. As he wrote in his diary, "The Holy Spirit forcibly impressed me that it was not my calling to shed the blood of the scattered remnant of Israel, but to be a messenger of peace to them."

Appointed by Brigham Young as the "Special Apostle to the Lamanites," Hamblin spent the rest of his life as the LDS ambassador to the native population, learning their languages, sitting by their council fires. In the sacred Hopi village of Oraibi, Hamblin broke bread with elders who told him his arrival had long been foretold by shamans.

Eventually weary from his travels, Hamblin was given a last task by

Brigham Young. He led a group of pioneers to the edge of the White Mountains and became presiding elder of the Round Valley Branch of the Little Colorado Stake. He's buried in the woods of the Apache-Sitgreaves National Forest, where his gravestone reads PEACE MAKER IN THE CAMP OF THE LAMANITES.

"It is a tremendous history," said Dr. Hamblin, who, like his namesake, had just been elected president of Round Valley Stake.

Bill Cooper had a different take on LDS history. As far as Cooper was concerned, the Mormons were a "power structure that controlled staggering resources and was organized for absolute authoritarianism." They were just one more branch of Mystery Babylon.

In a 1993 broadcast entitled "The Godmakers," Cooper told the audience that Mormons believed that "if a married couple produces many children and conforms to the teachings of the church, when they die, they will be gods and be given a planet of their own."

What crap this was, Cooper said, bemoaning the sheeple's capacity for self-delusion. "Where do these people get their egos? *'I'll be a god!'* Yeah, sure you will."

Later, in a 1996 broadcast called "Truths about Mormonism," Cooper said that he lived "in Mormon territory." The vast majority of LDS members were "good, honest, wonderful people," Cooper said. But that didn't negate the fact that Joseph Smith was a 32nd-degree Freemason, who at the moment of his death was heard to shout "Oh Lord, my God, is there no help for the widow's son?," the traditional Masonic distress call. Beyond that, Cooper said, the LDS Church followed "apartheid" racial policies, to say nothing of the fact that an abnormally high number of LDS members joined the CIA and FBI, working in "covert operations, black projects, and intelligence-gathering organizations."

During the siege, Cooper got into a dispute with Stephen Udall, a member of the Eagar City Council. Cooper said, "Where I live, you can't walk one hundred yards without running into a member of the Udall family." Most of them were "nice, wonderful people." But Councilman Udall was snooping around, invading Cooper Hill space, having driven up the approach road that, typically enough, was called Udall Street.

Cooper went out to inform the councilman about the "situation," and why access had to be restricted. "If an innocent person happens to be here when the federal government decides to come up here and kill us, they could be killed themselves," Cooper told the audience, explaining how he went outside with Crusher and told Councilman Udall quite reasonably that if he wanted to come up "this mountain," it would be best to call first.

Udall said he wasn't going to do that. Udall Street was a public thoroughfare and he'd drive up it anytime he wanted. He said he had some property up on the hill he wanted to sell and had come by to check if the road-paving project had been finished to his satisfaction.

Cooper was enraged. As he told the audience, he'd been trying to get that road paved for five years with no response from the city council. During the monsoon season, the mud could be half a foot thick. In the winter the road froze solid. He paid his rightful local property taxes, went through the proper channels, without result. But when "a Udall" wanted to his sell property, suddenly the work was done.

This was out-and-out corruption, a criminal act, Cooper railed, opening the phones. He wanted to see what people in the Round Valley had to say about Udall, but he doubted anyone would have "the guts" to call. This was because, Cooper said, Councilman Udall "happens to belong to a prominent church in this valley which appears to control everything there is.

"If you live in a town that is mostly populated by Mormons and you are not a member of the church, you are going to be shunned in politics, business, and society," Cooper declared.

"They should have learned their lesson in the 1800s that you should not do that; based on their own experience of being discriminated against," Cooper bitingly declared. This was the way the forces of Mystery Babylon always acted, he said, playing Hank Williams Jr.'s defiant "A Country Boy Can Survive" to underscore how fed up he was with the Round Valley's grandees.

The standoff with the feds took a turn in August of 2001 when Dr. Hamblin wrote a letter asking the Apache County Sheriff's Office to look into the Cooper case. "I wanted *someone* to do something," Hamblin told me when we talked.

The Apache County Sheriff's Office has a long and colorful history dating back before Arizona statehood. Rawhide Jake Brighton was county deputy when he hunted down and killed the outlaw Ike Clanton outside of Springerville. Later came the red-haired gunfighter Commodore Perry Owens (1887–1888). Jacob Hamblin Jr. was sheriff in 1915–1916 and again in 1919. But no one held the top job as long as C. Arthur "Art" Lee, sheriff from 1973–1999.

When the Cooper siege began, Sheriff Lee was a main advocate of nonintervention. He was adamant about not allowing "a Ruby Ridge in my county." As far as he was concerned, Lee told the FBI, Bill Cooper could live in the community "for the next fifty years and never receive a traffic ticket." He agreed with Special Agent Fillerup that storming Cooper Hill just "wasn't worth it."

Fifteen years later, he hadn't changed his mind, Lee told me when we spoke in November of 2016. Now into his eighties, Lee said "Things would have been different if I was still sheriff that night, that's for sure."

But Art Lee was not the sheriff in 2001. When he retired in 1999, he appointed thirty-seven-year-old Brian Hounshell, a former prison guard, to finish out his term. Many thought Hounshell was just a placeholder until Lee's son Clint was ready to take over the job. As the elder Lee said, "Before I put Hounshell in, I made him promise that the department would be run the same way it had been. He gave me his word on that.

"Well, he went about as far south from that as you could," Lee said. "In twenty-six years as sheriff, that was the biggest mistake I ever made, putting that guy in there." Hounshell was nothing but "a hard-charger, a bull in the china shop. Can't say I got much use for the man."

It was true that Hounshell was a different sort of Apache County sheriff. He had nothing to do with the old-line Mormon pioneer families. He'd been brought up around the Navajo Nation, where his parents ran a trading post. He spoke Navajo, had deep roots on the Rez, and pretty much didn't give a fuck what Art Lee wanted. In 2000, rather than step aside as had been assumed, Hounshell ran for sheriff on his own, and won. Once in power, he surrounded himself with several of his old correction facility buddies.

"He loved getting his name in the newspaper," Art Lee said. It was this quest for publicity, Lee contended, that prompted Sheriff Hounshell to take up Dr. Hamblin's case against Bill Cooper, celebrity madman of Eagar, Arizona.

On August 29, 2001, the State of Arizona on behalf of the Apache County Sheriff's Office issued a warrant charging "William Milton Cooper" with two felony counts aggravated assault and another for reckless endangerment against Scott Hamblin and his family. A plan was being devised to bring Cooper to justice.

The first date scheduled for the Apache County Special Response Team (SRT) to take Cooper Hill was September 11, 2001. These plans were canceled due to what the Arizona Department of Public Safety (DPS) called "a possible security breach."

"They were going to come get him on 9/11! Can you believe that?" Doyel Shamley said. "The 'possible security breach' was that Bill was on the air for like nine straight hours that day, all across the country. I guess they didn't want to break into the middle of that."

On the morning of September 11, Cooper was awakened by a phone call from Allan Weiner, owner of WBCQ. "I was recovering from cancer surgery and I see the Twin Towers crumbling. It felt like the world was coming apart," Weiner told me when we spoke in 2015.

"It is in times like that you have to go with your gut. People want to know what happened and 99 percent of the media was going to tell them the same thing. I asked Bill if he would take the mic, be voice of WBCQ. I told him to stay on for as long as he could, call it the way he saw it. On this day more than any other, I felt that what Bill Cooper had to say was *essential*."

Opening the show by saying, "This is probably the worst day in the history of the entire world," Cooper's first order of business was to set up *The Hour of the Time* as a media command post, a clearinghouse for American patriots who could not trust mainstream news reporting. He'd done something like that after the OKC bombing, but this was a bigger situation, almost beyond imagining.

"I don't want to hear any rumors," Cooper declared, "nothing that came in 'mysteriously by fax,'" or repeated from the radio shows of his enemies, people like Bo Gritz, Art Bell Jr., or Alex Jones.

"The only people who should be calling this radio program today are those who have something to report that the country and world *absolutely needs to know*," Cooper declared. Early reports would be crucial. It was only a matter of time before "the official story," the one the authorities *wanted* you to believe, set in.

As the head of SCAR's Intelligence Service, Cooper briefed the troops. Airports had been shut down, borders sealed, the president and Congress had been taken to well-protected bunkers. That could mean only one thing: The country was under martial law, whether the government admitted it or not. As for the patriots out there, it was the time to go underground. As proved after OKC, the reaction could be fierce.

Misinformation was everywhere. Even in the Round Valley, 2,500 miles from New York and Washington, people were spreading rumors that someone was planning to blow up the high school. There were reports that the Red Chinese were moving in.

"There is no threat in the Round Valley. *I repeat*, no threat in the Round Valley," Cooper announced.

He had predicted the attack, of course he had. Everyone had heard him do it only two months before on the June 28, 2001, episode of *The Hour of the Time*. The terrible event that was going to happen and be blamed on Osama bin Laden had come to pass.

On C-SPAN they were interviewing Orrin Hatch, the Utah senator. With zero proof, Hatch was foaming at the mouth, demanding bin Laden's bearded head on a plate.

Cooper stayed behind the microphone through the afternoon, pausing only when Doyel brought him an Italian sub sandwich from Arby's. He chastised those who called for blind vengeance against Muslims, as if the immigrant behind the counter at the Circle K was somehow the mastermind of the plot.

The only proper course of action, Cooper said, was to send in a highly trained team of professionals "to hunt down and find the people responsible, bring them back to this country, try them in court, and if they're guilty, sentence them to whatever punishment is required." That's how it was done in a constitutional republic, Cooper said, in case everyone had forgotten.

The show highlight came about fifty minutes in, when a Jersey man called in with an item that had been reported on the Channel 7 local news but then deleted from the news stream, unmentioned by Dan Rather, Peter Jennings, and the rest. This fit the description of what Cooper was looking for, news suppressed by the keepers of the official story.

Someone on the eighty-sixth floor of one of the towers had apparently phoned a local reporter to tell him that he'd heard a massive explosion and that "the entire core of the building has been blown out." The man said he was trapped. He was going to die.

The caller said he was passing this on because "I thought it might say something about the structural integrity of those buildings."

"You said someone inside the building heard an explosion before the planes hit?" Cooper inquired, the notion beginning to crackle awake in his head. A moment later the scenario arrived, full-grown. Suddenly he knew that "it couldn't have just been the planes flying into the buildings." The planes "hit high up, in the top third or quarter of those towers; the impact could not have injured the integrity of the buildings' bottom core.

"Something blew up at the major structural core of the buildings down at the bottom," Cooper declared, 2,500 miles away from the scene. *"I can assure you of that."*

The WTC was "exactly" the same thing as Oklahoma City, Cooper went on. Just as "a truck full of fertilizer parked in the street could not have brought down the Alfred P. Murrah Building," jet planes did not topple the World Trade Center.

The Twin Towers were "steel-reinforced concrete" buildings, what they called "a hard target in military jargon," Cooper said. When he was in the Navy he learned that the "only way to bring down a hard target is with shaped, specially placed charges."

It was *not possible* that the impact of a 400,000-pound 767 jumbo jet traveling at 540 miles per hour could have caused such a catastrophic result, Cooper declared, harkening back to the story of a B-25 bomber that ran into the Empire State Building in 1945. It took out a couple of floors, but the building stayed up.

Cooper had found the lede. His next "recap" of the day's breaking news events began with his assessment that the towers had "collapsed upon themselves, all the way down to the ground . . . as a result of detonation of a series of shaped charges." It was, Cooper said, "a demo-lition."

Supposed to be arrested that very day, Cooper made the most of his reprieve. He laid out the rudiments of what came to be called 9/11 Truth, the first great conspiracy meme of the broadband age, a theory of the crime that generated a fury of obsession not seen since the Kennedy as-sassination.

It was a necessary story. For many of the younger generation, 9/11 was the biggest public event they'd ever experienced. Like Ezekiel and his wheel, like a broad-daylight shooting of a president, it was an instantly mythic moment, a once-in-a-lifetime event. It begged for explanation, reassurance, something that made sense.

9/11 *deserved* Truth, or at least the semblance of an effort. Instead, it got Osama bin Laden and his nineteen men with box cutters, along with a president too engrossed in *The Pet Goat* to call in the SWAT teams. The story insulted your intelligence, left you cursing in the dark.

"These people are arrogant, they love to flaunt what they're doing in our faces," Cooper told the audience. "They think they can tell you any-thing and you'll believe it. Not this time."

The "controlled demolition" scenario became a major strand of the early 9/11 Truth groups that began appearing around the country. Com-mencing in 2004, members of the NYC 9/11 Truth movement attended weekly meetings in New York's East Village at the 350-year-old St. Mark's Church, where Alexander Hamilton once dispensed pro bono legal advice and Allen Ginsberg read "Howl." It wasn't just the usual gray-ponytailed guys with the protruding R. Crumb eyes; there was a new demographic present, younger, more diverse, crust punks, business-men, schoolteachers.

There were Architects and Engineers for 9/11 Truth, Pilots for 9/11 Truth, Poets for 9/11 Truth. Scholarly papers were prepared on the col-lapse of WTC Building 7. For many, the fall of building number 7 be-came a focus. It was hit by no plane and was the home of numerous governmental offices, including the FBI, CIA, and Securities and Ex-change Commission. Many of the SEC files kept in the building were paper records, not yet digitized. When the forty-seven-story building tumbled to the ground, so did a lot of cases against market profiteers.

At the beginning at least, 9/11 Truth was being run with a sobriety that reminded an old hand of those super-earnest faculty teach-ins at the dawn of the Vietnam War protests. Parliamentary procedure was invoked, persistent interruption and intemperate outbursts were discouraged. But a critical corner had been turned. Too much had happened for anyone to have much faith in the official story.

When it came to possible Bush administration involvement, many 9/11 Truthers narrowed the theory of the crime to two possibilities, LIHOP and MIHOP, as in "Let It Happen on Purpose" and "Made It Happen on Purpose." Arguments could go into the night about that.

Not that Cooper cared. He'd done his work, he laid out the rudiments of the 9/11 Truth "controlled demo" narrative in about three minutes of real time, off the top of his head, even as the paperwork from the Cantor Fitzgerald office still swirled in the wind above the pile.

Cooper said his special prescience came from having his "finger on the pulse of everyone in this country who thinks and feels the way I do." The fact that the first version of the documentary *Loose Change*, the visual totem of 9/11 Truth, didn't appear until 2005—making some of the same claims Cooper did as events transpired—shows how far ahead of the curve he was, a conspiracy salesman without peer, a natural.

For Cooper, 9/11 completed one more fearful symmetry. On September 11, 1990, before a joint session of Congress, George H. W. Bush, who Cooper claimed, had been initiated as "a priest in the Temple of Isis while lying in a casket with a ribbon wrapped around his genitalia," welcomed the dawning of the New World Order with the blood ritual of the Gulf War. Eleven years later, almost to the very second, on September 11, 2001, George Bush the younger, Skull and Bones class of 1968, completed the full circle.

"Today our fellow citizens, our way of life, our very *freedom*, came under attack in a series of deliberate and deadly terrorist acts," Bush the younger said. The reason America was "targeted for attack" was "because we are the brightest beacon for *freedom* . . . in the world and no one will keep that light from shining." Soon the president would be sending in more troops to the former Babylon. Death would beget more death. Bush Jr. was the new Horus to Poppy's Kennebunkport Osiris. Cooper saw it coming, all the way back to *2001: A Space Odyssey*. He even got the year right.

For eleven years, patriots had held them off. Ruby Ridge, Waco, and even Oklahoma City were battles bravely fought, but lost, catastrophically lost. The 9/11 extravaganza was Mystery Babylon's victory jamboree, their unholy bombs-bursting-in-air bacchanal, their Fourth of July. The great work of the New World Order was complete.

One thing that bugged Cooper was that the newsmen and politicians were calling the people in the planes "cowards." These weren't cowards, they were "brave men fighting for their cause," Cooper said.

"They see our hypocrisy. They see our lies. They know what we've done . . . we killed thousands of civilians in Bosnia and Iraq. But because we did it, it is supposed to be okay? *It is never okay.* You can't expect someone to obey the rules when we have never obeyed the rules in our history. Ask a Native American sometime. How many tribes did we wipe out down to the last man, woman, and child, that don't exist on the face of Earth anymore? It wasn't because they were scalping white people going west in covered wagons. We did it because we wanted their land."

America was supposed to be about *freedom*, real *freedom*. Freedom could not be bought or sold. Freedom was the real magic of the nation, the sense that an individual could make up his mind for himself about what could be done and not done as long as he stayed within the boundaries of his Creator-endowed rights. Indefinable at its core, freedom was the one thing no meaningful life could be lived without.

All around, Cooper saw surrender. The C-SPAN feed picked up the sound of a woman crying. We need "something to keep us safe" from these terrorists, the woman said. "See what I mean?" Cooper railed at the audience, with I-told-you-so dismay.

He couldn't believe what he was hearing from the so-called patriot community. Bodies crushed under the buildings were still warm and people were calling *The Hour of the Time* to say they heard Sonny Bono was murdered because he was doing research on the Waco Massacre, and maybe that had something to do with the attacks.

"Sonny Bono hit a tree while skiing on a mountain," Cooper said, slowly, and hung up.

"There must be someone who is just sitting around cooking this stuff up," Cooper said, adding that he couldn't imagine "why people take this stuff seriously just because somebody says 'Look at this, it's really *true*, man.' Nobody checks, they just go out of their mind about it and pass it on to somebody else." Most nights he just turned off the news and went to sleep.

One brisk early morning about two weeks after the Twin Tower attacks, Cooper got up to make breakfast. He opened the stove door and sprung the hinge, yet again. He went outside to get his rubber mallet from the trunk of the '58 Chevy to fix it.

Then, Cooper told the audience in *HOTT* #1917, "the strangest thing happened . . . there was a large, a very large puma, a mountain lion, walking right across the driveway." The puma walked past the chickens, who scatter at the sight of a house cat, and they didn't react. Crusher was right there but he didn't bark.

"It was like they knew each other," Cooper said, still amazed, telling listeners how the big cat kept walking "right straight toward me." His .45 automatic on his right hip as always, he was thinking of shooting the lion, but something told him that was a "bad idea." He stood stock-still as the puma walked closer, sat down right next to him, and started to purr.

"This really deep-throated purr like cats do. *Real loud.* It sat there for a few minutes and then it got up and just walked away toward the south." Nothing like that ever happened before. "I'm not bothered by it, I'm not perturbed, just sort of weirded out," Cooper told the listeners, asking if they had any ideas about the incident.

A woman called and said the puma was Cooper's "guardian angel." She was Catholic, the lady said, and "St. John Bosco had a gray wolf as his guardian angel who would materialize whenever he was in danger from assassins or robbers or anything else that might be traveling around." That's who the cat was, the lady said, "your guardian angel, Bill."

According to Doyel Shamley, Cooper was in a relatively cheerful mood on the morning of November 5, 2001. He'd just put the finishing touches on his Vietnam novel, tentatively entitled *Cua Viet: The War on the River*. Based on his experiences as a river patrol boat captain, Cooper started writing the book back in the 1970s, working on it on and off through the eighties. He'd put the book aside when his flying saucer career took off but now felt the need to get it done. He thought he'd lost the manuscript until Doyel found it shoved between some boxes in one of the storage units Cooper had rented in town.

The story tells of a river patrol boat captain known only by his surname, March, a Navy Special Operations man in a black beret, the sort who, Cooper writes, "makes people nervous." The year before, March's boat was ambushed by NVA forces near Whiskey Nine, a rocky island off the main channel of the Cua Viet. The only survivor of the attack, the gravely wounded March spent much of the next year in the sick bay. The book opens on the day he returns to the jungle, a terse, hell-bent Conradian soul looking for revenge.

"I'm coming for you, Charlie," March says to himself as he choppers in over the defoliated, bomb-pocked terrain surrounding Dong Ha. "I'm going to pay you back, you bastards."

Months before, Cooper read some of *The War on the River*, a work in progress, on *The Hour of the Time*. "Well, I just don't know . . . I don't know about tonight's broadcast," he began, laying out "the parameters" listeners "must observe" while hearing the story.

"You've got to be in a dark room, because that's the kind of place we are going to visit. Sort of moody, and gloomy. You should be in a comfortable chair, you should be leaning back. You should close your eyes . . .

"Because . . . I am going to try to evoke some pictures for you. I want you to see the place. . . . *It is an incredible place.* Maybe two or three of you will recognize it. I don't think it could possibly be more than that . . . and if you do, then you and I are *very close.*"

Slowly, carefully, Cooper read of a "lonely, bleak, and sandy" world where "the wind courses from the north and east, cursing this place with cold, rain, and low, black, ominous clouds. The light filtering through casts its drab finger on the land striking shadows dead. It is a perpetual twilight that eats at the soul and spreads the specter of doom."

For the Vietnamese, the river provided "food and travel from dawn to sundown, when curfew began," Cooper read. "But for us the river is a mysterious, evil monster to be confronted each night, night after night, night upon night, endlessly, without any break, every single night."

There was a strange thing about Cua Viet, Cooper said at the outset of episode #1926, the final entry in *The Complete Cooper*. It was a brutal borderland where many died. Yet you never heard much about the place.

It was like the river "fell down through the cracks of the war," Cooper said. He'd spent a long time looking for people who served with him, "but I never found a single one of them."

This changed after he read the excerpt on *The Hour of the Time*. When the e-mails began to pour in, Cooper said he knew, "instinctively, that this was going to be a catharsis for healing, for bringing people together. . . . It has touched my heart, way down deep inside."

He'd been "hard at work" building a website for veterans of Cua Viet, Cooper told the audience. The site was only one page now, but it would grow.

"We need stories from people, pictures," Cooper told listeners that night, spelling out the site name, CuaViet.org, letter by staccato letter, three times. The web page was going to turn out to be "important," Cooper said. "More important than I ever dreamed."

Right then the phone rang. "Bill?" the caller said. "Why are you calling?" spat Cooper, recognizing the voice on the line. "I didn't open the phones. Stay off the damn phone!" A moment later, still fuming, Cooper said, "I can't believe how gross and inconsiderate so many people really are. . . . Well, I'm not going to let it bother me. I'm going to go on with this."

Resetting, Cooper said he would be devoting the evening's program to reading the "pages and pages and pages of e-mail" he'd received. "You're not going to believe what you're going to hear."

The first e-mail was from Jerry Lilly, a platoon commander with H-company, Second Battalion, First Marines. Lilly told how he and his men had barely escaped an NVA unit after a firefight. "We spent two months along the river and it was dangerous territory for us," he wrote, saying what a relief it was to see a PBR "on the duck pond." He remembered the river boat personnel as "tenacious and on a fluid medium . . . focused, always ready to unload. Men who have tasted the sting of the enemy are like that. Me and my men could actually relax a bit because we could see you at the ready."

"This next one is so important to me," Cooper said. "I gotta tell you, when I got this e-mail, I was blown away. I sat down and cried. Because all these years I always wondered what happened to my crew. *My crew!* You see, I was a boat captain. And I never could find any of them. Then all of a sudden in my e-mail box, here's what I read:

"*'Hey, Coop!* Don't sweat it, man. I understand. I couldn't kick the Nam thing either. Glad to hear from someone who actually knows the score.

"'I remember you talking about your wife and how you used to go to the movies at the Air Force Club theater. I still enjoy matinees because of that. I remember when we had a mine go off just as we got through one morning. I remember the ramp at Dong Ha. Saw an old high school buddy of mine there one night; he was a jarhead guarding the fuel tanks. I remember that U-boat that sunk somewhere around Two Lima. A guy had a picture of it on Military.com. It was weird seeing a picture of that boat again.

"'Remember that leper colony at Da Nang and that old half-sunken Jap ship? I think it was our boat, PB-44, in Da Nang, when we had that picnic on Spanish Beach and a couple of kids blew themselves up. Was that our crew? . . . I don't remember talking to you but once or twice up north. You got the silver star, didn't you?

"'Well, I'll stop the rambling. Got to get up and go to work tomorrow. Remember that old saying, "It don't mean nothing." Your engine man, Mike.'"

It went on like that, Cooper reading the e-mails, stopping to compose himself, reading some more. One e-mail writer even recalled Cooper's radio call name, Stinger.

That night, in addition to his now standard sign-off, "Good night, Annie, Pooh, and Allyson, I love you," Cooper added, "and welcome home, my long-lost brothers. You have no idea how much this means to me, and everyone else who has just been lost, since then."

There is no record of how Cooper passed the hours following the broadcast of episode #1926. Chances are he poured himself a few bourbons, sat in one of the few chairs not piled high with boxes. He could have practiced his trumpet or put on an album. It might have been the great Satchmo, his forever go-to guy, or perhaps another horn player, Harry James, Sweets Edison, Chet Baker, Miles Davis; the list was long.

The trumpet was "the holy sound," Cooper used to tell his old friend Jerry Etchey as they sat on garden chairs, scanning the skies over Area 51. "No xylophone ever brought down the walls of Jericho."

Meanwhile, the enemy moved into place. Eight weeks had passed since the sheriff's office aborted the 9/11 date to take Cooper Hill. But the strategy remained the same. It was essential to lure Cooper out of his house. No way did the department want to engage in a headline-grabbing shoot-out.

By this time the estimation of Cooper's firepower had grown in the minds of law enforcement. It was widely believed he had an AK-47 just inside his home's front door. Handguns were said to be positioned at windows throughout the house. Another worry was the so-called long rifle, a product Cooper often pushed on *The Hour of the Time.* He loved his long rifle, Cooper said on the show, bragging that he could hit a target with it from "up to a mile away."

The sheriff's office likely could have arrested Cooper up away from the hill. He was known to sneak out to eat enchiladas at Los Dos Malinos in Springerville. There were early-morning forays to the Safeway on North Main Street to stock up on glazed doughnuts. But just as the authorities chose not to pick up David Koresh on those solitary jogs outside Mount Carmel, the authorities never made a move to apprehend Bill Cooper. It was not the way these things are done.

The 311-page account later prepared by the Arizona DPS describes the authorities' version of what happened the evening of November 5, 2001. The report is arranged, *Roshomon*-style, as a series of interviews, with testimony from all the police personnel present, but a consistent story line presents itself.

At 6:00 P.M., members of the county's Special Response Team arrived at the sheriff's department's Eagar facility, adjacent to the Round Valley Rodeo Grounds, to go over the strategy devised for the takedown of the fugitive, Milton William Cooper.

Since it was essential to lure Cooper out of his house, the idea was to go with what had worked in the past. Officers were to proceed to Cooper Hill shortly before midnight, pretend to be partiers, and wait for Cooper to charge out of his house, screaming, as he had done so many times before. Once Cooper approached, he would be surrounded and arrested.

Devised by Apache County Sheriff's Office (ACSO) commander Andrew Tafoya, the ornate plan called for the participation of seventeen officers. Seven of these were assigned to the undercover (UC) vehicle, a tan 1989 Chevy pickup, which would park down the road from Cooper's house. Commander James Womack, up front with Deputy Matrese Avila, were to play the roles of lovesick teens out for a good time. Four other officers hid under a blanket in the truck while another cop, charged with the duty of "dispatching" Crusher should this become necessary, was crouched under the dash of the cab.

The second stage of the operation involved an Apache County Tactical Operations van, a recent addition to the department's expanding motor pool. Parked out of sight on a dirt road adjacent to North Clearview Circle, the tac van carried four additional officers, including driver Sergeant Charles Brown, and Sheriff Hounshell riding shotgun. Hounshell had been on vacation but returned home early to take part in the operation, bumping his chief deputy from the spot. As many in the Round Valley said, Hounshell "wasn't about to miss this."

At approximately 11:40 P.M., Commander Womack drove the UC vehicle up North Hillcrest Road above where it forks away from Udall Street. Once in place, a high-capacity boombox was turned up all the way. Womack and Avila got out of the truck and waited in the middle of the road. When Cooper arrived all hot and bothered, Womack was to say, "What can I do for you?" This was the signal for the officers in the back of the truck to go into action.

Around 11:45 P.M., the music started up, that headbanger shit Cooper wouldn't let Doyel play on *HOTT* because it was "inappropriate for a family show." Almost immediately, the officers reported, the exterior light at 96 North Clearview Circle snapped on.

Cooper appeared at his front door and got into his GMC pickup. This was a surprise to the sheriff's office. Their plan was predicated on Cooper arriving on foot, as he had in previous incidents.

"It was the monsoon, for fuck's sake," Doyel later said, commenting on the sheriff's department's strategy. "The worst one in years. Everything was muddy, slippery. There was no way Bill was going to walk, not with his leg. That's pretty much a no-brainer, I'd say."

Still, there was something odd about Cooper's behavior. Ordinarily, if Cooper chose to confront an intruder, especially one that arrived in the middle of the night, he would have taken Crusher with him. As Cooper often told the audience, the dog had "one purpose on this earth and one only, to protect me and my family." But on this night he left the Rottweiler chained to the bumper of the '76 Buick.

"Here he comes," said Commander Womack, who, according to testimony he gave to the DPS investigator, stood on North Hillcrest Road shielding his eyes from the glare of Cooper's approaching high beams.

According to Deputy Avila's statement in the DPS report, Cooper stuck his head out the window. "You need to get out of here. You can't be here." Desperate to get Cooper out of his vehicle, Womack and Avila attempted to engage Cooper in conversation. Womack said he and Avila "just wanted to build a fire and talk." Perhaps Cooper would like to join them.

"I'm calling the cops," Cooper told the undercover officers. "I'm going to give you ten minutes to be off this property, or the cops are going to be here." Then he backed up his truck to turn around and started back toward his home.

"He's moving!" Commander Womack shouted.

Commander Tafoya jumped out of the truck bed and began chasing Cooper's vehicle on foot. The rest stayed in the UC pickup, which was now in pursuit. It was just then the tac van lurched out onto the road, blocking Cooper's path.

"Sheriff's Office! Put your hands in the air!" Sergeant Brown shouted from the van's driver's seat, as he aimed his M4 submachine gun at Cooper's pickup. On the passenger side, Sheriff Hounshell was out of the van with his Wilson Combat AR-15, using the vehicle door for cover.

This seemed to be the end of the line for Bill Cooper, who, according to Sergeant Brown, stuck his arm out the window of the pickup "as if he were surrendering."

This was a ruse. First checking the position of Sheriff Hounshell, Cooper turned his gaze back to Brown. "He stared at me for a few seconds," Brown is recorded as saying in the DPS report. "Then he turned the pickup wheels right and accelerated directly at me."

Brown managed to jump on the running board of Cooper's "stepside" pickup. Reaching in the window, Brown attempted to "knock Cooper's hands off the steering wheel with the butt of the M4 rifle." Then he tried to grab the gearshift, to throw Cooper's vehicle into reverse. Both maneuvers were unsuccessful. Cooper stiff-armed the officer, which sent him sprawling, as Doyel said, "right on his butt."

Cooper's maneuver cleared the tac van but caused the pickup to swerve over a rocky outcrop, stripping the truck's exhaust system from the bottom of the chassis. A moment later, as Brown and Sheriff Hounshell pursued him on foot, Cooper's pickup came to rest in his circular driveway about thirty-five feet from his front door.

Apache County deputy Joseph Allen Goldsmith picks up the narration from there. A twenty-nine-year-old father of two, Goldsmith came to the ACSO in 1999 after working in the state prison system. Goldsmith's assignment that night was to be one of the four officers lying under a blanket in the undercover vehicle, waiting for Commander Womack's "go" signal. Now, having chased Cooper's truck toward the house, Goldsmith and his fellow deputy, Robert Marinez, were hiding amid the decaying motor pool parked in front of Cooper's house, with their pistols drawn.

Taking cover behind the limousine Cooper had bought for Jessica in hopes she would go into the car-service business, Goldsmith saw the suspect moving across the driveway. Cooper appeared to be running, Goldsmith said, "but he was not moving very fast due to the noticeable limp."

As Deputy Goldsmith moved in from the east, Deputy Marinez closed ground from the other side. Both officers were shouting, "Sheriff's Office! Stop!"

"No!" Cooper shouted back and kept moving toward his front door. With the shouts and Crusher snarling as he strained against his chain-link leash, it must have sounded like a thousand openings to *The Hour of the Time*.

"Cooper almost made it to the door located on the east side of his residence when Deputy Goldsmith saw Cooper reach near his waist," the DPS report says. Goldsmith said he then saw "an arm come up and then a muzzle blast and I heard a gunshot." The shots, in the direction of Deputy Marinez "exposed his (Cooper's) right side and upper right torso region," Goldsmith said.

At that moment, Goldsmith told the DPS officers, he didn't know that

Marinez had been shot in the head, or that his skull had been fractured, fragments of bone pushed into his brain. He couldn't know that in 2003 the Marinez family would sue Sheriff Brian Hounshell and Commander Andrew Tafoya for "willfully and maliciously" sending him into "a dangerous situation for which he was not properly trained or equipped." Likewise, Deputy Goldsmith didn't know that Rob Marinez would still be paralyzed more than fifteen years later. Nor could he have guessed that in the many invocations of Cooper's Truther martyrdom, rare is it that an online poster mentions the name Robert Marinez, except as yet another piece of collateral damage in the vast saga that Bill Cooper crafted for himself.

Then again, from all accounts, Deputy Joe Goldsmith was not part of the audience. He might have listened to Cooper's low-power FM station to hear some oldies, but he did not follow *The Hour of the Time*. He was not aware of Cooper's uncanny ability to understand the tricks and deception of the past or his knack to foresee the future. He didn't know Cooper's despair; his sadness; the depth of his disappointment in the human species, the American people, and himself.

What Deputy Joe Goldsmith did know, according to the report, was that "fearing for the life of Deputy Marinez and for his own safety," he "utilized a two-handed grip on his service weapon, aimed at the center of Cooper's torso and continued to fire." As he advanced, Goldsmith said, "he saw two or three more muzzle blasts from Cooper's gun toward Deputy Marinez."

Goldsmith got off nine rounds with his Glock .45. Asked by investigators "what he was trying to do when he continually shot at Cooper," Deputy Goldsmith said all he wanted to do "was stop Cooper from shooting." That was what he was taught to do: When someone shoots at you, keep shooting back until the enemy falls to the ground, which is what happened when Bill Cooper fell through space and landed, as predicted, on his doorstep.

Aftermath
The Cherry Tree

Cooper's body lay by his doorstep through the rainy night and well into the next day, about fifteen hours in total. There were a number of reasons for this. The first and most important priority was Deputy Marinez, who was taken off to have the first of several surgeries. Another reason was that Cooper, lying in a pool of blood just inches from his doorstep, wasn't officially dead, not yet.

In Apache County, a person is not dead as far as the State is concerned until the coroner pronounces them so. As chance had it, the Apache County coroner at the time was Dr. Scott Hamblin. Due to Hamblin's role in the case, it was deemed a "conflict of interest" for him to sign off on the body. The coroner of Navajo County had to be called, but, it being the middle of the night, it was going to take some time before he made the seventy-mile trip from Holbrook.

There was, of course, a third and generally unstated reason. Cooper had shot a cop, a young, well-liked officer with a family. If Cooper's lifeless body was getting rained on, screw him. It wasn't for some time after the shooting that someone threw a poncho over his body. "We're not barbarians," one cop was heard to say. Crusher was dead. Denied his chance to defend his master as he had been bred to do, the Rottweiler was shot while chained to the bumper of the '76 Buick. Later on, Rob Houghton's band, Cooper Hill, did a song memorializing the animal, accusing the authorities of killing a man "for saying grace, shot his dog to save your face."

Doyel didn't find out about Cooper's death until early the next morning, when he woke up to see half a dozen cop cars parked in front of his house. Roadblocks with sawhorses and flashing lights were set up at either end of the street.

Sergeant Frazier of the Eagar police was walking toward his front door. "I knew it was serious when I saw Frazier in a blue windbreaker with a big POLICE stenciled on the back, and those tactical pants," Doyel said. "That's not done much around here."

"Hey, Doyel, I need to talk to you," Frazier said.

The sergeant gave Doyel the news "just the way I would have wanted it delivered, straight up, 20:20. He just said, 'Well, I gotta let you know that Bill's dead.'"

As Doyel later said in a 2005 interview with Rob Houghton for the *Hour of the Time* website, Frazier took him up to Cooper Hill. "They needed me to identify the body because there wasn't any next of kin. Annie wasn't coming to do it. His family wouldn't, either. So they took me over to the funeral parlor, Jewkes, which is where they took him."

Driving past Cooper Hill, Doyel was surprised to see the extent of the police presence. "They had barricades up on the road, blocking everything off." No one knew exactly what was going on. There were rumors militias were mobilizing, thousands of militiamen were supposed to be heading toward the Round Valley to avenge Cooper's death.

"This one local cop by the barricades, he looked at me and says, 'Is this the day I'm going to die?' It was such a raw day, raining buckets and cold. I got him a cup of coffee."

The sheriff's office had a warrant to search Cooper's house. The way the document was written, Doyel told Rob Houghton in 2005, the cops were entitled "to secure anything in the house . . . any recordings that were a broadcast and any recordings of his thoughts, and any device that could be used to record those thoughts." To the sheriff's department, this included "VCRs, tape decks, computers," because he might write himself a note.

"So you can see the vastness immediately," Doyel said.

"We could have lost the entire library, basically," Houghton replied.

Everything Cooper had ever done was inside that house, the tapes that became *The Complete Cooper*, back issues of *Veritas*, boxes of unsold copies of *Oklahoma City: Day One*, originals of his UFO essays. It was a man's life's work that the police were ready to haul off to rot in the property room up in St. Johns.

But the cops did not enter the house. "They said sources had told them Bill had the place booby-trapped," Doyel told me. "I told them that was crazy. Bill couldn't booby-trap anything. He could barely get off the couch.

"They said they were going to blow the front of the house off to make sure there weren't any booby traps inside. That was their plan. *Serious!*"

That couldn't be allowed to happen. "I told them I was the fiduciary of Bill's estate. I had the responsibility to safeguard the house and property for the two beneficiaries, who were Pooh and Allyson. I had the paperwork. There was nothing they could do because it was all perfectly legal."

Doyel said he understood where the deputies were coming from. Anyone would. One of their guys was fighting for his life. "But I told them to consider the other side. Whatever Bill did, right now there were two little fatherless girls out there. They were going to need that house, the money it would bring. It was the only thing they had. At least let them go to college on it or something. If it got blown up, they'd have nothing."

Hearing this, the sheriff's office personnel went into a little huddle. They changed their stance and decided to send in their camera-loaded robots to check the inside of the house. But the robots could barely get past the piles of boxes and dirty clothes Cooper had left around. Little of forensic interest was found, no bombs, no booby traps.

After that, Doyel said, the sheriff's office "basically said fuck it." Their main mission was accomplished. They'd done what they came to do.

"That left me up there to clean up the mess," Doyel said.

"There was blood and hair and whatnot still lying around," Doyel told Rob in their interview. Already the smell was attracting rodents and birds. But worse than that, Doyel said, were "the thrill seekers" who came by later on. "They were all these looky-loos like crazy. Supposed militia, supposed patriots. They were all goofballs and fakes, coming up to look at the blood." Some of the "sick fucks" were actually scraping the blood off the ground for souvenirs.

"I was scrubbing for a good long time," Doyel said, "just trying to rub it away."

For the next few days, the shoot-out on Cooper Hill was big news. Network affiliates from Phoenix, channels Three, Five, and Ten, sent crews. *The Arizona Republic*, Cooper's least-favorite newspaper, played it big. But perhaps the most in-depth reportage was done by a then relatively unknown twenty-seven-year-old shortwave broadcaster from Austin, Texas: Alex Jones.

An intermittent listener of *The Hour of the Time* during his late teens and early twenties, Jones had interviewed Cooper on his program in the midnineties. "He was a little bit ornery when I'd get him set up for the interview," Jones later said, but Cooper was someone the younger broadcaster looked up to for a time, a role model of sorts.

By the late 1990s, however, as Jones's WWE-style libertarian surrealism gained traction in the marketplace, Cooper began attacking him. "We used to sit there listening to his shit, the way he was copying Bill, and laugh our asses off. We called him Apple Jax and Jabba the Fuck," Doyel remembered. Cooper almost never had a good word to say about a competitor, but his dislike for Jones went beyond the bile. He appeared to genuinely believe that the character Jones was playing on the radio represented a true threat to whatever remained of the American ideal.

For Cooper, the breaking point came in the run-up to the new millennium, when Jones went heavy on the Y2K data-apocalypse scenario. For Jones, the turning of the calendar to the year 2000 was not simply a computer glitch but a spark to set off a full-scale unfolding of a tech-based Book of Revelation. As thousands awaited the dropping of the ball in Times Square, Jones spent his December 31, 1999, broadcast playing the planet's last anchorman, announcing the eschatological events as they came across his desk.

"Cash machines are failing in Britain. Large amounts of explosives have been found in France," Jones reported with the grimness of Raymond Burr narrating Godzilla's destruction of Tokyo. The hits just kept on coming. "Hundreds of thousands are dead in Chechnya. . . ." Nuclear plants in Pennsylvania were shutting down for unexplained reasons, gas stations in Texas were running low on fuel.

Reports were coming in that a single man appeared to be orchestrating the catastrophe. His name, Jones said, was Vladimir Putin, aka Vladimir the Ruthless. Putin was on "an unbelievable power trip," Jones declared, describing the current Russian leader as a "creature of the IMF and the World Bank, a former head of the KGB." Putin had all the characteristics of "a demon." He was unveiling the New World Order "right before our eyes." It was "everywhere, out of control, pandemic."

Jones's millennialist reworking of Orson Welles's 1938 radio broadcast, "War of the Worlds," was not without its moments of inspiration, but Cooper detected a more pernicious quality. Jones had done no research, sought no truth. "He was just making it up straight out of his head," Cooper said.

What was happening right now was a deeply serious matter, Cooper told the audience. "It was news, *hard* news," Cooper said, because Jones wasn't simply one more radio hustler, someone in love with the sound of his own voice. Jones had an agenda. He was deliberately introducing a whole other level of "deception and fearmongering" into public discourse. There were a lot of broadcasters on the radio with no other purpose but to "stir people up . . . to keep them in a lather." But Jones, clearly the most talented of the crew, was "the *main* guy," Cooper said. All you had to do was listen to "the fear, excitement, and adrenaline in Alex Jones's voice," and you would hear the sound of the future, Cooper predicted.

It was a notion Cooper would not let go. Indeed, broadcast #1918 of *The Complete Cooper*, which aired on September 26, 2001, barely more than a month before Cooper's death, was entitled "Alex Jones, Liar."

Now, six weeks later, on the afternoon of November 6, 2001, in what can only be described as a changing-of-the-guard moment, Alex Jones was reporting on the death of Milton William Cooper.

"When he called me, I don't know if I'd ever heard of Alex Jones," said Glenn Jacobs, editor and publisher of the now defunct *Round Valley Paper,* who become known to the *Hour of the Time* audience as Glenn Judas Jacobs.

If Cooper ever made a male friend of his own age while living in Eagar, Glenn Jacobs, the wry newspaperman, oldies rock fan, and Vietnam vet was that person. But it didn't last. In the summer of 1999, after

Annie left with the girls, and Cooper began telling the audience he'd sent them out of the country for their protection, Jacobs became haunted by a dark vision. He began to think Cooper had murdered his wife and children.

After much deliberation, Jacobs reported his suspicions to local authorities. When Cooper got wind of this, he was stunned. "I made a friend in the Round Valley, or at least I thought I did," he mournfully told the *Hour of the Time* audience in an episode entitled "Glenn Jacobs, Informer." He had never really hated anyone in his life, Cooper said, but he just might hate Glenn Jacobs.

"That's how I became Glenn 'Judas' Jacobs," he told me inside his rambling home on North Poverty Flat Road, just east of Cooper Hill, where he's lived for nearly forty years. (Forward-thinking city fathers wanted to change the street name to Happy Hollow Road, but this was rejected by residents.)

Now in his midseventies and as genial an old coot as you might ever hope to meet, Jacobs explained his thinking at the time. "Bill said on the air that no one was taking his children except over his dead body. Then he said that being in these foster homes was a fate worse than death. When the girls disappeared so suddenly, I kind of put two and two together and got five."

Jacobs tried to say he was sorry. He ran a public apology in the *Round Valley Paper* saying, "Bill, I done you wrong." But Cooper never spoke to him again.

This didn't diminish Jacobs's respect for what he called "Bill's quest, his striving for knowledge and the truth that would set him free whatever that might be," Jacobs said. As for Alex Jones, however, he was not so sure.

"He asked me what happened and I told him," said Jacobs. "I told him that Bill went off his nut and headed down into town and waved his pistol in the face of the town doctor. I told him I knew Bill well, that if I stepped outside, I could see his house up on the hill. I told him that even if we had fallen out, I was Bill's friend, I was sorry he was dead. But what he did was aggravated assault and that's a felony in all fifty states.

"I told him that in my opinion, the Apache County Sheriff's Office didn't have much choice. Everyone knew Bill was serious about going out in a blaze of glory. If he got back into the house, he would have had a perfect field of fire. He could have killed a lot of people.

"But that's not what Mr. Jones wanted to hear. He wanted to hear that the feds had snuck up in the night and ambushed Bill, that the pressure of resisting the New World Order had gotten to him. I don't know if Jones cared about Bill Cooper, whether he lived or died. But that's what he wanted to hear."

Indeed, Jones's November 6, 2001, broadcast confirms Jacobs's version of the conversation. After a few pleasantries, Jones suddenly goes into attack mode as Jacobs refuses to accept the host's theory of the crime, which was based on a couple of news clippings. "Well, they obviously shot him in the back," Jones harangues. "How many times did they shoot him?"

Jacobs, the old newspaper man, protested in his high-pitched reedy voice. "I don't know that they shot him in the back. Nobody knows right now. When this kind of situation comes up, everybody shoots because everybody knows 'This is it.' It is a desperate choice."

"Well, he's got to be a pretty good shot to be pulling up in his truck and they jump out and he shoots one in the head," Jones threw in.

"It was bad-breath range!" Jacobs responded sharply, adding, "I detect the finger of God in this that a man can take two .45-caliber rounds to the head and still have a chance to live."

"Well, it's a good thing it wasn't a .357," Jones returned, blithely showing off his knowledge of ballistics. "The .45 deflects quite a bit. It's actually a weak round."

The show went from there, as Jones took some calls from around the country. Scott from Illinois wasn't buying Glenn Jacobs's story. He didn't believe that Cooper had gone down into town to threaten anyone. Jacobs clearly didn't have a clue about what really happened, "whether you call yourself a friend of Bill's or not," Scott from Illinois said.

Brian from New York said that even if the feds were not on the scene that night, they were clearly behind the murder. "They know how to push your buttons," Brian said. There was no way of knowing that the feds hadn't told the local law enforcement, "You guys go get him or you're going to jail for income tax evasion yourselves," he said. Brian was making "a very good point on that," Alex Jones said. In fact, none of Alex Jones's callers believed a word Glenn "Judas" Jacobs said.

In the days following Cooper's death, with the Round Valley full of law enforcement, the monsoon continued. "It really came down," Doyel said. "The sky turned black, like something out of a *Twilight Zone*. It was like they brought evil to the town."

Cooper's death caused Doyel to reorder his priorities. He was supposed to begin a new job working with little kids at Head Start on November 6. But, he said, "I had to call in to say I couldn't make it because my good friend got shot dead by the police." This wasn't the ideal thing to say on your first day of a new job, Doyel recognized. "They're looking at the TV news, thinking, 'Well, who did we just hire?'"

His immediate task was to arrange Cooper's funeral. Given the circumstances, it was difficult to find a local place willing to hold the service, but eventually, Doyel found a young preacher willing to officiate at the Presbyterian church in Springerville. Security was tight for the November 15 service. Low-flying helicopters were in the air. Police snipers were on rooftops around the church.

As it was, the turnout for the funeral proved small, fifty people at the most. No one from Cooper's birth family attended. As Ron Cooper told me, he had no sympathy for his brother, he had "a lot more sympathy for that deputy he shot." Annie, Pooh, and Allyson did not come. Those who did show up, however, represented a reasonable overview of the deceased's life and times. Bob Swan, Cooper's friend from the Hawaii dive business, the first man he ever told about the contents of Admiral Cleary's cabinet, flew in to say a few heartfelt words.

Also in attendance was Norio Hayakawa, supporter of Cooper's ufology period. Even after twenty-eight years working at the Fukui Mortuary in Los Angeles, Hayakawa had never quite seen a funeral like Bill Cooper's. "There was a lot of suspense," Hayakawa told me, saying the helicopters overhead and armed guards outside the church door were "unique."

Hayakawa's eulogy of Cooper has been reprinted several times, including in Commander X's *Death of a Conspiracy Salesman*. "The world will always remember Bill Cooper as an egotistic paranoia monger," Hayakawa's remembrance begins, going on to call Cooper an "obnoxious," "choleric," "self-aggrandizing," and "vengeful person" whose tumultuous life ended by a "self-fulfilled prophecy" embodied by "his violent act." But still, Hayakawa said, "we must admit the fact that he did indeed make a tremendous impact among hundreds, if not thousands."

Arriving with Hayakawa from Los Angeles was Anthony Hilder, the man who broke it to Cooper that half of Harlem was reading *Behold a Pale Horse*. Attired in matching black leather jacket, pants, and boots, Hilder spoke for an extended period, comparing Cooper to John Paul Jones, Emiliano Zapata, and Joan of Arc.

"Fifteen armed agents of this government, fifteen hundred, cannot kill Bill Cooper." Murdering Bill Cooper was a "major mistake" on the part of "the tyrants," Hilder declared, because "thousands will rise to take his place."

Hilder was followed by sundry militiamen lauding Cooper's ultimate sacrifice, but far more memorable was the appearance of Cooper's former wife Sally Phillips and her daughter, Jessica.

"I was working at this place in Eugene, Java John, when my mother came over in the middle of the day," Jessica told me from Coffee Creek Correctional Facility. "We drove over to the Taco Bell and my mother said I could order anything I wanted. Immediately I asked, 'Who died?' When my mother told me she got a call from the US Marshal, I knew. I barely heard her say 'Your father has been shot and killed.'"

Following her visit the previous year, the trip back to Eagar for the funeral was "hell," Jessica reported. She and Sally argued the whole way. Sally said that even if her marriage to Cooper had ended nearly twenty years before, it was important they be there. But as soon as they arrived, Jessica said, "these military types" did everything they could to "isolate us, like we didn't belong there . . . It was like they wanted to control my father's memory. I'd only seen him that one week, but he was my father. None of his other children were there. I thought I should try to represent them."

Sally gave a nice speech. Introducing herself as "the one before Annie," she said that regardless of Cooper's domestic failings, she wanted to "keep this family together." She envisioned an extended Cooper family that would include all of Bill's wives and children. She'd already reached out to Annie about this but hadn't heard back yet.

Sally's dream of uniting Cooper's friends and relations proved overly optimistic. She and Jessica got into an argument with Doyel as to who was going to keep the guest book. According to Doyel, they also tried to take the flag draped over Cooper's coffin. One thing went right, Jessica said. They played "I Miss You So" by the Cats and the Fiddle, the tune Cooper played the night he first read Jessica's e-mail. "It was," she said, "our song."

"You know what I was thinking about the whole time?" Jessica said from Coffee Creek. *"Allyson's shoe.* I saw it when I came to visit my dad. I thought they should have put Allyson's shoe into the coffin along with him. But those people, they'd never think of something like that."

Doyel had a somewhat different account of proceedings. As he told Rob Houghton in 2005, as soon as Sally found out about her former husband's death, "she started calling at like one in the morning, two in the morning . . . trying to cancel the arrangements because it didn't fit her schedule.

"We're talking about a lady who hasn't been around for twenty years. They showed up in a rental pickup, saying, 'Oh, we came to get what's ours. . . .' Then she tried to assert that she was a trustee, which was completely bizarre."

More than thirteen years later, Doyel hadn't softened his stance. In fact, he was pretty sick of everything about Bill Cooper, his life, death, and anything else. I'd been coming around, on and off, for the better part of three years. He'd agreed to tell the story of Bill Cooper as far as he knew it, but there was a limit.

I still had questions. I wanted to know, for instance, how Doyel thought about that fateful night, how he'd processed the gunfight over the years. In the beginning, Doyel said, "I felt like I fucked up. I felt I had a certain responsibility to protect him." But what it really came down to was: "He didn't call."

That was the arrangement. If Cooper felt an attack by government forces or anyone else was imminent, he was supposed to call. There'd been several false alarms, Cooper reacting to stray sounds and flashes of headlights. But on the night of his death, when the "jackbooted thugs" finally arrived, Cooper did not call.

I asked Doyel what would have happened if Cooper had called.

"You mean, if he called me up and said the feds had him surrounded?"

"Yeah."

"Well, I guess I would have gone."

"Really? What would you do, just charge up the road firing off rounds?"

Doyel, the military man, offered a crooked smile. "Oh, I wouldn't have gone up the road," he said.

It was a moot point now, because deliberately or not, Cooper didn't call. There was no need to take Doyel or anyone else with him. That went for Annie and the kids, too. In the end, Cooper's claim to have sent his wife and children away for their own protection regained a ring of truth. Thinking about it was a really melancholy feeling, Doyel said. It wasn't until everything was done, after he'd soldiered through the aftermath of the death and the funeral, that he sat down and started crying.

Then he let out one of his Okie cackles. "*Three feet!* That's how much he missed by: three feet!" Another couple of steps and Cooper could have gotten inside the house. You had to hand it to Bill, getting that far. But those who thought Cooper was going to shoot it out with the cops didn't know Bill Cooper.

"He was trying to get on the air, hook up with WBCQ," Doyel said. Broadcasting one's own martyrdom, that would have been a radio first. It would have been "immortality."

I had one last question for Doyel. I wondered why, after all the things he saw and heard up on Cooper Hill, everything he came to know about Cooper's past, all the bills he got stuck with after Cooper's death, the mortgage on the house he had to pay, why did Doyel work so hard to keep it all going? Why did he take the time to put together *The Complete Cooper,* do so many *Hour of the Time* shows, archive the papers? Certainly, there was no money in it.

It was fairly simple when you thought about it, he said. For one thing, as flawed as he might have been, Bill Cooper had a lot of it right. The things he thought, the stuff he said, needed to be saved; there was history in it. Besides, Doyel said, "who wants to be the one to chop down the cherry tree?"

In December of 2015, Doyel and his significant other came to visit us in New York. One Saturday night we were uptown, so I asked him if they wanted to see where they sold *Behold a Pale Horse* back in the day. They were game, so we went over. It was already past nine on 125th Street, aka Knowledge, Wisdom, Equality Path. But the booksellers were there with their tables. Some of them knew me by now, at least by sight, but who was this cracker-looking guy with the Army-issue buzz cut?

I told them this was Doyel Shamley, Bill Cooper's friend and former onetime right-hand man. "I know you," said one bookman. He had seen the younger version of Doyel on YouTube, providing a blow-by-blow re-creation of the shootout on Cooper Hill. "Pleased to meet you, Mr. Shamley," he said, offering due respect to anyone who knew the author of *Behold a Pale Horse.*

We next visited Doyel in Eagar during the fall of 2016, during the final days of his campaign for Apache County supervisor, District 3. It was a visit that would culminate in that evening at the Sugar Shack, November 8, 2016, the date Donald Trump was elected president of the United States.

Doyel's bid for supervisor, which he said started out "hopeless," had picked up considerable speed. He was, after all, clearly the better candidate. He'd been appearing at candidate forums with opponent Gary Davis dealing with land issues. Asked some tough questions, Davis had to admit he didn't know the answers. He suggested such queries be directed to "Mr. Shamley." Doyel would probably know, Davis said. Which, of course, he did, in cascading detail. All those hours of obsessive, insomniac autodidacticism, skills honed in no small degree from those long conversations with Bill Cooper, had turned Doyel into a walking database, a quick search engine.

He was also demonstrating some political savvy. Back in 2005, he had referred to Sheriff Brian Hounshell, who led the Cooper Hill shootout, as "shit that walks and breathes." In 2007, Hounshell had been thrown out of office for misuse of county funds (speaking on *The Hour of the Time,* Doyel took the position that the old enemy was innocent until proven guilty). But now Hounshell was back, working as an investigator in the Apache County attorney's office and still wielding a fair amount of power. So Doyel sounded him out, reporting that the former sheriff said he "wasn't for me but he wasn't against me," which, as strange bedfellows went, was an acceptable outcome.

But it was up on the Navajo reservation, north of Interstate 40, where the votes really were. While Gary Davis avoided the Rez, Doyel had been there many times. His military background was in his favor. His flyers proclaimed him "the only veteran in the race," which really meant something in a community where a high percentage of young people join the armed services. So did getting one of the last living Navajo code talkers, linguistic heroes of World War Two, to record a commercial for him. First the listener hears the tones of the breathy Navajo tongue that flummoxed the Japanese enemies. Then, in English, come the words, "Vote Doyel Shamley, Apache County Supervisor, District Three." Local government in Navajo land is organized into units called "chapter houses." There are twenty-four chapter houses in District 3. By election day, Doyel had been endorsed by all of them.

Even though barely 7,000 people voted in Doyel's race, the counting ran far behind the national election. Trump had been anointed king for days before it was finally announced that Doyel had slipped through by a couple hundred votes, not that he was resting on his laurels. He'd made a lot of promises. He said he'd work to get a first-class VA facility in the county so vets wouldn't have to go all the way to Phoenix to fill out paperwork. He said he'd fix the roads and work on getting reliably clean water to the Rez. A few months into his term there had been progress on those fronts. He'd helped set up centers for youthful offenders to offer guidance on getting their lives together. No cops were allowed inside the centers in uniform or carrying a gun. This didn't mean Doyel was becoming a closet progressive or anything. He still said plenty of outrageous things and sent out posts from Breitbart. But what did it matter as long as he represented the people he was elected to represent and was fair about it?

Whatever, it is working. Last time we talked, Doyel said the Navajo tribal leaders were pushing him to file for the 2018 State Senate race, which he did. If he wins, he'll represent not only the Navajos but the Zunis, Hopis, the White Mountain Apache, and the San Carlos Apaches, which he referred to as "Geronimo's crew." In sheer territory he'd be in charge of the largest State Senate district in the country, which he said was "a heck of a long way from *The Hour of the Time*."

Cooper's gravesite, Springerville, Arizona

The day before leaving the Round Valley, I made a last visit to Bill Cooper's gravesite on top of the hill in the Springerville cemetery, where sons and daughters of the American West have been buried for more than a century.

Since Cooper's death, Mystery Babylon had been busy, undermining the nation, shoring up the New World Order unveiled on 9/11. There was the Second Iraq War, the collapse of the economy in 2008, the divisive election of Barack Obama, followed by the even more divisive ascendance of Donald Trump. Remarkably, no matter what happened, the country remained almost perfectly split, 50 percent on either side, a status quo as frozen as the supposed balance of power between the US and USSR during the Cold War. With each tweak of the Hegelian Dialectic, the audacious dream of the American Republic laid out by the Founding Fathers in the Constitution grew dimmer.

If he'd been alive, Cooper would no doubt have been behind his RCA 44-BX microphone, saying he predicted each and every event. It was, after all, so predictable.

Over the final stages of my Cooper research, I more or less abandoned any attempt to categorize the radio shows according to a set chronology or subject matter. There was an uncanniness to it. I'd be pondering a question about the man and there he was, providing the answer, never the one you might expect.

Such was the case when, for no particular reason, I clicked on a Cooper YouTube entry posted by Veritas1984, bearing the title "There IS a God." Likely recorded in September of 1999 and missing from the *HOTT* catalog, the show found Cooper dealing with his quest to find and keep an audience.

"I knew from the beginning I would have to capture an audience and teach them what they needed to be taught," Cooper said. He'd sought an audience that would accept his challenge "to think and use your brains . . . to find the road that will lead you to a sincere and earnest and never-ending quest for the truth." Now he had that audience, Cooper said, a group "tested by fire. Literally." Not everyone would listen to him, Cooper admitted. Perhaps there would be only a few, a small band of apostles. But those who were willing to hear his voice, "you know who you are."

This was a true statement. I knew that because, to my surprise, I increasingly found myself part of Cooper's audience. It was a mysterious, wholly unexpected connection. Perhaps it began when, for a fleeting moment, I imagined I saw limo driver William Greer shoot President Kennedy in the head with a shellfish-toxin pellet gun. Or maybe it was when I saw Ol' Dirty Bastard reading *Behold a Pale Horse* on a Brooklyn street. Maybe it just came over me one night like an inhabiting ghost. Cooper's conclusions didn't really matter, the man said some of the nuttiest things. What mattered was the journey, the relentless search for truths that he latched on to like rafts in the storm. For sure, there was no arguing his basic insight: that something wasn't right, that there was something you couldn't quite put your finger on except to feel it in your bones, that you were a little less free than you were yesterday.

Then, by some crazy quirk of karma, I'd become Cooper's scribe, charged with the task of setting down the vicissitudes of his life and death. It might not be the version of those who lionized the man, or who hated his guts, but it was where my own research took me, the particular truth I found. As a member of the audience, I was entitled to it.

It is in this capacity that I offer the following Bill Cooper story, an item not available in *The Complete Cooper* or posted on YouTube. It involves Cooper's star-crossed daughter Jessica, and the Newark, New Jersey, rapper Andrew Kissel who, at the suggestion of Killah Priest, decided to call himself William Cooper.

During my conversations with Jessica, I sent her some money to buy an MP3 player so she might better survive the unholy racket of jailhouse living. This I was happy to do. I also sent along a copy of William Cooper's recently released CD, *God's Will*. Jessica listened to the album and liked it, especially the tune entitled "Secrets of Oz."

As previously noted, the track is based on L. Frank Baum's *Wizard of Oz* story, which rapper Cooper has theorized is really a metaphor for the collapse of the Gold Standard and the subsequent takeover of the US monetary system by a cabal of international financiers that led to the creation of the Federal Reserve Bank. Or, as William Cooper put it: "Hey yo! Tornado flow down brick roads of gold let the / truth be told / the genesis of the barcode / the black cloud that allows accounts to get closed / the dark side of the rainbow controlling the globe / a twister that twisted our forefathers' vision to an economic prison."

Jessica listened to "Secrets of Oz" in the Coffee Creek general population and felt like crying. Her mother, Sally Phillips, used to read *The Wizard of Oz* to her at bedtime. She loved that, Jessica said. Now, after so many sad scenes, being separated from her children, thrown in jail, at least Oz was being returned to her.

The fact that the rapper's name was William Cooper, that he picked the name on purpose, made a difference, Jessica said. "Listening to that, I felt like a little kid again, with both my parents together with me, reading me a wonderful story." Later, Jessica and William Cooper spoke on the phone.

"Wow, when I heard about that bedtime story thing, I almost started crying myself," William Cooper said. "To hear the daughter of Bill Cooper say I made her happy like that, being in that place, that's like the greatest compliment I ever got in my life."

For a man so uncomfortable in life, death became Bill Cooper, I thought, standing beside the man's grave. Doyel said he chose the site because, being on a hillside, it afforded almost the same view as could be seen from the back balcony of Cooper's home. It is, after all, beautiful, especially at sunset. The plaque, done in the military style, offered only the basics: Cooper's name, his rank—quartermaster first class Navy—his birth and death dates, along with a simple Christian cross. That was the short form, all the news that fit on a four-foot-square piece of bronze, which is the problem with tombstones.

Cooper saw himself as a messenger, a midnight-riding Paul Revere on the Pale Horse, warning of things to come, events that often turned out exactly as he said. He always thought that if only the sheeple would just wake up from their slumber, and listen to what he had to tell them, the nation could be saved.

Even at the end, a madman holed up in his hilltop home, he clung to the America he treasured but never really knew, the world of white picket fences and cherry pies cooling on windowsills, flags flying on the Fourth of July. It was a place where Buddy Holly was always on the radio and each human being was equally free to exercise their Creator-endowed rights.

If there ever was an American dream, this was it. Yet, like most American dreams, it was doomed. That was because, in Cooper's version, the ideal was never going to work because Mystery Babylon, or whatever other force, had invented an alternative world that stole the authority from the Creator and created a society of men, imperfect humans, infected with ego and every other deadly sin. In short, fatally flawed people like Bill Cooper.

Cooper said it himself, during the Porterville Presentation, when he talked about how he'd spent his entire life looking for the Devil, only to find the beast within his ample chest. It was this demon, Cooper often supposed, that kept him from achieving the happiness that he managed to grasp only briefly, especially during those nights with his daughter Pooh, broadcasting *The Hour of the Time.*

It was the same with America, home of the Republic conjured through the revolutionary alchemy by the Founding Fathers. The Constitution, the most sacred of texts in a world of fake documents, was the law of the land, yet the freedom offered lay forever out of reach. Filled with unquenchable hope and mandated belief in its own goodness, the nation was riddled with a savage history, nefarious, shape-shifting forces behind every smiling face. Things weren't what they seemed, not at all. It was a dichotomy that informed Cooper's overriding question, "What is real? What's deception, what should we be paying attention to? What is it that is driving us *insane?*"

If there is a reason Cooper stays relevant, why *Behold a Pale Horse* keeps selling after all these years (in February 2018, it spiked to number 17 on Amazon, even ahead of *Goodnight Moon*), it is in this quest, this single-minded resistance to accept an imperfect world. The America Cooper wanted was one in which Lucifer could finally be tracked down by honest G-men, arrested, and brought to court, where he would be afforded his unalienable Creator-endowed rights under the Sixth Amendment, which guaranteed even him "a public trial without unnecessary delay," "an impartial jury," and the right to face his accusers. People call Cooper "the father of the Truth Movement," which now includes nutbag stories like Pizzagate and a tireless news cycle of biased reporting on every side, much of the *New York Times* editorial page notwithstanding. While never one to bow to the faintest whiff of objective reporting himself, chances are Cooper would refer to such knee-jerk tribalists as "sheeple," those who tossed aside the rigors of the standard admonition in favor of unalloyed, unexamined blame. As an American alive in this day and age, it was something to think about, standing at Bill Cooper's graveside, the dark wind coming in off the mountains beyond.

Acknowledgments

Bill Cooper's singular vision spanned the full gamut of American strangeness. Each of Cooper's passions—extraterrestrials, secret societies, the militia world—opens its own rabbit hole. Such underground exploration requires guidance.

I must first thank Doyel Shamley, current Apache County (Arizona) District Three supervisor. Along with his cohort at *The Hour of the Time,* Rob Houghton, Doyel opened the Cooper archives to me and put up with a million questions, which he often wasn't all that keen on answering. Doyel and his fantastic partner, Eva Wilson, welcomed my wife and me into their home in Eagar and showed us a heck of a good time. Plus, Doyel taught us Brooklyn liberals to shoot, a skill that might come in handy when the jackbooted storm troopers Cooper always feared come for us.

Members of Cooper's various families, including his ex-wives Janice Pell and especially Sally Phillips, a grand soul, were kind enough to share their memories of the man. Thanks to Tony Pell, Cooper's only son, who spoke forthrightly about the father he never really knew. I am most indebted to Jessica Caulboy, the daughter Cooper had with Sally Phillips. Jessica and I spent many hours talking, and it was always an interesting and rewarding experience. She has a lot of heart. You go girl, because no matter what happens, you remain all aces to me.

I must acknowledge Cooper's last family, his wife Annie, and daughters Dorothy (Pooh) and Allyson. I know you only through the lens of what Bill said about you, but like many *Hour of the Time* listeners, I feel close to you.

I spoke with many people about Bill Cooper's uneasy passage through this world. All were insightful, no matter how they felt about the man whose life I was chronicling. Let me express my gratitude to Apache County residents Dr. Scott Hamblin and his lovely family, Glenn Jacobs (keep those e-mails coming, Glenn!), Nolan Udall, Deke Robart, and former Apache County Sheriff Art Lee. Thanks, too, to the people of the Safire Restaurant, the Round Valley Public Library, the Springerville Heritage Center, and the great Sugar Shack restaurant in Concho. Also thanks to Western Drug in Springerville, for having everything any sane person might need to buy.

In the ufology community, many people offered highly amusing, if bitter, memories of their onetime fellow traveler. First and foremost is John Lear, one of the most fascinating people in the world to talk to about almost anything. Great thanks to my friend Jeremy Kenyon Lockyer Corbell, filmmaker and modern-day Renaissance man, who provided the lay of the extraterrestrial landscape.

Additional commentary came from the always-thoughtful Norio Hayakawa as well as Linda Moulton Howe, Jacques Vallée, Stanton Friedman, the great raconteur Bill Birnes, Timothy Green Beckley (a prince), Jack Womack, and Don Ecker, whose outraged tales of Cooper were most damningly hilarious.

Thanks a ton to rapper William Cooper née Andrew Kissel, a man with a fierce intelligence and gentle soul. He and his producer, BP, are the sort of artists worth seeking out. The testimony of Killah Priest of the Wu-Tang cosmos, was illuminating. Thanks, too, to the late Prodigy, one of the all-time-classic New York rappers, whose insights into *Behold a Pale Horse* and its meaning were invaluable. This is not to forget the unforgettable Ol' Dirty Bastard.

Thanks to those who gave me their time, including the estimable Steven Hager and Busy Bee, who inducted me into the Pot Illuminati; Allan Weiner, the classic pirate radioman; former FBI agent Steve Fillerup; patriot chronicler Gary Hunt; and Paul Krassner, one of my all-time heroes. The late composer Philip Lambro was kind enough to speak with me about his friend Cooper.

Let me give special shout-outs to Bro. Nova and the booksellers of

125th Street; the historians of the Five-Percent Nation; podcast maestro Chris Murrow; Melody O'Ryin Swanson, the publisher of *Behold a Pale Horse*; and especially Anthony Hilder, to whom I could listen to all day long.

I'd also like to extend best wishes to the crew at the Skills and Research Conference held by Doyel Shamley. Mike V., Scott G., Chris R., Stephen, Jesse, and the rest: It was a time. Big thanks to the late Jerry Etchey. RIP to Fred Otero, the greatest backwoods caterer ever. Thanks also to Tom Lasala, who will always send up a joyful noise, however dark and raw.

As for the compilation of this book, several people need to be mentioned. These must start with my agent, Flip Brophy of Sterling Lord, and continue to my longtime friend and coconspirator David Rosenthal, who originally signed the book up at his Blue Rider imprint. At Dutton, John Parsley, Brent Howard, and Cassidy Sachs were key in bringing the project to light.

But, in the teasing out of the original manuscript, one man stands alone. That is Will Blythe, aka Roy Tarpley. Our weekly conversations were certainly among the highlights of this entire process. As you know, Roy, be you buried in Siberia or lording over City Island, you are my kindred spirit, always.

No book by me could ever exist without the presence of my family and friends. It was a lucky day when I married my wife, Nancy Cardozo, in 1980, on the historically dense date of April 20. Our three children, Rae, Rosie, and Billy, now all grown up, offered much trenchant commentary on the writing process. They know more than me now, which is the idea. This is not to forget the new granddaughter, Alice.

It is always good to know who your friends are, and in this case, my buddies remain steadfast. The evening that the great NYC man of letters Michael Daly and godfather Jonny Buchsbaum came over to read through parts of the manuscript on deadline night will forever touch my heart. Photographer James Hamilton, truly a friend indeed, came through, as he always does. Carl Gettleman offered amusing advice on Cooper and the whole "conspiracy" genre. Shout-outs to Captain Christina Brown and Mike Bell for friendship and a sweet writer's retreat, ditto to my sister Paula Jacobson, always the greatest. Thanks also to Carol Cardozo for explaining outsider electronics and Claire Curtis for the pulp UFO book collection. Ditto George Cardozo, the artist. That's not to forget Dan Christian and "conspiracy corner" at the KGB Bar.

In the end though, the greatest debt is to Milton William Cooper himself, the biggest rabbit hole of them all. Brilliant, tortured, prescient, duplicitous, lover, and hater, he was what he always wanted to be: an American.

Notes on Sources

Researching a book and attempting to get at the nature of truth when the main figure is a world-class fabulist presents its challenges. Is it important to get the story right as the storyteller tells it, or to follow the more traditional route of proof? What matters more, fact or metaphor? Often, with Bill Cooper, a middle path seemed appropriate. For instance, did Cooper actually see John F. Kennedy murdered on live television as he claimed in *Behold a Pale Horse?* Er, no. The Dallas motorcade was not broadcast, but that wasn't the point. Perhaps Cooper needed to say that to get to his further claim that Secret Service agent William Greer, the limo driver, shot Kennedy in full view of hundreds of people. After all, we are not listening to someone like Cooper for the facts, ma'am, just the facts. He is not Joe Friday. Herein lies the journalist's dilemma. To report such a story, you have to meet the storyteller at least halfway.

Cooper's short but antic career in the public eye began in the time of the mimeographed handout and ended at the dawn of the broadband era, but his legacy lives on almost exclusively on the web. By the time I finished this book, I'd collected several hundred bookmarks pertaining to Cooper and related topics. This was augmented by numerous Facebook pages, Twitter posts, and Instagram feeds, more than a few displaying tattoos of the cover of *Behold a Pale Horse* emblazoned on the arms and backs of fans.

Now, as always, the best source for Bill Cooper–related material remains www.hourofthetime.com. It is here that one finds not only the lineup of the Complete Cooper, but also a treasure trove of the HOTT Virtual Research Library. This includes dozens of pdfs of the volumes in Cooper's (and Doyel Shamley's) personal library, a wide array of material on such far-flung topics as animal traps and hide tanning, covert activities, secret societies, and a selection of survival manuals. Especially interesting are the various pdfs of Masonic lodge constitutions and manuals, many dating back to the nineteenth century.

A good deal of Cooper UFO material is available at the venerable www.bibliotecapleyades.net, an unbeatable gathering of information on everything fringe on this planet and beyond. For transcripts of many of Cooper's broadcasts and speeches, see http://deceivedworld.blogspot.com and AnoNews Vienna (https://viefag.wordpress.com). The Wayback Machine at http://archive.org/web has many of the *Mystery Babylon* episodes transcribed.

As noted, there are hundreds of Cooper YouTube videos, usually replays of popular broadcasts, like the 9/11 prediction playing over user-created images. Those illustrated with the artwork of David Dees, the R. Crumb of the libertarian right, are worth searching out. Blurry videos of lectures abound. A quick search will bring up Cooper's classic speech to the 1989 MUFON Symposium along with the full eleven hours of the Porterville Presentation. Active Facebook pages dealing with Cooper material include "William Cooper—Mystery Babylon" and "Bill Cooper—Exposing the New World Order."

There are several additions to the extended Cooper terrain that hold attraction for fans. John Lear's site, The Living Moon (http://www .thelivingmoon.com), is always fascinating. Comic relief can be found in the work of "dallasgoldbug" (WellAware1.com), who never tires of the idea that Cooper faked his own death and now occupies the body of fellow conspiracist Jordan Maxwell. Also bizarre is Barbara Aho's "William Cooper and the Three Bears," which asserts that Cooper is somehow a "false prophet" tied up with a satanic bloodline of the Merovingian Dynasty (https://watch.pairsite.com/william-cooper.html).

The most recent high-profile addition to the Cooper canon are the postings of "QAnon," a reputed government insider who claims to have access to classified information on the ongoing attempt of the so-called Deep State to overthrow the Trump administration. In February 2018, "Q," as he is known to the followers of his "intel drops," wrote of his deep admiration for Cooper and his work. Sales of *Behold a Pale Horse* immediately spiked, landing the twenty-seven-year-old book at number 17 on the Amazon bestseller list.

Selected Bibliography

Allen, Gary, with Larry Abraham. *None Dare Call It Conspiracy*. San Diego: Dauphin Publications, 1971.

Barkun, Michael. *A Culture of Conspiracy: Apocalyptic Visions in Contemporary America*. Berkeley: University of California Press, 2003.

Beckley, Timothy Green. *Round Trip to Hell in a Flying Saucer*. New York: DBA Global Communications, 2011.

Bernays, Edward. *Propaganda*. New York: Liveright, 1928.

Bird, Kai. *The Chairman: John J. McCloy, the Making of the American Establishment*. New York: Simon & Schuster, 1992.

Bourke, Joanna. *Fear: A Cultural History*. Emeryville, CA: Shoemaker & Hoard, 2006.

Bowart, Walter. *Operation Mind Control*. New York: Dell, 1978.

Coates, James. *Armed and Dangerous: The Rise of the Survivalist Right*. New York: Hill and Wang, 1987.

Corso, Col. Philip J., with William J. Birnes. *The Day After Roswell*. New York: Pocket Books, 1997.

Daniel, John. *Scarlet and the Beast. 3rd ed*. Longview, TX: Day Publishing, 2007. A key source for Cooper's *Mystery Babylon* series.

DeLillo, Don. *Libra*. New York: Viking Penguin, 1988.

Dick, Philip K. *Shifting Realities: Selected Literary and Philosophical Writings*. New York: Vintage, 1995.

Duverus, Delamer. *The Golden Reed*. Seligman, MO: D. Duverus Publishing, 1973.

Epperson, A. Ralph. *The New World Order*. Tucson, AZ: Publius Press, 1990.

———. *The Unseen Hand: Introduction to the Conspiratorial View of History*. Tucson, AZ: Publius Press, 1985.

Finkbeiner, Ann. *The Jasons*. New York: Penguin Books, 2006.

Frayling, Christopher. *The 2001 File*. London: Reel Art Press, 2015.

Friedman, Stanton T. *Top Secret/Majic*. New York: Marlowe & Company, 1996.

Fuller, Robert. *Naming the Antichrist: History of an American Obsession*. Oxford, UK: Oxford University Press, 1995.

Gilroy, Paul. *Against Race: Imagining Political Culture beyond the Color Line*. Cambridge, MA: Harvard University Press, 2000.

Gordin, Michael D. *The Pseudoscience Wars: Immanuel Velikovsky and the Birth of the Modern Fringe.* Chicago: University of Chicago Press, 2012.

Gulyas, Aaron John. *The Chaos Conundrum.* Halifax, Canada: Starhawk Publishing, 2013.

Gumbel, Andrew, and Roger G. Charles. *Oklahoma City: What the Investigation Missed—and Why It Still Matters.* New York: HarperCollins, 2012.

Hager, Steven. *Killing Kennedy: The Real Story.* CreateSpace Independent Publishing Platform, 2017.

———. *The Octopus Conspiracy: And Other Vignettes of the Counterculture from Hippies to* High Times *to Hip Hop and Beyond.* Walterville, OR: Trine Day, 2005.

Hall, Manly P. *The Secret Destiny of America.* New York: TarcherPerigee, 2008. First published in 1944.

Hamm, Mark. *Apocalypse in Oklahoma: Waco and Ruby Ridge Revenged.* Boston: Northeastern University Press, 1997.

Hofstadter, Richard. *Anti-Intellectualism in American Life.* New York: Knopf, 1962.

Howe, Linda Moulton. *An Alien Harvest: Further Evidence Linking Animal Mutilations and Human Abductions to Alien Life Forms.* Linda Moulton Howe Productions, 1990.

Hunter, Edward. *Brainwashing: The True and Terrible Story of the Men Who Endured and Defied the Most Diabolical Red Torture.* New York: Pyramid Books, 1961.

Isaacson, Walter, and Evan Thomas. *The Wise Men: Six Friends and the World They Made.* New York: Simon & Schuster, 1986.

Jacobsen, Annie. *Area 51: An Uncensored History of America's Top Secret Military Base.* New York: Little, Brown, 2012.

Jacobson, Steven. *Mind Control in the United States.* San Diego: Dauphin Publications, rev. ed. 2015. Originally published in 1985, this book was the basis for much of Cooper's six-part mind control series, on *The Hour of the Time.*

Jaynes, Julian. *The Origin of Consciousness in the Breakdown of the Bicameral Mind.* New York: Houghton Mifflin, 1976.

Jones, William E., and Rebecca D. Minshall. *Bill Cooper and the Need for More Research (UFOs, Conspiracies, and the JFK Assassination).* Dublin, OH: Mid-Ohio Research Associates, 1991.

Keith, Jim. *Saucers of the Illuminati.* Kempton, IL: Adventures Unlimited Press, 1999.

———. *Secret and Suppressed: Banned Ideas and Hidden History.* Venice, CA: Feral House, 1993.

Keyhoe, Donald. *The Flying Saucers Are Real: An Early Account of the National Security State.* CreateSpace Independent Publishing Platform, 2008.

Kinney, Jay. *The Masonic Myth.* San Francisco: HarperOne, 2009.

Lambro, Phillip. *Close Encounters of the Worst Kind.* Los Angeles: Lulu, 2007.

Lernoux, Penny. *In Banks We Trust: Bankers and Their Close Associates: The CIA, the Mafia, Drug Traders, Dictators, Politicians, and the Vatican.* New York: Anchor Press, 1984.

Lieb, Michael. *Children of Ezekiel.* Durham, NC: Duke University Press, 1998.

Marks, John. *The Search for the Manchurian Candidate.* New York: Times Books, 1979.

Miyakawa, Felicia M. *Five Percenter Rap: God Hop's Music, Message, and Black Muslim Mission.* Bloomington: Indiana University Press, 2005.

Monk, Buddha, and Mickey Hess. *Ol' Dirty Bastard: The Dirty Version.* New York: Dey Street Books, 2014.

Moore, Michele Marie. *Oklahoma City: Day One.* Eager, AZ: Harvest Trust, 1996.

Muhammad, Elijah. *Fall of America.* Chicago: Secretarius Memps Publications, 1973.

———. *Message to the Blackman in America.* Chicago: Secretarius Memps Publications, 1973.

Mutual UFO Network. *MUFON: 1989 International UFO Symposium Proceedings.* Seguin, TX: Mutual UFO Network, 1989.

Pabst, William R. *Concentration Camp Plans for US Citizens.* Sons of Liberty, 1979.

Perloff, James. *The Shadows of Power.* Appleton, WI: Western Islands, 1988.

Robison, John. *Proofs of a Conspiracy: Against All the Religions and Governments of Europe, Carried On in the Secret Meetings of Freemasons, Illuminati, and Reading Societies.* London: Forgotten Books, 1798. (Note: In addition to writing the first account of the dangers of the Illuminati, Robison, a Renaissance man of alarm, is also the inventor of the siren.)

Seldes, Gilbert. *The Stammering Century.* New York: New York Review of Books, 1927.

Sutton, Anthony C. *America's Secret Establishment: Introduction to the Order of Skull and Bones.* Walterville, OR: Trine Day, 1983.

———. *Western Technology and Soviet Development 1945–1965.* Stanford, CA: Hoover Institution Press, 1973.

Tabor, James D., and Eugene V. Gallagher. *Why Waco?* Berkeley: University of California Press, 1995.

Toronto, Richard. *Shaverology.* San Francisco: Shavertron Press, 2013.

Vankin, Jonathan, and John Whalen. *The 80 Greatest Conspiracies of All Time.* New York: Citadel Press, 1995.

Weiner, Allan H. *Access to the Airwaves.* Yakima, WA: Breakout Productions, 1997.

White, Ellen G. *The Great Controversy between Christ and His Angels and Satan and His Angles.* Battle Creek, MI: 1858. Reissued as *The Cosmic Conflict, Good and Evil Wage War for Planet Earth.* Oakland, CA: Pacific Press, 1983.

Wilson, Nolan. *The Minuteman Handbook: America's First and Last Line of Defense.* InfoTech Publications, 1995.

Wilson, Robert Anton. *Cosmic Trigger I: Final Secret of the Illuminati.* Grand Junction, CO: Hilaritas Press, 1977.

Wilson, Robert Anton, and Robert Shea. *The Illuminatus! Trilogy.* New York: Dell, 1975.

Index

About the Author

Mark Jacobson is a writer and journalist based in Brooklyn, New York. He is known for his explorations of the seamy side of urban life and for his offbeat and witty take on popular culture. Mark is a contributing editor at *New York* magazine and a frequent contributor to *The Village Voice*, *National Geographic*, *Natural History*, *Men's Journal*, and other publications. Jacobson's journalism has been the basis for the TV show Taxi and the film *American Gangster*.